LOVE AND NEED

LOVE

and

NEED

THE LIFE OF

ROBERT FROST'S

POETRY

ADAM PLUNKETT

Farrar, Straus and Giroux
New York

Farrar, Straus and Giroux
120 Broadway, New York 10271

Owing to limitations of space, all acknowledgments for permission to reprint
previously published material can be found on pages 499–500.

Title-page illustration by Dan Thoner / Shutterstock.com.

Library of Congress Cataloging-in-Publication Data
Names: Plunkett, Adam, 1987– author.
Title: Love and need : the life of Robert Frost's poetry / Adam Plunkett.
Description: First. | New York : Farrar, Straus and Giroux, 2025.
Identifiers: LCCN 2024034454 | ISBN 9780374282080 (hardback)
Subjects: LCSH: Frost, Robert, 1874–1963. | Frost, Robert, 1874–1963—
    Criticism and interpretation. | Poets, American—20th century—Biography |
    American poetry—20th century—History and criticism
Classification: LCC PS3511.R94 Z869 2025 | DDC 811/.52—
    dc23/eng/20240926
LC record available at https://lccn.loc.gov/2024034454

Designed by Patrice Sheridan

Our books may be purchased in bulk for promotional, educational, or business use.
Please contact your local bookseller or the Macmillan Corporate and Premium
Sales Department at 1-800-221-7945, extension 5442, or by email at
MacmillanSpecialMarkets@macmillan.com.

www.fsgbooks.com
Follow us on social media at @fsgbooks

1   3   5   7   9   10   8   6   4   2

For my parents,

for Berit,

for Maren,

for Mari

The way to a poem is through as many as possible of all the other poems that were ever written.

—FROST

We shall often find that not only the best, but the most individual parts of [a poet's] work may be those in which the dead poets, his ancestors, assert their immortality most vigorously.

—T. S. ELIOT

When I am sometimes unjustly praised I accept it as making up for the other times when I have been unjustly blamed. Such is comedy. The only other way to take injustice is the way of tragedy. There I maintain my mystery for no one to pluck the heart out of.

—FROST

I knock on wood to placate any devil who may happen to hear me.

—FROST

CONTENTS

———

LOVE AND NEED

I.

THE FREEDOM OF THE MOON

I.

Though he had watched the poet before, the first time he saw Robert Frost watching him was when the other students started to laugh.

He was Lawrance Thompson, a junior at Wesleyan University who, on Frost's last visit to campus, had something of a conversion experience to the poetry of Robert Frost. The poet had come to Wesleyan in May 1925, and Thompson, then a freshman, had seen him perform, running late to the Wesleyan Chapel and walking in to see Frost, his talk already underway, about to recite "The Freedom of the Moon." It was a poem that Thompson had not heard or read before. It showed the beauty of a new moon seen in different ways—alone in the sky, along with a bright star, and as a shining sliver in the water. The young man was obsessed—or, as he later said, addicted—and a year and a half later, in early December 1926, the addict found himself sitting before Frost in the library of Alpha Delta Phi, accompanied by a handful of his classmates, also aspiring poets who had anonymously submitted their work to be critiqued by the distinguished guest.

The other students laughed at the poem about Santa Claus that Frost had just read to them. Thompson had put thought into his poem about

Santa Claus. The situation in his poem, "Delusion," is that the child from whose perspective the poem is written has been told there's no Santa Claus but hopes there really is one anyway, even though he knows better. Thompson's peers showed no sign of seeing past the surface of the poem to its ironies—that the same adults who would find the child childish would also think like him, as with their faith in God, the adults lying to themselves about their childish habits of mind while the child at least saw himself clearly. The students just laughed.

As Thompson was failing to reach his audience, he saw Frost begin to look around the room as if trying to tell who had written the poem. Its author had no way to hide. Frost saw the blush on Thompson's face and held up his hand.

"Wait a minute," Frost said. "Wait a minute." And he proceeded to defend the poem at some length, looking again and again at its author as he gradually calmed down. The students eventually murmured their approval after Frost read them the poem a second time.

After the meeting had ended, Thompson tried to sneak past the students crowded around Frost so he could take his poem and go, but the poet turned and looked him over. Thompson had to say something.

"Thanks for saving my face," he said.

Frost said, "Stick around."

He did, and Frost brought him and a few other stragglers over to the house of Frost's host, Professor Bill Snow, where Frost sat down with each of the students in the course of a long evening talk by the fireplace. When he got to Thompson, he asked where the young man was from.

"New Hampshire," Thompson said, pronouncing it "New Hampshah."

Frost said he'd bet he'd slept in more towns in New Hampshire than Thompson had heard of. Thompson said he doubted this, as the son of an itinerant Methodist minister who traveled all over the state. Had Thompson ever heard of Raymond? Well, yes, he'd lived there as a boy. So they talked into the night, Robert Frost and the man who'd be remembered by posterity as his biographer and his betrayer.

II.

To hear Thompson tell the story decades later—in 1962, for instance, twenty-three years after he became Frost's official biographer and four years before he would publish the first of his biography's three volumes—he had not wanted to write Frost's biography. It was Frost who wanted him to.

The appointment that Thompson would later call an accident took place over the last weekend of July 1939 in the Green Mountain village of Ripton, Vermont. Frost had invited Thompson up for a weekend after Thompson had written Frost for permission to write a little book about his poetry, probably to be called "Robert Frost: A Critical Introduction." Frost had no trouble with Thompson's proposal, he wrote, but he needed Thompson's help with something else: his biographer, Robert Newdick, had passed away suddenly, leaving him at a loss for what to do about the archive Newdick had compiled. "You be thinking my predicament over," wrote Frost, "and come along when you can."

Thompson was well-qualified to advise Frost on the archive. He had established himself as an authority on Frost's bibliography, having put together in 1936 the largest exhibition to date of Frost's rare publications. The exhibition, and the corresponding catalog authored by Thompson (*Robert Frost: A Chronological Survey*), got Thompson his first job after graduate school, as curator of rare books at Princeton University, where he had since been promoted to assistant professor. At the time of Frost's writing him, Thompson had lately won over a number of critics with his first book, *Young Longfellow*, about the early life of the great nineteenth-century American poet. He had struggled with Longfellow's heirs about permissions and had talked the struggles over with Frost.

Yet what Thompson learned in Ripton as he talked with Frost late into the night was that Frost wanted help not in preserving his old biographer's archive but in impounding it. Frost had changed his mind: he no longer wanted a biography of himself published in his lifetime. Did he have a claim on his biographer's materials?

He did not, Thompson said—not even on his own letters if they had been in Newdick's possession, although he could prevent their being published. But Thompson sympathized. He knew that Frost had come to resent the man for prying into Frost's private life only to write about it in academic journals with little discernment. Newdick had come to figure as a kind of invasive species, an academic pest who bothers the trees while missing the forest for scholarly articles. Thompson had met Newdick a year earlier, running into him at the Jones Library in Amherst as the two researched Frost after the memorial service for Frost's wife, Elinor, in April 1938, and Thompson, who had already developed a "violent dislike" for Newdick's articles, disliked the man on the spot.

Newdick died in early July 1939. "I am told his mind ran on me in his last delirium," Frost had written to Thompson. "What is a miserable hero to say to a worship like his?"

On Thompson's way to Vermont, he thought of a plan. Frost could not impound Newdick's materials, Thompson said, but Frost could name an official biographer. The new biographer would agree not to publish his book in Frost's lifetime, and could serve as a buffer between Frost and anyone else who wanted to write his life. Frost asked Thompson whom to choose.

It should be someone Frost knew well and trusted, Thompson said—someone already middle-aged and with a national reputation as a writer. Frost asked for a name, and Thompson gave three: Louis Untermeyer, Bernard DeVoto, Carl Van Doren. No, no, no, said Frost, and told the story of his friendships with each of them to show why none would do. Then Frost homed in on the young man in front of him. Thompson protested; Frost insisted. "Your Longfellow is good enough to satisfy me." And as Thompson told the story decades hence, "It was this place where the accident occurred," the accident that "really made the difference."

Yet if this was a stroke of fortune or misfortune, Thompson had done about all he could to get struck. He had made himself an expert on Frost's poetry and a biographer of a poet he knew Frost adored and admired, had told Frost in letters that no critic had gotten him right, that he knew the world of the mill town that Frost had grown up in (Lawrence, Massachusetts) and the little towns and farms and woods north of Boston that Frost had made immortal in verse, that he loved him. When Frost asked him to be his biographer, "I said I wanted to," Thompson wrote in his journal a month afterward. "In Ripton," Thompson wrote to Frost the week after he left, "that which I timidly hoped came unto me."

On Thompson's drive along the pass through the hills out of Ripton, he saw a pair of bodies next to an overturned car by the roadside. "If I die in any such accident," Thompson told Frost in a letter, "you may tell my grieving friends (count 'em on the fingers of one hand) that my last words were quoted from Job: 'That which I feared has come unto me.'"

"I am not much of a man of fears," Thompson went on in his letter, "but I must admit that I have one fear in this respect," one fear in writing about Frost: "that I'll let you down."

III.

"You are the best loved poet in America without a question," wrote Frost's publisher, Bill Sloane, to the poet in 1939, and by any relevant measure he was. Frost in 1939 had earned more distinctions than anyone but a bibliographer would care to count—more laudatory reviews, more honorary degrees—and had won the Pulitzer Prize for Poetry more than anyone alive (three times and counting). His superlative prestige was also matched by real fame, and in this he was alone in his century. There had been poets in nineteenth-century America who were at once highly distinguished and widely read, eminent in literary as well as popular culture, literary culture being at the time more central to popular culture and poetry more central to literature than by the time Frost published his first book in America, in 1915. Henry Wadsworth Longfellow had in his time been at the top of a Mount Parnassus of poets beloved by laypeople as well as enthusiasts and specialists. By 1939, Frost was more or less the whole mountain.

He wore his authority lightly. When he talked to an audience—as he did in countless chapels and auditoriums across the country, mostly at colleges—he was all watchfulness and presence of mind, not premeditation or performed erudition. He wasn't scholarly or superior. He didn't lecture: he talked, but not to pander to the crowd or bare his soul. He seemed to talk about whatever came to mind before saying—not reading, but "saying"—his poems. His talks were impromptu homilies, spiritual reflections as if they were occurring before an audience's eyes and without the trappings of the form—the office of the minister, the topic in chapter and verse, the moral drawn for you. His talk was the performance of ordinary speech brought to wisdom. If his talk on one day repeated his talk from another, it still seemed more like speech than a speech. He would speak in a manner slow and easy, unassuming, reassuring, and then give a little change to tone or pace or make a little gesture, raising the question of a contrast between what he said and what he meant. His facial features struck his observers as unusually expressive, his hands as unusually active. He had glacial blue eyes and thick lips, a big head, a bulbous nose, and an unruly shock of hair he was always pushing up off his forehead. He spoke in an accent not often found in nature, a cross between Harvard, where he had spent a couple of years in the late 1890s, and the Yankee folkways in southern New Hampshire, where he spent a dozen years at the start of the century. His voice was an instrument of exceptional subtlety, as his friend Sidney Cox described it in 1928:

> It can be elfin, ribald, gargoylesque, serene, sinister, utterly convinced, altogether sceptical, tender like firm fingers pressing soil around a delicate plant, and full of emotion or hilarity. And it has a fringe of little vibrations round it that have suggestions of mystery and power like the purring of great dynamos. It is the unspoiled organ of an un-cowed human being.

The novelist Wallace Stegner wrote that Frost's speech was "one of the best things this civilization has produced."

The clearest record we have of Frost's presence is a six-line poem by Gwendolyn Brooks, "Of Robert Frost," radiant and modest like the modest radiance it talks about. Here we have a man with lightning in his eyes and heat conducted into his speech but still a man composed despite the lightning, not unsettled by his inspiration. His gestures are just so, "his brows" not too highbrow, not too lowbrow. Inspiration strikes him not from on high but from tapping deeply into "some glowing in the common blood," something shared by all of us but hard for all of us to see. The poem ends by drawing our attention to "Some specialness within"—not only Frost's, as one would expect in a poem about what makes him special, but our specialness within, some aspect of human potential like a lightning rod buried in each of us that he brings to life. "Some glowing in the common blood," she writes, "Some specialness within," as though to say that to name it more precisely would falsify the experience of it. Frost does not explain this specialness within, and yet his presence makes its presence felt.

Then there were the poems. What Frost seemed to perform, his poetry seemed to embody: simultaneous apotheoses of ease and of depth like points on an axis along which his world rotated. His was not a special world of his own, either, but a world his poems could draw you into, a world in which the thoughts and emotions of common experience have by some grace of insight been brought to wisdom for the space of a poem. If the wisdom didn't translate exactly into plain English, that was because the poems were written to be experienced just as they were. If the experience seemed not to lead to a little lightning of revelation, perhaps that was him and perhaps that was you.

Frost introduced his collected work with a poem that serves as an invitation into the world of the poetry:

The Pasture

I'm going out to clean the pasture spring;
I'll only stop to rake the leaves away

(And wait to watch the water clear, I may):
I sha'n't be gone long.—You come too.

I'm going out to fetch the little calf
That's sitting by the mother. It's so young
It totters when she licks it with her tongue.
I sha'n't be gone long.—You come too.

You can hear the invitation in at least four ways at once. "You come, too" is a suggestion, an insistence, a command, a plain statement. It has the levity of an offhand suggestion (I shan't be gone long; why don't you just come, too?); the anxiety of insistence (I shan't be gone *long*; why can't you just come, too?); the declarative firmness of a command; and the disarming literalness of plain statement, as you, the reader, have already heard what he's going to go do before he says, "You come, too," having gone with him in his imagination as one does in reading the poems. These intimations add up to a startling intimacy, as if we hear not only the phrase but a mind in its nakedness weighing how it means to use the phrase, why it means to use it, what it wants and needs of you. In listening to the invitation, we find ourselves already off on our way with him. It's an invitation we can't help but take. Frost called "The Pasture" a love poem unlike any other he knew.

IV.

"You do throw people off the track in your poems again and again," Thompson wrote Frost in his letter after driving out of Ripton. The subject of his future biography had, Thompson wrote, "a tendency to play hide-and-seek around a half-truth. You embrace a truth at times as though you were half lover, half fighter; with one arm you caress and with the other you plant a little rabbit-punch. What a helluva lover you'd make—in such a mood."

A week after writing to Frost, Thompson recorded his thoughts for himself in an ecstasy of nerves. Being invited to Ripton by Frost felt to him like being invited to Stratford by Shakespeare, and neither the challenge of his task nor the magnitude of his opportunity was lost on the anointed biographer. "My first reaction is one that will not leave me—my downright inability to do the task *worthily*," Thompson wrote in his journal. Yet the same man who protested to himself "I'm too young" could also tell himself "to work skilfully into your whole book a history of modern poetry." He was thirty-three years old. "I go back to talk more with him this week," Thompson wrote to himself. "If I knew how to pray I'd be praying now."

When he saw Frost later that week, he faced a proposal by Frost for what he thought at first was an easy test of literary interpretation: say what "The Schism," a poem in the latest *Atlantic Monthly*, which Frost had a copy of, meant.

The *Jewes* their beds, and offices of ease,
Plac't *North* and *South*, for these cleane purposes;
That mans uncomely froth might not molest
Gods wayes and walks, which lie still East and West.
—HERRICK

FROM holy to unhallowed scene
(Such alternation is our lot)
From cleanly straightway to unclean
A tincture never quite forgot.

From duty well or badly kept
Straightway to bed; but should a trace
Hint that we loved before we slept
We quickly turn aside the face.

The madman desecrates the Host.
And yet there's not a voice we hear,

No, not the pang that moves us most
To make our muddied lives run clear,

But through the body it will dart
Taking the flesh for sounding-board.
The plaited thorns would pierce no heart
Pierced they not too the sensual cord.

While flesh is flesh and through it stalk
Those unperturbed familiar beasts
That thrust their heads up in our talk
And slaver at our gravest feasts

No art that we can lightly find
Will cure the guilt they make us feel.
The ancestral schism of the mind
Pursues us like a dog at heel.

Yet say that love refused to take
The luxury before it thrown,
Or would not lash itself to break
Storm-like upon its longed-for zone,

Then how of all that we think good
Might the least spray put forth its flower?
Dead spring can leaf no waiting wood.
The withered womb starves every power.

I do not shame, remembering this,
To think how green tides gulped the land
With an insatiable kiss,
And left their dried foam on the sand.

The poem was by Theodore Morrison, director of the Bread Loaf Writers' Conference down the road from Ripton and a man whose life had in the last year become intimately entangled with Frost's. Frost had, in fact, just bought a house in which Morrison and his family would live in the summers while Morrison oversaw the Writers' Conference, which happened every August, so that Ted's wife, Kay, could work closely with Frost as his manager and secretary, with Frost just a short walk away. The property, the Homer Noble Farm, was a handsome 150 acres on a gentle slope a mile west of Bread Loaf. The Morrisons and their two children would live in the farmhouse half a mile up a private road, Frost by himself in a one-bedroom cabin uphill from the farmhouse.

Thompson thought "The Schism" was a poem about coming to terms with the physicality of sex. Recognizing the sex act as necessary for the perpetuation of life, the poem declares, "I do not shame," notwithstanding the ignobility of "mans uncomely froth" (a phrase from the seventeenth-century quotation, of the poet Robert Herrick, that Ted's poem takes as its epigraph). Thompson thought the poem was banal. Frost thought it was revelatory: a confession that Ted no longer slept with Kay, having recourse to onanism instead as a compensatory measure. Ted and Kay were married in name only, and Kay, whom Frost was in love with, was his.

V.

Thompson learned all about Frost's love when he visited the wintering poet six months later in Key West.

It had all started with the sudden death of Elinor, Frost's wife of forty-three years, in March 1938. She had died of a heart attack in Gainesville, Florida, where she and Robert were spending the winter with family. Frost told Thompson how he had paced outside Elinor's room after her heart attack while her doctors attended to her, trying to listen for her breathing. Her breaths were hoarse and intermittent, and then it was over. Frost went to bed sick and exhausted. While he lay ill with strep throat, his eldest daughter, Lesley, told her father in a fit of anger that no artist should marry. He agreed with her, he told Thompson, for a time. But his grief progressed from an awful sense of guilt to a kind of nihilism—or so it seemed to Frost. It was in this state, in which Frost felt as if nothing mattered to him anymore, that Kay had visited him over the summer and the two had a tryst. She seemed interested; he thought, *Why not?*; and so, he said, they did. Then the poet found himself in love. He was in love with a woman more than twenty years his junior, he sixty-two and she thirty-nine. She had two small children and a husband she had no plans to leave.

When Thompson's trip had fallen into place, he had written to Kay, "I am practically walking on air. . . . I should almost be afraid to have him know how much I love him." The trip would be the longest stretch of time he had spent with Frost. He had two weeks to talk to Frost, two weeks to keep the great man company and begin his biographical undertaking in earnest. Meanwhile, the great man had two weeks to miss his beloved, who had, he said, abandoned him after taking him to Florida and spending two weeks with him there.

He felt neglected after three days without hearing from her. After five, he put his biographer up to tricking her with a false warning. "GETTING SERIOUS," Thompson telegraphed Kay, Frost having been in poor health since a sudden trip to a Boston hospital in late December that kept him there for more than a month. Kay dutifully wrote, but it was never enough. Frost said to Thompson one night, "If I don't hear from her tomorrow, you're going to have your patient back in bed." "He tried to smile," Thompson recalled, "while his eyes filled with tears and his lips quivered."

In Frost's long talks with Thompson about his past, he made a major theme of how bad he was. Frost said he had been ruthless with Elinor, had gotten her to marry him by force of will. He had been "riff-raff," Thompson wrote—"a rebel," "an outlaw," "always a wild, lawless, immoral fellow at heart." His wife had suffered a life of disappointments. She had blamed him for some, such as not encouraging the children enough. She had wrapped up her hope in the children, only to have them disappoint her. She had always shared in his poetry but had never told him that she shared in his success. Frost said that she had always been eloquent in her silences, and he returned again and again in his talks with Thompson not just to what she said but to what she may have meant in purposive silence. She had hoped her children would never have children. Frost worried she had wished the same for herself.

Thompson reported to Kay after three days with Frost: "I am having the time of my life."

Biographer and subject walked together for miles on the balmy island. They took a walk with Robert Moses, had a talk with Wallace Stevens, saw John Dewey laid out in the sun; they made up games for themselves on the beach, collected shells, tossed rocks in the water, watched the waves. They talked about the act Frost referred to as "what they call love," which he described as "a mixture of strangeness and intimacy," as Thompson recorded, "the happiest time [being] the time when there is an even balance between the two."

"Like the difficulty of looking straight into eyes," said Frost, "the splendor of it is almost too much. We avoid it not out of false modesty but out of shyness for intimacy."

"We have gotten past being embarrassed by each others [sic] eyes," Thompson wrote to himself.

He made note of some qualities in his subject that were less than ideal: Frost's moody "ups and downs," his "self-recriminations," his tendency to misread his own past and to take resentments from his previous life out on his new beloved. Yet Thompson struck his old note to himself after seeing it all: "Lucky he doesn't know how much I love him."

VI.

And then something shifted. Something unsettled Thompson's feelings about Frost. It was a shift with no recorded epiphany, no dramatic scene, no revelation or realization saved for posterity, but the poet would never again be quite the same in Thompson's eyes.

When Thompson came home from his trip, he wrote to lover and beloved with separate counsel. He had come to believe that their entanglement was a catastrophe to which they had to put an immediate end. "The real trouble" with Frost, Thompson wrote to Kay, "is his truly pitiable dependence on you," yet he made the case in terms that betrayed a suspicion about much deeper troubles with Frost.

To Frost he made the argument, with chastising authority he would have found unthinkable a month before, that what Frost had to do was to let go and move on. Yet as he told Frost to change, he told Kay that Frost would never change unless she made him. "He has thrown the whole weight of his life on you, and has no freedom apart from you." If she cut him off entirely, he would survive. If she continued to see him and work for him, she could accept his dependence as a fact and try to accommodate it—but even this prospect seemed dubious. "Perhaps," Thompson wrote, "there is no way to satisfy the fierceness of his demanding and demanding."

The Frost he described in his letters to Kay was no longer the hero with whom he had the time of his life skipping stones, but an ornery, erratic old man. That Frost was in a bad way Thompson had known before he went south, but he came to feel that Frost was not only unwell in mind and body but responsible for his own suffering. The suffering extended to people around him, and the tendencies for which he bore responsibility were part of his character. Thompson wrote to Kay of Frost's backbiting, his tendency with the people close to him to "find fault with one to the other, and vice versa—his inevitable pastime!" Where he had reveled in the splendor of Frost's eyes, he wrote now of Frost's sadism—the "kind of sadism which you know so well."

This was the worst that Thompson had to say about Frost, and, perhaps revealingly, it was in response to Thompson's only charge against Frost that concerned him personally. Frost had told his biographer on one of their first nights together in Key West that he had granted permission to another critic, John Holmes, to write his biography, too. Kay assured him that Frost would support him and not Holmes, and Thompson went on with his work.

None of the evidence suggests that Thompson had second thoughts about wanting to write the biography. Though he worried for a time that Frost might get in his way, he seems to have suffered no crisis of faith at the prospect of writing the life of a sadist.

Perhaps Thompson still loved Frost or thought he did, at least. He said so in a few letters to Frost over the next couple of years, albeit in the midst of consolation or flattery. Regardless, it is a crux in any love story how much the lover sees the beloved as their own person and how much as an embodiment of what the lover wants. Thompson knew the poems well long before he knew the poet well, and professed his love for the poet when he hardly knew the man. If he fell in love with the art; if he also loved the idea of getting as close to it as possible—knowing it, living through it somehow; if he mistook his attachment to the art and his aspirational identification with it for actual love of the artist (he himself especially charming with new people), Thompson would not have been the first fan of an artist to do so.

As Thompson told the story decades later, he had fallen under Frost's influence with the force of a charismatic conversion. The young man who had rushed into the Wesleyan Chapel on a May evening in 1925 was not the same young man who walked out. The minister's son had been arrested by a poem about the spiritual experience of the literary imagination. And then the admirer shared his own literary effort with his hero—a poem about how faith when disappointed has a way of finding a new object to rest in—and found himself seen, understood. He devoted himself to poetry in the tradition of, and then to the poetry of, his new authority, and won his approval and trust. When the biographer was appointed and got to see his subject's private life intimately, he suffered a swift change of heart. Then he went on with his work, which would still be in progress when he died thirty-three years later, ten years after the death of his subject.

VII.

Though it is impossible to know what Thompson was arrested by in "The Freedom of the Moon" other than sheer beauty and grace, the poem he brought in to show Frost might offer a clue. "Delusion," Thompson's poem about Santa Claus, bears more than a passing resemblance to the poem of Frost's that set Thompson on fire, making it plausible that Thompson wrote the poem in emulation of the master, a signal of understanding and affinity, a way to take up Frost's poem in a kind of conversation and see how Frost himself would respond.

The poems are similar in form (two short stanzas), perspective (a first-person speaker talking about fantastical things they imagine), and tone (a disarming ease in manner, in tension with the difficulty of the matter). Both are manifestly poems about faith of some kind or other, both less obviously about the article of faith that Santa Claus celebrates: the entry of God into humanity with Jesus's birth. That the poems are both allusions to much the same subject is a sign that Thompson plausibly saw the main subtext of Frost's poem, which would not have been hard for a minister's son to discern.

THE FREEDOM OF THE MOON

I've tried the new moon tilted in the air
Above a hazy tree-and-farmhouse cluster
As you might try a jewel in your hair.
I've tried it fine with little breadth of luster,

Alone, or in one ornament combining
With one first-water star almost as shining.

I put it shining anywhere I please.
By walking slowly on some evening later,
I've pulled it from a crate of crooked trees,
And brought it over glossy water, greater,
And dropped it in, and seen the image wallow,
The color run, all sorts of wonder follow.

The first sign of Jesus in the poem is much the same as it was for the magi in the Gospel of Matthew: new and shining near the horizon. Images of the Nativity cluster around the "hazy tree-and-farmhouse cluster"—the tree and farmhouse like the manger in which Jesus is born, the haze like the magi's gifts of frankincense and myrrh, the jewel like those of the bejeweled magi. The speaker sees the new moon with a star in one instance, without one in another, just as a star appears over the manger as a sign of the Nativity in the Gospel of Matthew but not in the Gospel of Luke. (It was Frost's wont to allude to theological disputes.) All of this is in the first half of the poem. The second takes up the story from the next chapter of Matthew, in which John the Baptist (the "crooked trees" calling up John's quotation of the prophet Isaiah in Matthew 3:1) gives Jesus his baptism: "And Jesus, when he was baptized, went up straightway out of the water: and lo, the heavens were opened unto him, and he saw the Spirit of God descending like a dove, and lighting upon him" (Matthew 3:16). As Jesus ascends from the water and has a vision of God, so does the image of the moon when "dropped" in the water seem to come alive and lead to a transcendent vision: "And dropped it in, and seen the image wallow, / The color run, all sorts of wonder follow." The color runs like the Spirit of God lighting upon Jesus, the dove descending—wings extended—like a shining new moon.

This subtext exists alongside a more obvious text, in which the new moon is a figure not of the Nativity but of the free, creative imagination.

On this latter reading, the freedom of the moon is the poet's freedom *with* the moon, the freedom to make of it different images—jewel or ornament (itself a sign of Christmas) or otherwise, each shading into the ways we imagine the moon. The poet casually shows off his powers by giving us an image—"As you might try a jewel in your hair"—no less evocative for being entirely unexpected in scale. We play with jewels, he implies, while he plays with the cosmos. In the grand tradition of Romantic poetry, the world as it is seen can be reconstituted by his godlike imagination, which does not exist just to mirror nature as in the Classical tradition. That an artist's imagination should merely reflect nature is an idea the second stanza swaggeringly rebuts. The poet pulls the moon out of the trees and drops it in the glossy water (water being a conventional image of mind or spirit), and the "image" passed through the mind of the poet does not just reflect the moon but grows and "wallow[s]" (as if it were animate and splashing), comes to life.

The Holy Spirit begetting divine transformation, the artistic spirit forging creative transformation—each story coheres. How they cohere with each other is harder to say. To see the two new moons under identical aspect is to feel the convergence of two faiths, Romantic and Christian, that on reflection all but contradict. It is to imagine a union inevitably sundered if confronted by doubt.

How the problem appeared to the young convert in the Wesleyan Chapel, how much he was thrown from wonder at the poet's imagination to doubt of his own, is strictly unknowable. He might not have seen it as a problem at all, being instead simply moved by the beauty of an art no less powerful than that of the faith he was raised in. He might also have taken the resemblance of myths as evidence for the Romantic cause, the sign of an artistic freedom great enough to create a world religion as you might try a jewel in your hair. Yet "Delusion" might also offer a clue to a differ-ent way of reconciling the new moons: one can hear Frost's poem spoken with an irony like that of "Delusion." The implicit speaker of the poem, an arrogant poet—not Frost but a grandstanding stand-in for him—

believes his own imagination free but fails to see his having channeled the fundamental myth of Christianity. Frost's stand-in, however sublime his talents, is like the kind of grown-up implicitly mocked in Thompson's poem for thinking himself superior to the child but still engaged in wishful thinking on the matter of his faith. Thompson thought for some years that Frost shared his religious unbelief, so perhaps he thought his poem underlined a point he took Frost to be making.

Yet the irony of the poem might also bite in a different way. In fact an irony at the expense of the reader, not a hypothetical speaker, runs through the very myth alluded to in the poem, which offers reason to mistrust the imaginative freedom in which we readers may have gloried. Confronted with the problem of whether the "wonder" that follows the end of the poem is the transcendent wonder of the divine revealing itself or just the work of our imagination, we share the perspective of John the Baptist, not seeing the revelation directly but having to take it on faith. (Those of us inclined toward religious doubt can take this as a challenge: we may not have any direct experience of God, but neither did John the Baptist, who had to imagine it.) His story tells us that he imagines the revelation accurately after following through with the ritual commanded of him. It is only those like him in the New Testament who make the necessary changes to their own perspectives who come to understand Christ's teaching, those who become as children, not the wise men. The letter of Jesus's life may be unknowable—maybe Frost meant to make this point by alluding to the inconsistency between Matthew and Luke—but the spirit of his teaching is the truth and the way. Far from an adequate substitute for religion, the free imagination could be an idol, the worship of which distracts from the worship of God. The poem could even be spoken not in the voice of a poet pretending to be godlike but spoken as if in the voice of God, free to set the moon wherever He wishes and to reveal Himself to people as much and as symbolically as He pleases. It would not be the only time Frost wrote a poem in the hidden voice of God. Then again, this is not an especially pious thing for a poet to do, which serves as a reminder that the pious undertones of the poem could themselves present a false god, bringing the irony full circle. We can only imagine.

Frost never wrote another poem so representative of how he took himself as an artist. Nor did he ever write another so characteristic of how he would be taken by readers. By whatever force of attraction, the young man in the chapel had been drawn to a poem with graces and silences so plainly and beguilingly like those of the poet himself.

VIII.

The Song of Songs *is* hard.

—FROST, "THE CONSTANT SYMBOL"

Frost, when especially playful or vulnerable, was liable to conduct himself like an unfinished poem. He lingered on the strange within the familiar, the penumbra of doubt at the edge of the known. He let his mind rest in uncertainties such as the space between feeling and impulse, impulse and motive, between motives real and recalled. In private conversations, he often seemed to act as if trying out a role he halfway believed in. Where his poems would offer a perspective in delicate balance—often evoked to repel as it appeals, shown in clear and compelling detail along with an understory of reasons to question the perspective, another voice nested as an undersong inside it—Frost in person could betray the wildness without the exquisite composure. Where his poems would offer a perspective to stage a conversation in the minds of his readers, Frost the man could cast the people around him in roles they hardly knew they were playing.

When Thompson visited him in Key West, Frost had a chance to act out his grief. He saw the worst in everything his dead wife had not said, as he had read his wildest dreams into Ted Morrison's poem back in August. Thompson was there to tell his story, Horatio to his Hamlet, and much of what Frost told Thompson in Key West was the story of his life from the perspective of his guilt, his sense of unbearable responsibility. The tryst Frost said he had with Kay brought out in him a knot of emotions hopelessly entangled somewhere deep in the unwritten poem of his mind. Frost said he felt bitterness, spite, and resentment, but not toward whom or about what. "It was almost in spite and bitterness" that Frost chose to sleep with her, as though he could not be sure what his impulses were and whether they added up to a motive. It was "almost a kind of revenge for all the past"—for the past, Thompson wrote, but not on whom, not on Kay or himself or Elinor's ghost, although all were plausible objects of revenge. Frost's motives were a mystery to him. What he knew was that he had fallen in love and his wife of four decades was dead, and from such fixed points he drew all manner of constellations.

Frost had lost the woman he called "the unspoken half of everything I ever wrote." "Pretty nearly every one of my poems will be found to be about her if rightly read," Frost wrote to friends after Elinor's death, in April 1938. "But I must try to remember they were as much about her as she liked and permitted them to be. Without ever saying a word she set limits I must continue to observe."

Frost was as out of sorts that fall as he had been in his first weeks of grief, but he managed to write a poem that seemed to give life like nothing else to his confusion. She was like a "silken tent" to him, setting limits that bound him inescapably but imperceptibly unless the winds of fortune shifted. The poem is as intimate as he was with Elinor and as private as she had them be with others, a poem the experience of which, like that of his love for her, one can hardly begin to convey without feeling its nuances:

THE SILKEN TENT

She is as in a field a silken tent
At midday when a sunny summer breeze
Has dried the dew and all its ropes relent,
So that in guys it gently sways at ease,

And its supporting central cedar pole,
That is its pinnacle to heavenward
And signifies the sureness of the soul,
Seems to owe naught to any single cord,
But strictly held by none, is loosely bound
By countless silken ties of love and thought
To everything on earth the compass round,
And only by one's going slightly taut
In the capriciousness of summer air
Is of the slightest bondage made aware.

For all the complications in this one-sentence sonnet, the syntax that sways like a silken tent in the wind, Frost frames it as an elegy with the first two words of the poem, "She is," words that stand on their own grammatically, the pole and "sureness of the soul" around which all else wavers, like the possibility that her body had been a tent for her soul that survives in heaven, an earthly tabernacle become an eternal *house not made with hands* (2 Corinthians 5). Her existence is his deepest conviction or his hope against hope.

Lesley thought so well of the poem that she asked to have its first line engraved under her mother's name on the family tombstone. She said so to Thompson over dinner in December 1963, and Thompson was stunned: "I almost dropped my false teeth on my plate!" Lesley was surprised by Thompson's surprise; she knew the poem was written for her mother, she said. Thompson told her that Frost had told him many times that the poem had been written for Kay. Lesley continued to remember the poem from her mother's lifetime, but the line never made it onto the gravestone.

Frost wrote about his passion for Kay to his old friend and critical champion, the poet Louis Untermeyer, in November 1938:

I was thrust out into the desolateness of wondering about my past whether it had not been too cruel to those I had dragged with me. . . . Then came this girl stepping innocently into my days to give me something to think of besides dark regrets. . . . You can figure it out for yourself how my status with a girl like her might be the perfect thing for me at my age in my position. I wish in some indirect way she could come to know how I feel toward her.

The "girl" had just turned forty—he didn't always think of her literally. She was, for all her care and companionship, a perpetual fantasy to him, a source of hope no matter how much she troubled him. He would try to let her know how he felt with a sonnet called "In Praise of Your Poise," later renamed "The Silken Tent."

"The Silken Tent" borrows a figure from a poem in the first book of poetry Frost read as a child. In "The Bracelet to Julia," Robert Herrick ties a "silken twist" around the wrist of his beloved to show how loosely she's "bound" to him even though he's hopelessly bound to her ("thy bond-slave is my heart"). Her binding is only symbolic, but it's a symbol of the depth of his. It's possible that Frost felt an echo of similarity between his situation and Herrick's, both of whom felt the need of the women they were writing for while the women seemed free to decide. In any case, Frost collapses Herrick's figure of the difference between freedom and necessity in love into a figure of love swaying between them, *loosely* bound and loosely *bound*.

One of the problems at this point in the story is the relationship between attachment and abstraction. When Frost wrote a poem about something he loved, for someone he loved, to someone he loved, he gave a second life to something real. His poems about his farm survived the farm. We can go out to clean the pasture spring, having never known it in space, as Frost could go to it in his memory. If his poems take on a life of their own, though, what ties them to the people and places out of his attachment to which the poems grew? Why not make a poem inspired by his love for his wife into a poem about love for his secretary?

One could always appeal to the dependable caddishness of the literary imagination. The poet seeks fit words to paint the blackest face of woe and, having found them, repeats them to whoever might be cast in the role of beloved. This was not for Frost, whose poems about love, when written under the least inspiration, were not of lost or imaginary love but of love he really experienced. His flights of fancy were grounded by a woman who knew him all too well.

The sex in "The Silken Tent" seems silly at first, forced—the big central pole, the rope going taut, the pun some people hear in the title. Frost may have loved Shakespearean sexual punning, may have punned elsewhere on "country" (in "The Need of Being Versed in Country Things," a poem with an "awkward" "pump"), may have made countless innuendos to Kay in the fall of 1938, may have put "The Silken Tent," in a book dedicated to Kay, right before a poem with three "thrusts" in the first three lines ("All Revelation"), but wouldn't it be unseemly, even ghoulish, to bring sex into a poem that seems to liken your dead wife to a sort of temple in a field? Not necessarily, if you built your poem around an allusion to the greatest biblical love poem, itself read alternately as courtship and as worship: the Song of Songs.

The Song of Songs, book I, has a cedar beam and a tent in the countryside, "curtains of Solomon" associated with silk ropes, and a back-and-forth of sexual obliquities between lovers in which the lady asks the man whom her "soul loveth" where he keeps his tent at noon—midday—with the type of arcane simile in the first line of "The Silken Tent":

She is *as in a field* a silken tent

—FROST

For why should I be *as one that turneth aside* by the flocks of thy companions?

—THE SONG OF SONGS

Why should she have to seek him, her lover, her God?

Perhaps Frost was up to something in pointing out that the dew—the liquid form of frost, Frost's favorite pun—dries at about the same time the rope slackens. There is no way to prove this, as Frost, who had every reason to veil his sexual velleities for his friend's wife when he wrote about them in public, would have wanted, but one can see "The Silken Tent" as the gauzy aftermath of a tryst, metaphysical pillow talk in which there's no tension between his promiscuity and promises he made. Like the lovers in the end of book I, he imagines a cedar-beamed temple as a bower of love with a bed of grass. Tension returns in the end of the poem when the wind disrupts the lambent moment and reminds him of "capriciousness" and "bondage," the marital bond, the "seal" of love from the end of the Song of Songs: "Set me as a seal upon thine heart, as a seal upon thine arm: for love is strong as death; jealousy is cruel as the grave." His elegy comes back in response to this call—his devotion to Elinor bound, if so loosely, to his passion for Kay. "The Silken Tent," the first poem Frost is known to have written about Kay, was his last great poem about romantic love. It was also, but for the possible exception of "The Wind and the Rain," written at about the same time but most likely in the weeks before "The Silken Tent," the last great poem that Frost ever wrote.

2.

And Be the Measure

———

I.

Though possibly not the first poem Frost wrote about romantic love, the earliest that survives for posterity, "Twilight," was offered to St. Lawrence University student Elinor Miriam White in the fall of 1894 as the titular poem in the poet's first book, of which a total of two copies were printed, at the author's expense. *Twilight* consisted of five poems bound between covers of pebbled brown leather. Its author was twenty years old. The volume, despite its small circulation, would have a long and consequential afterlife as a result of events precipitated by its reception, in which Elinor, shocked to find Frost on the doorstep of her rental housing from which men were banned at most hours, sent him home on the spot. The poet was left to travel the three hundred miles back to his mother's house in the suit he had bought for the surprise. Frost tore up his copy of *Twilight*. His poetry would never be the same.

II.

Rob and Elinor met in the fall of 1891 at the start of senior year of high school. They had not met before, because Elinor, chronically sick, had done her previous coursework from home, joining her classmates at Lawrence High School only in their final year. She was still on track for valedictorian, as Rob discovered in the spring, surprised to have a rival for the title. Told as much by the head of school, who nonetheless said that Frost should be valedictorian on account of his more difficult course load— Rob had taken the Classical course, traditionally the college-preparatory alternative to the English course, which Elinor had taken—Rob insisted that the honor go to Elinor. They would be co-valedictorians at graduation in June.

Unsurprisingly, it was as scholars that their classmates would remember them. Rob and Elinor each exuded a scholarly dignity that accrues to distinction without affectation and aloofness without condescension. Both, though reserved, were not only respected but liked. Classmates recalled Elinor as "very pleasant and a favorite in the class," "a studious woman whose modesty was worthy of imitation," "a girl of rare spirit and refinement." One classmate remembered "Bob" as "a rather large framed lad with a tawny mane of blonde hair, rather dreamy eyed, with almost a pink and white complexion, although he was by no means effeminate." Another recalled Rob as "rather grave for a high school boy, though always pleasant to meet," another still as "always a perfect gentleman with the soul of a poet." A woman who sat next to Rob in their senior year recalled being "always deeply impressed by his wonderful intellectual ability, high ideals, and great literary genius. He always seemed to live in an atmosphere of lofty thoughts and high aspirations." As Rob "dwelt like a star, apart," one classmate recalled, his budding relationship with Elinor seemed like "sort of a Browning and Elizabeth Barrett affair," referring to the two titans of English Victorian poetry, who fell in love during Barrett's protracted invalidism. Rob's ethereality notwithstanding, he was invited to join the football team as a senior owing to a shortage of players, and "dumbfounded" his teammates by playing "like some wild animal let loose." "He had no fear," the team captain remembered. "Right then and there he became one of us."

The Browning and Elizabeth Barrett affair began in earnest in their second semester. Perhaps Rob had been too distracted in the fall by extracurricular commitments as well as agita such as the mysterious psychological malady of, and contraction of typhoid fever by, his younger sister, Jeanie, whose long hospital stay had also caused him to miss school. In any case, the courtship, once begun, was distinctly literary. Elinor gave him love poems copied out by hand. His first gift to her was a book of poetry by Edward Rowland Sill, a poet of high sentiment and thoroughly idealistic sensibility. He shared another new discovery shortly thereafter, the first collection of another American whose poems had won her posthumous fame, the recently published Emily Dickinson. In keeping with such tastes, Elinor had published an essay that spring in defense of idealism in fiction, as against the kind of realism whose representations of life tended in her opinion to denude it of the ideals and the active imagination that were themselves aspects of experience. Her essay, published in the Lawrence High School *Bulletin*, of which Rob had been editor in the fall before resigning over a thorough abdication of duty on the part of his staff, called for fiction that incorporated "the ideal, that element which is as difficult to outline as that far off hill against the sky, but which is surely the best of life and without which its portrayal must deteriorate." Calling for inspiration as exemplified by the poetry of William Wordsworth, she declared, "Whatever may be the resources of the various forms of art, the end is the same[:] . . . to idealize the commonplace events of our life, and to subordinate the literal to some high conception of the imagination." In this embodiment of an artist's "inmost thought and feeling" she thought art was most real.

Elinor defined realism, then fashionable in American prose fiction if not in poetry, as "that something which strips from life the glamour of fancy and imagination, and accentuates its sordid details." Seen realistically, her and Rob's lives had not been entirely easy. The illness that for years kept her from school, in relative isolation, was only the latest expression of a physical vulnerability pronounced throughout her childhood. Her father, once a minister in the Universalist church, had lost his faith and taken up carpentry, sowing an atmosphere of tension between her parents if not economic precarity. The Frosts were in that last respect less fortunate. Rob's father, William Prescott Frost Jr., had passed away when Rob was eleven, leaving the family with almost no money, having neglected to pay his life insurance premium. Rob's mother, Isabelle Moodie Frost (or Belle), took the casket and her children across the continent by train from San Francisco, where the family had lived since shortly before Rob's birth, to Lawrence, burying her husband where he had been raised and where his parents still lived. She had gone to the baggage car in Omaha and Chicago to check the casket, leaving her children on board. In Lawrence, she and the children lived for a time with her in-laws, a retired foreman from a local mill who kept house for a wife who devoted herself to reading about women's rights. Humorless and dour, they left their grandchildren and daughter-in-law feeling like the poor relations they literally were before Belle moved her family half a dozen miles north of the city to Salem, New Hampshire, where she found work teaching school as she had done before marriage. Her salary was modest and her jobs inconsistent, leading to a number of local moves and forcing the children, Rob especially, to contribute by odd jobs where they could. She considered apprenticing Rob to a local cabinetmaker in lieu of enrolling him in high school. It would have been quite the contrast with his father, who had not only gone on to Harvard but graduated with honors and an offer to stay on and teach. In the event, Rob, though not previously much of a scholar or even an especially regular student, passed the entrance examinations to Lawrence High School and began taking the train down to the school where his father had once distinguished himself.

Lawrence High School was in those days an unusually good place to learn high conceptions of the imagination. Its pedagogical strength was all the more unusual because Lawrence was largely a working-class industrial city, home to the largest mill in the country and a population that was almost half foreign-born, most from Ireland, French Canada, Germany. Rob's chief occupation as a student was Latin and then also

Greek translation, taught by a group of unusually gifted and distinguished women who, like Frost's mother, had gone straight from high school to teaching. Their instruction was so scholarly that Rob did not appreciate for years that the language he was translating for several hours a week was poetry. He took perpetual fascination in the history and literature of ancient Rome and Greece, especially Caesar, Cicero, Virgil, Homer. Such precedents complemented the biblical teaching he had received at length from his mother, along with the reading in vernacular literature, especially poetry, that had begun with her reading to him and his sister for years before he began to read books on his own around the beginning of high school. His early enthusiasms included the episodic schoolboy tales of Thomas Hughes, grand and adventurous histories and legends of pre-European America and pre-British Scotland (James Fenimore Cooper, Jane Porter, Walter Scott), Longfellow's poems in their great range and Whittier's in their abolitionism, and all the poetry of Poe in its dreamlike and gothic Romanticism. The book he probably read most often in high school was a brilliant work of popular astronomy, *Our Place Among Infinities*, which Rob inscribed in those years with a passage from the Romantic poet Percy Bysshe Shelley proclaiming the subordination of the vast material universe to the "Eternal Nature" that transcends it.

Having not studied English literature in high school, Rob was introduced to more of English poetry by Elinor. One can get a sense of the caliber of her education by noting that it sent her to college, a rarity for any American at the time that was all the rarer for a young woman without significant means. The kind of clipping that ran in the *Bulletin* speaks to the educational standards of the English course: "'92 Milton students find that other things have been 'Lost' as well as 'Paradise,' among which may be mentioned their remembrance of nominative absolutes and other little intricacies of English grammar." This sort of thing qualified as "gossip" at this public school in a New England mill town that routinely sent students to some of the best colleges in the country.

Elinor's valedictory talk was right before Rob's. Her speech,

"Conversation as a Force in Life," made the case that conversation among intimates could be not only fulfilling but inspirational to the extent that it fostered mutual understanding. Such an understanding demanded sincerity, however, which was served best not only by speech but by "sympathetic silence" in the absence of having something urgent to say. Rob's speech was an ode not to conversation but to solitary reflection, contending that one's greatness and originality were forged not in the thick of action but in retrospective contemplation, or "after-thought." Rob phrased his paean to Emersonian heroism in the language of Shelley, alluding to his legendarily daring example. The speech was crafted as an arch conceit, channeling an imaginary priestess who was unveiling an invisible "monument" to the invisible act of after-thought, consecrated by the singing that followed of the class hymn, also written by Rob. Observers noted his stilted delivery. Rob remembered his mortal fear of the crowd.

Rob had wanted Elinor to attend the Harvard Annex, later Radcliffe, near him at Harvard. She planned instead to go to St. Lawrence University in Canton, New York, a Universalist college, and Rob himself changed his destination to Dartmouth, where he could get a partial scholarship through part-time work for the school. Still, Rob and Elinor had the summer together, full of leisurely hours floating together on the Merrimack River near Lawrence. Rob read Elinor Shelley's *Epipsychidion*, the high-water mark of anti-institutional romantic idealism in English nineteenth-century poetry, casting state-sanctioned marriage as a degradation of the spiritual union of a pair of souls truly in love. The long poem, drawing extensively on the Song of Songs and dealing incidentally with the tension between the poet's love of two different women, builds to an extended description of a marvelous lone dwelling in the wilderness, the site "at the noontide hour" of "the fresh dew of languid love" by which the poet and the woman he addresses "shall be one / Spirit within two frames." On such terms would Rob and Elinor be bound in spirit if not yet wedded in the eyes of the state. They exchanged rings before summer's end.

III.

Years after the summer of 1892, a young acquaintance of Rob's at the time, whom he remembered as "little Susie Holmes," recalled Rob and Elinor passing through her parents' yard to the dock where Rob kept the rowboat he had procured for the summer to take Elinor out on the river. It was the same yard under whose pear trees Rob would lie on his back in the grass, telling stories to her and her brothers "all about," she recalled, "knights and dragons and prancing steed." Though the legends once seemed entirely original to Susie, she later thought they owed something to Tennyson's *Idylls of the King*.

The idyll of the summer, like that at the end of *Epipsychidion*, would not last. The lovers met reality with their departure for school. From the first, Rob found the atmosphere at Dartmouth almost uniquely unsuited to the life of the mind, with a campus full of geographically isolated young men engaged in perpetual hijinks and war games, in which he himself was an avid participant. The boisterousness distracted from schoolwork that did little to compel Rob in any case, less for the subject matter, which included Plato and readings of Homer in the original Greek, than the whole enterprise of working to satisfy a teacher's approval, which felt anathema to Rob at his new stage of life and education. He had come to feel, as he later recalled, that his education had reached the point where he wanted to "do the telling," which meant no longer wanting to be told. In his ambition and conspicuous pride, he felt a stark contrast between the rowdy hallways and the teacher-pleasing classroom on the one hand and "the after-thoughts of long nights beneath the universe" on the other. When Rob took long walks, often at nighttime, in the woods around Dartmouth, his classmates were perplexed. One can only conjecture just how much he missed Elinor as well as his mother, with whom, for reasons presumably not exhausted by financial circumstance and his fear of the dark, he had shared a bedroom before leaving for college. His mother was enough on his mind that, when he learned after Thanksgiving of the severe disciplinary problems with her class of unruly grammar school students in Methuen, a town between Lawrence and Salem, he resolved to take over her class and impose the necessary order. He packed his things and left without even a word to the dean.

The cause of his sudden departure has always been less than entirely clear. In addition to homesickness, a weak sense of academic purpose, and a desire to help his struggling mother, he chafed at Dartmouth under the financial conditions imposed by his fastidious grandfather, who asked for an itemized accounting of Rob's modest allowance. Such constraints set him apart from his peers, whose relative wealth seems to have made Rob feel a sense of shame. One can see as much between the lines of the closest thing to a contemporaneous account of his decision to leave school, written five years afterward: "The fact was I was in financial straits and I wasn't the kind that could serve for hire his own classmates in a menial capacity. An education wasn't worth it." Still, his decision to leave seems to have been overdetermined and always a bit of a mystery, even to himself. In this it was like other momentous departures Frost would make throughout his life.

Rob found himself, come winter, among a different kind of "rough boys" than those he had left. Having procured rattans in case his pupils' behavior called for corporal punishment, Rob had recourse to them with some frequency. An older boy once came at Rob with a knife, which he wrested away. Rob lasted at the school through the end of the term, after which he joined Elinor's mother and sisters in a rented house overlooking Canobie Lake near Salem, the women having gone to the country to support Elinor's sister Ada in her suffering from a nervous disorder as severe and mysterious as Jeanie's had been. With Elinor's father not accompanying the women, Rob helped out practically in his capacity as man of the house, moving from his mother's aid to that of his prospective mother-in-law. Elinor joined the household later that spring. Rob urged her to leave college and marry him, his concern now with conventional as well as spiritual matrimony. Elinor refused for the time being, on the grounds that Rob lacked a way to support them. The straightforwardness of her reason did not prevent the two of them from understanding it in strikingly different terms. Rob would come to think of her refusal as at best a judgment on the impracticality of his ambition to live as a poet, at worst a sign that her commitment to him was under threat from other men, doubtless some with better prospects, with whom she was associating at school. Elinor thought they would burden their families by marrying before they could provide for themselves. What for him was crushingly personal was for her an acknowledgment of economic reality. The spring of 1893 saw the beginning of what would later be called an economic depression but was then known as hard times, which persisted for much of the decade.

Elinor returned to college and Rob to his mother's house. Perhaps it was Elinor's recent refusal that prompted him to undertake the most outlandish scheme for employment he would ever attempt, endeavoring to act as a kind of promoter and manager for a man whose self-advertisement as a "Shakespearean reader" Rob had found in the newspaper. After booking a venue in Boston and alerting local critics, Rob was disappointed, even embarrassed, by the reader, whose elocutionary style lacked the slightest dramatic inflection of character. Rob meanwhile made a project of reading Shakespeare over the following months with a special ear for the tones of speech implicit in lines from the plays and the sonnets. Much of this reading took place in the unlikely venue of the Arlington Woolen Mills in Lawrence, where he worked through the following winter replacing lamp filaments and tending dynamos. The task allowed Rob and his co-worker, especially on quiet shifts overnight, to sit on their assigned roof above the dynamo room and, as Rob's old associate remembered, "read Shakespeare's thunders to the heavy machinery of the electric power plant, and [sing] his sonnets to the purr of the brushes on the big dynamos."

Rob's literary discovery in this period of most immediate consequence was a poem he found at the historic Old Corner Bookstore in Boston. Picking up a volume titled simply *Poems* by Francis Thompson, Rob happened on a poem called "The Hound of Heaven." Having only enough money for his fare home on the train, he bought the book and walked the twenty-five miles, reading "The Hound of Heaven" again and again. "If I could meet that poem again for the first time," he said many years later, "I'd walk the same miles and find them easy underfoot."

Rob was spellbound by Thompson's vision of God as a hound who pursued man no matter how much man fled Him. The poem was not only enthralling but literally inspiring, as he found on an afternoon early in the winter of 1894 when lines of a budding poem began to come to him in a cadence straight out of Thompson's incantatory poem. Rob bought himself a modicum of privacy by locking the door to the kitchen, the only heated room in the floor-through apartment he shared with his mother and sister. Feeling himself inspired, Rob wrote a myth about inspiration. His myth is told in an elaborate logic of symbolic associations, the poem spoken as if by someone who had once shared the perspective of a wind with whom he was united in spirit—hence inspired—and, when a wind, flew briefly at one with a butterfly in a figure of spiritual union. The lush formalities of the language hardly help to make this all clearer, the poem beginning, "Thine emulous fond flowers are dead too." As "The Hound of Heaven" inverts man's search for God into God's pursuit of man, "My Butterfly" inverts the search for inspiration into the spirit's pursuit of the being it possesses, reversing the canonical Romantic ode to the wind's inspiration, Shelley's "Ode to the West Wind," from Shelley's desire to join by imagination with the winter-bringing wind, to the mysterious exertions of the same wind to make the speaker at one in spirit with his butterfly. It is a figure of grace in pursuit of the graceful. In fusing Thompson's poem about grace with Shelley's atheistic poem of inspiration from spiritual forces other than God's, Rob borrowed something of Thompson's theodicy, which argued that God could not reveal Himself constantly or risk having man fall in love with His gifts rather than with Him. Similarly, Rob's myth is about the evanescence of grace despite the enduring love the spirit has for its embodied being. An elegy, "My Butterfly" reads like a spell that conjures the experience of grace as the poem describes its having passed.

Something in the poem felt different to Rob from anything he had written before. He submitted it to the New York *Independent*, a major national weekly whose interest in poetry had struck him at Dartmouth when he saw an issue with a poem on the front page accompanied by a substantial essay. The editors were delighted to publish "My Butterfly," as they told Rob with deliberate speed. It would be his first real publication. On reading "My Butterfly," the poetry editor called the rest of the staff over to listen because she had just discovered a poet.

Thine emulous fond flowers are dead too,
And the daft sun-assaulter, he
That frighted thee so oft, is fled or dead:
  Save only me
Nor is it sad to thee
  Save only me,
There is no one to mourn thee in the fields.
  The grey grass is scarce dappled with the snow,
Its two banks have not shut upon the river,
   But it is long ago,
  It seems forever,
Since first I saw thee glance
With all the dazzling other ones,
   In airy dalliance,
  Precipitate in love,
  Tossed up, tossed up, and tangling above,
Like a limp rose wreath in a fairy dance . . .

IV.

On March 28, 1894, two days after Rob's twentieth birthday, he shared his exultation in a letter responding to the man who had lately accepted his poem on behalf of *The Independent*. "The memory of your note," Rob told William Hayes Ward, "will be a fresh pleasure to me when I waken for a good many mornings to come." Self-conscious about the modesty of his formal education, about which Ward had inquired, Rob betrayed the wish that his poem would give a different impression:

> If you mean what might be called the legitimate education I have received when you speak of "training" and "line of study," I hope that the quality of my poem would seem to account for far more of this than I have really had. I am only graduated of a public high-school. Besides this, a while ago, I was at Dartmouth College for a few months until recalled by necessity. But this inflexible ambition trains us best, and to love poetry is to study it.

Rob might as well have said that he hoped the sophistication of his writing would compensate for the unsophistication of his pedigree. It was a remarkably candid admission for someone so manifestly self-conscious, a tension underscored in his professing self-doubt as he pronounced his self-belief:

> I sincerely hope I have done nothing to make you over-estimate me. It cannot be, though, for rather than equal what I have written and be satisfied, I will idle away an age accumulating a greater inspiration.

The remainder of Rob's editorial correspondence at the time was with Ward's sister, Susan Hayes Ward, poetry editor of *The Independent*. Rob's letters to her amount to the most revealing portrait of the artist as a young man in his own contemporaneous prose. They stand in contrast to the obliquities of his verse at the time as well as his retrospective prose, which was, when not partly inaccurate from discretion or forgetfulness, relentlessly cunning and thus strategic in its self-revelation even when he meant every word. Of all the arts Frost would master in his artistic maturity, none was subtler than his ability to discuss himself with such fine degrees of reserve and disclosure that the line between revelation of self and concealment of self blurred imperceptibly. Yet Rob had not, in the weeks and months after his twentieth birthday, so mastered what he would later call "the technique of sincerity." His self-consciousness was ingenuous, not mannered, and concerned nothing so much as his manner, or style, as he himself worked out the perennial mystery for young writers of the way to present their inner lives to the world.

While Rob's introductory letter to Susan, in April, concerned literary style in the context of the poem he was failing to revise in line with her editorial directives, his subsequent letter set out to revise the mistakes he had made in presenting himself in the first. "Since last I wrote I hope I have aged enough not to seem so callow and distasteful as I used," he wrote six weeks after first writing. "I have been thoroughly overhauled in search of affectations," he wrote, his search having found no affectation in writing such a sentence as a way to say he was trying to sound natural. It is the voice of young ambition to think it can be thoroughly overhauled in six weeks and to trip over itself in the awkward phase between self-consciousness and self-awareness like an adolescent deer not grown into its spindly legs. Awkward, too, is the combination of self-abasement and self-aggrandizement also characteristic of young aspiration, both so freely shared with the woman whom he regarded as the first person in two years to offer thoughtful praise of his work ("My thanks unlimited!"). He freely called himself provincial, worried that "My Butterfly" was better than other poems he could possibly write, and that he could not inhabit again its driving passion to revise the poem, and that they had perhaps better not publish the poem anyway and that, come to think of it, he had actually been childish to say so, all the while confiding that "to betray myself utterly, such an one am I that even in my failures I find all the promise I require to justify the astonishing magnitude of my ambition."

One can recognize the author of such correspondence in the poems Frost wrote in this period. They are the work of someone acutely conscious of his strange interiority, varieties of solitary and halfway-dreamed experience in which the poet is often conscious of feeling distantly watched. That such observation of him implies no comprehension is the plaintive implication of the end of "An Unhistoric Spot," also included in *Twilight*, in which the poet's reverie from lying under a tree and listening to crickets and thrushes is punctured by other people observing him rather less rapturously than he observes a spire of grass. The poem ends laconically, almost dolefully: "And every one that passes looks at me." It is such a state of inner isolation that "Twilight" by its language attempts to transfigure, its self-conscious "invocation" addressed to the half-light to draw it toward him in a figure of the spiritual union into which the reader of the poem, addressed as if she were twilight, is also symbolically drawn. In its straining toward the proper language to evoke a similitude of experience with the reader it addresses, in the conspicuous magnitude of its ambition, the poem is much like Rob's letters to Susan, with which the poem also shares the unmistakable awkwardness of rhetorical affectation. Where his prose was attempting to fit his intimate experience into a language of abstract formality, "Twilight" was representative of his verse of the time in attempting to fit his experience into the kind of elevated vocabulary from which he had borrowed as a senior in high school, the incantatory cadences of Shelley.

"Twilight" was the result of a self-conscious attempt to write another poem like "My Butterfly." If the earlier poem was a kind of spell, the later was all the more so. In the progress in "Twilight" from the speaker's feeling himself singled out by the melancholy gaze of the twilight to a grand pronouncement of the speaker's spiritual union with his reader, the poem seeks to elevate an imperceptible spiritual reality into the stuff of felt experience, transfiguring articles of faith into objects of perception, making things unseen seen:

TWILIGHT

Why am I first in thy so sad regard,
O twilight gazing from I know not where?
I fear myself as one more than I guessed!
Am I instead of one so very fair?—
That thou art sorrowful and I oppressed?

High in the isolating air,
Over the inattentive moon,
Two birds sail on great wings,
          And vanish soon.
(And they leave the north sky bare!)

The far-felt solitudes that harbor night,
Wake to the singing of the wood-bird's fright.

By invocation, O wide silentness,
Thy spirit and my spirit pass in air!
They are unmemoried consciousness,
          Nor great nor less!
And thou art here and I am everywhere!

Rob, in naming his book for the poem, offered Elinor what was in effect an analogy—that no separation of physical space would prevent her,
holding him first in her so sad regard, from being joined with him spirit
to spirit as are the lovers in *Epipsychidion*. If she did not feel as much every
moment, she had the poem to read for the spell to be cast.

     Though the poem was not original in either ideas or diction, one
could hardly doubt its sincerity. Perhaps that was part of the problem.
The year had seen Rob increasingly distressed by his and Elinor's far-
felt solitudes, and in his distress he grew jealous. With Elinor off in
college while he worked sporadically at odd jobs in Boston and taught
at another district school (as he told Susan ashamedly), Rob worried
that Elinor's interest was wandering. The details are obscure, but he
seems to have done some combination of accusing her of waywardness,
warning her parents of the waywardness and immorality of her going to
dances, imploring her again to leave college early and marry him (conventionally), suspecting her even of getting engaged to another young
man, and generally making a pain of himself in the role of jealous lover.

It is hard to know just how strained the relationship grew—and Elinor did agree to finish school a year early and marry Rob on condition of employment—but it was into an atmosphere of tensions begotten by his own difficulties with their separation, not an idealized world of lovers longing for their lived experience to reflect the intimacy of their spiritual union, that Rob showed up unannounced with his first book and was promptly sent home.

V.

Shortly after returning to Lawrence, Frost left home for New York once again, this time for New York City. There, on November 6, he boarded a ship with passage to Norfolk, Virginia, from which he went down to the Great Dismal Swamp, walking through the fabled stretch of wilderness in the moonlight. He walked for a time on a narrow plank bridge no more than a foot or so wide, his solitude punctured by the sound of someone behind him. It was another man—a "pleasant Negro" as Rob would recall him—holding an axe on his shoulder and singing. Rob's solitude was punctured yet again when the boardwalk reached an opening of water revealing a steamer that took Rob aboard.

Rob rode along to nearby Elizabeth City, North Carolina, where the boat welcomed a rowdy assemblage of drinkers and duck hunters. They sailed through Albemarle Sound to the Outer Banks, a long sliver of land off the coast, before turning back to Elizabeth City. A saloonkeeper who had met Frost during the voyage made inquiries to get him hired by a local newspaperman and by the principal of a local academy, who indeed looked into hiring Frost, who, after all the fuss, recused himself and started north, this time on foot. Rob spent a night in a lumber camp, was robbed by a brakeman on a freight train he had hopped onto, and spent another night in a homeless encampment—a "tramp's jungle," Frost called it—where the men sat and told tales of their travels. He made his way to Baltimore, where, broke and hungry, he appealed for help to a minister whose name he knew from his mother's reading, only to have the minister, a famous moral reformer, look him over coldly and hand him change, some of which fell to the floor. Days later, again hungry, Rob inquired about a job at a grocery store, where he worked for a matter of days before writing to his mother for passage home.

Susie Holmes remembered years later the day at the end of November when she and some of the Frosts' other family friends were gathered together, worried on account of the rumor that Rob had been lost in the Great Dismal Swamp, when the door opened to reveal Rob, who noticed his old friend Horace Smith in the group, who locked eyes with Rob before the two went straight for each other and started to wrestle in front of the crowd, rumpling their suits in the process. Little Susie Holmes, though "afraid one or the other of you would get hurt," "was glad you were home and had not been eaten by alligators or bitten by snakes."

On December 4, Frost wrote to Susan Hayes Ward: "The occasion is, or was, the appearance in print under your supervision of my first poem." "My Butterfly" had appeared in *The Independent* two days after Rob had left harbor in New York City. He had not noticed the poem's publication, for reasons he explained first literally and then experientially—"I for my part have been out of time a little while," something like unmemoried consciousness. Rob attempted to share his reaction to seeing his poem in print. At a loss for how to convey his inner state, he elaborated on various manners of presenting himself and their relative merits under the circumstances:

> Before proceeding further I perceive I must assume an attitude, or else endanger the coherency of my remarks, for my natural attitude is one of enthusiasm verging on egotism and thus I always confuse myself trying to be modest. It is my rule to be despondent to be dignified (or coherent) and I might be cynical for the same purpose, but really unless it be enthusiastically I am at a loss to know how to comport myself on the present occasion.

Having settled on enthusiasm, Rob enthused,

> You see I am just returned from experiences so desperately absorbing
> that I am nothing morbid now and can enjoy the poem as freshly as if
> it were but lately written and I had not since wasted eight months in
> ineffectual aspiration.

Frost was not alone in his enjoyment of what he had written. Maurice
Thompson, a prominent poet and novelist (no relation to Francis Thompson), wrote to William Hayes Ward upon reading "My Butterfly," taken
with the "extreme beauty" of the poem: "It has some secret of genius
between the lines." But Thompson worried that Frost's vocation would
lead him to poverty and wished for the young man to forget about poems.

VI.

Retrospectively, the crisis of rejection was among the most important
events in the early life of Frost's poetry, a disenchantment every bit as formative as the inspiration that struck with "My Butterfly." The departure
from his past made way for the earliest notes of substantial originality in
his art. At the time, however, Frost seems to have had no such idea, fearing
instead that he would never publish a poem again.

"Twilight" was the last product of Rob's youthful idealism, the last
time on record that he tried to articulate the deepest aspirations and convictions of his inner life through variations on the example of Shelley.
His imitations of Shelly were idealist first in the philosophical sense of
the term, the conviction that the physical world was less real than an immaterial realm of ideas, from which the world as it appears to the senses
is somehow derived. While Shelley's idealism was atheistic and Frost's
recognizably Christian, both were spiritual in their faith that the ideal
realm could be embodied in experience, not merely postulated as a matter of abstract conjecture. This spiritualism made Frost's Shelleyan work

idealistic in the quotidian sense of the term as well, in the faith that the
achievement of spiritual ideals could suffice to effect his ideals in life
and in love. Such was his faith in after-thoughts, in the world-reshaping
incantation of "Twilight," expressing an idealized language of an idealized world. It was a language of shameless conviction and breathless
grandeur, full of grand effect and rhetorical flourish, a language of emotions conveyed by declaration and their sincerity conveyed by elevated
rhetorical flourish, by the kinds of linguistic elegance and sonorousness
that rendered an emotion or a perception in something like its ideal form.
Boundless in the scope of its conception, this kind of writing would bring
the isolated soul by imagination into communion on a higher realm. In
this sense was Frost's first romantic poem Romantic as his work would
never quite be again.

"Twilight," Frost would later recall, "represents everything I had to
cleanse myself of." His departure led to wandering. So it is with many
young people cut off from a sense of self that once felt real but had come
to seem merely aspirational, a borrowed identity worn as if it were their
own. His departure from Shelley led him to wander for the rest of the decade in a swamp of largely underwhelming verse, minor forms and minor
emotions that did little to draw out the depths of his inner life, for which
his imagination would in time invent new and adequate forms. Though
each form of Frost's original invention owed something to his departure
from Shelley, the qualities Frost abandoned were varied and his rejections
not straightforward antitheses. They were instead a constellation of ways
to realize ends like those to which Rob's Shelleyan imitations aspired,
albeit by alternate means—paths out of Romanticism that managed to
satisfy something in Frost's prior ideals.

All of which raises the question of why Elinor's nervous deference
to the parietal rules of her lodging galvanized such a crisis of faith in
her suitor. Part of the answer, one suspects, is that Frost suffered a shock
of disillusionment. That an evocation of an ideal spiritual union hardly
sufficed to draw Elinor to him in any tangible way—that love, far from
being a force more potent than all social convention, held even less power

than visitation policy—was a natural argument that a certain kind of conventional idealism was hardly enough to realize the aspirations of love. Frost responded in the manner of the disenchanted believer who finds himself incapable of immediate acceptance of any part of the faith that has let him down, reacting against the whole to forestall further disappointment, running away into a literal wilderness. Having fled, however, he found himself desperately absorbed by what he came across on his travels. What entranced him was not any ideal but reality in its sordid details, in which he dwelled, as he wrote, out of time.

VII.

It was half a decade after the turbulence of late 1894 that Frost wrote his first truly original poem, a short lyric called "Flower-Gathering," also the first of his poems to transmute conventions of Shelley's lyrics into a form unmistakably his own. To do so, Frost did what much of his original poetry would continue to do, which was to repurpose the pith of different works across authors, genres, and centuries to make something substantially new, so new in most cases that its structural influences would be hidden from almost the whole of his readership. In the case of "Flower-Gathering," the animating influence was a song from Shakespeare's *Twelfth Night*.

Frost wrote his new kind of love story about a new phase of his and Elinor's love. Though it was written three years later, "Flower-Gathering" took its inspiration from a summer Frost and Elinor spent in a cottage in Allenstown, New Hampshire, on a kind of delayed honeymoon. The long-agitated wedding had transpired days before the previous Christmas (1895), after Elinor had finished college early and Frost had secured employment, setting up with his mother in the center of Lawrence a small private school at which Elinor would teach as well. The year 1895 had seen Frost in a number of jobs, each short-lived, including two on local newspapers, and had witnessed at least one painful fight over the course of their future, in which Elinor supposedly offered to give back her ring, Frost

CARPE DIEM

O Mistress mine, where are you *roaming*?   [A]
O stay and hear! your true-love's coming   [A]
    That can sing both high and **low**;   [B]
Trip no further, pretty sweeting,   [C]
Journeys end in lovers meeting—   [C]
    Every wise man's son doth *know*.   [B]

What is love? 'tis not hereafter;   [A]
Present mirth has present laughter;   [A]
    What's to come is still unsure: [B]
In delay there lies no plenty,—   [C]
Then come kiss me, Sweet-and-twenty,   [C]
    Youth's a stuff will not endure.   [B]

accepted and threw it into the stove and fled to Boston for an evening, only to come home to find his mother in possession of a letter of rapprochement from Elinor explaining that she had recovered the ring. The mood of that interval of Frost's interminable longing is best captured by his plaintive "Waiting: Afield at Dusk," a solitary poem rich in sensations that intimate the presence of another. Incomparably more absorbing than "Twilight" in its atmosphere, "Waiting" suggests that Frost learned to draw his readers to his experience when he lost hope of uniting himself with them, moving on from spiritual union to a nighttime daydream of union, from twilight to the dusk that ensues. The sun had risen by "Flower-Gathering," a poem of a morning in Allenstown, where Elinor was pregnant with their firstborn.

FLOWER-GATHERING

I left you in the morning,	[/]
And in the morning **glow**,	[B]
You walked a way beside me	[/]
To make me sad to go.	[B]
Do you know me in the gloaming,	[C]
Gaunt and dusty gray with *roaming?*	[C]
Are you dumb because you know me not,	[/]
Or dumb because you *know?*	[B]
All for me? And not a question	[/]
For the faded flowers gay	[B]
That could take me from beside you	[/]
For the ages of a day.	[B]
They are yours, and be the measure	[C]
Of their worth for you to treasure,	[C]
The measure of the little while	[/]
That I've been long away.	[B]

The poem could hardly look less like "Twilight" on the surface, the outing to pick flowers and the cosmic pronouncement, but their dissimilarity in scale belies a mutual ambition of the poems to reach a kind of apotheosis of shared imagination with the person they address. The difference is that "Flower-Gathering" goes about drawing in its audience not by callow pronouncement but by an act of staging so subtle that the reader is hardly aware of having been cast in the drama at all.

"Flower-Gathering" is a dramatic lyric wrapped in an old mannered form. The poem draws on the tradition of carpe diem poems, in which by convention a suitor bids a maid be his mistress, impressing upon her in courtly fashion the brevity of life and youth and the urgency of acting on the passion they share (most famously, perhaps, in Andrew Marvell's "To His Coy Mistress"). Frost in "Flower-Gathering" transforms this performance of courtship into words between lovers, as you can see by reading the poem alongside its literary source, a song by Feste the Clown in Shakespeare's *Twelfth Night* excerpted in the anthology Frost knew best and loved most, Francis Turner Palgrave's *Golden Treasury*, as "Carpe Diem."

The woman is not withholding in Frost's poem; he is "roaming," not she. Frost's is spoken not as an entreaty to intimacy but as an imagined conversation between intimates, tender and anxious, the speaker away from his lover not from having been denied her figurative flowers but out of his love of literal flowers. The tone of "Carpe Diem" hovers under Frost's poem as an undersong of the pressures of time and the sweetness of the day's joys, halfway hidden by three unrhymed lines in each stanza that ruminate more than they sing. It is as if we listeners can hear the speaker try to sing to himself on his walk but disrupt his fanciful ideal with the pressures of the actual—as if we can hear him try at and partly succeed in fitting his situation to the old song. The tone is made anxious by his misgivings. Unlike the speaker of "Carpe Diem," assured of his devotion as one could only be to an abstraction and not a real person, the speaker of "Flower-Gathering" is uneasy with his choice of going out to pick flowers and not spending the day with his lover, to choose autonomy rather than presence at the cost of a day's separation.

It turns out that in his ambivalence between separation and closeness he misses her enough on his walk to imagine at length what he will say on his return. "I left you in the morning," he begins—an address that makes sense not as something literally said to a lover, for whom it would be too obvious to mention, but as something he imagines saying as a light accusa- tion: "You walked a way beside me / To make me sad to go." He guesses at her quiet, harmless manipulation, although one wonders whether he needed any help in being made sad to go. Then he imagines her seeing him as he is now in the evening, "in the gloaming" rather than "the morning glow," and wonders whether she's imagining him truly as he's imagining her. She keeps her silence in the theater of his mind—because she knows him or because she does not? He loses track of the fact that he's only imagining this, as we readers, too, lose sight of the line between his imagination and his reality and are thrust into the lovers' ambiguous space between projection and perception. The trope in carpe diem poems of the woman's silence, conventionally a mirror for the suitor's projected ideals and an excuse for his eloquence, is here a self-conscious mirror for the speaker's insecurities in his attachment, all the more aching because the separation is so brief and her hints so slight at begrudging his journey. Is she silent because of a mistake about him or, as he seems to fear, because she knows him well enough to give her pause? Then he proceeds to defend himself.

After dwelling on their separation in the first stanza, he begins the second by imagining their reunion. "All for me?" he imagines her asking, and not about the flowers he will have brought her: about him. He imagines answering in a way that would reconcile his ambivalence. "They are yours, and be the measure / Of their worth for you to treasure": he urges her to be the measure of their worth. The poem ends with him trying to persuade her as in conventional carpe diem poems but with an aim that could hardly be more different—to imagine that he parted from her only to bring back these flowers for her, that what he does in his autonomy is not for himself but for the relationship. His request extends from time spent in search of flowers to time off in his head making poetry, "measure" also referring to the rhythm of a poem (as Feste the Clown uses the word in *Twelfth Night* about poems of precisely this measure). He urges her to be the measure of his poems, judging their worth, as a measure of their time apart, the poems keeping time just as he and she do in their imaginations: "The measure of the little while / That I've been long away." So gracefully is everything arranged in their reconciliation one can easily forget that the speaker is still on his own and we have not heard her answer.

The pronouncement of "Flower-Gathering" is spoken with such reserve as hardly to sound like a pronouncement at all. Yet, appearances aside, it hints at scope and scale to rival the pronouncement of "Twilight" in the sense that "The measure of the little while / That I've been long away" could span time and space in her estimation of worth. As intimacy is attempted by an elaborate if nearly invisible stagecraft that casts the listener in an almost active role, subjects of aesthetic weight and philosophical heft, the sublime and the beautiful and the spiritually true, are introduced under the most modest of auspices. Each tendency was part of the general way in which the young Rob Frost learned to communicate a portion of his inner life in all its unwieldy complexity: by figures written to entice his readers to follow paths in thought and sensation resembling the paths he had gone down himself. Frost would codify this idea four decades later in his essay "The Figure a Poem Makes," as he would later define poetry itself as "a carefully measured amount of all you had to say." "What more is needed to measure the changes of an indefinite thing than an indefinite instrument?"

The question, posed later by Frost to himself as a matter of general principle, applies also in the context of Elinor's experience as figured in "Flower-Gathering." If the fallout from "Twilight" made it untenable to treat her psyche as idealized abstraction, it meant that he had to approach it as an indefinite thing. Having once imagined himself taking the measure of the cosmos "alone . . . in the after-thoughts of long nights beneath the universe," he found himself taking the measure of the woman all but sitting back to back with him as he wrote.

3.

THE SWEETEST DREAM

———

I.

While the change of the young poet from aspirational Shelleyan to the measured author of "Flower-Gathering" involved a transformation like caterpillar to butterfly in which the latter bears little outward trace of what it had been, the next stage of his artistic maturity involved a change altogether more subtle, a different rhythm of flight. The change from "Twilight" to "Flower-Gathering" was that from casting a spell to casting a scene, to staging with his audience a kind of drama that was, if not a play, then play. The stage thereafter saw Frost's role in the drama change from casting himself to something altogether more subtle. This shift, invented once again with benefit of lessons from Shakespeare, widened the range of the movements of thought Frost could incline his readers to share with him, by complicating the relationship between who he was and what he said. That his path to a wider breadth of intimacy with his audience involved a more elaborate kind of ambiguous distance says something about the strange and conflicted position in which he found himself in the second half of the 1890s, a position one can trace to the circumstances in which his earliest poetry came to his mind.

II.

It was on a windy afternoon in March 1890 on a long, dusty walk to his grandparents' house, in Lawrence, after a day of sophomore year, that Rob began to hear as if from elsewhere a voice speaking the lines of a ballad. It was a tale of Spanish treachery and Aztec revenge. After the death of Montezuma in Tenochtitlan, the Spanish commander, Hernán Cortés, plotted a midnight escape from the occupied city. Their machinations discovered, the remaining Spanish forces climbed over the bodies of their fallen comrades in their struggle to escape. Rob was enchanted. Some power in him had conceived all at once a ballad of nearly two dozen stanzas, after which, he later said, he knew he would never want to do anything but write poetry.

Rob had learned about the flight from Tenochtitlan in one of the first books he read for himself. Accordingly, his story followed in factual outline the account he had previously read, trading historical accuracy for thematic clarity and dramatic emphasis as one does when adapting narrative prose into balladic verse. In theme, however, Rob's story broke with its source material decisively. The chapter in *History of the Conquest of Mexico* by William Prescott, "Noche Triste," was, despite the author's pronounced admiration for Aztec civilization, a colonialist portrait of "barbarian" slaughter and Spanish victimization, while Rob's poem, "La Noche Triste," shifts the narrative emphasis to heroism on both sides. The vengefulness of Rob's Aztecs comes off as eminently justifiable, their success a sign of martial sophistication rather than savagery. Instead of ending his ballad on Spanish suffering as Prescott does, Rob shifts to the Aztecs' perspective, as he draws the ballad's didactic encapsulation in the penultimate stanza:

> The flame shines brightest e'er goes out,
> Thus with the Aztec throne,
> On that dark night before the end,
> So o'er the fight it shone.

To this paean to faded glory Frost adds an ironic conclusion at the expense of colonial pretensions:

The Montezumas are no more,
Gone is their regal throne,
And freemen live, and rule, and die,
Where they have ruled alone.

"Freemen" rule over a land where once the Aztecs had ruled free of them.

Behind the poem was not only Prescott's *History* but another one of the first books Rob read on his own, *A Century of Dishonor*, Helen Hunt Jackson's searing indictment of American treatment of the American Indian. Rob admired Indians as much as he despaired over what colonization had cost them, comparing them to the majestic North American chestnut devastated by a European disease. After depicting the Spaniards' lust for gold as shameful in "La Noche Triste," Rob would in time for Thanksgiving of his senior year of high school give voice in another poem to a Native chief's scorn for the moral pretense at the heart of the Thanksgiving holiday: "'Thanks!' I hear their cities thanking that my race is low in death."

The poems were the young Frost's small contribution to a long-standing New England literature of sympathy with "Indians" and opposition to government policies at their expense. The chief, or sachem, in Rob's Thanksgiving-themed "The Sachem of the Clouds" happens to be not only a chief but a wizard, appearing in a mystical mist and blowing across the hilltops with a vengeance as righteous as that of "the Montezumas" before he blows away.

III.

Rob's earliest efforts at poetry consisted mostly of attempts to express the imperceptible or the impossible. His second poem was spoken by a wave. Julius Caesar descends from the sky in another poem from high school, the revived hero declaiming, like the chief in "The Sachem of the Clouds," before turning to vapor. His poems written from the inaccessible past and the impossible perspective and the fantastical scene, his legends, visions, and dreams, tell of experiences outside the bounds of worldly experience like the incantation of "Twilight." All were Romantic expressions of the spirit's transcending material constraints—through time, across perspective, into inanimate matter or even the revelation of things unseen by empirical means. "Twilight" had all the above. The rare poems with none in Rob's early years read like expressions of Romantic frustration, stories like "An Unhistoric Spot" of the isolated spirit unable to transcend its self-consciousness into something beyond itself. Frustrated Romanticism, in contrast, characterized the poems after *Twilight*, their vastness and grandeur reduced to modesty as their penetration of the impossible was reduced to a realistic perspective in which acts of the imagination were treated principally as psychological experiences rather than spiritual visions, a skepticism Frost began to reconcile with his earlier confidence in the balancing act of "Flower-Gathering" in 1899. That such a story started in Tenochtitlan doubtless owes something to the poet's earliest dreams.

Frost as a boy invented an elaborate story of a peaceful tribe in a secret canyon undisturbed by European encroachment. He fantasized in high school about running off to live with an unconquered tribe in Mexico, and well into his adult years would sometimes think of himself among the imaginary tribe of his childhood in the minutes before sleep. Just so did his first daydream in poetic form concern indigenous Americans free of European settlers, if only for a time. If one takes for granted in the interpretation of childhood dreams that a fantasy of welcome escape, begun in early boyhood, has something to do with the home from which he dreams of escaping, might his poem of escape have been born of those sources as well? "La Noche Triste" was written four years after the passing of Frost's father. At age eleven, having lost the Copperhead father who named him after Robert E. Lee, Rob moved to a part of the Union that saw the old southern cause as a moral abhorrence. Frost as a boy had immense admiration for the lost father who stood for a cause regarded as immensely shameful in Rob's new surroundings. Seen analogously, the world of "La Noche Triste" is one that dissolves the tension between filial piety and social ignominy. An occupied nation (as William Prescott Frost Jr. spoke of the South) repels its occupiers righteously rather than, as the conventional wisdom had it, barbarously. Instead of civilization threatened by savagery, heroism shone on both sides. The flame shines brightest e'er goes out—so, too, for the man whose gravestone Rob visited weekly along with his family? With its distant setting, the poem avoids the shame of bringing up the cause as it was or the dissonance of acknowledging the issues not reconciled in life as they are in the sweet dream of poetry.

IV.

On his son's recollection, William Prescott Frost Jr. was a drinker, carouser, and curser; fiercely competitive, partisan, and principled; stern and unpredictable; brilliant and brutal. Rob once pettily disobeyed his father and embarrassed him in front of someone they knew and was whipped in response with a dog chain. It was years after his father died before Rob said his name. Frost still thought in his own final years that his father might have lived to be a senator.

Among Rob's earliest memories was a ferry ride from San Francisco to Oakland, taken by the family to send his father off to Cincinnati as a delegate to the Democratic National Convention in the summer of 1880. Rob was six years old. He remembered his father waving goodbye as the train left the station and coming home with a campaign biography of the nominee, General Winfield Scott Hancock, a war hero who had fought for the Union at Gettysburg and Fredericksburg. Rob took the book, with its blue cloth and gold letters, as a present for himself. His father, after learning that Hancock had marched in James Garfield's inauguration parade after losing to him, lit the book with a match and threw it into the fireplace.

It was the custom in those days for elite pedestrians to race one another in walks lasting almost a week. Frost recalled his father once defeating the famous, record-setting pedestrian Dan O'Leary, albeit with a head start, over six days and six nights—a story that turns out to have been substantially embellished, perhaps before Frost ever heard it himself. He also remembered his mother blaming the race for her husband's tuberculosis (then called consumption), a disease that did not prevent him from regularly swimming out into the bay to a buoy while his son watched from shore, the man disappearing from sight until the buoy started to sway in the water.

William Prescott Frost Jr. had hated his own father, resenting his strict Yankee namesake. The young Will was not allowed out after dark, his parents locking him in his room at night, only to have him let himself out the window with a rope ladder he made. Will's parents, among the local minority of states' rights Democrats, had so persuaded their son of the Southern cause that he fled south from Lawrence with an eye to joining the Confederate army, getting as far as Philadelphia before the police apprehended him at his parents' behest. He would have been no more than fourteen. He refused to take a cent from his father after turning fifteen. For his part, Frost was troubled by his ancestors' Civil War politics well into adulthood, recalling also that the meaning of the Copperhead symbol had been clear to him as soon as he heard it: "Some of my ancestors were what they call Copperheads politically—and I knew what that meant, don't you? Mean little snake the Copperhead is."

After standing out at Lawrence High School, Will went on to Harvard, where there was no one to lock him in the bedroom. He ran with a rowdy and hard-drinking set among whom he was known for his prowess at cards. Enterprising as he had been in high school, Will tutored his way through college, leaving with more money than he began with, and graduated second or third in his class, winning a prestigious Bowdoin Prize for an essay. In addition to such distinctions, Frost recalled a minor scandal involving his father, a local madam, and an attempt to blackmail her. The police got involved, his family straightened it out, and he could have stayed on and taught as an instructor at Harvard had he been so inclined. Instead, he went west.

Will took a job after college as principal of a small private school in Lewistown, Pennsylvania. Needing an English teacher for Lewistown Academy, he chose to hire a woman who had been highly recommended, Belle Moodie. She was teaching at the time in Columbus, Ohio, where she had been raised after emigrating from Scotland as a child after her father, her sole surviving parent, had perished at sea. Frost learned of the figure his parents had cut as teachers from an old pupil of theirs who wrote to him almost half a century later, having seen his picture in the paper. The old pupil, one Elizabeth Beckwish of Albion, New York, fifteen years old in the fall of 1872 under the tutelage of Moodie and Frost, remembered William Frost for his dignified bearing. "Your dear mother," she reported, "was adored by the girls." Beckwish remembered Miss Moodie's efforts at proper instruction to a seemingly indifferent class, her warmth and generosity, her hair that she once let Beckwish unpin and see fall almost down to her knees. "Then came little signs of a budding romance between the two teachers. Trust girls of fifteen or sixteen to scout a romance." Soon after the marriage at the end of the school year, Will and Belle moved to Columbus, from which Will left for San Francisco to find work.

He got a job in the decidedly unprofessorial environment of a newsroom whose windows were shot in his first months on the job. The paper had published something that incurred the retribution of some members of the local stock exchange; the newsmen were tipped off; nobody was killed. Will himself brandished a revolver when a doctor arrived at their home to deliver their first child, threatening to kill the man if something went wrong for his wife. Rob explained the story later by saying his father loved his mother so fiercely that it drove him almost crazy with fear.

Will moved from the *Bulletin* to the *Post*, where he worked briefly
alongside Henry George, the autodidact political economist who would
become the country's most-read intellectual at the end of the century.
His analysis of inequality in *Progress and Poverty* (1879) helped to inaugu-
rate the Progressive Era in politics. The *Post* was strongly identified with
George's proposal for a single tax on the value of unimproved land and
other natural resources, a theory to which Will and Belle both subscribed.
In addition to his father's work for the paper, Frost remembered a series of
his father's increasingly prominent roles in Democratic politics—writing a
pamphlet for a congressional campaign in 1880, chairing the city's Democratic Party, running for tax collector of San Francisco with an eye on
Congress, his candidacy ending with a miserable loss.

Rob was in and out of school. Though he remembered malingering,
an old friend of his mother's who lived for a time with the family said that
Rob was often quite sick. Whatever the cause, it gave him long hours to go
around town with his father. They would eat lunch together at the counter
at Levy's saloon, the unofficial headquarters of the party, for whose boss,
the famously unscrupulous Blind Boss Buckley, Will often acted as fixer.
Frost later said he had been raised in saloons, running off on errands for
his father, following him from one saloon to the next. Frost would grow
up to hardly drink at all. Will would take his son along to the slaughterhouse for his regular cup of warm cow's blood, a treatment at the time for
consumption. Father and son would see the cows killed. Frost was afraid
of the dark, so his parents let him keep the door open to his bedroom,
from which he would listen for hours after his bedtime to his father talking with his friends in the living room, the men going over fine points of
the war, refighting the battles again and again.

Frost remembered his father laying out a map before them and showing the seven sections into which he thought the country would be divided.
In addition to teaching his son separatism, Will taught that there were
no honest Republicans, only hypocrites and demagogues who waved the
bloody shirt, exploiting the pathos of their military service for electoral

gain. Rob spent much of the election of 1884 with his father, the first year the Democrats won the presidency since the end of the war, with Grover Cleveland victorious. The boy walked the city streets with his father, saw the rows of stenographers in the Democratic Party headquarters, ran off to city hall on errands, "did what I could by marching and shouting and burning oil to throw the country to Cleveland." It was Will's last year to live.

Frost as an adult called his father importunate and impatient, unable to follow a regimen for his disease. He kept drinking, tried quack cures, talked of convalescing out on "the Islands" (Hawaii) but did not even rest in San Francisco. Will was chronically dissatisfied, risking too much in the stock market, too sullen to speak to his wife for weeks at a time. Frost told the story of his father in light of his own class motto from high school, "Vincit qui se vincit," "He conquers who first conquers himself," an encomium to the self-control he thought his father tragically lacked. Will left his family almost penniless. Sometimes he hit his son for a minor offense, sometimes not. Rob, six or seven years old, lost a dime on an errand once and told his mother, who prayed for him—and Frost's father brushed off the loss. Other times his drunken father sent Belle running out into the street in fear, taking her children with her. She returned to Lawrence with Robbie while pregnant with Jeanie and stayed far from San Francisco for months, pleading from Columbus that her husband take care of himself so they could grow old with each other.

In retrospect, Frost said at times that his father had clearly been fond of him, that his brutality had been mixed with love; at other times he said his father had been inscrutable and that he could never tell if his father had cared about him. Jeanie for her part recalled that "Papa was an incorrigible tease, and not perhaps especially fond of children but he certainly thought a lot of us." His memory haunted her long into adulthood as it had when she was a girl. "I thought his ghost followed us from San Francisco to Lawrence."

In Frost's recollection, Will would start drinking in the morning and come home at night with liquor on his breath. He would lie down on the couch and have his son lie beside him, falling asleep while Rob, his father's warm breath in his face, lay there, afraid to move. His father came home early one day in March 1885 in another man's arms and died the next day while Rob and Jeanie were off playing as per their parents' instructions. Will had given Rob advice the night before, making him promise not to go out in the streets after dark.

V.

The surviving reminiscences about Belle Moodie Frost paint a less agonized picture. "A great teacher." "That rare personality." "A constant delight to us children." "One who seemed to radiate love + understanding." "One of the finest women who ever lived."

With her long, thick hair and soft Scottish burr, her large, bespectacled brown eyes, her ethereal aspect and gentle dignity, Belle Moodie Frost made quite an impression. One former student remembered her playfulness and her "delightful sense of humor." Another remembered her humor suffusing even her religious instruction, imparting deep religiosity but nothing like pious severity. "In her Sunday-school class," her former student recalled, "she impressed us with the idea that God was always very near, that he was kind and loving, and loved children especially; which could have been the basis for the little boy's thinking that sunshine was God's smile." The little boy was Frost and Elinor's first child.

The old students of Belle's remembered her reading to them and telling them stories, helping them through all their work. One student surmised that Belle had not been the best mathematician, but none doubted her study of scripture and her chosen Swedenborgianism (then called the New Church). Others wondered at the economies her condition demanded given her lot as a mother raising two children alone on a schoolteacher's salary, the more than Yankee thrift such a life would require, and the unfailing pride she nonetheless showed. An old student, who revered Belle as "one of the people who made the deepest impressions on my early life," recalled why Belle said she preferred Easter to Christmas: Christmas may be the "merry time," but Easter is the "joyous time." Belle delighted a group of children once when they persuaded her to sing "Auld Lang Syne" and she followed through in a thick brogue. More than one person recalled the confidence she had in her son.

Rob said his mother did not openly encourage his poetry or even discuss it. "My mother was very fond of poetry, and, while she never said so, I always felt that underneath she wanted me to write."

The Belle of his recollection was unmistakably the same woman the others recalled—independent-minded, gentle, cerebral, proud, strong, and long-suffering. Frost would remember her as a natural teacher and the inspiration for his becoming a teacher himself. She read volumes to her children, such as the poetry of Poe, Shelley, and Keats in that order; Browning, Burns, and his fellow Scot George MacDonald; Bryant, Emerson, and Wordsworth—a distinguished reading list that attests to the lesson her son learned from her that the poems good for children were equally good for adults. In prose, she read her children romances, histories, novels like the episodic *Tom Brown's School Days* and the socialist utopian fiction *Looking Backward* by Edward Bellamy. Frost said he didn't read a book to himself before his "fourteenth year," so much did his mother read to him. She passed along her religion to him with more piety than others remembered, put off when her son teased her about straying from doctrine. Yet his own later account of her religion stressed not doctrinal conformity but spiritual searching. Raised Scotch Presbyterian, she became an Emersonian Unitarian from reading Emerson's essays and a Swedenborgian from reading Emerson again, himself admiringly critical of Swedenborg's mystical system of symbolic, Neoplatonic "correspondences" between physical and spiritual things. Frost remembered his mother's faith as profound, serene, and mystical. She believed in the possibility of "second sight," extrasensory spiritual perception that Frost associated with her native Scotland. Belle would improvise on stories from Genesis for her children's benefit and write fairy stories with a strong component of didactic moralism. "The Land of Crystal," about spirits who inhabit a realm halfway between heaven and earth, stressed the evils of giving in to a melancholy disposition. Belle also reviewed books for the *Bulletin*, such as an illustrated edition of Herrick that caught the eye of her young son, and published poetry on Browning's example.

Frost never knew why she went to her in-laws' in Lawrence when her husband died rather than to her own extended family in Columbus. He thought his mother must have been too proud to go back to Ohio. He himself remembered thinking that the country was at risk without his father. Belle talked of her dead husband as a lost great man, a perspective that incurred Frost's only direct criticism of his mother anywhere in the record, well into the years of his adulthood. "Some people cant resist tragedy," he wrote. "My mother couldnt. Nothing could have saved her but my father's death. It was wretched, pitiful, wicked, but she was hopelessly committed to it." He called her attitude toward her late husband "Romantic."

VI.

When Frost wrote to Susan Hayes Ward of *The Independent* two days after Christmas in 1896, he struggled to convey why he had not written more often of late. The answer had something to do with the rut of ineffectual self-consciousness in which he found himself stuck. "As nothing that happens matters much and as most of my thoughts are about myself I am always at a loss for likely subject matter," he wrote, adding, "I am the father of a son if that is anything." Elliott had been born in September.

The passage is representative of the years between Frost's disenchantment with *Twilight* and the renewed inspiration of "Flower-Gathering" five years hence. In life as in literature, Frost had lost the sense that the depth of his inner life was communicable or, for that matter, worth communicating. The birth of his first child seemed to him marginally worthy of comment. Having conveyed little of his inner life at the time to his editor, he conveys little to posterity as well, leaving hardly any record at the time of his own sense of his changes of mind. His external circumstances, however, tell a story consistent with his later recollections of these years in which he, not finding a suitable place for himself in society, departed for a farm in New Hampshire.

After writing to Ward on December 27, Frost stood trial on the twenty-eighth for the only time in his life. He had punched the man who lived upstairs from the apartment he, Elinor, and Elliott shared with his mother, having offended the wife of his housemate and been affronted gravely in return. Frost's trial resulted in a minor fine of ten dollars, but a more substantial shame, in which the judge, a friend of the family's, was quoted in two local papers dismissing the accused as "Riffraff." The word stuck with Frost for the rest of his life. Perhaps he wrote to Ward the day before his trial to get ahead of the news, or to remind himself of a place where his name was untarnished.

Frost's main occupation in 1896 was as a teacher, a job he saw as in tension with his primary ambition. The summer offered a reprieve as well as an opportunity to learn a great deal of botany from his friend Carl Burrell, who passed along his special interest in orchids. (Frost would distill his solitary botanizing walks of that summer in "Flower-Gathering.") The fall occupied Frost once again. Feeling his time consumed "to the exclusion I fear of things more lofty" and his nerves frayed by the noise of the classroom, Frost eventually had the idea for a change. He would go back to college, this time at Harvard—a thought that occurred to him while reading Tacitus, the great cynical realist among Roman historians, in the original Latin. Frost pleaded his case by letter to the dean of men at Harvard on September 11, 1897, stressing his ample qualifications, his flexibility under the unusual circumstances, and the urgency of his situation ("Let me say that if I enter college it must be this year or never"). He trumpeted his own "general intelligence (!)" while misspelling "honerable" and, before correcting it, "knoledge." He was enrolled within weeks.

Frost's second chance at college lasted longer than the first—almost two academic years. He read a number of authors in Latin and Greek who would become important to his later poetry, especially Virgil, for his pastoral *Eclogues*, as well as his Greek model Theocritus. Frost felt affronted by an instructor of English composition who seemed to mock his pretensions toward being a writer of poetry. Though Frost may well have heard the slight correctly, the instructor would later recall having been intrigued by Frost's ideas about poems' tones of speech. Frost also took a number of courses in philosophy, though he would later say that the teacher from whom he learned most, at Harvard or anywhere else, was a man he never actually met, that is, the great philosophical psychologist and psychological philosopher William James, who was to Frost's chagrin on leave while he was at Harvard. Belle worried that free-thinking Harvard would shake her son's faith. If anything, Harvard reinforced it in the person of the philosophical aesthete George Santayana, whose impious irreverence toward the American creed, the idea that all men are created free and equal, piqued Frost's moral indignation for decades to come, as Santayana's general skepticism of religious truth inspired Frost's strident criticisms of the terms of Santayana's skepticism.

As in Frost's first stint at college, his reasons for leaving, though somewhat mysterious, had more to do with separation than with school itself. His academic record was unimpeachable, even distinguished, and he would later recall his first year at Harvard as one of the best in his life. After that year, however, he had a strange spell of chills and pains in his chest, for which the doctor, suspecting tuberculosis caught from his father and long in remission, suggested a move to the country. As his second year at Harvard began, Frost felt the strain of living alone, which he had avoided in his first year by convincing Elinor to move to Cambridge with him, where they were joined by her mother, then at odds with her father. Frost commuted back to Lawrence often, also teaching once a week at his mother's school, as he had worked the evening shift as a principal at another school nearby in his first year in Cambridge. Yet he was, in his second year, a husband and a father living alone with a wife due to give birth in the spring. Frost later cited other familiar agita such as restlessness, distaste for petty academic competition, and a lack of time to write on his own. He left Harvard at the end of March, with the dean of men attesting in writing that he was "sorry to lose so good a student" and that Frost's dismissal had been honorable (the dean spelled it correctly). Frost returned to Elinor and Elliott in Lawrence—and his old pains persisted.

Frost made a plan to do as his doctor prescribed. Having once enjoyed keeping hens in his parents' yard in San Francisco, Frost found himself admiring a set of chicken coops he saw on a walk from Lawrence into Methuen. He introduced himself to their owner, who offered Frost eggs and practical help if Frost wanted to raise hens on his own. Frost did, and soon had a loan from his grandfather (at interest), two hundred eggs, and a rental of a barn and a floor of a house in rural Methuen, to which the small family moved, with the addition of their first daughter, Lesley, born on April 28, 1899.

Though they were only walking distance to Lawrence, life in Methuen was a world apart. Frost enjoyed the work greatly both for itself and for the leave it gave him to be out of doors, which made him feel better indeed. His new life afforded him far longer stretches of time in Elinor's presence than during the long years when one of them was in school or working at a school. Under this confluence of circumstances, his writing got immeasurably better. While one can hardly isolate the most important cause behind the flowering of "Flower-Gathering," it stands to reason that this transformation of the romance of vast absences into the romance of intimacy had something to do with the newfound regularity of their intimate life, the drama of the poem something to do with the domestic dramas that were now allowed to occupy the ages of a day.

As it happened, Belle was far more unwell than her son. On a trip to Boston for a procedure she thought would be routine, her doctor diagnosed her with inoperable, terminal cancer. Jeanie fainted on hearing the news. Belle dissolved her school, already struggling without her son's help, and after trying a series of sanitariums—which Frost compared to her husband's sampling of quack cures for tuberculosis—she moved in with her son once again. Alas, her cancer was not the only illness disrupting the idyll in Methuen. In July 1900, Elliott, then a gentle child of three with his grandmother's brown eyes, ran a fever and failed to sleep through the night. Frost asked his mother's doctor, paying a house call for Belle, to examine his son. The doctor recommended no urgent treatment. Soon, Elliott developed a high fever. Frost and Elinor called for a doctor who had seen their son before, and he chastised them for not bringing him earlier when he could have done something for Elliott. The child had cholera infantum, he said, and would be dead before morning.

In the unfathomable aftermath, Frost's symptoms were worse than ever before. He blamed himself, he cursed God. Elinor renounced her belief in any God who could let such a thing happen. Frost responded with a poem that answers her (and perhaps his) forlornness much as "Flower-Gathering" had answered her (and perhaps his) anxiety, dropping its readers into a conversation whose stakes they can hardly understand until it is well underway.

STARS

How countlessly they congregate
   O'er our tumultuous snow,
Which flows in shapes as tall as trees
   When wintry winds do blow!—

As if with keenness for our fate,
    Our faltering few steps on
To white rest, and a place of rest
    Invisible at dawn,—

And yet with neither love nor hate,
    Those stars like some snow-white
Minerva's snow-white marble eyes
    Without the gift of sight.

As a thinly veiled marital argument, "Stars" is less a pure apology than a more familiar kind of marital conversation in which the apologizer misses no chance to defend himself. "Stars" is about the instinctive persistence of the will to believe as much as its potential benightedness, the poem prompting its audience to imagine a series of things that, according to the poem, most likely don't exist but that, once imagined, are hard to tease apart from the world on which they are superimposed. "How countlessly," the poem begins so that one thinks to count the stars that don't blend in with high snowdrifts, that don't care about our fate, that don't want to see us through to a heavenly place of "white rest," that neither love nor hate us, that are not the "snow-white" eyes of a goddess but a "snow-white" statue's eyes, which have no sight. The stars congregate, like congregants, and constellate into Minerva, among the twelve Roman gods in the zodiac, known for her bright eyes, which could see in the night like an owl (her symbol), and for her wise and dispassionate intercessions in the fates of men. She would act "with neither love nor hate" but not indifference, with "keenness"—piercing eyes and wisdom. She turned Medusa into a monster. She blinded Tiresias but, to lessen the pain of her punishment, gave him the gift of being able to listen prophetically. Her name derives from "goddess of the moon," perhaps from "mind of god." She was not there.

    Time passed. Practicalities obtruded. Having neglected some of his duties as hen man in the morass of his grieving, to the point that chickens were walking in and out of the house, Frost had earned his family a pending eviction from the landlady upstairs. He found a farm on the outskirts of Lawrence. Elinor's mother, however, had heard of a farm for sale on thirty acres across the border in Derry, New Hampshire, set along the Londonderry turnpike two miles south of the village. Elinor met with Frost's grandfather in Lawrence to tell him about the property, which he agreed to buy for them if it passed the inspection of Frost's uncle Elihu Colcord. Frost's grandfather also covered Frost's obligation on the farm near Lawrence, however begrudgingly. Frost moved his family north around the end of September, to be joined, as his grandfather wished, by Carl Burrell to help with the farmwork. Belle moved to a sanitarium also in southern New Hampshire. In buying the farm, William Prescott Frost Sr. wanted his newly rooted grandson also to set himself up in a practical enterprise that he would stick to longer than the others at which he had tried his hand since Lawrence High School. Frost had seldom lived anywhere for more than a year. He would stay at the farm for roughly a decade in the literal sense, but in a deeper sense he never did leave.

VII.

[Shakespeare's] lyric power lies in the genius of the piece. The sonnets, though their excellence is lost in the splendor of the dramas, are as inimitable as they: and it is not a merit of lines, but a total merit of the piece; like the tone of voice of some incomparable person, so is this a speech of poetic beings, and any clause as unproducible now as a whole poem.

—EMERSON, "SHAKSPEARE; OR, THE POET,"
in *Representative Men*, marked in Frost's copy in use before
the turn of the century, prized for the rest of his life for
the scribblings Elliott had made in the book

One of the first poems Frost wrote in Derry was a sonnet called "Mowing." Nothing else in his poetry would ever seem so distinct from what he had written before or be so important to what he would write after. He would regard the poem in retrospect as both a singular landmark in his style of writing and an encapsulation of his way of thinking. Stylistically, he saw "Mowing" as his first "talk-song," the first of his poems to realize its beauty from the tones of actual talking. Among its lines was the rare idea that he openly declared as a creed, telling an audience later in life, "Just for once, there's one of the keys to all my life [and] thinking in one line," the line that is the climax of the poem, "The fact is the sweetest dream that labor knows."

His two pronouncements about "Mowing" suggest an obvious relationship between them, with his style itself a realization of the creed, the fact of actual speech tones wrought into a sweet and dreamlike poem. The less obvious key to all his life is that the creed managed to set him apart from both of his parents, contravening their very different ideals.

The greatest ambitions of William Prescott Frost Jr. were partisan and political victories, the sweetest dream of his labors not fact but victory—about which his son thought him often deluded, in pursuit of which his son thought him often unscrupulous. The subtler contrast than that with his father's cynicism was with his mother's idealism. The *fact* is the sweetest dream that labor knows—the fact, not the idea, not the ideal; the here and now and not the hidden world or the hereafter. One might suspect Frost of pronouncing realism superior to idealism, but this is precisely what he does not say, calling fact not superior to dream or ideal but the sweetest dream itself. His creed is not a riposte to the idealism of his mother and his earlier self but a way to reconcile its sense of a world known through imagination with his later sense of a world known mostly through observation. The creed declares that the richest aesthetic experience of imagination, the sweetest dream, is to be had by using the power of imagination to contemplate the world at hand.

In effect, the creed is Frost's explication of a famous passage from Emerson's essay "The Poet" on the universal symbolism to be drawn from all worldly things: "The highest minds of the world have never ceased to explore the double meaning, or, shall I say, the quadruple, or the centuple, or much more manifold meaning, of every sensuous fact." This proliferation of meaning from a simple observation is that which the creed seeks to explain and, by its ambiguities, exemplify. Of the creed's manifold meaning, the double meaning most fundamental is of realist and idealist visions of knowledge, the *fact* as the sweetest dream that labor knows or the fact as the sweetest *dream* that labor knows, as if the facts of the world, like dreams, were knowable through imagination. It is the contention of the creed that one could fruitfully pursue these distinct visions of knowledge by the same means. In imagining the sensuous fact, one might know something of its manifold meaning as well.

The creed set a standard for the rest of Frost's poetry. In much of his work after "Mowing," and in all of his best, contentions of an idealist or otherwise spiritual nature, when present, would not be presumed or asserted but implicit in a story coherent by the standards of the plainest common sense. This would involve great compactness of meaning and implication, often of ideas that seem almost but not entirely adequate to the world from which they are drawn, manifold meanings unfolding themselves. As Frost's first poem of this kind, "Mowing" has a profusion of meanings without the clarification that would come from later prunings, which would give his readers greater sense of direction. You can avoid losing yourself in the ambiguities of "Mowing" by keeping in mind a central ambiguity encapsulated by the creed: Is the speaker of the poem, in trying to understand the "whispering" of the scythe as he used it for mowing, asking the realist question he seems to be asking or the idealist question he seems to be trying to avoid? How literally does he take the metaphor of "whispering" as he dreams the fact?

MOWING

There was never a sound beside the wood but one,
And that was my long scythe whispering to the ground.

What was it it whispered? I knew not well myself;
Perhaps it was something about the heat of the sun,
Something, perhaps, about the lack of sound—
And that was why it whispered and did not speak.
It was no dream of the gift of idle hours,
Or easy gold at the hand of fay or elf:
Anything more than the truth would have seemed too weak
To the earnest love that laid the swale in rows,
Not without feeble-pointed spikes of flowers
(Pale orchises), and scared a bright green snake.
The fact is the sweetest dream that labor knows.
My long scythe whispered and left the hay to make.

With its tricks and its traps, the poem makes a game for its readers of the kind of interpretive experience it describes. It pulls us into plausible interpretations of what "Mowing" is intimating to us, only to cast them into doubt like the idea that the scythe whispers the poem's creed. For those encountering the creed for the first time as it appears in the poem, without benefit of outside context and clarification, the elusiveness of the creed's meaning gives it the sheen of a treasure and the slipperiness of a dream. "The fact" sounds precise but is perfectly indeterminate in magnitude, from the smallest particular to the whole of the natural world. And what fact? To know a dream is either to realize it or to know it as an unfulfilled aspiration. There is also the hint that labor might know what the self does not, inviting the interpreter to try the preceding distinctions on the ambiguous "labor" and wind up in a cloud of foggy ambiguities, repeating the simple-sounding line in hope of clarification, dreaming the line as the poem dreams the fact. Does the scythe whisper the creed? Of course not—if you leave the labyrinthine poem seeing it as the work of a disabused realist. From another angle, however, the speaker might be a kind of fastidious idealist, one who casts off a host of false intimations before hearing from the scythe's whisper an epiphany in the form of the creed.

Each of these readings has a distinct precedent in literary form to which "Mowing" alludes. In fact, the poem owed much of its break-through in style to its fusion of the two forms, embedding a Romantic lyric of inspiration in the distinctive ambiguity of a properly Shakespear-ean sonnet.

It is in the lyric of inspiration that the speaker might hear her scythe whispering the creed. Such lyrics, best exemplified by William Words-worth and later by Longfellow, are poems proceeding from specific ob-servations, often of nature and the poet's responses thereto, to a broader idea, drawn from experience but proclaimed with the validity of a general insight. This kind of poem presents itself as the literary embodiment of spontaneous inspiration, the elevation of everyday life into spiritual truth. Immediately preceding the climactic spiritual contention of "Mowing" is an allusion to a dream that proves to be truly visionary in the archetypally Romantic ballad "Christabel" by Samuel Taylor Coleridge, the dreamt-of "bright green snake" encoiling an innocent maiden symbolized in the form of a dove. What might have made Frost think of a Romantic dove sweet-hearted enough to let herself be encoiled by a nasty little snake is not altogether hard for students of his biography to imagine.

A lyric of inspiration makes a claim to sincerity. In this it is un-like the sonnets of Shakespeare. The sonnets may well be sincere, but their style gives one reason to doubt. Lyrics of inspiration begin with an experience, like a walk in a field, or a personal reflection like a note in a diary, where the sonnets begin in the middle of dramatic reflection. Lyr-ics of inspiration end with a precept for all kinds, whereas the sonnets, if they end with a precept at all, may well be making a pronouncement for dramatic effect. One can see as much in the sonnet of Shakespeare's to which "Mowing" owes a deep structural debt: Sonnet 60, called "Revolu-tions" in Palgrave, two pages away in the anthology from the excerpt of Shakespeare's *Twelfth Night* that served as a model for "Flower-Gathering." As "Mowing" dwells throughout on the work of his scythe, "Revolutions" dwells on the work of the cruel hand of time ("And nothing stands but for his scythe to mow"). More important than any particular debt of "Mowing" to its precedent is a model of conveying self-consciousness without letting it either consume or paralyze the writing. Shakespeare does so in the sonnets by writing out of a discrepancy between style conceived and style revealed, showing a mind partly at odds with its own outward expression. It is the distinctive drama of the sonnets to intimate such inner conflict as a matter of style—not character or plot, but the sheer pressure of articulation. Shakespeare stages this drama by means of the attitude the speaker of the sonnets takes toward his own words, an ambivalence that one can call make-believe. Some poems are spoken in character, which makes the speech a fiction. Some poems are spoken by the poets themselves in propria persona, and between these poles of explicit fiction and self-revelation exist a thousand shades of ambiguity. Make-believe in poetry is any kind of speech that, like children's play, neither claims to represent reality nor requires a willing suspension of disbelief to make sense of. Make-believe can coexist with any characterization of its speaker, ambiguous or clear. It is in itself dramatic without the context of drama, performative without the staging of performance, and the make-believe of Shakespeare's sonnets is that of a monologist with a mask and a mysterious backstory and background. His speech, ostentatiously fanciful and dramatically forceful, seems to bear on something important offstage. The stakes of the speech feel vital even though they remain obscure. This make-believe is a kind of obverse of a conventional (not a Shakespearean) dramatic character, not someone acting realistically on an assumed identity but someone acting unrealistically on no definite identity at all.

Frost's adoption of make-believe is easiest to see not in "Mowing," on which so many streams of influence converge, but in his other sonnet of 1900, "Choice of Society," whose model in Shakespeare was Sonnet 66, not far from Frost's other Shakespearean models in Palgrave. A mature revision of "An Unhistoric Spot," "Choice of Society" takes from its precedent much of its world-weary affect—its hermetic misanthropy, melancholic to the point of comic despondency. Frost's sonnet begins,

"Tired of the trees sometimes I crave my kind," much as Shakespeare's begins, "Tired with all these, for restful death I cry." Shakespeare's speaker halfway pines for death in disgust with society; Frost's lies down in a graveyard for company. Shakespeare's melancholy verges on comedy in its extremes of overstatement in listing the faults of the world, its world-historical eloquence marshaled to articulate something that looks a bit like a bad mood. Frost's verges on comedy but in pacific understatement, never budging from the pretense that the dead and the people he spies at a distance in the village are themselves the company he needs to ward off his loneliness. And yet each poem's comedy of self-misconception could also be a comedy of persuading its audience by feigning, each a way of courting our sympathy. Sonnet 66 ends, "Tired with all these, from these would I be gone, / Save that, to die, I leave my love alone," as in "You're all that keeps me alive." "Choice of Society" invites our pity by the spectacle of desperation and the example of someone too sad and stoical to ask for our help. In neither Shakespeare's performance of vulnerability nor Frost's of invulnerability does the reader have a definite clue about character or context, yet the poems draw us into a relationship with their speakers, albeit a relationship mediated by the veil of make-believe. And it is behind such a veil that the epiphanic creed of "Mowing" is reached.

In Shakespeare's sonnets as in Frost's, characterization without character would not be possible without the poems' tones of speech. The tones evoke a recognizable kind of speech, like the almost luxuriant despair of Shakespeare's "Tired with all these, for restful death I cry," the lonely languorous boasting of Frost's "My breathing shakes the bluet like a breeze" (from "Choice of Society"). The tones realize a type of person more fully than any description of them. Yet the realized speech is not a realistic way for people to talk outside the wildest flights of their imaginations. So it was that Frost cast aside his mother's Romantic example not for realism but for a way of writing that contained his qualified spiritual reflections within a frame that neither propounded nor disclaimed them. Frost learned from Shakespeare a kind of writing that leaves us with

Emerson's impression of "the tone of voice of some incomparable person," the "speech of poetic beings," not a character to understand, but a fact of humanity for the reader to dream.

VIII.

Though Frost was still in San Francisco when he began to daydream of going off to live with a peaceful tribe undiscovered by anyone else of European descent, it was the years since the death of his father that saw him always somewhere out of place. A Californian in New England; a poor child in a prosperous family; a rural student among city folk; a Copperhead's son in the Republican North; a scholar among college students; a man of unfailing artistic ambition among practical Yankees; a poet who could hardly place his work after major early publication; a Shelleyan youth who had lost the faith but had found no new gods; an idealistic young lover in a world of realistic constraint; a man without work he could keep for more than a matter of months; a move-about; riffraff; a husband and father and evening principal among freshmen in college; a provincial believer among the skeptical elite and an educated skeptic among the faithful; someone conscious throughout of his place in the eyes of society as a loafer among laborers and a man without respectable vocation. Then, bereaved and evicted, he moved across the state line to Derry. It was a dozen miles away and a different realm. His "Choice of Society" was solitude on a hill with a vantage of chimney smoke in the distance. His vocation, or calling, was the whisper of his scythe that he strained to hear and read into, his labor the mowing of pastoral convention told now from experience. Having achieved a measure of distance from the society of his origins, he achieved a measure of distance in his writing. It was a style that managed to be at once entirely present but never quite explicable and therefore always somehow out of place. The whole remainder of his literary achievement would owe something to this novel way of making himself understood by holding a range of complexities together in mind, folding their shades of ambiguity into the vicissitudes of a character speaking while maintaining an intimate relationship with his listener. Sonnets or not, everything hereafter owed something to Frost's achievement in make-believe, which was soon to proliferate in his first sustained years of original work, yielding a wide range of forms united by an invisible architecture of mourning.

4.

NOT FIND ME CHANGED

———

I.

Later collections of Frost's works begin with a walk across the road from the farmhouse to clean the pasture spring that fed the gentle brook that flowed under the road through a culvert and ran through the woods across the bottom of their farm. His first book of wider circulation than *Twilight*, *A Boy's Will*, moves about a hundred feet east from the spring and into the cellar hole his children would play in, the "Ghost House," a poem that flies northeast across the farm, from the raspberry brambles on the cellar walls to the grapevines on the fences near the hardwoods, and west through the mowing field and the footpath in the orchard. The places in his poems are imaginary, to be sure, but they came from somewhere— the pasture lane and the path through the garden above the farmhouse, the house's east window in a violent snowstorm, the orchard white with apple blossoms in the spring, drops of water falling in the brook in the moonlight, the porch whose steps led down to the yard and the alders, the pastures Frost and Elinor walked in at twilight.

In a strict and literal sense, the early years in Derry were no more sheltered from the harshness of circumstance than the years that preceded them. Frost lost his mother in early November and buried her next to his son. Free from the judgment of Lawrence, Frost began to feel the judgment of his neighbors in the country for what he thought they thought was his incompetent farming and therefore his irresponsibility toward the family that depended on him. He had to borrow more from his grandfather to settle a debt. Elinor was too sad for months to put curtains on the windows. Frost's nerves were poor and his old symptoms hardly improved. The first winter was so cold that water froze on the floor of his kitchen when he spilled the pails he carried back from the pump.

Under these circumstances, though, he wrote "Mowing." It was the first in a series of poems that transfigured his local surroundings into the terrain of his imagination as they transfigured his experience into a story more faithful to his inner life at the time than any literal autobiography could have possibly been. Taken together, as Frost collected them a dozen years later in *A Boy's Will*, the poems of the early years in Derry make up a spiritual autobiography on the model, as we shall see, of another young poet from a half-century before torn about how to mourn his past without abandoning it. Among the most striking parts of this hidden architecture is how little one could infer the broader design from the absorbing experience of individual poems, absorbing as the experiences behind them presumably were for Frost himself, beginning with the first on his journey, a poem about the long thoughts of youth.

II.

The first poem of *A Boy's Will*, written in 1901, is a sonnet about leaving people behind. Its epigraph gives a hint of its speaker's breathless hope: "The youth is persuaded that he will be rather more than less himself for having forsworn the world."

INTO MY OWN

One of my wishes is that those dark trees,
So old and firm they scarcely show the breeze,
Were not, as 'twere, the merest mask of gloom,
But stretched away unto the edge of doom.

I should not be withheld but that some day
Into their vastness I should steal away,
Fearless of ever finding open land,
Or highway where the slow wheel pours the sand.

I do not see why I should e'er turn back,
Or those should not set forth upon my track
To overtake me, who should miss me here
And long to know if still I held them dear.

They would not find me changed from him they knew—
Only more sure of all I thought was true.

Endless woods and open land and open road is the world as it stretches before the speaker, the youth. He will arise and go into a world rising to meet him, will depart from people who might set off and find him, will transform himself in an act of self-realization, will go boldly without risking much and without letting go.

The youth goes nowhere. He proclaims to go off to the wilderness and congratulates himself at some length. He turns his back on people by imagining their running after him, declaims his fearlessness in literal "doom" and "gloom" rhetoric, his cliché of an end rhyme following an opening rhyme pair, "trees" and "breeze," once parodied by Alexander Pope. How seriously should we take a declaration of solitude that steals a phrase from Shakespeare's famous sonnet on the constancy of love ("Love alters not with his brief hours and weeks, / But bears it out even to the edge of doom")? How much can we trust a poem whose original title upon publication in *The New England Magazine*, "Into Mine Own," was just as silly a mixture of archaism and idiom at the time? How much are we supposed to trust this pompous, grandiloquent, self-satisfied kid?

And yet his words have grandeur within their grandiloquence—the wide eyes with which he draws us into his confidence ("One of my wishes"), the mythic assurance of "I should not be withheld but that some day," the singularity of the "highway where the slow wheel pours the sand," the line slowing, nearly halting, like the pour. The youth may be a little ridiculous, but since when was youth anything but? Without costing him any composure, his conviction in his journey is weighed down by his fears and his doubts and the vagueness of his ambitions. With every reason not to be, he's sure of himself. Likewise, in reading his poem, it's hard not to be taken by his passion even as you doubt its justification, hard not to be swept up by his language even as you notice its conventional badness, believing in his words despite yourself. It's hard not to feel like the youth.

"Into My Own" is a kind of make-believe new in Frost's poetry. Its epiphany turns not on the revelation of an idea but on self-revelation. Its characterization, though still lacking a character, is of the character type of a youth, whose self-revelation one is made to feel and doubt much as he surely feels it and doubts it. One is left to look for the line between self-belief and self-idealization, between idealistic and idealized language. One is left with the shape of a wish that cannot quite find expression in what is wished for, articulated in a language that works against the wish. It is a story of self-consciousness about the originality of the youth's literary style, a poem called "Into My Own" that is full of borrowings. To come into one's own was also idiomatically to come into one's inheritance, willed rather than literary. (Frost's grandfather died in the summer of 1901 and left him the farm on the condition that he not sell it for a decade.) To come into one's own, in the context of the poem, is also to come into one's own thoughts, mistaken or revelatory, "Only more sure of all I thought was true." The poem is a story rather familiar to a certain poet's youth of the unboundedness of self-belief and the fear of his self-belief as a mere sham, the association of self-belief with solitude and solitude with fear, the need, beyond what he can explain, to go.

III.

Following "Into My Own" in *A Boy's Will* is a poem about having gone. Stasis rather than adventure, rootedness rather than venturing forth, the fine delineation of a local environment and not a limitless, indefinite expanse, the consolations of stability and not the boundless hope of youth—all are part of dwelling in "Ghost House," written in 1901 like the poem of adventure that precedes it. Its epigraph, "He is happy in the society of his choosing," refers to a society of ghosts. Yet he does seem rather happy, considering. He seems unaware that his companions are dead. From his world of exquisite loneliness, he speaks of his strange isolation in a way that seems to court the sympathy he disclaims. His listeners are left at a loss as to whether he's fighting tears or stifling a grin, but for all that his psyche remains a mystery to us, his mysterious world is clear as day as he moves his listeners through it, weaving our attention in a pattern that takes us back and forth and in and out of reality. The pattern is established in the first four of the poem's six stanzas:

> I dwell in a lonely house I know
> That vanished many a summer ago,   *Imaginative unreality*
>   And left no trace but the cellar walls,
>   And a cellar in which the daylight falls,   *Movement downward*
> And the purple-stemmed wild raspberries grow.   *and upward*
>
> O'er ruined fences the grape-vines shield
> The woods come back to the mowing field;   *Physical reality*
>   The orchard tree has grown one copse

Of new wood and old where the
    woodpecker chops;   *Movement away*
The footpath down to the well is healed.

I dwell with a strangely aching heart
In that vanished abode there far apart   *Imaginative unreality*
    On that disused and forgotten road
      That has no dust-bath now for the toad.   *Movement downward*
Night comes; the black bats tumble and dart;   *and upward*

The whippoorwill is coming to shout
And hush and cluck and flutter about: *Physical reality*
    I hear him begin far enough away
    Full many a time to say his say   *Movement toward*
Before he arrives to say it out.

Such a pattern in the speaker's surroundings primes the reader to expect
a similar pattern as the penultimate stanza begins to describe the speaker's
strange company:

It is under the small, dim, summer star.
I know not who these mute folk are   *Imaginative unreality*
    Who share the unlit place with me—
    Those stones out under the low-limbed tree   *Movement downward*
Doubtless bear names that the mosses mar.   *and upward*

Then instead of beginning the sixth and last stanza with the naturalism we
have been led to expect, the speaker dwells on the mute folk whom he dwells
with, ineffably realer to us for their position in the pattern of attention:

They are tireless folk, but slow and sad,
Though two, close-keeping, are lass and lad,—

With none among them that ever sings,
And yet, in view of how many things,
As sweet companions as might be had.

If we expected movement away or movement toward in the end, our expectations are unmet as in the beginning of the stanza. The folk are his companions: they stay.

Perhaps the youth is happy in their company. One precedent suggests that he is. The youth, though bereft of human companionship, is aesthetically satisfied in his loneliness, and "Ghost House" alludes throughout to a poem whose conclusion is a famous paean to the sufficiency of aesthetic experience in a vision of the good life, Keats's "Ode on a Grecian Urn":

"Beauty is truth, truth beauty,"—that is all
Ye know on earth, and all ye need to know.

As in Keats's ode, the youth looks upon and communes with a series of creatures who will never speak to him, including a pair of proximal but imperfectly satisfied lovers. The cellar hole is something of an urn, "leaf-fring'd" and open on top. One can even hear "Ghost House" as an ode in praise of the ghost house that he haunts about. Keats famously used the preposition "on" in his title as a substitution for the conventional "to" in his expounding the sides of the urn, and Frost in turn plays on "on" in his first line by using "in" where one would first expect "on": "I dwell in a lonely house I know / That vanished many a summer ago." Frost's is an Ode in a Ghost House, fittingly so because his speaker may in fact be a ghost.

This strange possibility of posthumousness—the idea that the speaker, having forsworn the world, left it entirely—would seem to undercut his professions of flourishing. There is precedent, too, for this nightmare of solitude. "Ghost House" alludes throughout not only to Keats's ode but to a little fable of Emily Dickinson's that she herself wrote about the ode,

spoken from the point of view of a ghost. Frost would have encountered
Dickinson's poem in the volume of her work that he bought for Elinor in
the spring of senior year. The ghostly speaker of "I died for beauty, but
was scarce" tells of having passed the night buried in a tomb adjoining
the cell of one who died for truth "Until the moss had reached our lips /
And covered up our names," silenced by moss covering the names on their
gravestones as Frost echoes in the penultimate stanza of "Ghost House":

> It is under the small, dim, summer star.
> I know not who these mute folk are
> Who share the unlit place with me—
> Those stones out under the low-limbed tree
> Doubtless bear names that the mosses mar.

Dickinson's devotee of beauty fails to grant the identification of beauty
and truth that the devotee of truth is confident in, suggesting that aesthetic satisfaction might not suffice for the good life, might even delude a
devotee of beauty who forswears the world into a false sense of satisfaction
in his imaginary companionship.

Like "Into My Own" before it, "Ghost House" amounted to a new
and more complex kind of make-believe. It combines the mystery of its
speaker's tone with the mystery of its speaker's identity, the poem spoken not only *in* ambiguous character but *by* an ambiguous character. The
question lingers of whether the youth is serenely appreciative or stoically
desperate, whether to take his beautiful testament as the truth. It is a fair
question for a young man gone into his own in pursuit of his art, committed to dwelling in an imaginative realm whose excesses could isolate
him or lead him astray, and yet Frost in posing the question brings us
vividly into the realm of his dwelling, of his doubts and serene satisfac-
tions, of the literary ghosts who keep him sweet company. "Sweet" is not
only a Keatsian turn of phrase in its sublime entanglement of aesthetic
experience and spiritual intimation but is in fact a word Keats used that

way in the ode to speak of the unheard melodies of the figures on the urn. Keats, whose works Frost knew so well before reading a word of them himself, would remain a profound influence on the rest of Frost's writing. So would Dickinson, whose fable modeled the perspective for Frost's poem, in which he drew on her unparalleled genius for ventriloquizing the wildest things in the most natural ways. Frost's borrowing marked him as the first poet of any significance to fall under her influence.

"Ghost House" is also the first salient instance of a peculiarity of Frost's protracted intimacies with his literary forebears, which is that he borrowed often from poems that themselves borrowed conspicuously from earlier poems, adding his part to a conversation between a pair of familiar ghosts. Their work had kept him company during his years of relative literary isolation. They may well have been as sweet companions as he could have had.

IV.

When Frost told a friend in the weeks after Elinor's death in 1938 that he was "afraid I deceived her a little in pretending for the sake of argument that I didn't think the world as bad a place as she did," he effectively paraphrased the third poem of *A Boy's Will*. That poem, "My November Guest," written in the first years in Derry, is addressed to "My Sorrow," a figure who prefers the dying time of year to the thriving one, with whom the speaker of the poem feigns disagreement. Yet the nature of Sorrow as a figure is as ambiguous as the nature of the denizen of "Ghost House." She seems at first like a conventional allegory but shows herself as her own person at the end of the first stanza, walking beside him. She flickers between realities throughout the poem—feeling, spirit, vision, woman—raising the question of the stakes of the speaker's purported disagreement with her, whether those of domestic harmony or emotional delusion or spiritual enlightenment or spiritual mistake, depending on the nature of his Sorrow. The tone is correspondingly ambivalent, his levity underscored

by a hushed weight that builds to a dramatic revelation: he believes her.
The poem demonstrates what it describes. He sees "the beauties she so
truly sees" (as if she were among his mute Keatsian companions), sees such
beauties in the conventionally unbeautiful scene, and, by the seemingly
simple enchantment of his profession of trust, inclines his readers to share
in the beauties as well.

My November Guest

My Sorrow, when she's here with me,
    Thinks these dark days of autumn rain
Are beautiful as days can be;
She loves the bare, the withered tree;
    She walks the sodden pasture lane.

Her pleasure will not let me stay.
    She talks and I am fain to list:
She's glad the birds are gone away,
She's glad her simple worsted gray
    Is silver now with clinging mist.

The desolate, deserted trees,
    The faded earth, the heavy sky,
The beauties she so truly sees,
She thinks I have no eye for these,
    And vexes me for reason why.

Not yesterday I learned to know
    The love of bare November days
Before the coming of the snow,
But it were vain to tell her so,
    And they are better for her praise.

Although the poem has the form of a soliloquy, like a sonnet, it has the hidden drama of a play. The play is staged between three perspectives—the speaker's, his Sorrow's, the reader's—in a drama of disclosure and withholding, a game of intimacy. In the last stanza, we learn of his withholding the feelings he shares with his Sorrow. That is his game with her, which he lets the reader in on. His game with us is to reveal her perspective and his perspective on her but not reveal her nature. We see her as an outline of what he sees of her, or of what he tells us he sees of her. We see traces of her walking "the sodden pasture lane" in the first stanza; of her talking eagerly in the second; of her questioning him in the third, perhaps without words. We hear his reply before we learn that he intends not to tell her as well.

Perhaps he might relent. One can hear a halfhearted sigh in his "But it were vain to tell her so." This would set up the drama of perspectives to resolve like a comedy in the old, Shakespearean sense, with the boundaries between lovers at the point of dissolution. He has adopted her perspective—his sorrow is that of his Sorrow. In adopting her perspective, he has learned to love her for something idiosyncratic about her and personal to her, seeing her beauty of soul as she sees beauties in November days. This is much the same attitude that Shakespeare adopts in the sonnet beginning "When in the chronicle of wasted time," which Frost would have first read in Palgrave under the title "To His Love," a poem in which the sonneteer claims distinction from the tradition of love poetry before him by virtue of his singular appreciation of his beloved's beauty, which even exceeds his description. (The sonnet shares its final rhyme with that of "My November Guest": "days" and "praise.") The game we witness between Frost and his Sorrow on this interpretation is like the final trick a lover plays when he and the audience already know that lover and beloved will fall into each other's arms at the end of the scene.

Yet with the play suspended in mid-action, one can also spy hints of tragedy—tragedy not in the sense of a horrible outcome but that of insoluble conflict. That "it were vain to tell her so" could mark an insoluble boundary between him and his Sorrow. No matter how he feels, she will not believe he truly shares her feeling. His sorrow is there *with* him; the beauties are what *she* truly sees; he *knows* "the love of bare November days," but we do not know that he feels it, exactly. In this slant of light, the poem reads as a description of his visitation by something from which a part of himself will always be at a remove, like the arresting melancholy in the aftershock of grief, like a spirit other than his own. Such is the subject of the poem to which "My November Guest" owes its most substantial debt, the third canto of *In Memoriam* (1850), an extended elegy that Alfred, Lord Tennyson wrote for his friend Arthur Hallam, casting himself as a kind of spiritual Hamlet in mourning. The poems bear a striking resemblance. Frost's poem begins "My Sorrow," Tennyson's "O Sorrow"; the poems are written in the same meter (iambic tetrameter) and in much the same form, four stanzas in which a couplet (a pair of rhyming consecutive lines) is surrounded by another pair of rhyming lines. Each poem tells of fellowship with a female figure named Sorrow who sees a world of dying fields and bleak skies under whose surface she can sense something potent. Tennyson's poem ends on the question of whether to trust Sorrow's perspective. Frost's ends on an answer in the affirmative that he may or may not have inflected with make-believe.

The play is suspended. The lovers might align or stay perpetually distinct. The speaker might give himself over to the spirit who taught him so much. The game might be at her expense or, if Sorrow is as deluding a spirit as Tennyson says, at the speaker's expense. We can hardly tell how the story will end. In this we are like a voluble young man in love with a woman given over to communicating by silence, melancholic by temperament as he was in his grief, unsure of their alignment in spirit despite everything he tried to learn from her perspective, a commitment to which the poem is an undoubtable testament. It would be Elinor's favorite poem of her husband's. The problem of idealized language, elsewhere a question of potential self-delusion, has the potential to be something like the opposite in "My November Guest" in its elevation of the unlovely into something beloved by the grace of her vision. The poem sets the problems of self-deception and self-articulation in balance with the old problem from *Twilight* of the communion of souls.

Like the two poems before it in *A Boy's Will*, "My November Guest" was a new achievement of style, incorporating the make-believe of the sonnets into the perspectival drama of "Flower-Gathering" and the ambiguities of character of "Ghost House." The poem is distinctive not only for marking Frost's greatest complexity and sophistication of style in his first book. It also offers a clue like no other poem in *A Boy's Will* to an organizing principle in the book of profound literary and biographical significance, the spiritual autobiography of *In Memoriam*, a Dantean journey through the sorrows of grief.

V.

Each of the first nine poems in *A Boy's Will* bears a resemblance to the corresponding canto of *In Memoriam*. The ninth poems in each sequence intone prayers to the wind; the eighth poems tell stories of eager lovers abandoning hope when they look into the homes of their beloveds, each love story mentioning wind and a singular flower. The seventh poem in each sequence is about a dark house before daybreak, with premonitions, precipitation, and a narrator unable to sleep. In the sixth poems in each sequence, the poets use a similar frame tale to illustrate a sense of cosmic meaninglessness and loss: a female figure expecting someone home from his travels whom, as we learn in the end of each poem, she will never see again. The fifth poems in each sequence are about what can be known about nature and what taken only on faith, as well as the parallel questions about people, each of the poems comparing "words" and "weeds." The fourth poems in each sequence wonder about the effect of trouble on the young heart's "desire." The third poems are "My November Guest" and the canto beginning, "O Sorrow, cruel fellowship," respectively. The second poems have trees with limbs reaching over or into gravestones, in each case called "stones," which in one poem "bear names" and in the other "name the underlying dead." The speaker of each poem uses the resting place of the dead to imagine himself among them. Frost's poem, "Ghost House," is in a modified *In Memoriam* stanza like "My November Guest." And the first poems in each sequence are impassioned expressions of hope for a distinctive kind of journey of the soul: to move beyond the limits of their earlier selves without the loss of their old loves. Frost quoted a line from canto I of *In Memoriam* on the same day that he paraphrased "My November Guest" in relation to his lost wife: "Let darkness keep her raven gloss."

In Memoriam was the product of almost two decades of writing. In this it was like *A Boy's Will*. Although Tennyson's endeavor was spurred by the death of his friend, the elegies also show his own transformation through the process of grieving. He called his book "The Way of the Soul," which could serve as a subtitle for Frost's book as well. Each of the books is a form of spiritual autobiography, a story of self-becoming less in relation to the secular world—the literal, factual, and personal—than to the world of the soul. The point of the books is not to record events faithfully, although some events are recorded; nor is the point to preserve experiences such as they were. The point is to show how the poets came to their ideas of transcendent authority and came to see themselves in light of it. Symbolism means using the perceptible as a figure for the ineffable; spiritual autobiography is using your life as such a figure.

These spiritual autobiographies were written during roughly the same years of the poets' lives, mostly their twenties and thirties, and each was written about an indefinite stage in the early part of those years. Frost called his "The Record of a Phase of Post-adolescence"; the poets also used the word "youth." In fact, they use the word in a similar way—as part of a frame tale that draws a measure of distance between the poet at the time of publication and the relatively youthful and unsettled speaker of the poems. Tennyson writes toward the end of his preface, "Forgive these wild and wandering cries, / Confusions of a wasted youth." Frost tells of someone similarly unsure and unsettled in the prefatory glosses in his table of contents, "The youth." The framing of the poems as spoken in youth gives the poets each a mask that is hard to tell apart from his face. The poets can alternately inhabit the poems, letting readers identify them as the speakers, or disavow identification with poems set in an indefinite past. The poets' similar vagueness about chronology permits them a similar privacy. They each compress years of reflection and struggle into the space of a handful of seasons, setting their sequences of poems in the overlapping chronologies of linear and cyclical time. Those chronologies serve respectively as analogues for personal and impersonal time, time considered in human and divine terms. Their stories of spiritual progress are tempered by repetition, leaving at the heart of these figures of spiritual youth the sense that one never outgrows it entirely. Youth in its passion and doubt, and passion to rid itself of doubt, is a figure for a spiritual condition, of which we moderns remain capable our whole lives, in which one can always still feel like the youth.

Frost's and Tennyson's books are both made up of short poems in rhymed verse. The books each have a single speaker, at least at first blush. Relations between poems are loose; narrative threads are mostly obscured. In the absence of much backstory or plot, narratives emerge as series of episodes. The poems have just enough external event to frame the episodes as internal events—ways of being. They are mostly reflective more than declarative or associative, conversational more than declamatory or cryptic, inner conversations shared with an audience. The main difference is in the staging.

The way of the soul for Tennyson's speaker is to be torn between ideas and emotions throughout his self-transformation. Taken alone, the cantos are ambivalent; the sequence on the whole is resolute. You can see the resoluteness by comparing repeated phrases and scenes within *In Memoriam*, parallels that serve to show different ways of reacting to similar emotional conflicts. (This parallelism of episodes, in far more elaborate form, is also the organizing principle of Dante's *Divine Comedy*, the canonical spiritual verse autobiography in Western literature, on which *In Memoriam* is modeled in ways such as the number of cantos and the rhyme scheme [to which Tennyson adds a line, rather as Frost adds a line to the beginning of Tennyson's four in "My November Guest" and "Ghost House"].) Like Tennyson in *In Memoriam*, Frost organized *A Boy's Will* in three parts, like Dante's three stages of the afterlife or the three years of Tennyson's elegy sequence. The three parts of *A Boy's Will* correspond loosely to three stages of mourning, the first to the youth's spiritual attachments in their vagaries and their vexations, the second to the spiritual commitments he resolves to keep, and the third to moving ahead. Unlike Tennyson's and Dante's examples, however, Frost's sections are neither symmetrical nor structured in terms of parallel poems between sections whose shades of difference betoken spiritual growth. That is because Frost condenses so much inner conflict into the space of individual poems, especially the poems of attachments, which include "Into My Own," "Ghost House," "My November Guest," "Stars," "Flower-Gathering," "Waiting," a revision of "Choice of Society" called "The Vantage Point," "Mowing." Parallel states between poems in *A Boy's Will* are less important to the work than parallel states within individual poems, his ambivalence embodied in an intricate balance of ambiguous perspectives staging an invisible drama, as "My November Guest" is balanced between the sonneteer of "To His Love" and the mourner of Tennyson's third canto, as "Ghost House" is balanced between Keats's aesthete and Dickinson's ghost of Keats's aesthete. In fact, "Into My Own" balances parallel states from within *In Memoriam* itself, one from the beginning of Tennyson's journey and one from its visionary conclusion, the wish for self-transformation and the parallel testament over a pair of late cantos of a self as it has been transformed. Recall the declaration at the end of "Into My Own": "They would not find me changed from him they knew—/ Only more sure of all I thought was true." This couplet of Frost's is much like the last stanza of Tennyson's canto 123, a declaration that he will dwell in his spirit, constant to his own inner life and thereby not leaving his old self and his old loves behind:

TENNYSON	FROST
But in my spirit will I dwell,	
And dream my dream,	Only more sure of all I thought
and hold it true;	was *true*
For tho' my lips may	
breathe adieu,	
I cannot think the thing	They would not find me changed
farewell.	from him they knew

In the preceding canto, Tennyson steals away into the bared spiritual landscape he yearned for. He insists, as Frost does, that the absent dear to him be with him.

TENNYSON	FROST
O, wast thou with me, dearest, then,	And long to know if still I held them *dear*
While I rose up against my doom,	But stretched away unto the edge of *doom*
And yearn'd to burst the folded gloom,	Were not, as 'twere, the merest mask of *gloom*
To bare the eternal heavens again . . .	

It is the very climax of Tennyson's spiritual odyssey. He regains the unfettered imagination of his boyhood as the freedom of youth joins to the power of maturity in his envisioning his lost beloved friend brought back to him in spirit at last.

> . . . And like an inconsiderate boy,
> As in the former flash of joy,
> I slip the thoughts of life and death;

And all *the breeze* of Fancy blows,
　　And every dewdrop paints a bow,
　　The wizard lightnings deeply glow,
And every thought breaks out a rose.

Tennyson's concluding line, "And every thought breaks out a rose," is much like Frost's, "Only more sure of all I thought was true"—apparent affirmations of the whole of their *thought*, though Frost hides his misgiving in his very note of triumph.

　　Why did Frost hide that his book was a book about mourning? He did not hide that it was a book about loss, borrowing his title from a well-known poem of Longfellow's called "My Lost Youth," all of whose stanzas end with the lines "A boy's will is the wind's will / And the thoughts of youth are long, long thoughts." A boy's will has the force of the wind and like the wind can blow whichever way, but the long, long thoughts of youth can make his lost youth blow back to him. Longfellow's couplet unites the psychological and spiritual senses of "will," the will blown with little discipline or direction in a boy's mind but never lost in a man's reflective spirit. Frost also adds an ambiguity to Longfellow's line in cutting it down to a phrase. A boy's "will" could be his last will; it could be the inheritance by means of which he comes into his own. Yet "My Lost Youth" is a poem of rejuvenation by memory, while *A Boy's Will* is also a book about mourning. It mourns the poet's youthful ideals, even the undoubting spiritual vision that embodied them. Its penultimate poem is "My Butterfly," glossed with the epigraph "There are things that can never be the same," such as that poem's way of envisioning spiritual life from the vantage of a breeze that is a spirit. The book's hope for a renewed clarity of spiritual vision at the culmination of mourning is implicit in the powerful allusion to Tennyson's climactic vision in the very first lines of Frost's book. Yet by the time he published his book, Frost had become too private to disclose revealing facts behind much of his work even as he wanted as ever to share the texture of his inner experience. Perhaps it was as a compromise between these conflicting impulses that he set up a situation in which one had to look very carefully to see the logic of grief in his book and to notice its relationship to the boy with his grandmother's eyes who had passed like a breeze.

Though not a literal story of mourning, *A Boy's Will* suffuses its every texture in an atmosphere of mourning like the mist in "My November Guest" that turns her gray wool silver. The poems are tinged throughout with a sense of amorphous loss, the other side of which is a depth of gratitude for, even an awe toward, the dark trees scarcely swaying, the footpath and cellar hole, raspberry and grape-vines, the sodden pasture lane and the snowdrift under stars and the mowing field, the daydream that could be a haunting and the haunting that could be a vision, the affectation that could be genius, the dream that could be fact and the fact whose bare existence is the sweetest dream his work knows.

5.

OTHER FAR

———

I.

Frost would come to remember the first half of the first decade of the century as an extended interval of familial solitude, the farmhouse like Walden Pond with wife and children in tow. (Lesley was joined by a brother, Carol, in 1902, Irma in 1903, and Marjorie in 1905.) Once his life became more public, Frost would speak of this earlier time with wistful hyperbole—no callers at the house for eight years, out twice after eight in eight years—as well as a more doleful hyperbole about being lost to people after feeling unable to live among them. However, the living room of the farmhouse looked out on a thoroughfare that was only steps away. Frost's recollections were fictional embellishments of a life lived in a great deal of genuine privacy for better and for worse. For worse, professionally; for better, domestically, intellectually, aesthetically. Frost not only wrote almost all the poems in *A Boy's Will* in those years but began to develop the style for the two kinds of masterpieces he would write in the early years of the following decade, the narrative poems he would publish in his second book and the lyrics he would publish in his third. Many of the habits of mind that would characterize his work of the next decade grew out of his life of domestic labor and domestic attachments, farming and fatherhood. Farming was in fact an unsolitary pursuit, from which he learned enough about his neighbors to fundamentally change his perspective for the rest of his life, gaining a sustained admiration for the depth of their practical knowledge and the profundity of their values and the unstudied grace of their habits of speech. He was especially taken with the custom of "changing works," in which neighbors took turns helping one another with tasks on their farms, undertaken for Frost out of a distinctive lack of admiration of his competence and diligence as a farmer. Their judgment, not extended to his pragmatic housemate Burrell while he lived in the farmhouse until 1902, weighed on Frost. Not even his prose writings for widely read poultry journals, short stories and reporting, dispelled local impressions of his acumen. He embarrassed himself with the readership of *The Farm-Poultry* in 1904 by flagrantly mischaracterizing the roosting of geese, an error he tried to cover up elaborately by writing a letter to the editor in support of himself in the voice of an authoritative poultry man he had come to admire and befriend enough for the latter to consent to the ruse. These publications aside, the years were short on professional momentum. Frost took his family to New York City for a month in 1903 and made overtures to editors that went nowhere. Despite publishing poems in substantial periodicals at a respectable clip, he was deeply frustrated with editors' lack of greater interest in his work and wondered what was so strange about his poetry that prevented it from wider acceptance. This frustration may help to explain the delay of more than a decade between his sending Susan Hayes Ward a set of poems "with a view to a volume some day" and his submission of *A Boy's Will* in manuscript a dozen years later. With whatever justification, he felt that the world did not recognize him. The feeling began to change in 1906, when, with four children to support and with dimming prospects of regular income from writing, Frost returned to people in the form of formal employment, sharing what he had learned in relative solitude with the broader world as he would in one way or another for the rest of his life.

II.

The most extensive contemporaneous record of the Frosts' daily life in their years on the farm is a series of journals that Lesley kept regularly beginning in February 1905, shy of her sixth birthday, celebrated with banana pudding and cake. Early journals tell of her playing in the pasture and swinging birches, family sleigh rides in winter, the cow escaping from the barn and needing to be chased down in the snow, trips with her father in the wagon to Derry, and walks into their neighbor's woods. The journals tell of her mother going off to look at the stars by herself while the others competed to be first to see Venus. She and her father like to go on walks together, she noted. He told her any number of stories and encouraged her to write out stories of her own.

Her father tended to have an easy time with children. Perhaps this was because of his years as a teacher or the example his mother set for him, perhaps because his imagination rested so often on aspects of life where the boundaries between imagination and reality are porous, as they are for the young. Frost himself saw no boundary between caring for children and teaching them, writing in his notebook, "Loving children (which is teaching)."

The Frosts' most formal means of instruction, per Lesley's journals, was a game called "playing school." The curriculum as of October 1906 was as follows:

> almost every day about ten o'clock mama calls us in the front room
> and we have to sit up on the sofa and tell storys then we have to count
> 12345 and then we sing a song and then read and then we do a b c d
> and when any one says a word right he gets the word and then we sing
> another song and then we do our exersizez and then we march around
> the room once or twis and then march out into the kichen to show papa
> how we can do it.

Naturally, Lesley learned a great deal. Nowhere is this more apparent than in the grasp of botany she demonstrated well before her eighth birthday, her stories populated by, inter alia, daisies, dandelions, dahlias, phlox; white and purple clematis growing on the stone steps out to the orchard; cherry blossoms flowering white and quince blossoms flowering red; hepaticas and cinquefoils spelled as well as one might expect by someone whose main teacher was careless of spelling, "hapaticas," "singuafoles." A story from June 1906 has her father showing her different species of orchids on and around the property—snake-mouthed orchids (rose pogonias) in the cranberry bog, lady slipper, arethusa, causing her to reflect, "i like snake mouth and arethouses best i think."

Lesley seems to have had much of her father's attention in these years while her mother looked after the younger children. To judge from Lesley's stories, her father seemed disinclined to prepare lectures. He seems instead to have merely spent time with her, very often on walks, sharing what was of interest to him or telling her more about what struck her interest. Her stories record "papa" (sometimes "rob") giving her a fantastical explanation of a crow's flight and a precise description of a phoebe's call. Father and daughter blackened a glass to look for the sunspots that appear the day after the northern lights, which once, after her bedtime, he woke her up to go see.

The subjects in which she demonstrated knowledge unsurprisingly mirror her father's particular interests. Not all of them were natural and local. Her story "About War," a fine articulation of just-war theory for an eight-year-old, argues, "The best reason we have for a war was the reason for the civil war the reason to free the slaves." Lesley recounted a war game she and her father played to reenact the Eastern Theater of 1862. The game appeared in a journal entry of August 1907, a stretch of time with unusually large gaps in her journals and no mention of her mother, who had lately suffered yet another harrowing loss, giving birth to a daughter, Elinor Bettina, who died shortly after childbirth. Her parents left almost no record of the tragedy other than eventually putting her name on the family gravestone. Frost seems to have done his part to distract his eldest daughter with trips to Derry and the woods and "our war game," far more elaborate than games Frost devised for the younger children like trying to bite an apple hanging from a string, a Halloween favorite.

Of course Lesley knew a great deal of poetry. "Poems are very pretty sometimes," she opined, adding, "I like wordsworth and shaksperes best." She recorded which poems of each she liked most and, elsewhere, what she liked most about Wordsworth's writing. "I like Wordsworth's poems about best of all, he makes them so pretty and gives you such a picture that he sees, and he likes to have something in his poems that caried something in his mind." She extended her observations to favorite lines in "The Solitary Reaper," "The Daffodils," "The Rainbow." ("The prettyest line in that is, a rainbow in the sky, i like that because you can see a rainbow in the sky now.") She offered the same kinds of impressions and observations in a later story about the six books she read from out of the hundred and twenty-five in the front room's big bookcase. Among her favorites were Palgrave, Matthew Arnold for his captivating, troublous plots, "Coldridge" for the only poem of his she read, his *Ancient Mariner*, and Tennyson for his lovely stories of long, long ago, especially his stories of King Arthur.

She quoted another poem of Tennyson's, a ballad called "The Brook," in a story that encapsulates the family's attitude toward the Derry farmhouse as well as anything her father ever wrote. "Our farm has interesting places to travel to, just like the world, though you do not have to journy so far as in the world," she wrote in "journeys On The Farm."

> We go to some place almost every day that it is good enough to go to and that is only when it is nice, but when it snows we sometimes dress up and go tramping out to the gate. When it shines we go everywhere on our farm though we have been there a hundred times.

Among her favorite places on the farm was the stand of alders through which Hyla Brook ran, which reminded her of Tennyson's poem. ("It reminds me of the brook that said 'I sparkle out among the fern to bicker down the vally.'") She also loved to play in the grove and the pasture and the field across the road. "All these places that I am speaking of we travel to about every day and play in each one half an hour and play that half an hour is half a year at some far off place in the world."

III.

Her father expressed similar sentiments about the brook that ran seasonally through their alder woods in a poem called "Hyla Brook." Frost began the poem, a near sonnet, in 1904, so one assumes that the stream of influence ran, if at all, from father to daughter. Like her story, his poem is about a constant appreciation of familiar places on the farm even in their less illustrious seasons. His poem may also recall Tennyson's Brook, which sings, in its refrain, "For men may come and men may go, / But I go on forever." Frost imagines his brook dried up in June and "out of song." To see the brook going on nonetheless requires an act of imagination as well as a constancy of attachment, virtues his poem celebrates as it shows how painfully hard they are to live up to with a brook or any other thing that one loves and has seemingly lost.

HYLA BROOK

By June our brook's run out of song and speed.
Sought for much after that, it will be found
Either to have gone groping underground
(And taken with it all the Hyla breed
That shouted in the mist a month ago,
Like ghost of sleigh-bells in a ghost of snow)—
Or flourished and come up in jewel-weed,
Weak foliage that is blown upon and bent
Even against the way its waters went.
Its bed is left a faded paper sheet

Of dead leaves stuck together by the heat—
A brook to none but who remember long.
This as it will be seen is other far
Than with brooks taken otherwhere in song.
We love the things we love for what they are.

As in the best storytelling, the conclusion is as unforeseeable beforehand
as it seems necessary in retrospect: *We love the things we love for what they are.*
After the poem's twists and turns, solid ground. After sentences that bend
and flow for fourteen lines (a sonnet's length), a one-line declarative sentence; after fourteen lines of unusual rhymes for a sonnet, the most familiar rhyme for the form in our language, a quatrain of ABAB, ending
with a line of perfectly regular iambic pentameter; after crosscurrents of
shifting descriptions, a conviction; after a sonnet's worth of imagination
and memory, preservation and loss, the present and lasting and real. The
"brook to none but who remember long" is a brook to those who remember it by means of this poem, who can know what it is despite appearances
just as a work of art can preserve the essential in a thing despite the passage of time. Surface fades, but love worth its name sustains essence. We
love the things we love for what they are.

     Yet the path to the triumphant conclusion has a curious undercurrent.
The poem shows us a brook without "song and speed," perhaps buried
underground (and with it the hyla frogs that sound loudly with their
mating calls in spring ["taken" with the stream underground like the
Hylas of legend, a fair young beloved of Heracles, who disappeared after
his abduction by nymphs of the spring of Pegae, in love with his beauty,
and was never seen again], frogs that had shouted in the mist "like ghost
of sleigh-bells in a ghost of snow," a figure of faded song and speed [the
sleigh-bells having rushed away]—an echo in an echo and a reverberation
of the frogs in mist, an echo in itself of sight and sound, all compressed
into a brief parenthetical about the brook's having maybe gone underground as against flowering in jewel-weed [silver underwater, orange when

not], the riverbed showing no signs of the water that flowed there). The poem does not show us the brook.

So we readers are told with great feeling to love the things we love for what they are by means of a description that on close inspection tells us what the brook was and will be and might be, not what it is.

One effect of the tension is to underline the difference between what something is and what it seems to be. The poem asks us to hold the brook in mind despite descriptions, just as the speaker of the poem tries to hold it in mind despite appearances. As time alters the thing, imagination preserves it, and we readers in the little act of constancy the poem asks of us can feel the ache of loss and anticipate the grace of renewal. It takes the smallest hint to think a life is like the brook, once alive like youth with "song and speed" only to be buried underground or transformed in its decomposed elements into matter that gives no trace of its ghost, a soul to none but those who remember the person, including He who goes on forever. And what does the passage of a season or a lifetime matter to an immortal God who loves us for what we are—immortal souls? Our constancy in holding the brook in mind—the little, graceless brook, as small to us as we are in the great order of things—is a figure for God's constancy in holding on to us immaterially, as if we, too, could fade into nothingness, only to flow again with song and speed when the snow melts in the great spring of being, "other far" than the spring we can see.

The poem has thus delivered a sermon on imagination as an aid to constancy. Yet this reassuring sermon sits in tension with a cautionary example in which imagination works against constancy without even noticing its mistake. The question turns on an ambiguity of syntax implying that the speaker might not in fact be sitting with a dried Hyla Brook but imagining how he will remember the brook once it's gone. The brook by June is "out of song and speed" but not necessarily dried up. The poem begins in present tense and doesn't return to it till the tenth line, the start of just the third sentence, at which point we don't know whether the line "Its bed is left a faded paper sheet" (and so on) refers to the present of the poem or to an imagined continuation of the second sentence, which for eight lines imagined where one would find the dried brook "much after" the beginning of June. *Its bed is **then** left*, it could mean, or *Its bed is **now** left*, the former raising the possibility that the speaker's grand act of imagining the brook to preserve it comes at the expense of losing sight of the little brook running slowly and song-lessly under his nose. Perhaps his sense of its diminishment leads him to anticipate missing it so powerfully that he loses it while it's still there, and the poem of his that had seemed like a noble elegy, preserving the essence of the brook in extended description, is just so much aggrieved sentimental lamentation that would mourn the thing preemptively from attachment to what it had been at the expense of appreciating or even noticing what it has become. A tone that sounds like relative equipoise in the face of loss can mask a whiny somnolence in the same words. The poem, which has shown us something of how it feels to love a thing for what it is, shows us something of how hard it is to see a thing as what it is if you love it.

Thematically, "Hyla Brook" is a counterpart to "Mowing," the former a poem about the vexed role of imagination in knowing some-thing ostensibly absent, the latter about the vexed role of imagination in knowing something ostensibly under your nose. The poems are in this sense two sides of the same fundamental problem of Romanticism: the relationship between imagination (make-believe or otherwise) and knowledge. Fittingly, the poems—both irregular sonnets—each borrow from long visionary poems by Coleridge, "Hyla Brook" far more sub-stantially. It owes much of its sequence of imagery and even the theme of its concluding precept to that favorite of Lesley's, *The Rime of the Ancient Mariner*. As she explained the plot, "Somebody did something wrong and that made them have trouble." Specifically, the mariner, his ship waylaid "in the land of mist and snow," did shoot an albatross with his cross-bow, sending him on a long nightmare of an odyssey and precipitating the death of his crew. That crew, in a parched and protracted doldrum, is briefly reinhabited by a sudden procession of ghosts who produce in their host corpses a song of resounding and orchestral proportions that shortly subsides into "A noise like of a hidden brook / In the leafy month of June." The mariner is left to wonder what continuity there is between these silent reanimated bodies and the crewmen he knew. Haunted by the voyage he is doomed to remember in perpetuity, the mariner draws a moral in conclusion about constancy in love regardless of the scale of the beloved:

> He prayeth best, who loveth best
>   All things both great and small;
> For the dear God who loveth us,
>   He made and loveth all.

So ends the mariner's speech. He who remembers long would have us love the things God loves for what they are.

Frost had borrowed from longer poems and transformed them before—often, as here, from the manifestly sublime to the apparently modest that nonetheless carries an imaginative arc like that of the source poem. This borrowing from the *Mariner* was new in scope and scale, however, drawing together central images and a central idea of a much longer poem that Frost himself knew well and writing a compressed and original work out of the conflicts between them. Though similar to the borrowing in "Into My Own" of two poles of *In Memoriam*, the difference is signal: that was a borrowing between two states of mind in short lyrics, whereas this from the *Mariner* is between an experience and its meaning in the context of a longer work refashioned by Frost into a story of his own. The result in the case of "Hyla Brook" was a new and more abstracted kind of make-believe that would be essential to his masterpieces of the following two decades, both the lyric poems and the narratives, for whose inception Frost borrowed similarly from another poem in the volume in which Coleridge initially published his *Mariner*, *Lyrical Ballads*, his famous collaboration with Wordsworth that was an experiment in adapting the ballad, a verse form associated with vernacular and even childlike storytelling, into literary art by means of unliterary language, the language of everyday speech. Frost developed his narrative style through his borrowing from Wordsworth's "Ruth" in that volume, as the present work will discuss shortly.

What makes the make-believe of "Hyla Brook" different from that in the poems before it is the absence not only of character but of characterization as well. Personality is all but absent from the speaker of "Hyla Brook." There is no meaningful backstory for the reader to infer. The conflict of the poem turns on the meaning of its central idea on its own terms, not also on the relation between the idea and the type of person who had it. There is no type of person to speak of. The reader shares with the speaker the components of the drama of the poem: words susceptible to distinct inflections of speech that indicate different ways of thinking and feeling in the context of the poem. Where make-believe involved characterization without character, this involves tonal inflection without characterization. Frost would come to call this aspect of his style the sound of sense.

IV.

When Frost composed a letter in verse to his old friend and former housemate Carl Burrell in the doldrums of the winter of 1906, it was in the voice of the mariner. Frost even adapted Coleridge's balladic verse form to tell of the family kept inside in "the time of snow" and afflicted by maladies and strange alterations of consciousness like the adrift passengers on the mariner's ship. Beset by poor respiratory weather as described by a made-up Coleridgean word ("coughter"), Frost the mariner ended his mock tale of woe with a nod to the means requisite for future escape:

The Hermit good lived where he could
I would be down in the tropics
Where there are no gales of coughter more
But I cannot muster the kopecks.

The desire to go south may have been just a passing fancy, but the desire
to earn more was real. Frost was seeking employment by February.

"It Was a Banner Occasion," proclaimed *The Derry Enterprise* of March
9, 1906, in regard to the prior Friday's "Annual Supper of the Men's
League of the Central Congregational Church" in Derry Village, New
Hampshire. The "Pleasing After Dinner Program" had included one
"Robert L. Frost," introduced "as the author of an original poem, which
was read by the Rev. C. L. Merriam, pastor of the Central church." Frost
sat next to the reverend, too anxious to read it himself. It was the first
reading of a poem of his to the general public. He made a vain attempt to
hide behind an iron post. Frost met a trustee of Pinkerton Academy who
arranged for him to interview with the headmaster, and Frost was teaching high school English within weeks.

Frost would later claim to have gotten into the situation by happenstance. His story went that he, down in Lawrence from Derry to ask for
letters of recommendation to apply for teaching jobs in lower schools,
happened to run into an old acquaintance, Reverend William Wolcott,
who had told him years before that his poems sounded too much like
talk. It was not the only time that Frost in his retelling would run into
helpful associates on the street at just the point when he needed their
help. In any case, Frost told Wolcott he was looking for work, Wolcott
recommended that Frost call on Reverend Merriam in Derry, Frost did,
and Merriam asked the self-conscious farmer, whose poetry he had heard
of from Wolcott, whether he might want to read a few of his poems
to the Men's League and perhaps help himself get hired at Pinkerton.
Frost returned in a few days with a couple of poems for Merriam to
look over, one of which was the poem Merriam read to the crowd, "The

Tuft of Flowers." Though Frost would later claim to have written the poem years before the occasion, vain as ever to conceal the pains he took in his own self-interest, his first recorded account of the poem, from 1913, tells a different story:

> [*A Boy's Will*] comes pretty near being the story of five years of my life. In the first poem I went away from people*; in the one called a A Tuft of Flowers I came back to them actually as well as in words verbally for I wrote that poem to get my job in Pinkerton as little Tommy Tucker sang for his supper, and Brer Merriam read it for me at a Men's League Banquet in Derry Village because I was too timid to read it myself.

> * and college

Frost often bragged about never having written poetry "to order," but he granted again decades later that "The Tuft of Flowers" had been an exception. He was less forthcoming about the other occasional verse he wrote in his tenure at Pinkerton.

"The Tuft of Flowers" tells the story of an old job of Frost's from the summer of 1893—turning over bales of grass to dry their bottom sides after a mower had taken his scythe to the grass at dawn and left one side to dry in the morning. The solitude of his task causes the speaker to muse on the solitary nature of labor until a butterfly disrupts his melancholy by flying over to a tuft of butterfly weed that the mower's scythe had evidently spared. This discovery so enraptures the speaker that the mower becomes his kindred spirit, present before his mind's eye and mind's ear, causing him to invert his earlier musing about the solitude of labor in favor of a resounding conclusion about the imaginary fellowship present in all labor:

> 'Men work together,' I told him from the heart,
> 'Whether they work together or apart.'

The poem mirrors Frost's insight, oft repeated, that he grew to appreciate his broader community by "changing works" with people on neighboring farms, taking care of tasks for one another even in the other's absence. It also seems to bear some hints of the occasion. Its revelation about imaginary fellowship reaches a crescendo of imaginary "brotherly speech," an apt phrase for a Men's League and also an echo of Wordsworth's demotic description of poetry in the "Preface to *Lyrical Ballads*" as the "language" of "a man speaking to men" (also a language children could understand). The main analogy between farmwork and literary work at the heart of the poem—itself an apt kind of analogy for a farmworker auditioning to teach—was an analogy so close to the heart of Frost's philosophy of teaching that it looks prepared for an audition, his description of the mower's attitude toward the flowers, which is also the teacher's attitude toward his material:

> The mower in the dew had loved them thus,
> By leaving them to flourish—not for us,
>
> Nor yet to draw one thought of ours to him—
> But from sheer morning gladness at the brim.

Just as the mower shares his spirit not by reaching out to the turner but by his example of noticing things in the world by sheer spiritual pursuit, so does the teacher of literature teach best by demonstrating his response to what moves him most.

"The Tuft of Flowers" is also manifestly a poem about poetry. Its scythe-wielding mower and miraculous butterfly call to mind the earlier poems of his in which such characters feature, as if Frost were reaching back through his earlier poems to encapsulate them. He often said that "sheer morning gladness at the brim" was the state out of which poetry should be written, rather like Wordsworth's "spontaneous overflow of powerful feelings" from his "Preface." Frost's figures for teaching and writing blur into one another in an auspicious beginning to the life of work he had in store for himself as a literary teacher.

V.

A number of Frost's former students at Pinkerton remarked more than half a century later on the state of his hair. "He used to come in the classroom in the morning like he slept in his clothes and hadn't combed his hair." "Always tossing his head back to get a lock of hair out of his eyes." "He would lounge against the teacher's desk, hair and clothes rumpled, hands in his pocket, and quote poetry most of the period." One woman remembered him as "blond with the bluest of blue eyes which were partly concealed by 'half mast' lids[,] . . . wont to gaze into space and discourse more to himself than to the class and I am sure he was often quite unaware of us." The same woman recalled him as "interested in the lives of birds and small animals," "easily distracted by accounts of unusual behavior of any of nature's creatures," and inclined to "ask endless questions," even following her to "a little bunny hiding place I had discovered under the branches of a small hemlock": "Fortunately there were two bunnies waiting when we lifted the branches and he was enchanted." "He was gentle and shy," she remembered, "and I could understand why his wife looked so adoringly at him and worked so hard for him."

The work referred to was both domestic and agricultural. According to a former student's father, "that damfool Frost" had been "shiftless" and unable "to cope with any form of farming," leaving "machinery where last used and weeds and brush were allowed to accumulate all over" and leaving a great deal of work to his wife. Their neighbors, who regarded Elinor as "out-going and well liked," "helped her in many ways, ploughing and preparing a small garden and seeing that she had a winter's supply in the fall."

Surprisingly few of his students described him as having been lazy.

One remembered him as a very exacting corrector of writing, another as a careful editor of her writing, others as an encouraging reader. Someone remembered him patiently working with four Chinese exchange students to practice basic English. Perhaps he remembered himself as a lazier teacher than he was out of a lingering shame about his neighbors' estimation of his farming. Yet his students understood and accepted his unusual manner of teaching far more than his neighbors did his unusual manner of farming. There were exceptions. A pair of students worried that much of what he said had been beyond most of the class, whether from a lack of aptitude or interest in poetry, and yet each of these students expressing reservations expressed appreciation, too. "To those of us who loved poetry he was a delight," one wrote. Another, with dubious grammar, testified that "he got me to writing poetry."

"A remarkable and outstanding teacher," someone wrote. "There was never any question of discipline in our class," wrote another, because the students "were spell-bound by his personality." Another remembered trying to study as a freshman while sitting in the room where Frost taught Senior English and ending up "spell bound" as well.

Someone remembered Frost's fondness for the rhythms of Kipling's poetry, as in "Mandalay"; another recalled that a favorite poem of Frost's had been "Daffodils" (maybe Wordsworth, maybe Herrick). Probably one reason his old students remembered these individual poems almost sixty years later is that their teacher had them commit so much writing to memory. The students "memorized numerous passages from Macbeth, Julius Caesar and As You Like It." He promised one girl a copy of his first book of poems, whenever published, for memorizing twenty-five poems from Palgrave (though he seems to have forgotten his promise when a book of his was published years later, to her chagrin). A number of students recalled him as demanding and exacting about their memorizations. One remembered him "very indignant" when she couldn't memorize "part of Washington's Inaugural Address . . . overnight." Another remembered Frost's "wrath" when a student would begin a recitation with the word

"Well." "He would thunder 'When you recite to me, don't begin with "Well."'"

Frost's style of discipline as both teacher and parent seemed to involve few rules, strictly enforced, like his style of verse. "He stood for no foolishness," wrote one man, "but he was also friendly and helpful. I remember when we used to go to the ball field to practice baseball he would come down and play with us and give us a few pointers on the game." The football team seems to have been his favorite. A former student remembered his suiting up in proper uniform to play in practice with the second team. "I can assure you that we did not put on kid gloves when we tackled him," one man remembered. "He asked for no special treatment and he got none."

Frost's tenure at Pinkerton began inauspiciously. Carrying some of his shyness from the years on the farm, he felt out of place as a poultry man, out of place as a teacher at his level without a college degree. He struggled at first to gain his students' respect, having to draw a hard line when one of them insulted his farmer appearance with an anonymous message on the blackboard. He had to cut his first semester short when he came down with a bad case of pneumonia. Soon enough, however, he grew into the role and then some. His shyness turned into its opposite. He served as students' confidant about troubles they had in other classes, took students on long walks, had groups of the boys over to the farm on Saturday mornings to talk and play games, took a group of "three or four of us boys to a Lodge some distance from Derry Village for a week-end." "I do not recall what we did during the day," one remembered years later, "but I have never forgotten how we sat entranced until after three o'clock in the morning listening to him talk."

With some students, Frost grew especially close. One was Emma Pearl Goldsmith, one of whose old friends remembered her as Frost's former "star pupil": "He took a great interest in her work and if I remember correctly aided her in going to college." Another student with whom Frost became close was a boy named Harald Abbott, who would later recall the summer after his graduation as a kind of extended tutorial held on the branches of a cherry tree in Frost's yard. The sessions were much like those Frost would have with dozens of others, mostly younger men, over the years. "When I finally said I had to go and started off he would accompany me slowly along the road," Abbott recalled. "At intervals we would stop," during which Frost "would continue his talk, sitting on a stone wall." "He wrote me rather often," Abbott wrote. "I cannot understand quite why."

Another student, Clarissa Hall, thought that Frost had taught them to observe the little things of life, largely natural, "to the fullest extent possible." It was a lesson in which a classmate of hers found the meaning of much of Frost's teaching, that he "in his quiet way taught us that we did not have to seek beauty in far off places." Hall compared this kind of instruction to Lesley's recollections of her father's teaching, published after his death. "He taught us as he did his children."

VI.

In 1907 as in 1906, Reverend Merriam read a poem of Frost's on his behalf at the annual Men's League banquet at the Central Congregational Church. "The Lost Faith" was an oration in verse in celebration of the lost ideals of the Union cause in the Civil War. Though written to order, the poem is an irreplaceable artifact in the history of Frost's poetry, doing much to clarify the relationship between the initial and revised drafts in Frost's first attempts at original narrative verse. The initial attempt borrowed from Wordsworth, the revision from Browning. As it happened, "The Lost Faith" itself borrowed from a poem of Browning's, one responding to Wordsworth with rage.

In 1845, in a poem called "The Lost Leader," Browning excoriated Wordsworth with the indignant moral fervor of youth. It is a poem with the peculiar condemnatory force of disappointed adulation, even disgust, charging Wordsworth with having abandoned a generation of disciples by surrendering his commitment to freedom and art for the tawdry goals of money and laureateship. In "The Lost Faith," Frost excoriated the generations succeeding the men who had fought for the Union for forgetting the cause for which the soldiers had served. Like Browning's, Frost's charge is of abandoning an ideal of noble devotion for the pursuit of lesser goods—for "things," Frost writes, "that were not beautiful and bright." He speaks in "The Lost Faith" not as Browning does on behalf of a generation of idealists but on behalf of a generation that seemed to be losing the highest ideal of the nation, the American creed, expounded by Lincoln in his paraphrase of Jefferson in the Gettysburg Address: "Four score and seven years ago our fathers brought forth, on this continent, a new nation, conceived in Liberty, and dedicated to the proposition that all men are created equal." Lincoln's proposal of the creed was a strange kind of poetry, something between history and exhortation and decree, not a straightforward statement about Americans' actual motivations over the course of their fractious history but a reminder of the ideal on the basis of which their nation had from the first claimed legitimacy, a calling to heed the ideal in pursuit of the Union cause in the great civil war, and a decree that it was this ideal for which the army of the Republic would stand. It is in this sense of idealistic history, not idealized history, that Frost recounts the creed as "the soldier's dream":

> No less a dream than of one law of love,
> One equal people under God above!

Frost in his couplet outdoes even Lincoln in drawing out Jefferson's phrase into a vision of the promise of the American republic: not only equal law, not only the self-evident *truth* of all created equal, but a law enacted on earth that realizes the same equality as people share in God's love—not merely a people equal under God, but one equal people under God. These ideas had fallen out of fashion in the "latter wisdom" of the country, cynical after the failures of Reconstruction and the Southern revision of history on which the war had been pursued by the North for material interest rather than moral purpose, a myth called the Lost Cause that was the opposite of the Lost Faith. The creed had also lost purchase in light of the increasingly prominent idea, forcefully rejected by Frost in the poem, that American races were too different biologically to be equal, a modern intellectual trend that gave a scientific veneer to a deep strain of American racism. Frost ends his poem with a thundering rhetorical crescendo denying that the unfashionableness of the creed has the slightest bearing on its truth. Though the dream may be passing from the world, it is nonetheless truer "than all the hopes the years abate from youth" and truer than anything a wandering soul might find about the heavens in the hours before sleep.

"The Lost Faith" was published in *The Derry News* on March 1, 1907. Frost tried more than once in those years to publish the poem that revisited the ideas of "The Lost Faith" in narrative verse, "The Black Cottage," thinking an editor might want to time it with Memorial Day, then called Decoration Day to mark the custom of decorating the graves of Union soldiers with flowers and flags. Editors rejected the manuscript from Derry, perhaps because the poem submitted in honor of the soldier's dream looked so much like a dismissal.

"The Black Cottage" is a monologue of a minister taking a silent narrator through an abandoned cottage that once belonged to a widow whose husband died in service to the Union cause. Stylistically, the poem is typical of Frost's major narrative verse that was soon to proliferate, its spare, unrhymed pentameter full of what Frost would proudly call "an everyday level of diction that even Wordsworth kept above." The poem was not always so. The draft that survives of it was written in a rhymed and lushly poetical tetrameter. Frost dated the draft to 1905 or 1906, implying that he found his way to revising it after writing "The Lost Faith" to order. As the only early narrative for which an unpublished draft survives, "The Black Cottage" is the only fossil record

showing the emergence of the narrative verse that would make Frost's
reputation.

The draft of the poem began with a poem of Wordsworth's, "Ruth:
Or the Influences of Nature," which tells the story of an old woman
living alone in the woods. Wordsworth's poem, also in Palgrave, is an
initially tragic retelling of the biblical story of Ruth, taken by her new
husband to a foreign land not to join her new people (as in the Bible)
but to be abandoned by her base and meretricious betrothed and put in
a madhouse, only to recall her childhood love of solitude in nature and
then escape to find peace in a life of solitary indigence and natural grace
under a greenwood tree. Frost's draft of "The Black Cottage" is, like
"Ruth," whose ballad stanza Frost adapted, about a woman living alone
in nature when travelers pass by, a woman who inspires the narrator's
pity (ruth) for her "loneliness," her having lost a husband, her dubious
sanity, and the quickened pace of her aging. Ruth is figuratively an "in-
mate" for Frost and literally for Wordsworth, and each ends his poem
with the narrator imagining her in an earthen burial mound by means
of the word "mould" at the end of a line in the last stanza, a "hallow'd
mould" for Wordsworth and an "oozy meadow mould" for Frost. The
difference between the phrases encapsulates the difference between the
perspectives of the poems, the spirited pronouncement of "hallow'd"
and the dispirited observation of "oozy meadow" in its watery lugubri-
ousness. Wordsworth purports to know her experience, whereas Frost
wonders what we can know of her. Wordsworth declaims his perspective, while Frost writes his poem out of questions of perspective implicit
in the language he uses. His reader is brought to question the woman's
perspective on her surroundings (and by extension on her life) and the
perspective of anyone who passed the house and imagined the woman,
such as we readers and even the narrator. Wordsworth tells us of her love
of nature; Frost shows us her perspective in free-indirect narration, the
long grass (untended) flowing river-like to her door as in a van Gogh:
"The long grass that flowed in from o'er / The fields all day to her

closed door." Frost's deviation from Wordsworth actually shows a self-conscious bridging of two of Wordsworth's major concerns, the subject's capacity to understand its object of consideration and the poeticality of his diction. Frost worked through the former problem by means of the latter. The poem ends on the question of whether his Ruth ends up where she wants to be, as Wordsworth's did, the final stanza hinting in its lushness of language at the way her description of her surroundings could sustain her pleasure in her pain with a languorous magical glamour—or the flight of poeticality, unparalleled in the poem, is just a sign of the narrator's getting carried away with himself and losing sight of her experience in his embellishment of her life's pathos. The pleasure in her pain may be his.

Frost's transformation of "The Black Cottage" from this version into the one he would publish was a rewriting in an alternative genre. Themes and stray phrases persist; the rest is transformed. The poem grows more than three times in length, its rhymed tetrameter relaxes into unrhymed pentameter, the sentences sound like sentences and not chiefly lines of verse, and its universe fills out its details distinctly and realistically, leaving a charged and oneiric world like that of Poe's poetry for the believability of realism. Accordingly, woman and narrator become characters with explicit historical context, she—now deceased—a war widow devoted till the end to her husband's principled sacrifice, and the former narrator—no longer the poem's actual narrator but its monologuist who spends the poem describing her extensively—a minister who knew her as his congregant. The new narrator, who happens upon the abandoned house on a walk with the minister and walks through it with him, is nameless, silent, and otherwise unidentified, briefly relaying the context of the minister's monologue at beginning and end with reportorial spareness.

One effect of this transformation is to hide the perspectival drama of the earlier version. A conflict close to the surface in a lyric world of verbal embellishment and self-conscious imagination is harder to see in a

narrative world of people and history. The conflict is all the murkier because the minister, unlike Frost's narrator in the earlier draft, seems not
to question his own perspective. He talks with a chatty authoritativeness,
reinforced by his ecclesiastical office and not questioned or even interrupted by the narrator, that makes his perspective seem almost incidental
to the curious woman whom he describes at such length. What stands
out in the minister's telling is the old cottager's eccentric stubbornness
of principle:

> One wasn't long in learning that she thought
> Whatever else the Civil War was for
> It wasn't just to keep the States together,
> Nor just to free the slaves, though it did both.
> She wouldn't have believed those ends enough
> To have given outright for them all she gave.
> Her giving somehow touched the principle
> That all men are created free and equal.
> And to hear her quaint phrases—so removed
> From the world's view to-day of all those things.

For a sense of how Frost might have actually felt about the minister's treat-
ing her conviction with bemusement and pity, consider the character of
Browning's from whom Frost adapted his worldly-wise minister: Bishop
Blougram, brilliant and specious, a disgrace to his calling.

"Bishop Blougram's Apology" appeared in Browning's *Men and Women*
(1855), a collection of poems spoken by an assortment of characters
and personality types, written in Browning's characteristically expansive
range of forms. The poem is a dramatic monologue and an "apology" not
in the modern sense but in that of the classical term "apologia," a formal
defense or justification, in his case defending himself against the moral
condemnation he imputes to the silent journalist he talks at across the
dinner table over a last glass of wine.

Like Frost's minister, Blougram is conspicuously worldly. The two are both in the world and of it, concerned with man's esteem to the point of subordinating truth—each fixes on the word—to the standards of society and not the divine. Truth for them is timely, contingent on their historical period, not timeless as one would expect as a precondition of faith. They trust the spirit of the age. Their extended pontificating monologues are each spoken in unrhymed pentameter to silent interlocutors and framed but not interrupted by brief narration, each ending on a note of sudden escape to a faraway and relatively unpopulated land, the minister to an imagined fantastical Bethlehem and Blougram's interlocutor to Australia, as far from the bishop as one could get under the sun.

While the bishop is magisterial and domineering, the minister is unassuming, chatty. This doubtless helps to explain why scholars have missed the clerical parallel, though clues to the minister's character are there for the discerning. Despite his years of visiting the old woman, he can't remember whether her husband died at Gettysburg or Fredericksburg, a major Union victory or an overwhelming defeat. He proves himself repeatedly obtuse and unashamed of his obtuseness, attentive at all times to the opinions of the people around him and showing no sign of his own convictions. He wanted to drop a line of the Apostles' Creed about the descent into Hades to accommodate "non-believers in the church," wanted to change liturgy in deference to the faithless, relenting only to avoid upsetting the woman, though it perplexed him that the ritual acknowledgment of man's capacity for evil could have meant something to a woman who believed that her husband died fighting it. The minister seems to think of truth as what people tend to believe at the time, a vacillation he regards as unavoidable but lamentable. He ends the poem with a lofty, poetical fancy of ruling a desert land "I could devote and dedicate forever / To the truths we keep coming back and back to," seemingly unaware of the injunction in the Lord's Prayer, Matthew 6:10, "Thy kingdom come, thy will be done on earth as it is in heaven."

If the minister seems reasonable, it's because he sounds like he cares. He's sad that the world passed the old woman by, sad when the world loses its truths—so sad that he imagines himself shepherding the truths like one of the three kings protecting a version of "the babe born to the desert" who, far from dying for man's sins as a paragon of self-sacrifice, never leaves Bethlehem. Yet the minister's care is in each case shorn of judgment, let alone action. His sentiment, a sign of caring, takes the place of engagement. He feels sad instead of responsible. As in the poem's rhymed draft, the final flight of poeticism intensifies feeling at the risk of distorting its object. Words get away from him, implying that, by a similar sentimental self-deception, his earlier response to the woman's conviction, his ruth that had seemed so reasonable, was wrong.

Through Blougram, Browning voices a series of finely articulated arguments, only to disclose that he had scattered among his convictions a series of seductive ideas he didn't believe, a rhetorical habit of Milton's Satan. Through the minister, Frost leaves his readers with a series of compelling ideas and no means within the poem of judging which he agrees with. Browning befuddles his audience as Blougram does his. Frost does the same while barely showing his hand, leading his unsuspecting reader to think that the poem was written to dismiss the unfashionable belief of his subject even though its purpose was rather the opposite. By making her case in the minister's words, Frost tempted those of his readers susceptible to the minister's perspective to judge her on the minister's terms before realizing the shallowness and moral vacuity of his, and perhaps of our, dismissal. The poem delivers the sermon of "The Lost Faith" by alternate means, not in an excoriation of the faithless but in an unassuming satire by means of which the faithless might come to doubt their own perspective as Frost doubted Wordsworth's perspective in "Ruth"—a means of persuasion so subtle that many a reader might think their doubts had come to mind with no one trying to persuade them at all.

"The Black Cottage" doesn't look much like "Hyla Brook," but the styles that emerged with each poem turn out to have similar origins as well as similar ends. As Frost's personal concern shifted from mourning the losses of his youth and the loss of his youth to loving children, which is teaching, the concern of his writing shifted from conveying self to others to understanding others himself, a problem taken up in *A Boy's Will* only in the context of his relationship. The problem of understanding others was the subject of "Hyla Brook" and both drafts of "The Black Cottage" as well as the poems of Coleridge, Wordsworth, and Browning from which Frost borrowed for them. In their respective aspects of the problem of understanding other people, Frost's styles of lyric and narrative verse correspond to Coleridge's and Wordsworth's respective contributions to *Lyrical Ballads*, the former about the subterranean currents of the imagination hidden in everyday life and the latter about the imagination present in everyday life. Frost would find forms in his most sophisticated lyrics and narratives to incline his readers to experience the ambiguities he saw in such acts of imagination without reference to himself at all.

These ends would remain in his greatest work, but their origins would grow invisible. One could say much the same of his teaching, an exercise in drawing out the imaginations of his students, including his children, toward the things they loved without reference to the mower who had left them out in the sun.

In later years, Frost would opine that teachers do not improve their students but have the privilege of "being occupied with the idealizing part of people's nature." These years of the youthful formulation of ideals, in Frost's case a reconstitution of ideals in the shadow of disappointment and grief, were the years of solitude in Derry and the years of *A Boy's Will*. Having passed this phase of life, Frost occupied himself with the idealizing parts of other people's natures. He who had been too timid to read aloud his job application of a poem addressed his classes with composure, then authority, then a spellbinding charm. With a personality to perform, he performed more of himself, and, curiously enough, his poetry grew more impersonal as his personal life expanded decisively from the solitude of Derry. He began to develop something largely absent from his life so far but essential for the rest of his life: intimate and revealing friendships, beginning with the star pupil Frost discovered in his sophomore English class.

6.

THE TRAVELER AND THE ROAD

I.

The friendship began in the fall of 1907. John Bartlett, fifteen, was in his first term at Pinkerton, in what would now be called the tenth grade. He had turned in precisely one theme for Junior Middle English, about a cave in the Pawtuckaway Mountains, north of Derry. As was his wont, Frost joined a group of the boys tossing a football after school one afternoon. Bartlett could remember the rest twenty years later:

> Frost happened to come near me. He asked several questions concerning the Pawtuckaway Mountains, where the "Devil's den," about which I had written, was located. I answered them awkwardly; I was a shy boy. In a matter-of-fact way he observed that I was a fellow who had ideas.
>
> That was all there was to the conversation, as a spinning ball came my way, but I can see Frost, and the fall mud, and the football bucking machine, and the boys, as I recall it.

Bartlett came away with a distinct impression. "He seemed, during this conversation, to be possessed of several hundred times the interest in me that other teachers had." They would be friends as long as Bartlett lived.

Though the two were of course not growing up together, they were in their different ways coming up together through Pinkerton. Bartlett's was the first class Frost saw from start to finish. The two would flourish together over the ensuing three years, often with each other's help. Frost coached Bartlett and his junior middle classmates to victory in competitive debate against the seniors, supplying his side with more elaborate answers than was the custom, showing up the senior class, some of whom had been giving their farmer of a new teacher a hard time. Frost directed Bartlett as a marvelous devil (Mephistopheles) in the *Faustus* Frost put on as part of a series of plays, spanning centuries of English drama, that were at once novel in selection and compelling in performance, Mephistopheles rushing Faustus (Harald Abbott) into the grand piano onstage. Frost advised Bartlett in running a literary magazine he would still praise decades later, practiced with the football team of which Bartlett was captain, and not only marched back to town with the team after their season-ending victory but penned jingling verse in Captain John's honor. Bartlett was in his senior year when their English class received a visit from the superintendent. For the period, Frost directed much of the discussion toward Bartlett, who especially impressed Superintendent Morrison by questioning the scholarly footnote in their edition of Milton's *Comus* that equated "charity" and "chastity." Morrison would not only approve of Frost's methods but single him out to give a talk on his teaching to a meeting of teachers in nearby Exeter, a distinction that not only showed up Frost's rival on the faculty, who had teased him for his lack of a college degree, but set Frost up for consideration as headmaster at Pinkerton and eventually for his appointment to a higher level of education in his next job, training teachers at the state Normal School in Plymouth, the lower gateway to the White Mountains. The rise began for Frost by directing a single classroom discussion toward the boy he would remember as the best student he ever taught. The student Frost remembered as second best, Bartlett's co-valedictorian, was soon also his wife.

Margaret and John Bartlett delighted Frost and Elinor with the parallels to their own story, which only grew when John dropped out of college, at Middlebury, shortly after matriculation. He and Margaret decided to go off to Vancouver in search of adventure and, perhaps more importantly, a respite from John's asthma. Frost and Elinor thought of joining them there.

II.

Bartlett's was one of three consequential friendships Frost formed in these years. One of the other two was also with someone much younger than Frost, the other with someone much older.

Frost met his older friend by happenstance in the summer of 1906. Having suffered from hay fever toward the end of previous summers in Derry, Frost went alone in August 1906 to Bethlehem, New Hampshire, north of the hay fever line. The little town next to Franconia sits at the northern seat of the main pass through the White Mountains. Finding its hotels full, Frost asked around for places to stay and was referred by an Irishman he met to another Irishman by the name of John Lynch, from whom Frost rented a room in his farmhouse. Frost took to the thoughtful and laconic man with a long white beard, and to life on the farm with its easy rhythms and views of the mountains, returning in subsequent summers with his family in tow. The families enjoyed long nights on the porch, Frost regaling the crowd but also listening to the distinctive Irish wit of his new friend with its discernment and dryness. Lynch exemplified a kind of father that Frost's father was not—self-contained, responsible, able to take life with great humor, and not disfigured by the force of ambition. Frost appreciated profoundly the way Lynch appreciated life, seeing in his very way of talking a depth of sophistication and reserve that amounted to a kind of embodied philosophy. Frost listened for such understated dignity and modest nobility in the speech of other rural working-class people of the region he met in these years, such as the careworn wife of the man on whose property the Frosts camped near Lake Willoughby in northern Vermont in the summer of 1909.

The Frosts' return to Derry in the fall set in motion the circumstances through which Frost would meet his younger friend at Plymouth Normal School. Pinkerton's new principal, Ernest Silver, was impressed by the teacher who had so impressed the superintendent. When Silver was asked to lead Plymouth Normal School beginning in the fall of 1911, he asked Frost to join him. Frost agreed on the condition that he would stay for only one year. The terms of his grandfather's will would allow him in the fall of 1911 to sell the Derry farmhouse from which the Frosts had already moved in the fall of 1909 to a rented place in Derry Village closer to Pinkerton and schools for the children. Frost and Elinor intended to sell the farmhouse and go somewhere new. Silver accepted Frost's terms, hiring his teacher of English to teach psychology and the history of education to women in training to be teachers themselves. So it was that Frost found himself chaperoning a dance along with another new member of the faculty, fifteen years his junior, who would be Frost's devoted friend for the rest of his life. Yet the friendship began less auspiciously than its destiny would suggest.

Neither man would seem to have made the right impression. Frost, thirty-seven, nonchalant and rumple-suited, struck Sidney Cox as objectionable. Cox, a young twenty-two, was someone inclined to object. When some women he had gone to college with at Bates, a Baptist college at the time, had gone off to a dance, faced expulsion for waywardness, and been reinstated on the strength of student protests, Cox disagreed with the protesters. He was a preacher's son, one who had taken sixty-three courses in college. His was the kind of fastidiousness that Frost had to poke at. One of Frost's socks was tucked over the top of his boot at the dance. Cox let his disapproval be known, Frost said something to the effect that Cox should go off and grade papers, and Cox did go off, speculating to another teacher that perhaps Frost had failed to get further in life at his age because of a penchant for drink.

The two went on a walk together the following day after school. Cox would remember Frost's calling him to the principal's office, though Frost would cast some doubt on the memory. In any case, the impression Frost made on the walk was nothing short of transformative. "After the walk I had with him that afternoon," Cox recalled, "I had accepted him, and thereafter when I felt a discrepancy between some attitude of his and what I had always supposed, the presumption in my own mind was that what I had always supposed was wrong." Though technically his colleague, Frost would be the greatest teacher Cox ever had.

To the students Frost was actually assigned, he came across much as he had to his students at Pinkerton. Being more established and authoritative, he was more uninterested in formal rules such as showing up on time to teach or preparing lessons beforehand. In his conspicuous laziness, he seems to have been even more engaged with his students' inner lives and even more widely appreciated by them. Their memories were more effusive than those of his students from Pinkerton. "A friend first and then a teacher." "So kind, so gentle and always seemed to be much interested in each of us as an individual that we soon felt that he was not just an instructor but a real friend." "[Elinor] was a sweet motherly lady and we all loved her as well as her husband." "We all loved him." "Often when he came to class he would say that at an early hour that morning, say two o'clock, he had taken the seven mile walk to Rumney to think about things." "I, and others, feel quite sure many days he came to class with no preparation whatsoever. He would simply tell us to write a theme on whatever came to his mind first. . . . [and] would then slouch down in his chair for the entire period." "He induced me to play tennis and often."

With striking consistency (if not perfect uniformity), Frost's students remembered feeling not only inspired but especially recognized by this aloof man, distinctly seen by him. Such was the impression made by a mind that made a show of following its own inclinations rather than those of propriety and then turning to find you of great interest. One woman whom Frost taught at both schools, Clarissa Hall, "recall[ed] very vividly one day his asking me to remain after the class was dismissed that we might continue our discussion on predestination." The two of them discussed the subject for four hours, so long that Hall went to bed "supperless."

Silver tried to keep Frost after his first year, but he and Elinor were set on departing. The farmhouse was sold. They daydreamed about going off to Vancouver near John and Margaret but settled on a different kind of adventure across the Atlantic instead. A coin flip determined their course for London rather than Vancouver, Frost later claimed dashingly, inconsistently, and rather implausibly. The truth was that he was determined to make it as a poet, as he confided in Bartlett, saying it would happen in the next three or four years or never, and London was the literary center of the English-speaking world. Frost had made it as a teacher and seems to have expected teaching work to be open to him when he returned to the country, given Morrison's support and despite the warnings of Silver. As a poet, he had reason for confidence, having published more in the preceding half-dozen years than in the dozen before that. Still, at nearly forty, he had yet to publish a book. Someone might well wonder why he had not gotten further in life by his age.

The departure, while exciting, was not without a sense of loss. In an unpublished poem about selling his farm, Frost imagined the longing his older self would have for the farm:

> Only be it understood:
> It shall be no trespassing
> If I come again some spring
> In the grey disguise of years,
> Seeking ache of memory here.

His older self, essentially unchanged, would be merely hidden "in the grey disguise of years." He would come again for the "ache of memory," not the pleasure of memories and not the return of lost time.

III.

John Bartlett, John Lynch, and Sidney Cox were each a different kind of friend for Frost. Lynch was a model, Cox a disciple, Bartlett something harder to categorize. That he was something between the best friend Frost had never had and the son Frost had lost only begins to explain the relationship. Cox's relationship with Frost, though easy in one sense to classify, was no easier to explain. Frost would spend decades insisting that this young man who was manifestly his disciple not be his disciple. Looking up to Frost put Cox in such a vexed position that he spent a lifetime trying to understand it. Every disciple of Frost's would do the same, as would almost everyone whom Frost grew close to as an adult. Intimacy with Frost exposed you to the byzantine complexity of his inner life, of which no small part was the complexity of Frost's reserve, his will to conceal his inner life and to reveal it as well, his unparalleled ability to do either or both in the simplest words in the language. The intimacy in his poetry was one thing, subject to his shaping and therefore little threat to the parts of his life he wanted to keep private. Intimacy in life involved a different kind of exposure, as he had learned with Elinor over long years.

Given the complexities involved in being close to Frost, his friendships are doubly revealing. They are revelations of the ways he showed himself or hid himself and of the conditions under which he chose the one or the other or some ambiguous admixture of both expressed in some variety of make-believe. The conditions of his self-revelation were never straightforward, often requiring not only privacy, not only friendship, but the specific kind of friendship to draw Frost out in a particular way. Demonstrably, he needed his friends, and to judge by how many of his finest essays were letters and his finest talks conversations, his need for his friends was intellectual as well as emotional. Bartlett, for instance, was not only a good student making his teacher look good but a participatory audience in front of whom Frost could realize his potential as a teacher. Frost's intimates were each a different kind of audience with whom Frost engaged in a different kind of drama, each with its disclosures of character and mysteries of motive. The story of Frost's life was to a great extent the story of such revealing and beguiling intimacies.

In Cox, Frost had a young man who would take his every word seriously. It made Cox the perfect recipient of Frost's teasing, Frost's hectoring, Frost's sermonizing and testing. Most importantly, it made Cox an eager audience for a number of the ideas most important to Frost over the years, beginning with the increasingly philosophical ideas with which much of Frost's poetry was occupied in Plymouth and the ensuing years abroad in England, a sojourn best appreciated by starting not with the Frosts' voyage across the ocean but Cox's pilgrimage up to Franconia to see the newly repatriated Frost at the end of July 1915.

When Cox arrived at Frost's newly purchased house in Franconia, he was disappointed to find a young and unusually erudite professor already visiting Frost. Cox would have been impressed by the scholar had he not seemed in Frost's presence "like a fire-fly in full moonlight."

Frost's hands were brown and hairy; his face was unshaven. He sat on top of a packing box in front of his house with his guest, the professor, Joseph Warren Beach, when Cox arrived with his traveling companion, a young German named Alex Bloch. The house was only somewhat unpacked despite their having been there for a couple of months. A door was off the hinges, set against the wall. "The tea," wrote Cox, "was poured from a measure for milk, and the soup which I think was the staple was served from an earthen mixing bowl with a large spoon instead of a ladle." Robert and Elinor made no apologies. Cox was enthralled, writing pages on end to his parents in the hope that they could gain "some conception of the joys of my visit—the rich spiritual feast." They talked for hours on end the first night. Robert walked Cox and Bloch partway down the hill toward the inn and turned around for home to milk the cows.

The farmhouse, gray and gabled, was backed by acres of fir trees that Cox called Frost's Christmas tree woods. The house looked east to Mount

Lafayette and the rest of the Franconia Range. A thick fog known as the dragon often stretched through a gap in the ridgeline.

Cox exhausted a thesaurus's worth of superlatives in his description of his days at the farm. The hospitality was the warmest, the most unaffected; the table talk was the most interesting; the children were the most attractive for "vigor and sweetness of character." The first appearance of Elinor made his heart leap. "This Franconia Range across from the house and tent would furnish a splendid subject for a series of studies by a great sober landscape artist." Cox's hosts were "the very finest people," chief among them, of course, "Mr. Frost." He worried that his diary failed to capture Frost's presence. "It leaves out the strong, sweet, laughing, earnest, sympathetic, scrupulously honest, frank and hearty yet always controlled spirit of the man." Cox did his best to draw out the depth and measured intimacy of Frost's presence:

> Every thing he says comes from deep within him specially for him or them he talks with. Nothing he says is learned or even merely reasoned. It is experienced and felt. He does not use the word love with flippant frequency but love fills and overflows him. It never gushes.

Frost's reticence with his affection left Cox a touch insecure. Cox could have used a pour if not a gush, lamenting that Frost "did not in all the time I was there make a single friendly speech to me." Cox was reassured after Frost said, "Old friends are best" and later signed the back of a photograph for him, "Your old friend R.F."

Frost may not have gushed with affection for Cox, but he seemed to talk especially well when Cox was listening. His stray remarks to Cox in a matter of days in Franconia make up a better introduction to his way of thinking than anything he ever wrote for publication. Frost preferred Emerson to Whitman, he said, and Shakespeare to modern dramatists like Ibsen and Shaw. The latter had meanings they tried to embody in their plays; Shakespeare embodied situations out of which meanings arose.

There was less insight to gain from abstract speculation than from what Frost called "special cases." He was for unsystematic philosophy. He thought that systematic philosophies all followed from fallible premises outside the system itself. The premises determine our thinking more than our reasoning from them, and our backgrounds determine much in our premises. Our minds are guided by simple desires imperfectly known to ourselves. It was necessary to resist some of your own emotions and fine to take some small pleasure in the tragedies in your own life. The words in a poem must be "inevitable," not merely fine. We stand in relation to our faculties of reason like a man at risk of drowning on an ice floe. Reason is what lets him avoid error in navigation. What drives him is "an unanalyzed desire to get home."

IV.

The movement homeward of Thought had been the climax of a poem Frost had written in Plymouth and sent Cox from England in July 1913. The poem, "Bond and Free," was a draft of a lyric fable about Thought and Love. Its tone was light, its thrust sincere. In style and scope, "Bond and Free" was representative of Frost's great lyrics of the period even in draft form. The poem was stylistically like "Hyla Brook" in its impersonality, in the sense of framing a drama whose resolution would turn on ideas or aspects of experience not particular to the characters or types involved. This implies a great ambitiousness of scope in articulating ideas or aspects of experience somehow shared by a general audience—the literary equivalent of sharing his perspective with Cox in long improvised talks. The style of "Bond and Free" was as ambitious as its scope. Like almost all the other great lyrics written in the years after "Hyla Brook"—"To Earthward" is a startling confessional exception— "Bond and Free" used not only the impersonal make-believe of "Hyla Brook" but at least one other earlier style of make-believe, making for ambiguity in the kinds of ambiguity on which the poem turns. Dreadfully abstract as this sounds in theory, in practice it is anything but, which was among the great achievements of Frost's lyric style: to contain the growing complexity of his poetry in forms that were no more difficult than those preceding them, that were in most instances simpler, belying the turbulence one is made to feel under the surface. Cox could hardly have been prepared for what awaited him by the three words Frost wrote at the top of "Bond and Free" as he sent it to Cox along with two other manuscripts with these three words separating it from the others: "This is best."

"Bond and Free" is in a distant sense an impersonal variant of "My November Guest." Its figurative abstractions Love and Thought are embodied figures like Sorrow but with no "My" to qualify their existence. Yet "Bond and Free" is even closer in spirit to the two poems from which it borrows substantially, each an instance of the kind of seventeenth-century poetry known generally, if loosely, as metaphysical for its vivid embodiment of abstract ideas in philosophy and theology. Frost encountered a good deal of such poetry at a young age through the editorial selection in *Parnassus*, an anthology of the favorite poems of Emerson, whose own verse was largely metaphysical in his own distinctive key. Frost would draw on metaphysical poetry as his own poetry sought to vivify his own ideas, which meant inclining his readers to experience the conflicts and uncertainties implicit in his own ideas.

In Frost's draft of "Bond and Free," Love is grounded, Thought is boundless. Love clings and Thought soars. Yet beyond the initial impression of Thought as majestic and Love as hidebound and homely, Frost leaves the reader with a hint of suspicion that Thought might be a little too pleased with herself. She seems to see herself as heroically bold and independent, free of any constraint by physical laws or emotional ties. In a sign that she might overestimate her own capacities and not comprehend the force of her own attachments, she traverses the heavens, only to find herself flying back to earth, as if drawn homeward for no reason she can give.

Bond and Free (draft)

Oh, Love has earth to which she clings,
And circling arms and hills about,
Walls within walls, to keep fear out;
But Thought has need of no such things;
For Thought has a pair of dauntless wings.

Oh, Love has left on lawn and lea
Her print in many a flowery place,
From straining in the earth's embrace;
And such is Love, and glad to be!
But Thought has kicked her ankles free.

Thought cleaves the interstellar gloom,
And sits in Sirius all night long,
And comes at daybreak, winging strong,
With the smell of burning on every plume;
While Love has slept in a little room.

The poem is clearly told from Thought's perspective—not in the first person, but in free-indirect narration, which follows a perspective through the words of another. This point of view helps to explain not only the favorable descriptions of Thought relative to Love but the strange ways that Love is described. Love has "circling arms and hills," a pair of things so different in scale that only Thought in her detachment from earth would draw the two together in description. (Even the use of "circling" as against "encircling" makes Thought sound as if she were from another planet.) Perhaps it is this distance that makes Thought describe the object of Love's embrace as the earth. Maybe Thought is set to find another kind of embrace if it enters the "little room" that Love had slept in.

    As readers of the poem, we hover with Thought in the end at the threshold of Love's "little room." We are in something like the position of Satan in his first approach to Eden in *Paradise Lost* when he sets sight on Adam and Eve's "narrow room," the Garden of Eden. Milton's Satan, like Thought, is wingèd and "dauntless"; they both escape their fetters; they talk themselves up out of pride. Sirius was known in English literary tradition for its changing colors, like those of Milton's Satan in his flight down from the sun toward Paradise. Satan's wings are often said by Milton to be burning; on his descent, he is "inflam'd." The Paradise that he discovers—entirely new to him—is thick with hills and different layers of walls. He sees the dwellers in the Garden "Imparadised in one another's arms" before they retire to their bower, wherein "the rites / Mysterious of connubial love" were duly observed before bed. Satan whispers to Eve as she sleeps. His hope is to "taint / Th' animal spirits" or "raise / At least distempered, discontented thoughts, / Vain hopes, vain aims, inordinate desires, / Blown up with high conceits ingend'ring pride." In the midst of his temptation, he is caught of a sudden by a pair of angels and taken away.

The reader of Frost's manuscript who hears the allusion may be surprised to find something like the devil in her ear. Although the poem hews to Thought's point of view, in tracing her path and admiring her we resemble Thought less than contented, unsuspecting Love, Love in the position of Eve in her temptation. We hear grandiose temptations from a source that hides its nature. Like Satan's disguise, Thought's is imperfect. Like Satan's temptation, Thought's might leave an air of discontentment even with her true nature revealed. Who would not want to cleave the interstellar gloom instead of being bound, by fear of fear, to earth?

The draft leaves its readers to sit with the temptation. The version Frost would publish three years later offers us a way out. In addition to some relatively minor changes from the manuscript—Thought becomes male, for instance, and it's clear that he alights on the "earthly room" but left for us to infer that Love has been sleeping there—the revised version adds a stanza at the end to make the case for Love:

His gains in heaven are what they are.
Yet some say Love by being thrall
And simply staying possesses all
In several beauty that Thought fares far
To find fused in another star.

"His gains in heaven are what they are" is quite the snub for the rebel archangel who tried to gain command of Heaven, only to be damned eternally for his pains. As Satan could never tolerate, Love is thrall (a Miltonic word); Love is earthbound. Yet the last stanza offers the case that what Thought seeks, Love possesses (a Miltonic and a biblical word)—possesses "in several beauty," a Miltonic construction and an odd one to the modern ear. We might expect something more like "varied beauty" or "several beauties," but neither phrase has the same meaning as Frost's. Frost uses "several" in the antiquated sense of "separate and in the manner pertaining to each," as in "They went their several ways." There is no idiomatic synonym in modern English for "several" as Frost applies it to a singular noun like "beauty." The strangeness of the phrase impels a reconsideration of the case for Love. The point is not what we might have first thought, that Love possesses any number of beauties, but that the possessions of Love reveal themselves as beauty experienced in all its pertinent forms. In other words, *Some say that what Thought knows without having, Love has without knowing.* In other words, *Some say the sense of beauty is Love's way to know what it has.*

It is a beautiful idea. Perhaps Frost believed it. One would nonetheless be mistaken to infer that the poem is written to persuade us of the case for Love that it presents. "Some say," he writes; they may be wrong. The case for Love is a small counterweight to the adventures of Thought. The beauty of its appeal could be its own temptation to disregard Thought under the sway of beauty, casting aside the True in the classical Platonic triad of the Beautiful, the True, and the Good. Such a casting aside is rather like the vanity of Milton's Eve, her admiration of her image in the water, that stirred her discontent and made her open to temptation. (Eve's attraction to her own image would be one of two scenes in *Paradise Lost* from which Frost borrowed to write a poem about knowledge and doubt, "For Once, Then, Something," in 1917, the other scene being a parallel section in which Satan is confronted by his own daughter [Sin] before departing hell to fly toward earth, the complex of parallels about reflection, misperception, attraction, and temptation showing just how well Frost knew these early books of Milton's epic.) In "Bond and Free," the appeals of Love and Thought are impossible to weigh without our knowing what it is that Love possibly has and Thought seeks. What Thought fares far to find fused in another star, what Love might have fused in itself like the double star Sirius, persists as a beautiful mystery.

The phrase "bond or free" recurs throughout the New Testament in the King James translation to refer to the distinction between free people and people in bondage. Frost's phrase seems similar at first, with Thought free and Love bound, but the story of the poem is of human capacities that frustrate the binary—Thought free to soar but bound in its course and Love bound to its object but free to enjoy it and free from Thought's peregrinations. In other words, we are ourselves bond and free. It is a vision of humanity familiar from *Paradise Lost*, the central problem of whose theology was to reconcile humanity's freedom to sin with the omnipotence of the God who created the world and its laws to which humans are ostensibly bound. We are bond and free like Milton's Adam and Eve, bound to each other, bound not to eat from the Tree of Knowledge, bound to their omnipotent creator but free to give in to temptation.

If fables are usually written to explain the inexplicable, what was "Bond and Free" written to explain? A clue can be found in another poem to which "Bond and Free" owes an obvious debt, "The Definition of Love," a fable of a poem by Andrew Marvell, Milton's contemporary. Marvell's fable would explain how two people can love each other entirely without being entirely one with each other. Frost's would explain a division not between lovers but within the soul itself.

The poems take place in worlds of personified abstractions and granular detail. They are fables in which the scale shifts suddenly from love to cosmos to a single pair of wings. The personified abstractions— Love and Thought for Frost, and for Marvell love and Fate primarily with supporting roles for Despair, Impossibility, and Hope—are characters with minds of their own. Each is at once an aspect of the human condition and part of a little fanciful tale, at once the stuff of treatises and bedtime stories. The tension that results for both Frost and Marvell between the lightness of their tones and the depth of their thinking marked what T. S. Eliot would define as the essence of metaphysical wit.

Love and its partner are separated for at least part of each poem by the vastness of space. Love in each poem is both binding and bound. The poems each rhyme "see" and "be" in that order and "thing" and "wing" in that order (though Frost uses "wings" rather than "wing"). In Frost's manuscript, "Love" is the second word of the poem as it is in Marvell's, and the pair of first lines scan identically and rhyme with each other internally—"Oh, Love has earth to which she clings," "My love is of a birth as rare." The last stanza in Frost's revised version is, like the last stanza of "The Definition of Love," a stunning and ultimately elusive summary of the poem's meaning that ends the poem on a use, plural in Marvell and singular in Frost, of the word "star."

The parallels to "The Definition of Love" serve to show by way of contrast what Frost intended with his revision of Marvell's metaphysical fable. Marvell's story is of "perfect loves" ensnared in a reality in which they cannot realize themselves, while Frost's story is of love that can never be perfect, love with paradise lost. Marvell's love is Platonic. Its essence is Idea, something capable of being grasped by thought. One ascends in Platonic sublimation from love of beautiful individuals to love of the beautiful in itself, an Idea in the world of forms apart from the world of material things. This kind of sublimation is precisely what "Bond and Free" denies. Thought cannot be the perfection of Love if Thought is bound to be at a remove from it. Frost's Love is non-Platonic; its essence is not in an idea one can abstract away from the object of Love. What the essence of Frost's

Love is, though, he hardly implies. One can say he leaves Love undefined, but the presence of Milton offers a suggestion. Frost follows Milton and centuries of Christian tradition in showing a world in which the intellect can deceive as well as lead, tempt as well as discipline. And his evocation of human capacities would seem to follow Milton's diagnosis of the human condition. Frost's Love is bounded but potentially transcendent in a way that Love could never know. Frost's Thought is limitless in potential but in need of definite bounds. So is humankind in Milton's postlapsarian world, forever severed from knowing divinity and left with only one another and the faith that human love, undertaken for whatever purpose, intimates a love of God for humanity that can only be taken on faith.

V.

One of the funny things about the letters Frost wrote to Cox from England between December 1912 and February 1915 is that he's always exhorting his younger friend to be more self-reliant. Self-reliance for Frost meant independence from ways of thinking that would drown out the authority of your own spirit. Cox's schoolteacher fastidiousness was one such habit of mind on account of its preoccupation with rules and conventions, and Frost accordingly peppered his letters with pleas to overlook mistakes of spelling and grammar and in particular the spelling errors of Frost's own, which he told Cox were meant for his training in the practice of ignoring them. Frost even misspelled Cox's first name in his first letter from England: "Sydney," not "Sidney." Frost's letters are full of his own ideas pronounced in bold, intriguing, and elegant terms. His observations have the force of proclamations, not least on the subject of Cox's need to do his own thinking.

Frost was well aware of the ironies involved in his manner toward Cox. They did not make him stop. "I will scold you more in my next letter," he promised in one letter. "I preach," he wrote elsewhere, "but this is the last time." It was not. Frost continued preaching self-reliance to his friend.

The ideas animating Frost in his letters to Cox in these years, like the ideas animating his poetry at the time, amounted to an unsystematic philosophy of the human spirit. Frost's first sustained prose on the subject, the letters go a way toward showing how his conception of spirit framed how he thought about "these things that we cant reduce to a science anyway such as literature love religion and friendship," matters he thought the spirit couldn't but touch on. The letters also go a way toward clarifying how his thinking on the spirit had changed since the old faith of "Twilight"—yet they clarify only so much because they leave much of his thinking implicit. He tended to convey his views by assertion rather than argument, by statement rather than exposition. Their means of appeal was not theoretical coherence or explicitly reasoned inference but, as in poetry, direct claims on his reader's judgment and imagination, on what his reader felt and thought. It was left to Frost's younger friend to work out the thinking behind ideas like the following:

> You do right to damn grammar: you might be excused if you damned rhetoric and in fact everything else in and out of books but the spirit, which is good because it is the only good that we can't talk or write or even think about. No don't damn the spirit. (ca. November 26, 1913)

> I can always find something to say against anything my nature rises up against. And what my nature doesnt object to I dont try to find anything to say against. That is my rule. I never entertain arguments pro and con, or rather I do, but not on the same subject. I am not a lawyer. I may have all the arguments in favor of what I favor but it doesnt even worry me because I dont know one argument on the other side. I am not a German: a German you know may be defined as a person who doesn't dare not to be thorough. Really arguments don't matter. The only thing that counts is what you cant help feeling. (September 17, 1914)

> Your opinions are worth listening to because you mean to put them into action—if for no other reason. But there is no other reason as

important. What a man will put into effect at any cost of time money life or lives is what is sacred and what counts. (December 1914)

Literature is the next thing to religion in which as you know or believe an ounce of faith is worth all the theology ever written. Sight and insight, give us those. I like the good old English way of muddling along in these things that we cant reduce to a science anyway such as literature love religion and friendship. People make their great strides in understanding literature at most unexpected times. (January 2, 1915)

In these letters as in Frost's other writing, he proceeds from the assumption that we are each in possession of a spirit. He makes no attempt to explain it; he denies the possibility, in fact. Its origins, its scope and limits, its commonality or variation, its physical or nonphysical nature—all of these are problems he thinks are insoluble. (Not that he didn't wonder.) His ambition was not to explain the spirit but to live by it. Self-reliance was for him as for Emerson reliance on that in yourself which is spirit. Insight was apprehension by means of the spirit. Poems were insights embodied in form sufficient to communicate them or else they were worthless. The spirit manifested itself in a certain kind of experience, which Frost often identified with that which you can't help but feel. His unsystematic philosophy coheres as a guide to the attainment of that kind of experience.

Frost impressed upon Cox to respect his own judgment more, to respect others' less, to pursue the ideas he will act on and not get stuck on excessive thoroughness or rule compliance. This self-respect and freedom from deference were important for self-reliance, Frost thought, but he did not identify self-reliance with these qualities. They were enabling conditions—whether necessary or not Frost didn't say—but not sufficient conditions. They prepared you for spiritual insight but did not guarantee it. Nothing could guarantee it other than what you could not help but feel, which is not the same as what you merely feel strongly. The former is not only compatible with testing your feelings with reflections but rather implies such a test as part of that despite which your feelings persist. Frost's formulation implies sentiment but not sentimentalism—attention to your feelings but not to the exclusion of your judgment. Frost's disavowal of weighing arguments might give the impression of disavowing careful thinking, but in light of his other writing the criticism is clearly not of the goal of careful reflection but of weighing arguments as a means to that goal. He thought that the habit had the potential to drown out the feelings of spirit and was in any case superfluous, since the arguments came to him anyway when he needed them in conversation. He also thought that the lawyerly habit gave the false impression that the problems were more susceptible to answer by reasoned argument than they actually were.

It was this general skepticism about the power of reflection to answer the questions it poses itself beyond a reasonable doubt that made the bulk of Frost's more abstract ideas about ways the spirit might try to resolve the questions it happens to ask. Accordingly, the ideas he shared with Cox clustered around methods of obtaining spiritual experience in general and especially in the writing, reading, and teaching of literature. Frost was a prophet of self-cultivation in the form of "muddling along in these things that we cant reduce to a science anyway such as literature love religion and friendship."

No idea animated Frost in England like what he called "the vital sentence" or, in a letter to John Bartlett, "the sound of sense." An evocative theory of much of Frost's own practice, the idea behind the vital sentence was that the essence of good writing was its ability to convey tones of speech that the reader could recognize in the experience of reading. The sentence could be seen not as it usually was, as "a grammatical cluster of words," but as a sound in itself that a careful writer could affix to the page and a careful reader could hear as it was meant to be spoken. The grammatical sentence in reading is mostly a "clue" to the vital sentence that it conveys. The vital sentence in the process of writing has to arise "in an imaginative mood" and cannot be invented at will. With vocal tones observed carefully with the writer's "hearing ear" and affixed properly in a poem, "every word used is 'moved' a little or much—moved from its old place, heightened, made, made new." In other words, the "audile imagination" allows for a clarification of meaning that is also a clarification of the spirit, something the writer could not help but feel. Cox was borrowing Frost's idea for an article on education, and Frost said he himself would "do a book on what it means for education" if he didn't always wind up writing poetry instead. Frost also told Cox that Edward Thomas, a writer with whom Frost had grown deeply close over the course of 1914, "thinks he will write a book on what my new definition of the sentence means for literary criticism."

Frost as a thinker is often compared to two of his great influences, Emerson and William James. The comparisons are apt to a point. With Emerson he believed in the reliance on that in yourself which is spirit, but Emerson had a far more elaborate and mystical conception of the spirit than Frost did in maturity. Frost did believe in a supranatural aspect to spirit, but in maturity he almost always presented his ideas about it to the public in a way that required nothing other than naturalistic observation or mere common sense. He would talk to audiences about saving their integrity, for instance, if they preferred not to think in terms of saving their souls. Where Emerson's conception of spirit is Platonic, a transcendent essence, Frost's is Aristotelian in a general sense, realized in the natural world and gradually apprehended by careful observation of one's inner and outer worlds. One could always speculate about the nature of the spirit one observed, and much of Frost's poetry is indeed the fruits of such speculation following his observations, his insight and his sight as he called them. But between observation and speculation was always a leap whose bounds Frost had painfully grown to respect.

Frost shares a picture of human decision-making with the philosopher and psychologist William James, whom Frost admired so much in his early twenties. Frost's sense that our actions and beliefs should depend on what we can't help but feel is similar to some of James's formulations.

Both of them stressed the vital importance of what Frost called, on James's inspiration, believing the future in, committing to a belief in cases in which you can't evaluate sufficient evidence to know whether to hold the belief but could benefit from acting according to it. Yet despite these profound agreements with James, Frost was not a Jamesian pragmatist. James's pragmatism involved a categorical skepticism of conventional notions of truth, skepticism according to which truth simply was that which it is better to believe, not, for example, what corresponds to reality. Frost expressed no categorical doubt about the nature of truth or our ability to know some truths about ourselves and the world. His skepticism was general but not categorical; it applied widely but was not a theory in itself, applied in the consideration of particulars but not in the formulation of a cohesive philosophy.

As a corrective against comparisons of Frost to Emerson and James, consider an influence on each of them to whose habits of mind Frost's are more directly analogous: the sixteenth-century French essayist Michel de Montaigne. All of Montaigne's essays serve to investigate one question: "Que sçay-je?" or "What do I know?" which he had written above his desk and Frost had written in French in one of his notebooks. Like Montaigne, Frost was interested in reflection unbound by subject matter and unguided by the drive to subsume his ideas under a comprehensive whole. The two were theoretical as well as observational, granular and unsystematic. Their chief ambition and greatest rigor was in working out their own natures to determine what they thought about a given subject. Their depth and breadth of skepticism made each of them generally disinclined to think they had settled fine matters of theoretical debate and inclined to present their ideas to the public as little more than matters of preference. (They also presented themselves as far less assiduous than they were.) Their commitment to following their natures led to careful insights on a wide and heterogeneous range of subjects and also to oversights and embarrassments. Each of them was thorough enough in his skeptical reflection on his own nature to expand the kinds of questions we ask of ourselves—

Montaigne far more than Frost, to be sure. He was almost never banal, whereas Frost could be dogmatic and repetitive especially in later years. While the essay is a form of writing that can easily contain a wider range of ideas than verse—and Montaigne also invented the essay as we know it—the intricacy of Frost's form allowed him to expand the range of experiences we have in asking questions of ourselves and perhaps of our spirits as well.

VI.

In 1913, "Bond and Free" rewrote a source poem's conflict between characters into a conflict in the nature of the soul. It was not the only such poem that Frost wrote in those years. Another—also tetrameter with four five-line stanzas and in a similar rhyme scheme—was the poem that would become Frost's most famous and arguably the most famous poem in all of American literature, "The Road Not Taken." On Frost's recollection, he began his unassuming monumental work sitting alone by the fire in a cottage in Ryton, Gloucestershire, on a dark night in the last weeks of 1914. He and Edward Thomas had lately been walking. Thomas had a habit of peering down the paths at a crossroads, unsure which path to take. Frost sent a draft of the poem to Thomas from Franconia in early 1915. Thomas failed to recognize himself in it, let alone to recognize the main poetic source of the poem and the role that the source put him in. The source was "Etienne de la Boéce" by Emerson, a poem named for Montaigne's dearest friend and the subject of Montaigne's essay "On Friendship." Frost would go on to describe his friendship with Thomas in something like the superlative terms that Montaigne used for his own boon companion. Montaigne's essay is a description of ideal friendship as one of harmonious wills, and Emerson's poem is a sort of essay in verse to the effect that he'll serve his friend best if he relies on himself. Frost's poem dramatizes the will's uneasy harmony with itself.

THE ROAD NOT TAKEN

Two roads diverged in a yellow wood,
And sorry I could not travel both
And be one traveler, long I stood
And looked down one as far as I could
To where it bent in the undergrowth;

Then took the other, as just as fair,
And having perhaps the better claim,
Because it was grassy and wanted wear;
Though as for that the passing there
Had worn them really about the same,

And both that morning equally lay
In leaves no step had trodden black.
Oh, I kept the first for another day!
Yet knowing how way leads on to way,
I doubted if I should ever come back.

I shall be telling this with a sigh
Somewhere ages and ages hence:
Two roads diverged in a wood, and I—
I took the one less traveled by,
And that has made all the difference.

To be sure, "The Road Not Taken" echoes with a number of sources.
The poem is both an amalgam and an archetype, like "Bond and Free."
The archetype is that of the crossroads, the primal scene of choice or the
workings of fate, the place where Oedipus slays his father as it had been
prophesied. The poem bears hints of other uses of the archetype Frost
would have known. Emerson contrasted "the old and trodden round" with

"a new road to new and better goals" as paths to choose in life in his essay
"Circles." William James used the figure in a pair of essays Frost knew
well about the momentousness of choice and the problem of free will. But
only one poem that Frost would have plausibly known uses the archetype
of the crossroads to pose the question of what path to choose before settling on the newer path in anticipation of all that the choice would mean
for his soul. "Etienne de la Boéce" culminates in the vision of a path in
which "The traveller and the road seem one / With the errand to be
done," which finds reformulation in the first lines of Frost's poem: "Two
roads diverged in a yellow wood, / And sorry I could not travel both, /
And be one traveler. . . ." Emerson's vision recurs again at the end of Frost's
poem in meaning if not again in phrasing, when Frost writes, "Two roads
diverged in a wood, and I—/ I took the one less traveled by, / And that
has made all the difference." It is a vision of the harmony of the will, the
traveler (the person) at one with their errand (their will) and the road, the
world in which the traveler's will is enacted.

Frost tended to recall the onset of "The Road Not Taken" in terms
too poetical to describe the composition of actual poetry—"a dark winter's night," a "stormy night" with him "sitting by a big fire in a house kept
by a keeper all alone." However accurate a recollection of the night when
he first thought of two roads diverging in a wood, his memories resonate
with the scene of ideal convergence in "Etienne de la Boéce":

> . . . if I could
> In severe or cordial mood
> Lead you rightly to my altar,
> Where the wisest muses falter,
> And worship that world-warming spark
> Which dazzles me in midnight dark,
> Equalizing small and large,
> While the soul it doth surcharge,
> That the poor is wealthy grown,

And the hermit never alone,
The traveller and the road seem one
With the errand to be done;—
That were a man's and lover's part,
That were Freedom's whitest chart.

Frost in memory sits alone in a cottage like Emerson's hermit, his "world-warming spark" a fire and a storm, his "midnight dark" a dark night. As, in "The Road Not Taken," Emerson's last line is transformed into Frost's, the archly symbolic proclamation of an optimal path for his future, "*That* were Freedom's whitest chart," made into a line that could come up in conversation, "And *that* has made all the difference."

Emerson's ending is hypothetical, not predictive. It imagines a mystical path toward a friendship like Montaigne's with la Boétie that Montaigne describes as such a rare perfection of its kind that he wonders if the world produces such a friendship every three hundred years. It was a friendship with no admixture of interest. The circumstances that had brought about their harmony of wills were inexplicable and fated. It was as if their wills were lost in each other in a spiritual union effacing the seam that had marked their distinctness. This is the condition of which Emerson's path is a vision.

"The Road Not Taken" is the only poem of Frost's that not only is famous in its own right but has been subject to a famous interpretive debate. There is the poem of graduation speeches and inspirational posters, the poem of car commercials (really), in which the speaker takes a hard and lonely road that makes him who he is. The speaker has made himself the master of his fate, the captain of his soul. (No wonder Frost first read the poem in public at a graduation ritual—the Phi Beta Kappa ceremony at Tufts College on May 5, 1915.) This earnest interpretation was eventually challenged by an ironic one that sees the self-determination as a farce. The roads seem different to the speaker for only a moment. He offers his conclusion that seems so triumphant not after having taken the less-traveled road but in anticipation of the way he'll come to remember it. The conclusion is not retrospective but said in anticipated retrospection, in which the speaker imagines his future self misremembering the roads as distinct and congratulating himself for his bravery and self-determination. There is no evidence that he made a meaningful choice between roads or that the road he took determined his character any differently than how the other would have done. The earnest interpretation is of a will in harmony with itself over time—the person at one with his will and the world that formed his character according to his will. The ironic interpretation is of a will in disharmony, the person not clearly responsible for a choice that will be meaningful, consequential, or formative. The traveler and the road may seem one with the errand to be done; whether they are is another matter.

If the problem with the earnest interpretation is that the facts seem not to support it, the problem with the ironic interpretation is that the readerly experience of the poem pulls stubbornly against it. "The road less traveled" would never have entered cultural memory if the end of the poem wasn't so powerful. The final declaration builds to such a crescendo not by hyperbole and sentiment, the exclamations of the previous century, but by restraint and steadily progressing conviction and clarification that feels as if it fits the crossroads story perfectly, feels that way as you read the poem and hold in mind the experience if not as you analyze the poem and parse the facts of the case. In other words, it feels like an epiphany. You'd have to read the poem with the dispassionate suspicion of a pedant not to feel the epiphany rise out of the lines.

One way to reconcile the rush of epiphany with the undercurrent of irony is to assume that the latter takes precedence over the former, that Thought undermines Love. It follows that Frost wrote in cynical mockery of naive inspiration. But what if he meant not to argue one side or the other but to capture something of the relationship between them in the mind's attempt to grasp at itself? The motive for the poem would amount to skepticism rather than cynicism, not a denial of epiphanic self-realization but a questioning of it in the form of interior drama.

One of the subtler mysteries about the poem's setting is the amount of time that passed between the speaker's pause at the crossroads and his saying the words of the poem. Indeed, part of the reason the epiphany feels genuinely retrospective is that the first three stanzas had been purely retrospective. This indeterminate setting raises the prospect that the speaker's memory has betrayed him the other way around, fooling him into misremembering the roads as more similar than they actually were. Maybe he stood at the crossroads a long time before and is relaying the poem ages hence. Maybe he had long believed that his choice of road had made all the difference but has come to doubt this story about himself and with it the memories the story is made of. Who hasn't ever doubted a memory on the grounds that you too badly want it to have happened exactly that way? If the speaker is willing to doubt his future memory in the last stanza, it's hardly a stretch to suppose that he doubts his present memories elsewhere in the poem.

So it is that what had sounded like a bit of triumphal personal history, like the kind of self-congratulation in which a man of a certain age indulges at a family gathering on the front porch after dinner, comes to sound like something more revealing. The setting of the poem sounds less like a regaling than an inner monologue, less like a speech than the tentative rehearsal for a speech in the theater of the mind. And so it is that we find our interpretive conflict also playing itself out in the speaker's self-interpretation. It's possible that his doubt is the cold truth about a myth of himself that feels too good to be true. It's possible that his epiphanic self-realization is the deeply felt truth that his doubt picks apart by analysis. Belief and doubt twirl around in his mind as their interpretive analogues, epiphany and irony, rotate in our minds—as if some part of the boundary between us and the speaker had collapsed, the seam between us nowhere in sight. So it is that we find ourselves entangled with the speaker in something like friendship as Montaigne described it and Emerson envisioned it, albeit in a messier form than how they depict it—in parallel uncertainty, harmonious disharmony.

Among the many curiosities of Frost's poem is how often people mis-remember its name. People say, "The Road Less Traveled," not "The Road Not Taken"—a sign of how powerfully people remember the epiphany in which the former phrase is used. It's easy to forget that the first three stanzas of "The Road Not Taken" are about the road not taken, and possible to wonder if what animates the speaker's doubt might not be his epiphany but rather the choice he wound up making. You can hear the whole poem spoken in the wistfulness of old possibility and the longing for a life he'll never know. You can hear him tell this whole poem with a sigh. What had sounded like doubts that the two roads were different come to sound like reassurance that he hadn't missed out. The final stanza sounds less epiphanic than rueful, as if to say that although he harbors these longings now, his mind will unwittingly invent a myth of his own self-determination as a way to protect his future self from having to sit with the pain of dwelling on what might have been. If we hear the rue as epiphanic, it's all the more evidence of the myth's power to change memory's course.

Suppose, then, that he's right, or potentially right. Then we readers stand in relation to him as in another manifestation of friendship, the kind that can witness your deepest uncertainties and remember you as you were, long after you've forgotten yourself.

7.

THE CURIOUS COVENANT

———

I.

Although Edward Thomas passed away on the Western Front on Easter Monday 1917, it was nineteen years later that Frost remembered their time together in verse. The poem was "Iris by Night," published in April 1936. Like other elegies Frost wrote in the period, "Iris by Night" builds to an optical epiphany that leaves the reader to draw the line between perception and the imperceptible. Atypically for an elegy, "Iris by Night" is animated more by wonder than loss. Iris was the goddess of the rainbow in Greece as well as the rainbow itself, and in English is a flower whose varietals cover the spectrum—Adam and Eve's bower in Milton's paradise is bedecked in "Iris all hues"—and an iris is also the colored part of the eye that encircles the pupil, expanding or contracting to govern the amount of light the pupil lets into the retina. The goddess of the rainbow, a rainbow, a flower, a part of the eye: an organ of vision, something concrete, something ephemeral, and something beyond.

"Iris by Night" recasts in dramatic form a figure from another poet's verse that had been self-consciously figurative, Robert Herrick's "The Rainbow: Or Curious Covenant," as Frost had done in "Bond and

Free" with "The Definition of Love" and would go on to do in "The Silken
Tent" with "The Bracelet to Julia," the poem immediately after "The Rainbow" in the volume of Herrick that Frost knew from childhood. "The
Rainbow" elaborates the conventional tropes of the beloved's scorn as a
storm and her beneficent gaze as a parting in the clouds, a rainbow after
rain as her eyes look into her lover's. "Iris by Night" follows "The Rainbow"
in its course from overstated deluge (both poets use a form of the word
"drown") to rays of light that coalesce into miraculous rainbows that seem
halfway animate and that the poets end their poems by describing in terms
of a formal relationship uniting the pair of people involved for all time, a
"Curious Covenant" in Herrick and in Frost a "relation of elected friends":

FROM "IRIS BY NIGHT"

A wonder! Bow and rainbow as it bent,
Instead of moving with us as we went
(To keep the pots of gold from being found)
It lifted from its dewy pediment
Its two mote-swimming many-colored ends,
And gathered them together in a ring.
And we stood in it softly circled round
From all division time or foe can bring
In a relation of elected friends.

A "covenant" is a contract, from the Latin *convenire*, come together. Its stron-
gest connotation is the biblical covenant between God and God's chosen
people. "Elected" likewise means chosen, with a strong connotation of
chosen by God. Perhaps it was something of a corrective to end the poem
on a note of resolute choice after having famously written about Thomas's
difficulty in choosing, a corrective just as Frost says in beginning the
poem that they were "one another's guide," neither following the other as
Frost was always telling people lest they think his influence on Thomas

had been decisive, and as Emerson had written in "Etienne de la Boéce." "Relation" derives from the Latin *relatio*—a bringing back, restoring. A relation is also what Thomas wasn't quite to Frost but what Frost said he might as well have been, calling him "the only brother I ever had" weeks after he died.

"Iris by Night" as a story is something between a fairy tale and a tall tale. Frost strikes a tone between fancy and exaggeration, between embellishment his audience is meant to disbelieve or meant to believe. He tells the story with such finely textured realism in each line to make the reader all but suspend disbelief in the whole—all but suspend it, that is, until the final four lines. The first two of those concluding lines would seem to trigger any disbelief that the reader suspended, asking us to believe in a rainbow encircling them. The penultimate line would seem to underline the point by saying they were ensconced from all division that could be brought on them by "time or foe," the two things that did in fact divide them in time. And yet the final line recasts everything before it in a miraculously plausible light. It is not the circular rainbow that renders the two indivisible but instead their relation. A relation is by its abstraction not subject to the ravages of time. A relation of elected friends is a curious covenant, fanciful but nonetheless conventional. "Elected" pulls the meaning toward the fancy of the rainbow goddess Iris choosing to mark them with a singular miracle. But it is not just as people that they're marked: it is as "friends," a word nowhere before in the poem. The sudden appearance of "friends" as the very last word makes it seem as if it were the friendship itself that was the singular miracle, the relation that could stand any threat of division, the choice that felt chosen by something beyond them for all they could see.

II.

The man whose friendship Frost would remember as if it were a singular rainbow—wondrous, expansive, and touching transcendence and provi-

dence, somehow both evanescent and timeless—was born four years after
Frost in the outskirts of London, an ocean and a continent from Frost's
San Francisco. Thomas nonetheless had more meaningfully in common
with Frost than any of Frost's other friends, the two sharing an uncanny
range of similarities in addition to poetic genius. They were sons of stern
political-functionary fathers and doting mothers; children raised in ambiguous class positions; late bloomers and young lovers of Shelley and
therefore isolated young souls; men who married women with whom they
fell in love at sixteen or seventeen following an initial disdain of conventional marriage after reading Shelley's thunderingly anti-conventional
Epipsychidion aloud with their respective beloveds; naturalists; raconteurs
with great need for solitude; melancholics capable of unusual joy; men
of pronounced self-consciousness and mysterious reserve; young fathers
with strange ailments who moved their respective families to the country
around the turn of the century; men devoted from their early years to
poetry without another ideal to distract from it, enamored of the odes of
Keats, *In Memoriam*, Milton, Herrick, Thomas Hardy, George Meredith,
Shakespeare with special reference to the sonnets, and later, emphatically,
Yeats. Frost and Thomas both thought of poetry as a product of the
spirit. Thomas doubted that his spirit could produce. He wanted nothing
more than the faith he couldn't bring himself to feel. His sense of possible
faith for himself was subtly but meaningfully different from Frost's, since
he considered himself a pagan of sorts while Frost was a heterodoxical
and skeptical Christian. The two were different in temperament as well,
Thomas principled and fastidious where Frost was slippery and lazy by
outward appearance. Still, the two arrived at profoundly similar aesthetic
standards, values, and ambitions before they had the slightest knowledge
of each other. Frost found recognition as a poet at a time he considered
late in life, in England, not without Thomas's help. Thomas found recognition as a poet only after he died, having found his way to writing poetry
after he grew close to Frost.

Though it would be more than nine months until they met, they

were a mere fifty miles apart at Christmas 1912. The Frosts had sailed
for England four months before. Thomas wrote in a Christmas letter
about the torrents of rain: "The rain up here is incredible. It is like living
before the creation." He ended the letter with the refrain of "The Wind
and the Rain," a song sung by the Fools in *King Lear* and *Twelfth Night*. Frost
wrote his first letter to Cox from England on the day after Christmas, ap-
pending a slight poem about the rainy climate he had found overseas. It
ended with a lesson in English meteorology beginning with an image out
of Coleridge's *Mariner*:

> The bird was the kind that follows a ship,
> The rain was salt upon my lip,
> The hill was an undergoing wave,
> And the gate on which I balanced brave
> Was a great ship's iron railing.

> For the breeze was a watery English breeze
> Always fresh from one of the seas,
> And the country life the English lead
> In beechen wood and clover mead
> Is never far from sailing.

III.

The Frosts set sail from Boston Harbor on August 23, 1912, aboard the
SS *Parisian*. The ship "skirted along the north coast of Ireland" on the last
night, as Elinor wrote, the family finding "the dark, wild looking head-
lands and mountains very beautiful." Carol looked out of his porthole after
bedtime on the last night as the *Parisian* glided up the River Clyde toward
Glasgow, watching ripples on the water and lighthouses glowing onshore.

On the morning of their arrival, they boarded the train to London.
Lesley admired the purple hills, which brought to mind "the people who

in the wars with England had crouchingly crept among that heather and over those hills to escape from either the Scotish or English." The train arrived in London in the evening. They called for rooms in a hotel and took a cab there, "feeling greatly excited," wrote Elinor, "at being all alone, without a single friend, in the biggest city in the world."

They settled in a cottage in Beaconsfield, west of London, after a week of "theatre" in the evenings and days of Frost looking for houses while Elinor took the children into town. A highlight was the zoo, where Irma was struck by the monkeys and Marjorie by the elephants. The place they settled on was stucco and covered with vines, near the house of G. K. Chesterton, whose writing Frost admired, and a few miles from the cottage where Milton wrote *Paradise Lost*. Frost described the setting with its high hedges and distant views of London lights in a confessional letter on September 15 to Susan Hayes Ward ("one of the very few mortals I feel in any sense answerable to"). He confided the length to which he was willing to go in order to write poetry and establish his reputation at last. "My soul inclines to go apart by itself again and devise poetry. Heaven send that I go not too late in life for the emotions I expect to work in." He was right not to stay in America, he wrote, "if only for scorn of scorn— scorn of the scorn that leaves me still unnoticed among the least of the versifiers that stop a gap in the magazines." Skeptical as he was about travel as a source of inspiration, he evidently believed in it as a means to the mental space he needed for writing. In the event, the location also had the virtue of leading him to his first publisher, M. L. Nutt, who accepted the manuscript of *A Boy's Will* on October 26.

Frost was as reticent about the book's publication as he would later be about the book's sources in a tempting letter to Cox, which advised his friend not to follow Tennyson's example in naming his own inspirations (preaching Frost hinted he didn't quite practice himself). For every story he told about his life in which everything works out by remarkable chance, often involving a walk he just happened to take, there is usually another story in the record that hints at a hidden intention. Though he would later say he found his publisher on the chance recommendation of a columnist who wrote about local walks and whom Frost had approached weeks before for advice about lodging, he said at the time that he approached the firm of David Nutt because it had published the work of a minor poet he admired, W. E. Henley, famous to posterity as the author of the stirring "Invictus." Henley's *Poems*, with its subtle interplay of Romanticism and Stoicism, had met disapproval from other prominent editors before Nutt. Perhaps Frost noticed this story in the book's introduction and, feeling his circumstances analogous to those of its author, submitted his manuscript to the publisher of strange spiritual poems that no one else would take. Frost was a little deflated when the publisher accepted, out of concern that the easy acceptance of his manuscript indicated its "safe mediocrity." He tended to deprecate the book gently even after its release and positive reception. Still, he was grateful for the social world to which he felt his book offered him access—the company of some of the more eminent writers in the English-speaking world.

His entrée into literary society begins with another remarkable chance. Harold Monro, a poet and editor, was proprietor of the new Poetry Bookshop, at whose grand opening, a publicized event, Frost simply happened to find himself. One wonders if he really was just out for a walk that passed 35 Devonshire Street in London on the evening of Wednesday, January 8, 1913, in time to join a planned gathering of prominent poets. Regardless, he met a poet there who struck up a conversation, recognizing him as an American because of his shoes. Frost would later apologize in case his manner had seemed awkward:

> You will take my word for it that there was nothing in my sleeve: I showed just what I felt. I was only too childishly happy in being allowed to make one for a moment in a company in which I hadn't to be ashamed of having written verse. Perhaps it will help you understand my state of mind if I tell you that I have lived for the most part in villages where it were better that a millstone were hanged about your neck than that you should own yourself a minor poet.

The poet Frost met, F. S. Flint, had worked closely with Ezra Pound, to whom he mentioned Frost shortly, sending Frost a calling card at the end of the month for "the countryman poet of yours whom I mentioned to you." Pound would be Frost's first literary proselytizer and, soon after that, his first literary enemy. Frost and Thomas would discuss their disregard for Pound at their first meeting nine months later, having missed each other at the Poetry Bookshop.

Frost's countryman poet Pound would go on to become the single most influential figure in English-language Modernist literature, influential as poet and translator but even more as impresario: conduit between dozens of writers, codifier of aesthetic philosophy, grand arbiter of taste. No one else would do more to promote an aesthetic standard that made difficulty a prerequisite for quality in modern writing. Pound was at twenty-seven already known for his influence, having published several books and served as Yeats's secretary, self-appointed editor, and fencing instructor. He once threw Frost over his back suddenly in a restaurant while demonstrating a move of jujitsu. Frost referred to him as "my dazzling friend," "the stormy petrel," "my particular friend Ezra Pound the dazzling youth who translates poetry from six languages." "Someone says he looks altogether too much like a poet to be a poet," Frost wrote, calling him, once their relationship had soured, "that great intellect abloom in hair."

The two met when Pound received Frost at his flat in Kensington. (This story is as Frost told it consistently, sometimes adding that he was just walking through the neighborhood and remembered Pound's address when he happened to spot it.) Seeing Frost, Pound asked why he hadn't come sooner. He asked if Frost had a copy of *A Boy's Will*. Frost didn't—the publisher had yet to release it—so Pound declared that they'd go to Nutt's offices and get a copy. They got one and walked back to Pound's flat, Pound holding the first book of Frost's that Frost ever beheld. Pound sat down to read it and asked questions as he read. At one point he laughed—Frost ventured he knew what Pound laughed at. Pound said something to the effect of, "You don't mind our liking this, do you?" Of course not. Pound sent Frost on his way and began to draft a review.

Pound showed Frost around. In a matter of weeks, he introduced Frost to writers and editors, aspirants and eminences. Pound told Frost to call on T. E. Hulme, young and brilliant aesthetic philosopher, himself, since Pound and Hulme had fallen out. Pound in 1914 would tell another New England émigré, Thomas Stearns Eliot, about his countryman Frost. Pound took Frost to Yeats's flat in London, where Yeats held court on Monday evenings in a candlelit room that looked to Frost more like a shrine, conducting himself, Frost wrote, like "a man in some dream he cant shake off." Frost considered Yeats the greatest English-language poet alive. Pound appeared at Yeats's in a purple coat with gold buttons; inside, he literally lay at Yeats's feet. Frost would write to himself years later that "Yates is a kite with a one Pound tail."

Frost gushed about his new choice of society to Ernest Silver, a man whom Frost had come to think of as constitutionally envious and petty (and whom Frost incidentally owed money). He very much meant to stoke Silver's envy, as he confessed in a letter to Bartlett that revealed him delighted by the new company but skeptical of it nonetheless:

> [A Boy's Will] has brought me several interesting friendships which I can tell you about without exciting any jealousy in your breast because you know that I care more for you and your opinion of me (formed when I was fifteenth in command at Pinkerton) than for the opinion of all the rest of them put together. Yeats has asked me to make one of his circle at his Monday nights when he is in London (and not in Dublin). And he told my dazzling friend Ezra Pound that my book was the best thing that has come out of America for some time. Of course we needn't believe that.

Whether Frost in fact believed it and was trying to temper his effusiveness for Bartlett as he tried to gloat for Silver, we can't know. What is clear is that Frost had come to see the literary world in London partly as a publicity game: one sold books through reviews and met reviewers out in society.

Pound "has found me," wrote Frost, Pound having made a reputation already for discovering writers. Pound "sent a fierce article to Chicago denouncing a country that neglects fellows like me. I am afraid he over did it and it may be a mercy all round if it isn't printed."

The article appeared in the May issue of *Poetry: A Magazine of Verse*. It begins by praising Nutt at the expense of American editors, characteristically tasteless. Though "Mr. Frost's book is a little raw," it has the virtues of being natural, simple, unaffected, sincere. Pound describes the book as a partly elevated kind of folk poetry, with the directness and vitality often lost in oversophistication. If Pound evidently did not read the work carefully, to judge by blatant inaccuracies of straightforward paraphrase, it was Pound's express opinion that one did not have to read the book carefully. "One reads the book for the 'tone,' which is homely, by intent, and pleasing, never doubting that it comes direct from his own life." The praise is less damningly faint than it sounds. Pound was in the business of excoriating modern literature for coming from books more than experience and had even pronounced the founding of a movement in 1912 whose cause was the writing of poetry unmediated by all forms of bookish cliché. Pound thought that Yeats had done more than anyone else to revivify English-language poetry by elevating the common language and mythology of Ireland to the sophistication of literary form—so being regarded by Pound as a writer of folk poetry was at least as much compliment as condescension. Frost, after waiting almost two decades for this sort of recognition, thought this kind of praise was certainly better than nothing. He could not say the same for Pound's likening the surroundings in the book to a "middan" (Irish for trash heap) or for his false story about Frost's uncle and grandfather, an embellishment of Frost's own embellishment shared offhand and presumably in confidence, making Frost out to be his relatives' victim as he had been that of American editors: "His grandfather and his uncle had disinherited him of a comfortable fortune and left him in poverty because he was a useless poet instead of a money-getter." When Elinor saw that, she cried.

Other reviews were more straightforwardly appreciative. Frost sent one to Bartlett in June along with a detailed scheme whereby Bartlett, affecting disinterestedness, would write a letter to the *Derry News and Enterprise* about Mr. Frost's recent achievements, demonstrating Frost's standing to people whom he felt had underestimated him. Frost was less than forgiving later that month of Pound's execution of a scheme similar to his own. "He had a finger in the writing of his own review, did he?" wrote Frost to Flint about Pound. "Damn his eyes! An arrivist from the word go." The review that Frost sent to Bartlett had been written by Flint in *Poetry and Drama*, a magazine founded and run by Harold Monro. Frost thanked Flint for his discernment in contrast to Pound's condescension:

> Ezra Pound manifestly made a mistake when he thought he knew how to praise my poetry for the right thing. What he saw in them isnt there and what is there he couldn't have seen or he wouldn't have liked them. I have to thank you for the word "subtlety" in your review. The poems are open. I am not so sure that the best of them are simple. If they are they are subtle too.

Frost's earlier notes about Pound had been tempered in their reservations. This letter was almost splenetic. Something within Frost had burst.

Frost's outburst found expression in a number of poems he never published. "Poets Are Born Not Made" mocks Pound's pretense that Frost owed his success to him—"my father-in-letters," it calls him. Frost's poem is written in lazy free verse (or vers libre—verse with no regular meter), mocking the lazy free verse that Frost saw Pound as propagating. Frost mocks the swaggering immodesty of Pound's theorizing for the movement Pound called Imagism:

> The merit of the poems is the new convention
> That definitely locates an emotion in the belly,
> Instead of scientifically in the viscera at large,
> Or mid-Victorianly in the heart.

"The poems" here referred to were written by Pound's Imagist disciples whose work Frost took Pound to have urged, sculpted, and planted quickly in publication by means of his cultural power. Frost treated the subject years later in a rough sketch of a play, to which he gave three provisional titles: "Two Poets," "A Poetical Boss," "If Art Came to America." Ezra Pound is the poetical boss (how much like "political boss") who operates like a boss of Tammany Hall or another American political machine, an operator of a "wonderful manufactory" in which one can sit and watch the machine efficiency of "poems and poets made at one and the same stroke." Ezra Pound is "Amos Poise"—four-letter name of an Old Testament prophet followed by a surname that is a five-letter monosyllable beginning with "Po" and projecting conspicuous confidence. Poise bestrides his Poetical Headquarters pronouncing things like "Take out every other line," very much like Pound's unsolicited editorial advice for Frost's work. Portraying Pound as Poise implies that Frost saw them as the same kind of bully, one who wields power by leveraging his relationships to the benefit of clients and the detriment of rivals and uncooperative marks. If a political boss corrupts democracy by diverting the will of the people to the interests of party, a poetical boss corrupts the writing of poetry by diverting poets' individual taste to the whims of the boss's authority. It might be revealing that Frost used the figure of a party boss to dramatize his illegitimate "father-in-letters," since Frost knew something of political machines from the saloon out of which his father worked under Blind Boss Buckley for the San Francisco Democratic machine.

Frost wrote another piece of vers libre about Pound that reads like a confession of what he would have told Pound in perfect honesty if he had been able to say it:

I am a Mede and Persian
In my acceptance of harsh laws laid down for me
When you said I could not read
When you said I looked old
When you said I was slow of wit

I knew that you only meant
That you could read
That you looked young
That you were nimble of wit
But I took your words at their face value
I accepted your words like an encyclical letter. . . .
I was willing to take anything you said from you
If I might be permitted to hug the illusion
That you liked my poetry
And liked it for the right reason. . . .

I suspected though that in praising me
You were not concerned so much with my desert
As with your power
That you praised me arbitrarily
And took credit to yourself
In demonstrating that you could thrust anything
    upon the world
Were it never so humble
And bid your will avouch it

And here we come close to what I demanded of you
I did not want the money that you were distributing
    among your favorites
      for two American editors.
        Not that.
All I asked was that you should hold to one thing
That you considered me a poet.
That was [why] I clung to you
    As one clings to a group of insincere friends
      For fear they shall turn their thoughts against him
        the moment he is out of hearing.
The truth is I was afraid of you

He was willing to accept Pound's authority as a priest accepts the dictates of a papal encyclical. He wanted to be called a poet. He was afraid.

Edward Thomas, too, was once enamored of Pound. Like Frost's admiration, Thomas's swiftly turned to condemnation, but while Frost changed his mind in a matter of months, Thomas regretted his praise of Pound within weeks. His volte-face was in the spring of 1909. Having first seen Pound as "a great soul" with a "vague large promise," Thomas came to see him as a false prophet full of "meaningless suavity" and little substance: "Having allowed the turbulent opacity of his peculiarities to sink down we believe that we see very nearly nothing at all."

Although Thomas in 1909 was not in search of Pound's help or recognition as Frost would be in 1913, there was still a sense in which he had wanted something from Pound. Pound's early work promised something for which Thomas as a reader and critic of poetry was restlessly searching—a return to the essentials of poetry unmediated by dominant styles. Thomas saw in Pound someone defiant of any convention that would produce poetical effects rather than poetry. In this sense, his first assessments of Pound are strikingly similar to Pound's first assessment of Frost—rough in execution, vague in ambition, but original in perception and faithful to his own originality. Simple, direct. As Pound would praise Frost as "not post-Miltonic or post-Swinburnian or post-Kiplonian," Thomas praised Pound in a more exhaustive series of negations. Noting that all the forms Pound wrote in "are subdued to his spirit," Thomas called his poetry "the old miracle that cannot be defined"—the spirit imbued into words, not possessed by the words of other poems.

Having suddenly ceased, Thomas's infatuation with Pound would never resume. He had words to say against Pound on the day he met Frost through a mutual friend in October 1913 at St. George's, a restaurant in St. Martin's Lane where Thomas often spent his afternoons. Frost wrote to Flint a few days after meeting Thomas to invite Flint to meet the two of them soon, quoting a demand of Pound's for fealty that typified the poetical boss in Frost's eyes:

Would you think it too disloyal to the man "through whom alone you have a market for your poetry" (I quote) to meet with me some afternoon or evening a person who loves Pound as little as the critic Edward Thomas? Figure that out at your leisure and give me an answer in the spirit in which it is meant.

IV.

Thomas found himself in October 1913 at a spiritual crossroads. Having spent half a decade in passionate pursuit of spiritual experience without an article of faith, he had lately convinced himself that no spiritual experience was possible for him without something to believe in. Spiritual experience without faith was the promise of a school of thought called aestheticism, which had exerted a deep influence on Thomas until he excoriated it in a book-length study of an exemplary aesthete, Walter Pater, published early that fall. One can see Thomas's impasse in his case against aestheticism—that its attempt to reconcile religious doubt and spiritual life led only to false hope.

Aestheticism as Thomas saw it exemplified by Pater was an ersatz religion, a cult of intellectual beauty. Pater had sought religion as it felt "possible for the modern mind" and, failing to quell his doubts in the tenets of conventional faiths, abstracted their substance away. Pater would find transcendence not through divinity but through exposure to a generalized plane of beauty. It was a faith not in a supernatural force by which to transcend experience but in the force of a kind of experience to approximate or evoke the rapture of transcendence. Thomas accused aestheticism of a profound failure on its own terms. If its intention was to revitalize experience, its effect was to sterilize experience. Its idealization of beauty at the expense of other values inclined its adherents not to elevate their other pursuits toward congruence with this primary interest of beauty but rather to neglect or suspend their other commitments insofar as they yielded effects other than that of the beautiful. Pater's concern for strange effects as against meaningful causes led him to overlook the aspects of life other than the narrowly aesthetic, and, by treating those strange effects outside their human context of a balance of values and cares, to distort the original strangeness of effects into the conventionality of appreciation in the manner of a connoisseur. The aesthete, Thomas charged, was a spectator of life, bereft of the ecstasy that was the heart of spiritual life.

Thomas saw Pater's values reflected in his style of writing and his style as a culmination of a hundred years of bookish artificiality in English writing. If Pater's ideal for writing was scholarly, Thomas set against it an ideal that one could call intimate—an ideal nearly identical to Frost's, which Thomas explained much as Frost did. The writer would write as they spoke—a commonplace standard that Thomas revivified by pointing out the conditions that made the standard so hard to meet in practice. Writing as you spoke meant not just writing words that sound abstractly like speech but writing as you actually would speak in the moment you imagined. Such writing could exist only insofar as its authors imagined themselves as they would act in the world. They would write not from books but from life.

For Thomas, Pater had been a false god of whom the book was an intellectual exorcism. Thomas shared Pater's sense of urgency about the spiritual impasse to which aestheticism offered a solution. He also shared the sense that spiritual experience for him would be pagan, achieved by practice rather than the faith or dogmas of institutional religion. He disagreed that such paganism could be spiritual without a sense of supernatural reality. Thomas had declared belief in 1908 in the reality of the soul and the greater reality of the soul's imagination to that of the physical world, having gained his conviction by reading a spiritual autobiography by Richard Jeffries, *The Story of My Heart*. Yet Thomas feared he lacked imagination himself. He had written much of a book in early 1913, *In Pursuit of Spring*, a travel narrative that was manifestly a pilgrimage west from London to the Quantock Hills, where Coleridge had the vision of "Kubla Khan," a place in Thomas's description in which Coleridge's imagination was somehow more real than the physical land, Coleridge giving the land its reality.

Thomas thought of poetry as the response of the spirit when it could feel the concerns of daily life as parochial. His daily concerns in the beginning of 1913 were mounting. He was chronically overworked with all the writing assignments he took on, unable to write to his satisfaction in a way that would "touch natural things 'with a large simple emotion'" (quoting his friend Gordon Bottomley) because "I go about the world with a worried heart and a note book." In addition to being overworked, he had for the last couple of years gotten fewer reviewing commissions and less money. He had informally separated from his wife, Helen, and their three children out of fear that his melancholy was too much for them to bear, melancholy he described as a dull flat shore, elsewhere as an extreme of self-consciousness or void of personality or crawling along at the edge of life wondering why he doesn't go over the edge. He had been prescribed all sorts of cures for his condition, then called neurasthenia, but he thought that what was wrong at the heart of himself could be put right only by spiritual means. By the end of 1912, he worried about his ability to make money by any form of writing. He felt that someone was out there to help him but he didn't know who.

Although it presented a practical obstacle, his relative lack of commissions for articles freed him to spend more of his time on books and stories that he simply wanted to write. In September 1913, Thomas lay in bed one night trying to make rhymes for a poem, not getting beyond "ember" and "September."

V.

A week and a half after Frost and Thomas met at St. George's, Frost wrote to an old friend from Plymouth, Gertrude McQuesten, a dramatic reader who was planning to travel to London. "I may yet live to see you read in public something from my own dramatic work." Frost was referring to the poems in his second collection, most of which he had written in an inspired stretch over the previous year in England. Frost explained why the work would be more appropriate for her reading than the first book had been:

> You will say they are dramatic. The form is something I have partly devised for myself. . . . Laurence Binyon speaks of my muse in A Boy's Will as a shy muse. It would be strange if she wasn't that, for I was a shy youngster when I went away by myself in to the Derry woods to write it. But shyness is a thing one can't keep if one wants to. Once I fled from everybody. But I find I am only a little abashed by the only human in my later days. At least I grow less and less afraid of imaginary people. The new book proves that.—I call it "North of Boston."

Frost gave McQuesten an overview of the poets and writers she would encounter in London—the shallow, callow literary society Frost encountered at Hulme's salons, most of whose attendees were partisans of one literary method or another, eager to judge each other on their allegiance to a program for writing rather than their merit, achievement, or personal taste, dining out in Soho and pronouncing on poets it was important not to have read. "I should like these fellows in and out of motley," Frost wrote of these men who were fools in his eyes, reminding him of newly trained teachers overly "devot[ed] to method." "My real intimates are of another kind," Frost continued. "Gibson is my best friend. Probably you know his work. . . . He will be of the Gloucester colony. Abercrombie is already living in Gloucester. Be sure you are up on the works of these two when you come to see us."

Wilfrid Gibson and Lascelles Abercrombie were two of a handful of poets planning to live near one another in the countryside near Gloucester. The poets were united under the auspices of a common style they called Georgianism, which they had promoted over the last few years in a surprisingly popular anthology of their Wordsworthian colloquial verse.

After Abercrombie made a public call for a return to Wordsworth and Milton, Pound challenged him to a duel—a scene Frost later re-created for Amos Poise and Ethelred Vest, Poise's poetical foil.

The Frosts moved to their cottage in Ledington, on the border with Gloucestershire, in the beginning of April 1914. They arrived to fields full of daffodils, the golden flowers made an emblem of English spring by Wordsworth and by Herrick before him. Frost wrote to Cox on May 18 about the walks and the solitude:

> We are on a lane where no automobiles come. We can go almost any-where we wish on wavering footpaths through the fields. The fields are so small and the trees so numerous along the hedges that, as my friend Thomas says in the lovliest book on spring in England, you might think from a little distance that the country was solid woods.

Remote as they were, they were not isolated or unsociable. The typically abstemious Frosts drank cider with company—Gloucestershire was cider country—and Elinor even took to smoking. The colony of poets had come into being. As Frost wrote to Cox, "The important thing to us is that we are near Gibson."

Come summer, Elinor wrote to her cousin Leona in awe. It was "a beautiful summer," "a glorious summer." "The weather has been al-most perfect since the middle of April." Elinor effused about their spare sixteenth-century cottage with exposed beams and floor tiles, the hedges and pastures and daffodils, the cuckoo, primeval bird of spring in English verse, which "sang all day long" for weeks after the Frosts' arrival. "I wish I could make you feel what a lovely country this is," wrote Elinor. She had lately gotten over an awful exhaustion from "housework and teaching [her children] and the excitement of meeting so many people constantly." One visitor had been especially welcome. "Edward Thomas, who is a very well known critic and prose writer has been here with his two children and he is going to bring his whole family to lodge near us through August. Rob and I think every thing of him. He is quite the most admirable and lovable man we have ever known."

Thomas had first arrived on April 22. He was predictably careworn, working away at yet another book that felt like drudgery to him, though he had ended his separation with Helen in February at what Frost would later say had been his urging. Thomas and Frost had seen each other regularly since they met in October, but it was these visits to Ledington that would be hallowed in amber for both of them. Thomas had not known the area. It had the freshness of discovery for him—flowering apple trees, "a concave meadow, in April strewn with daffodils," "not the first cuckoo, but the first abundance of day-long-calling cuckoos," "the first nightingale's song." Thomas would later recount in an essay, "This England," the lambent ease of his days in the area walking and talking with Frost. "Three meadows away lived a friend, and once or twice or three times a day I used to cross the meadows, the gate, and the two stiles" to the Frosts' cottage, "the little house of whitened bricks and black timbers." Their long, leisurely walks put them in constant view of a high hill that looked like an optical illusion: "Again and again we saw, instead of solid things, dark or bright, never more than half a mile off, the complete broad dome of a high hill six miles distant, a beautiful hill itself, but especially seen thus, always unexpectedly, through gaps in this narrow country, as through a window." It was from this high hill that Thomas "saw with Frost" a rainbow that seemed to him "like the first that ever was."

So inspired was Thomas after this first visit that he was even thinking of "taking to verse." Frost encouraged the idea, and possibly even suggested it before Thomas did, citing passages of prose in Thomas's *In Pursuit of Spring* that already made for poetry as good as any English verse being written. Thomas was inspired, too, to write "a book on speech and literature," drawing out the ideas of Frost's that he himself had touched on in his book on Pater. It was an idea Thomas saw spectacularly put to practice in *North of Boston*, which he read in typescript in June. He was at a loss as to how to describe his reaction to Frost. He would make up for his inarticulateness with three separate reviews of the book that remain the book's best introduction more than a hundred years later.

Other reviewers praised Frost for his method. He helped most of them to it as he never would again for other books, probably inferring that if reputations were made in literary London on the appeal of method, he would do well to declare one. "When you are in England do as the Romans did," he wrote to himself as one who would conquer. What set Thomas's readings of *North of Boston* apart from those of other critics was his sense of the book as an achievement of subtly monumental originality. "This is one of the most revolutionary books of modern times, but one of the quietest and least aggressive," began Thomas in the first of his reviews. "It speaks, and it is poetry." The review proceeds to explain why this amounted to a quiet revolution in abandoning the trappings of poetry for its essence, going back as Wordsworth had "through the paraphernalia of poetry into poetry again." Not a return to Wordsworth: a return like Wordsworth's in his own time to the old indefinable miracle.

Thomas's summaries of poems from *North of Boston* show a book without poetical subjects, sensational emotions, stock narratives, characters playing to type—a fictional world observed from life. As the poems' material is free of bookish cliché, so is the language. Informality did not imply simplicity, as Thomas was careful to note: Frost's was "the ordinary English speech of a man accustomed to poetry and philosophy." Nor was the range of diction generic or broadly representative rather than "perfectly Mr. Frost's own." Likewise with Frost's influences. "I have not met a living poet," Thomas wrote, "with a less obvious and more complicated ancestry."

"One and indivisible" was how Thomas described the experience of reading the poems. They possessed the virtues both of longer narratives and of compact lyrics, yielding "drama with a lyric intensity which often borders on magic." The poems showed "the beauty of life seen by one in whom mystery and tenderness together just outstrip humour and curiosity"—the best definition of Frost's character ever attempted.

VI.

On August 3, Thomas and his son, Merfyn, set out to join the Frosts for the month in Ledington. On August 4, Britain declared war on Germany. On August 6, Frost and Thomas beheld a lunar rainbow on their walk down from the commanding summit of May Hill.

War meant, among other things, a collapse of the literary economy on which Frost and Thomas depended. Thomas would have even fewer reviewing assignments. Frost, whose proceeds from the sale of the farm were dwindling and who had made no money thus far on his books, would not be able to sell many books in England. Regardless of what happened with the war, their time together in England was scarce.

Like Frost in "Iris by Night," Thomas would later memorialize their time together in August as an apotheosis of friendship. It was the longest stretch of time they spent near each other. Frost had grown demonstrably closer to Thomas than to the man he had lately called his best friend. Gibson, of whom Thomas himself was no fan, had published in July one of the few less than glowing reviews of *North of Boston* to appear, rehearsing Pound's condescending clichés. For Thomas, the friendship with Frost may have meant so much not only in itself but as a respite from marital tension that his devoted friend Eleanor Farjeon, who joined the two briefly in Ledington, said was worse than she had seen it before. Farjeon was awestruck by "Edward's relaxation in Robert's company": "The humour of the two friends was in perfect accord." She never saw Thomas so relaxed and open with anyone else, comparing his innermost self in general to "the Cretan Labyrinth." Her impression comported with Thomas's account to Helen that he felt more at ease with himself around Frost than with anyone else—completely at ease but for the slightest awareness of wanting Frost to approve of him.

With war came a predictable social resurgence of self-superior nationalism, which brought with it a pressure for Thomas to fight. By October, he had come to feel that his particular love of his country obliged him to do something for it. The country he loved, as he explained in "This England," was not the country of martial triumph, naval empire, political tradition, or even literary culture, none of which he mentioned. This England was the stretch of land in Gloucestershire and Ledington that Thomas had come to only late in life to pass consummate days with a friend:

> All I can tell is, it seemed to me that either I had never loved England, or I had loved it foolishly, aesthetically, like a slave, not having realized that it was not mine unless I were willing and prepared to die rather than leave it.

Foolishly, *aesthetically*. His rejection of aestheticism obliged him to subserve his enjoyment to a commitment in service of more than enjoyment. What that commitment was he did not say.

Though it would be months before Thomas enlisted, he had nearly made the agonizing decision in November shortly before another visit to the Frosts. They had moved to Abercrombie's vacant place in the village of Ryton, a cottage on Lord Beauchamp's estate that Abercrombie stayed in by special arrangement. On Thomas's visit, he and Frost were accosted by a gamekeeper who patrolled the grounds and ordered them back to the cottage, they having no rights to walk the preserve owing to their humble station as cottagers. After retreating, Frost grew angry, walked up to the gamekeeper's cottage with Thomas in tow, and threatened to have it out with him, only to retreat again in the face of the gamekeeper's shotgun. The incident would linger for both Frost and Thomas, for Frost as a gross instance of English class stratification, whose worst example was Gibson, who was of a superior class position and unwilling to help. The encounter lingered for Thomas as an episode in which his bravery was challenged and found wanting: Frost, not he, pursued the gamekeeper to fight. This was also the visit of Thomas's in which Frost later remembered beginning a poem about his friend's protracted deliberations about the path he should take in a yellow wood.

VII.

Frost began "The Road Not Taken" that winter on a couch in Abercrombie's cottage, thinking of Thomas, how "no matter what road he took, he would always have missed not having taken the other." Frost got only as far as one stanza. He would finish the poem in the spring and send it to Thomas from Franconia. The poem's subject did not know what to make of it.

Thomas at the time was vacillating between enlisting and undertaking the financial and practical risk of pursuing his fantasy, joining Frost in New Hampshire. Recriminating himself for lacking the faith of a "believer" to make up his mind, Thomas sought Frost's advice in one letter after another. The great concern for Thomas was to earn enough in New Hampshire to support Helen and the children. Frost dutifully responded with a pair of letters detailing how Thomas could make a living by farming and by writing, respectively—letters Thomas received, he told Frost, "in the king's uniform." How history might have been different but for the delays of wartime mail.

Thomas wrote to Frost of his decision. "I wish I could explain how it came about. But I don't quite know." He asked that his friend "try & forgive me everything." Frost responded not with forgiveness but with praise. He praised his friend for coming to his decision in his slow, tortuous way. "All belief is one," Frost wrote. "And this proves you are a believer." Frost asked his friend to "have a volume of poetry ready for when you come marching home."

VIII.

Thomas's poems about Frost are all longing. In the first, "A Dream," from early July 1915, Thomas loses Frost only to find him again in the moment before waking to say, "I shall be here some day again." It was a resolution, a prophecy, a wish. Thomas's next poem about Frost was a lament for lost time. "The sun used to shine," written ten months after "A Dream," recalls their walks together in Ledington as in an irrecoverable past. It is the poem's sleight of hand to fold the rhythms of their old easy hours into the seamlessly accelerating cycles of the passage of time. The sun sets over the course of the poem from the heedless walks and flowers to the moonrise and then to a faceless procession of other men in the same place, the particulars of memory blurring into the indistinctness of general experience:

> And other men through other flowers
> In those fields under the same moon
> Go talking and have easy hours.

Thomas wrote the poem a year into officer training. It would be another half a year till deployment. He wrote to Frost regularly and frequently, but Frost sometimes failed to keep pace, leaving Thomas's letters unanswered for weeks or even months, as in the exasperated weeks before Thomas heard from Frost at last and, scholars suspect, wrote "The sun used to shine." Frost never offered much of a reason for letting his half of the correspondence subside. Though no less sincere than Thomas's letters to him, Frost's letters to Thomas are more measured, implying that he approached this kind of intimacy with a different kind of reserve.

In contrast to the abjectness of Thomas's poems about Frost, Frost's poems conceived with Thomas in mind tend toward reticence or obliqueness. In "The Road Not Taken," Frost confounded where Thomas would have confessed. "Not to Keep," sent to Thomas just before he wrote "The sun used to shine," is a poem about reticence, in this case the reticence of a soldier on leave and of his wife who learns that his leave is temporary and that he will have to return to the front. The drama of the poem, as in so much of Frost's treatment of tragedy, is the chasm between how much the characters have to communicate and how little there is to say.

For all his inwardness, Thomas was far likelier than Frost to bare his soul. This difference in kinds of reserve had something to do with circumstance and something to do with sheer differences in temperament, but more important than either was a subtle difference in values, fine shades of difference hard to see unless the two poets are thrown into relief. For all that the two seemed to share a spiritual vision of literature, they were actually heirs to subtly distinct traditions that assigned different values to emotional expression itself. Thomas was a Romantic in the sense that he believed in the possibility of experiencing some form of transcendence without reference to his own moral conduct. Frost was non-Romantic in the sense that he believed in a general connection between transcendence and divine regard for what he did or thought, echoing most strongly, where this connection was concerned, the theistic and thoroughly non-Romantic tradition of Puritanism. The hovering sense of God's justice and mercy inclines the Puritan to value experience for what it allows them to do either in outward conduct or in inner life, whereas Romantics' sense of transcendent possibilities in the absence of theism or moralism inclines them to value experience as an end in itself. This goes a way to explaining why the spiritually distinct pair of friends would regard their emotions differently under conditions of intimate friendship. Passionate emotions, sentiments, are a means to action (outer or inner) for a Puritan and, for a Romantic, the important action itself. It was thus according to type that Frost would have less to express in the context of a remote and stable friendship to which his sentiments could not be put to much novel use, whereas Thomas in his letters shared his life and bared his soul. It was also according to type that Frost as a poet would subordinate to the cause of the relationship sentiments Thomas would have expressed.

One to two years after learning of Thomas's death an hour after sunrise on Easter Monday 1917, Frost wrote Thomas a poem. It is the only published poem of Frost's addressed to a named contemporary. "To E. T." is striking for its lack of the lamentations or encomia one would expect from a poem of public mourning. For an elegy, the poem is unsentimental to the point of coldness, even teasing, beginning with the line "I slumbered with your poems on my breast," a line that one could reasonably construe as something less than an endorsement of the poems' ability to hold an audience. The poem seems distinctly lacking in the warmth of personal intimacy—seems so unless you hear the poem as what Frost would have actually told Thomas if he had been able to write him a letter about seeking him out in a dream. What seems like emotional distance in the public gaze turns out to be the greater intimacy that refuses to perform itself and speaks as if no one else were listening.

To E. T.

I slumbered with your poems on my breast
Spread open as I dropped them half-read through
Like dove wings on a figure on a tomb
To see, if in a dream they brought of you,

I might not have the chance I missed in life
Through some delay, and call you to your face
First soldier, and then poet, and then both,
Who died a soldier-poet of your race.

I meant, you meant, that nothing should remain
Unsaid between us, brother, and this remained—
And one thing more that was not then to say:
The Victory for what it lost and gained.

You went to meet the shell's embrace of fire
On Vimy Ridge; and when you fell that day
The war seemed over more for you than me,
But now for me than you—the other way.

How over, though, for even me who knew
The foe thrust back unsafe beyond the Rhine,
If I was not to speak of it to you
And see you pleased once more with words of mine?

The depth of feeling shows itself slowly. Frost slept with the poems on his breast out of longing, not boredom. There is a sense of deflated expectations within the line "Like dove wings on a figure on a tomb" in its fall from transcendent symbol (dove wings) to commonplace abstraction (figure) to the cold reality of the tomb. Yet dove wings pointed downward are also a potent, conventional symbol on old New England tombstones like those Frost would have seen on his family's weekly trips to his father's grave, the dove descending a symbol of an untimely death like Thomas's and a symbol of the Holy Spirit, conduit of heavenly grace, with which Jesus is imbued after the Resurrection on Easter in the Gospel of John after Mary Magdalene finds his tomb empty and assumes that it must have been looted, unable to see Jesus risen before her.

Though Frost did not believe in the Resurrection, he did believe in the possibility of spirits surviving their bodily hosts imperceptibly, as if Thomas might be haunting in spirit about Frost's figure of a tomb in a way that he, like Mary, could not see. This sense of ambiguous separation is a signal part of the famous elegy to which Frost's poem alludes, Catullus's lament for and farewell to his brother, which like "To E. T." emphatically addresses its subject as brother (or *frater*) in the middle of its tenth line, also the final line in Catullus's poem. "Atque in perpetuum, frāter, avē atque valē" is Catullus's parting: "And in perpetuity, brother, hail and farewell." That is, he is perpetually praising and saying goodbye and yet perpetually hailing, perpetually greeting, an undermining of his spare sense of closure like the point at which Frost arrives after ten lines.

Such is the elaborate background of the straightforward foreground of Frost's poem. He wishes for the chance to tell Thomas to his face that he had realized the ideals he had aspired to as soldier and poet. (Thomas did not live to see his poems published under his actual name, having published under a pen name, Edward Eastaway.) Though Frost's wish might look at first like any other dream of someone lost, it carries the hope of the dove wings. Frost might not have hoped for a literal encounter with Thomas's spirit (though who knows?), but he did believe that the faithful work of the spirit could be of eternal significance. This was the explicit thesis of Frost's later poem "A Soldier," which he said was about Thomas—that acts of dedication position the spirit in a realm beyond our discernment. To be soldier and poet was not just as Thomas the Romantic would have conceived of them, to have certain experiences enabled by certain ideals, but to have made something of that in himself which was immortal. Frost wanted to tell him. He wanted to see Thomas pleased, seeing what he otherwise could only take on faith.

Frost wrote to Helen after Edward's death to call her lost husband "the bravest and best and dearest man you and I had ever known." To another acquaintance he called Thomas "more beautiful" than Thomas's beautiful poems. To another he called Thomas "the only brother I ever had." "1914 was our year," Frost wrote. "I never had, I never shall have another such year of friendship."

Before publishing "To E. T." in *The Yale Review* of April 1920, Frost wrote to the editor to explain why he had not written something already. "As yet I feel too much the loss of the best friend I ever had," Frost explained. "And by that I dont mean I am overwhelmed with grief. Something in me refuses to take the risk—angrily refuses to take the risk—of seeming to use a grief for literary purposes." Frost would have his wish of not seeming to take such a risk. The poem he addressed to Thomas would seem to make no use of his grief. The later poem that made use of his grief would seem not to be about Thomas at all.

IX.

[Thomas's] concern to the last was what it had always been, to touch earthly things and come as near them in words as words could come.
                                                    —FROST, OCTOBER 22, 1917

After the slumber of "To E. T.," there is a dawn in the next poem in Frost's *New Hampshire* (1923), "Nothing Gold Can Stay." "To E. T." entertains the

perception of a spiritual reality whose loss from experience is the subject
of the compact and wrenching "Nothing Gold Can Stay":

> Nature's first green is gold,
> Her hardest hue to hold.
> Her early leaf's a flower;
> But only so an hour.
> Then leaf subsides to leaf.
> So Eden sank to grief,
> So dawn goes down to day.
> Nothing gold can stay.

"Nothing Gold Can Stay" would seem to refuse the consolation for which
"To E. T." had held out a fantastical hope, affirming in general the sense
of permanent loss against which "To E. T." held out hope in the particular
case. The poems would seem to balance each other in phases of grief like
parallel cantos of *In Memoriam*, setting the particularity of the person lost
in the context of universal loss without reference to the particular, not
seeming to use a grief for literary purposes. One wonders about the particular grief Frost meant to hold in balance, noticing that "Nothing Gold
Can Stay" moves between a day's and a life's cycle with the sudden finality
of lost time as Thomas does in "The sun used to shine." One notices, too,
the resignation to a loss an hour after sunrise and the identical scansion
of the poem's eponymous last line to Thomas's pseudonym, with which
the poem's title rhymes: "Nothing *Gold* Can Stay," "Edward *East*away."
The pseudonym, that vessel for hidden identity, charts the literal course
of the sun after sunrise away from the east, as in the following passage
from which Frost borrowed in Wordsworth's legendary ode on the loss
and recovery of a sense of immortality:

> The youth, who daily farther from the *east*
>   Must travel, still is Nature's priest,

> And by the vision splendid
> Is on his way attended;
> At length the man perceives it die *away,*
> And fade into the light of common day.

The Immortality Ode, known in Thomas's writings as simply the Ode, is the preeminent poem of English Romanticism on the subject of our fall from spiritual to quotidian, earthly perception. The Ode traces the feeling of wonder to its roots in childhood when the world seemed resplendent with heaven. Wordsworth begins the Ode by recollecting a lost time in the green of his youth when the green of the world was gold to him, "A time when meadow, grove, and stream, / The earth, and every common sight / To me did seem / Apparell'd in celestial light, / The glory and the freshness of a dream." The vision fades in the passage cited previously, to which Frost's poem bears a depth of similarities. Wordsworth's passage is punctuated by jolts in perspective in its two final lines—line five into seeing the sunrise as the duration of youth, line six into seeing the end of youth and the end of the sunrise at once in the faded "light of common day." These are also the perspectival shifts of Frost's final two lines:

So dawn goes down to day.   *The length of youth in the length of a sunrise*
Nothing gold can stay.   *The ending of sunrise and youth*

Frost condenses the passage out of effortlessly perceptible immortality into the line preceding the couplet above, "So Eden sank to grief," an unassuming five words that also fold Wordsworth's story of lost immortality into the story of humanity's lost paradise in Genesis, that older, theistically moralistic story of our lost immortality. Frost had followed Wordsworth's Romantic story alone in an earlier draft, showing the light of a mature reverence for nature as a partial approximation of "that first golden light." By adding Eden's grief, Frost took the poem out of the realm of experience alone and into the metaphysical loss underlying it.

Frost's earlier draft condensing Wordsworth's poem was actually not an elegy at all. In revising his draft into an elegy, Frost drew on an unrelated poem about the finality of loss from the volume of Herrick's that Frost remembered from childhood. The poem was "To Daffodils":

> Fair Daffodils, we weep to see
> > You haste away so soon:
> As yet the early-rising Sun
> > Has not attain'd his Noon.
> > > Stay, stay,
> > Until the hasting day
> > > Has run
> > But to the Even-song;
> And, having pray'd together, we
> > Will go with you along.

> We have short time to stay, as you,
> > We have as short a Spring;
> As quick a growth to meet Decay,
> > As you, or any thing.
> > > We die
> > As your hours do, and dry
> > > Away,
> > Like to the Summers rain;
> Or as the pearls of Mornings dew
> > Ne'er to be found again.

"To Daffodils" has flowers disappearing in morning, the brevity of youth, and in the most striking parallel to Frost's poem a figure of day rising that feels conventional at the start of the poem but actual in the end, the particular imbued with the breadth of the general point and declared with finality in the final line of the poem. Frost might have thought of the sun shining in Thomas's first visit to Ledington in the spring with the fields blanketed with golden flowers, or thought of the words Thomas used to come near to them.

The Immortality Ode would have been familiar to Frost as the penultimate poem in Palgrave, where Frost would have seen the Ode preceded by a little poem of Wordsworth's about what Frost called "nature piety," or piety toward nature, expressed in the joy Wordsworth hoped he would feel throughout his life at the sight of a rainbow.

8.

THE LINE WHERE MAN LEAVES OFF

I.

As Frost would tell the story ages hence, he disembarked in New York City from his voyage back from England in February 1915 and chanced upon an unfamiliar magazine in a newsstand, *The New Republic*. He discovered that this new American magazine of politics and culture had printed a review of the version of *North of Boston* published in America. This meant that *North of Boston* had been published in America. Frost called on his newfound publisher, Alfred Harcourt at Henry Holt, who cut him a check, sorely needed, as an advance against royalties. The editors of *The New Republic* also cut Frost a check when he called on them, having recently published a poem from *North of Boston* that would later become famous, "The Death of the Hired Man." On Frost's way up to New Hampshire, in Boston, he called on the woman who had written about him in *The New Republic*, the prominent poet and critic Amy Lowell, and met Ellery Sedgwick at *The Atlantic Monthly*, William Stanley Braithwaite at the *Boston Evening Transcript*, the philosopher William Ernest Hocking at Harvard, and a number of others. Then, having become a public man, Frost went up to Franconia in search of a farmhouse.

He found his farmhouse. He did not find John Lynch, who had passed away in Frost's absence, robbing Frost of the chance to share stories from his trip. Frost was not so unfortunate with John Bartlett, who had lately returned from Vancouver owing to troubles with Margaret's health and their financial prospects. The circumstances allowed Bartlett to watch his old teacher give a talk in May at a private school in Cambridge. The talk was the first for which Frost was financially compensated and the first at which he expounded his ideas relating to the sound of sense, here under the auspices of what he called "the imagining ear." Thus did Frost's old student chance to witness the beginning of a great career in extemporaneous lecturing and poetry reading.

These early months of Frost's repatriation set the tenor for the next year and a half, balancing an active public life with a domestic life of relative seclusion. Frost called his place in Franconia a mountain fastness, a geographically fortified stronghold, whose security he left rather often to give the lectures that quickly became a main source of income, alongside publishing poetry and collecting some residual remittances from his grandfather's estate. His circulation in the world of letters brought him no greater friend than Louis Untermeyer, a critic who had already emerged as a champion of Frost's work in the spring of 1915 and who would become a preeminent anthologist of American poetry, Frost's very much included. Untermeyer, a poet himself, was a Jewish autodidact with left-wing politics and a jewelry factory of his family's to run in New York City. His circumstances allowed him to introduce Frost to the literary world of the city with its bohemians and radicals. His stature, devotion, and wit, which included an insatiable appetite for punning against all better judgment, drew Frost into an unusually regular correspondence of an unusual kind. If Frost in his letters to Louis was a friend revealing himself to a friend, he was also a performer performing for another, not to mention a man of some reputation writing to someone working to maintain it. One can see this bewilderingly ambiguous mixture of revelation, performance, and guardedness even in the incomparable confessional letters that Frost wrote to Louis in their early years of friendship, such as his lament in May 1916 that his activeness in the literary marketplace had sapped the private wellsprings of his poetry: "The poet in me died nearly ten years ago. . . . The calf I was in the nineties I merely take to market. I am become my own salesman." The last sentence alludes to Tennyson's famous lament in "Ulysses": "I am become a name."

In one sense, Frost's plaint was less than entirely serious, creative frustration played up for effect. In another sense, Frost's words were quite revealing. He had become a name, and it was changing the way he wrote poetry. The anonymous self of his earlier verse was in some new poems becoming the persona Frost had taken to market. This was to the detriment of his poetry in much the way that he feared or pretended to fear, replacing the intimacy of a self sharing its experience in all its uncertainty and ambivalence and ambiguity with the charming performance of self that was the work of a showman or salesman. The change was fortunately gradual and never total—and it would usher in a few masterpieces of a different kind than Frost had written before—but the change had begun and was largely, eventually, for worse. Frost was wont to say that what begins in felicity ends in publicity, an explanation of his distaste for weddings that he thought could also be said uncharitably of his own career.

The other changes in Frost's style at the time were of a piece with his emerging persona. Each brought new kinds of achievement eventually taken to excess, each a new kind of flourishing that buried the seeds of poetic decline. Some of his narrative poems began to abandon the spare realism of the poems in *North of Boston*, whose plots unobtrusively embodied imaginative conflicts like those his lyrics were about, for a more fanciful narration that showed an active imagination in the story's very conception. Some of his lyrics also began to abandon their own kind of realism in narration insofar as they no longer sought to embody the drama of a person talking, shifting attention further to the intricacies of ideas and impressions themselves. All of these budding trends involved a shift in relative emphasis from experience to reflection, a product, no doubt, of Frost's newfound occupation performing himself and discussing his ideas, and his newfound social position among writers and scholars. It had been some time since his peers had been farmers and rural tradesmen. When he asked some friends of his in Franconia whether they would be at one of his first readings in town, he was chagrined to find them present as servants. He had published in *North of Boston* an incomparable monologue of resilience and vulnerability under conditions of economic and social marginality called "A Servant to Servants," but he would never again write such an intimately observed work about the poor, having become a lecturer to paying audiences and a writer among eminent writers.

These changes in style were not all for the worse. At their undramatic best, his reflective lyrics would embody ideas and impressions with an elegant compactness unmatched in his earlier work. Such a style at its best is wit and, at its worst, cleverness, versified thinking rather than poetry unfolding in its own movements of thought. However, most of Frost's compact reflective lyrics of the time were in fact quite dramatic despite an extreme simplicity of surface, concealing depths like "Nothing Gold Can Stay." (And how dramatic are the sounds of the poem in their own right, "Her hardest hue to hold" with the near rhyme of "her" and "hardest" unwinding over the course of the line like a futile attempt to hold sky.) His emerging styles were at their subtle best when integrating styles developed previously, taking the form of short and simple reflections with an astonishing sequence of perspectives embedded unobtrusively; poems written at once in propria persona and with the artful distance of make-believe; lyrics with the concreteness of narrative staging or narratives with a lyric grace of conception, such as a potentially revelatory story about the private life of Rob and Elinor's marriage based on a tall tale he heard of spotting Paul Bunyan's wife in a sliver of moonlight.

II.

One can trace the lineaments of "Paul's Wife" in a pair of letters Frost wrote to Untermeyer in the early years of their friendship. "Elinor has never been of any earthly use to me," wrote Frost to his friend in a pique over Amy Lowell's portrayal of Elinor in a piece of writing in 1917. Lowell had made Elinor out to be "the conventional helpmeet of genius," Frost wrote—"an unpardonable attempt":

> She hasn't cared whether I went to school or worked or earned any-
> thing. She has resisted every inch of the way my efforts to get money.
> She is not too sure that she cares about my reputation. She wouldn't lift
> a hand or have me lift a hand to increase my reputation or even save it.
> And this isn't all from devotion to my art at its highest. She seems to
> have the same weakness I have for a life that goes rather poetically. . . .
> She always knew I was a good poet, but that was between her and me
> and there I think she would have liked it if it had remained at least
> until we were dead. I don't know that I can make you understand the
> kind of person.

Frost ended his letter to his critical champion, as ever, with a hint that the remarks above might be of earthly use to him. "Amy means well and perhaps you will come to our rescue without coming in conflict with Amy."

In Frost's denial that Elinor was of the slightest "earthly use" to him, the adjective was signal, confining any usefulness of hers to a separate realm. In saying so as he doubted his ability to explain himself, Frost struck a note like a description he gave of "Paul's Wife" as "about the kind of person who refuses to share socially his spiritual possessions." Whether his refusal was a matter of emotional possessiveness or a spiritual fastidiousness not to pretend to share something impossible to share is a question the poem invites the reader to ask.

The giant lumberman is distinguished in Frost's retelling for his extraordinary sensitivity on the subject of his wife. Someone had only to mention her to send the giant running away. His mates in the lumber camp speculate that she might have left him, that he might be ashamed of her, until they catch their first glimpse of her and find that she emanates light. Shouting at the sight of her literal radiance, they disturb her solitude and her light flickers out like a firefly's. A campmate surmises that Paul was "what's called a terrible possessor. / Owning a wife with him meant owning her." The campmate fails to surmise another potential motivation in Paul's categorical rejection of all earthly terms to describe her:

> . . . a man like Paul
> Wouldn't be spoken to about a wife
> In any way the world knew how to speak.

Paul's privacy looks to the world like possessiveness. It feels to him like a response to an enchantment that fades with witness by anyone other than him and his wife.

This aspect of the myth was Frost's revision of another major source for his poem, Yeats's "The Song of Wandering Aengus," which Frost had taken up with Yeats at one of his Monday salons. Rather as Yeats's Aengus discovers his beloved transformed from a fish he had caught and laid on the floor, Frost's Paul saws his wife out of a log of white pine from which she emerges fully grown. The girls emanate light in each legend. Yet the legends—each an alternate myth of the creation of Eve—tell very different stories of how the enchantment is lost, implying different accounts of the human condition. The girl absconds in Yeats's poem and engenders her beloved's eternal pursuit in an archetypally Romantic figure, humanity ever stretching toward its ideal like the lovers wrought on Keats's urn, ever in pursuit of re-enchantment. The enchantment of Paul's wife does not fade, but it is consigned to privacy. Frost probably came as close as he ever did to explaining the point in June 1915, in a letter to Louis, then a new friend, saying Louis could tell he was in fact a realist, as often described, by virtue of "how I fell in love."

> The realist always falls in love with a girl he has grown up and gone to school with, the romanticist with a new girl from "off somewhere." Thats not to say that they dont both fall in love with the respective girls for what they dont know about them. Mystery draws both on; only in the case of the romantic it is a more obvious mystery—a less mysterious mystery.

The more obvious mystery is liable to fade, one might extrapolate, while the more mysterious mystery is harder to share and harder to put into words.

III.

The idea of different mysteries, one ideal and one real, illuminates a related poem of Frost's from England, "To Earthward," that evokes like nothing else in his writing the change in his sensibility away from the young poet of *Twilight*. "To Earthward" begins by recalling the poet's old, idealized way of thinking and feeling in words that recall the words of another poet, Longfellow's in "A Day of Sunshine," a poem that practically defines the sensibility of that old Yankee Romantic.

Gentle, graceful, careful, cheerful, "A Day of Sunshine" describes a day of perfect weather that the poem feels as spiritual ease intimating holy rapture. It is a vision of transcendence through an ordinary experience. The force of merely being out in the world on the "perfect day" is enough to ravish his very being:

O gift of God! O perfect day:
Whereon shall no man work, but play;

Whereon it is enough for me,
Not to be doing, but to be!

Through every fibre of my brain,
Through every nerve, through every vein,
I feel the electric thrill, the touch
Of life, that seems almost too much.

Summoning the winds with the incantatory phrase of King Lear in the storm ("Blow, winds!"), the poet calls them not to wreak sublime destruction in their overwhelming power but just to blow the peach and cherry blossoms, the former feeling to him like the fire Lear calls forth in the storm:

Blow, winds! and waft through all the rooms
The snow-flakes of the cherry-blooms!
Blow, winds! and bend within my reach
The fiery blossoms of the peach!

The poem ends by articulating the ideal of which the poem is an imperfect realization:

O heart of man! canst thou not be
Blithe as the air is, and as free?

"To Earthward" recalls Frost's own old ethereality, his own sense of the overwhelming force of the slightest sensation. "I lived on air," Frost wrote, describing a gentle "touch" that "seemed almost too much" like Longfellow's "touch / Of life, that seems almost too much." Frost calls to mind Longfellow's "fiery blossoms of the peach" in his recollection of another blossom's supersensuous charge: "The petal of the rose / It was that stung." It was only fitting that a poet who owed so much to Longfellow's influence should frame the change in his sensibility in terms of his deviation from what he once shared with his forebear. The poem tells of how Frost, who once quivered at the slightest touch for its intimation of a perfect whole, had come to crave the imperfect and the overwhelming force of sensation of earth.

To Earthward

Love at the lips was touch
As sweet as I could bear;
And once that seemed too much;
I lived on air

That crossed me from sweet things,
The flow of—was it musk
From hidden grapevine springs
Down hill at dusk?

I had the swirl and ache
From sprays of honeysuckle
That when they're gathered shake
Dew on the knuckle.

I craved strong sweets, but those
Seemed strong when I was young;
The petal of the rose
It was that stung.

Now no joy but lacks salt
That is not dashed with pain
And weariness and fault;
I crave the stain

Of tears, the aftermark
Of almost too much love,
The sweet of bitter bark
And burning clove.

When stiff and sore and scarred
I take away my hand
From leaning on it hard
In grass and sand,

The hurt is not enough:
I long for weight and strength
To feel the earth as rough
To all my length.

One could call the first half of the poem "To Heavenward," an evocation of spiritual ease that recalls his earlier perspective as if from outside, unable to feel as he once felt, spoken in words that pare down what
"A Day of Sunshine" (or "Twilight") embellishes. The second half, "To
Earthward," is about strain rather than ease, not the blithe pleasure intimating perfection but the pleasure bound up in resistance. On this point
Frost figures the felt experience of lovemaking with an almost synesthetic
climax, "the aftermark / Of almost too much love, / The sweet of bitter
bark / And burning clove." The erotic charge in the poem is undeni-
able. Something like Longfellow's "electric thrill" hovers in Frost's every
terse line of building anticipation and impartial satisfaction. The terse-
ness shows a kind of reverence for overpowering experience, the language
a dizzying array of strong words for craving and phrases for shadows of
sensation. The first line alone is a kind of poem in miniature, "Love at the
lips was touch" evoking both love and the act of love, lips in the courtly
English and the vulgar Latin, thereby invoking the idealized sense of "To
Heavenward" that a kiss brought idealized love to reality, as well as the

carnal memory of "To Earthward" when touch and not resistance was enough. The final stanza expresses something of an opposite to the latter perspective, longing for resistance brought to its apex:

> The hurt is not enough:
> I long for weight and strength
> To feel the earth as rough
> To all my length.

Like the first line, the last stanza seems to signify something sensational as well as symbolic. The longing is the opposite of that in "A Day of Sunshine": not total weightless ease and freedom in air but total roughness pressed to earth. Not elevation: possession. Possession in every nerve and vein by the real for which nothing can substitute, spiritual possession for which all sensation was welcome and no feeling on earth was enough.

IV.

The first of Frost's poems spoken in the persona of Frost the Poet was his Christmas card for 1915. "Christmas Trees" tells the story of men from the city in search of trees in the country. The narrator, piqued at first to feel his surprise visitors turning his beloved woods into something to buy, is all the more piqued to hear their low offer. Showing how outside interest can impinge on private life by turning art into commerce, the poem also lets on that the narrator's aestheticism can be its own negotiating tactic in what the poem calls "the trial by market everything must come to." Frost sent the poem to Louis from his Christmas tree woods in Franconia with an illustration by Lesley and then put the poem, lightly revised, after "The Road Not Taken" in the beginning of his next collection, *Mountain Interval*, published before Christmas in 1916.

Mountain Interval, though well received, did not make anything like the impression of *North of Boston*. Perhaps this had something to do with its relative diffuseness of form and of theme. Though the book was a master-piece that included a number of the best poems Frost would ever publish, it was less a unified work than an assortment of work, and therefore not the sort of thing that makes for an event. His publisher had wanted an-other book from him, and Frost was in no position not to part with his Christmas trees.

Having lectured widely, Frost had grown weary of lecturing as early as the end of 1915. It seemed to Elinor, reasonably, like a drain on his health and a distraction from writing. It was therefore a welcome surprise in the summer of 1916 when a pair of Frost's new acquaintances showed up in Franconia to offer him a position at Amherst College, beginning the following spring. His appointment was announced to the Amherst men in chapel toward the end of fall semester, accompanied by a reading of "The Road Not Taken" that met with great applause. Thus began the next stage in Frost's vexed and extraordinary career as a teacher, henceforth at the level of education he had twice begun but never completed.

Frost had reservations from the start. "I've been up to my ears in the work of other writers," Frost complained in May 1917 about his students, "young hopefuls that don't really give me much hope." He looked forward to ending his foray in professing after the semester and getting back to Franconia until a good enough offer from Amherst brought him back in the fall on a more permanent basis. His appointment was unusual if not unheard of in American colleges at the time—hiring a practitioner of an art to teach it as a professor—and Frost's hiring was a testament to the open-mindedness and foresight of the two men who had hired him, Al-exander Meiklejohn, president of the college, and Stark Young, a popular professor in the English department. It was ironically their philosophies that Frost would cite as his cause for resigning in a huff in the spring of 1920. The conflict was and remains a minor scandal—was for Young and Meiklejohn at the time and is in retrospect for Frost—and the scandal is liable to persist in the absence of reliable evidence to settle the facts of the case.

Young, who was homosexual, was accused of trying to seduce a number of his students. Frost, in his frustration with Meiklejohn's lack of
response, has been accused by posterity of homophobic intolerance. The
truth is hard to suss out. It is both a common myth with a devastating
history that gay men could and did prey on young men in their charge
and also the story Frost heard in this case. As cited, Frost's intolerance
was for the violation of students' sexual boundaries, not the sexuality of
the accused. Homosexuality in other contexts provoked Frost's judgment
but not his intolerance, as when he ran into a friend who had been arrested for having pornographic photos of young men and Frost put his
hands on his friend's shoulders and asked, "What is it? The Greek vices?"
Though tolerant by the standards of his time, Frost was undoubtedly and
sometimes unforgivably a creature of prejudice, which happened to be
the main philosophical concept underlying his protracted conflict with
Meiklejohn.

An optimistic rationalist, Meiklejohn believed that a liberal education
should aim for the eradication of prejudice. Frost, an anti-rationalist in
the tradition of Burke and Milton, believed that in matters beyond the
purview of reason one was guided best by passion that one might as well
call prejudice. Frost levied the charge that Meiklejohn was irrational in
practice for eliding limits of reason, and shared with colleagues such as
George Whicher the suspicion that Meiklejohn's idealistic optimism was
cover for a cult of personality that impoverished the education it purported to enlighten. Rather than eradicating prejudices, Frost thought,
Meiklejohn was inculcating different prejudices—for vague enthusiasm rather than sober reflection, for an airy Romanticism rather than
a classical conception of one's own capacity for evil, for cosmopolitan
reactions against parochial attachments rather than sustained loyalties,
for the charismatic authority of Alexander Meiklejohn at the expense
of one's own inner sense of authority. Such was what Frost described in
May 1919 to Lesley, by then a sophomore at Barnard, as "the conflict now
on between the aesthetic anti-Puritan anti-American Meiklejohn-Youngs

and the anti-aesthetic Puritan-American Frost-Whichers." Frost thought his own position was dangerous to Meiklejohn because "rationalistic and anti-intellectualistic," meaning against the intellectual's posture that all ideas of value were amenable to open debate, that classroom debate would inevitably improve the ideas rather than just drawing participants toward consensus with the winner. Frost had had enough by the start of spring semester in 1920, imprecating Meiklejohn as he pronounced his decision "to leave teaching and go back to farming and writing."

V.

Had Frost been a more systematic thinker, he might have ventured a clearer delineation at the time of the limits of reason and the realms of thought that warranted the felt conviction he called prejudice aside from the realms of "literature love religion and friendship," his old list for Cox. But Frost was not a system builder, and he would spread his skepticism over different cases in the poetry, prose, and talks of the rest of his lifetime. The case of Meiklejohn draws out nothing more clearly than Frost's skepticism of education conceived as a group exercise rather than a relationship between student and teacher. If Meiklejohn's purported model of the classroom was the debating society, Frost's was the nurture involved in "loving children (which is teaching)." Frost's looseness of manner as a teacher depended on a simplicity of method whose principles are largely encapsulated in a comparison he once drew between students learning to write and children learning to feed themselves.

A toddler with food in hand might first succeed in making contact with his cheek, then his eye, until "by luck he hits his mouth," his masterstroke reinforced by his mother's cooing encouragement. "The added pleasure of his mother makes him do it every time." It was Frost's contention that the way of the pen mirrored the course of the spoon. A student learning to write might strike an inspired note or two in a series of stabs, after which triumphs Frost thought it incumbent on the teacher, like the mother, to praise the good work achieved partly by luck, letting students know on the teacher's authority when they had achieved a "literary moment."

Frost's comparison is representative in a number of ways, one of which is his example of responsive maternal reinforcement. It captures how Frost was inclined to react to students' writing, preferring encouragement rather than criticism, few interventions rather than many, and praise rather than evaluation against an abstract standard, praise that described the work directly rather than comparing it with other attempts or to noteworthy achievements. Frost loved to mock teachers who saw themselves as vessels for information or enforcers of rules—"Miss Pains" he called one functionary, and another one "Mr. DeGree." Frost set himself up as a person in whose pleased reactions his students could take pleasure. His general aim as a teacher was not to impose external discipline or offer external incentives but to cultivate his students' natural impulses, with particular attention to impulses that, like those of the spoon-wielding toddler, bore no clear relation to literary ambition. One such impulse was the shame "when others get the idea before they do" (though he warned not to "cultivate shame . . . before the instinct for it makes itself apparent"). Another impulse was the satisfaction of devising a winning retort to someone after the moment had passed.

Frost was by no means distinctive in seeing an analogy between sophisticated kinds of teaching and early stages of nurture. He stands out for how far he took the analogy in practice—well into the years of education when by received wisdom most learning was informational and most teaching didactic or disputatious. He considered the cultivation of impulse into initiative the most important aim of education. Initiative did not imply ambition necessarily—he said that the "lack of initiative" he regretted in his students was "in getting up notions to surprise, shock, and amuse me," and he meant it. This sort of throwaway initiative was for him merely an undistinguished manifestation of the spirit's attempt to orient itself in a world of material, an endeavor he regarded as the aim of almost all human thinking, an aim for which he thought poetry offered a first-rate education.

The great heritage of Puritanism for Frost was its commitment to what he thought of as poetry. He effectively defined both poetry and Puritanism as the "renewal of words," elaborating in the context of Puritanism that renewal comprised "a stubborn clinging to meaning,—to purify words until they meant again what they should mean." In poetry, the purification of meaning fostered a corresponding purification in those who came close to it, cultivating reactions of pleasure in words as poetic imagination renewed them. Yet Frost knew that such pleasures took time and could not be forced. Where one cannot bring oneself to take pleasure in what one has come to value, one is left with ideals. Frost conceived his role as a teacher not as imposing ideals on his students but being around to guide the "idealizing part of people's nature," so active at their stage of life. It was Frost's conviction that the task of purification, extending to our deepest loves and profoundest ideals, began with our first forms of self-sustenance.

VI.

Purification of sensibility was the subject of Frost's most comprehensive talk on literary education. Given in November 1930, the talk brought out ideas implicit in Frost's thinking for years, reframing the question of education in poetry as that of "Education by Poetry," the title given to the talk's republication in prose. Education by poetry, for Frost, is education in judgment and taste insofar as they deal with metaphor. To the extent that our thinking is metaphorical, poetry is a measured way to take the metaphors of thought, comprising a balance of thought and feeling for which Frost offered the characteristically vivid figure of "enthusiasm . . . taken through the prism of the intellect and spread on the screen in a color."

Frost went so far in the talk as to say all thinking was metaphorical. One wonders how much measure to take him with (though the idea has received more systematic treatment in recent years by the likes of cognitive scientists such as George Lakoff and the polymathic Douglas Hofstadter). By metaphor Frost meant not only the rhetorical device narrowly construed, distinguished, for example, from simile or synecdoche. Frost meant metaphor to encompass every bit of speech, writing, or thought that involved "saying one thing in terms of another" or "saying one thing and meaning another." Analogy perhaps comes closest to Frost's meaning— indeed, it is Hofstadter's preferred term to draw together the various figures under a single mental function rather than an assortment of rhetorical forms—but Frost preferred "metaphor," perhaps because it does the better job of implying how much of our saying one thing in terms of another is implicit and unwitting, hidden in common sense and plain language. He offered the audience for "Education by Poetry" examples drawn from the sciences such as "health" as used in Freudianism (for which a contemporary audience could substitute every extended application of the phrase "mental health"); "evolution" as it extends outside the domain of biology to things like "the evolution of candy"; and the old scientistic notion of the world as a machine, which Frost treats as a metaphor in hiding.

If all thinking is metaphorical and all metaphor deserves to be taken with more or less belief or circumspection, poetry offers a way to respond to metaphor along with a complex and ineffable balance of credence and doubt—a balance of thought and feeling all but impossible to express outside the experience of what Frost called coming close to a poem, which someone could do by writing poems or reading them with the right sensitivity. The goal is to be "at home in the metaphor"—able to see its insightfulness without being fooled into taking it as literal truth. However accurate as a description of poetry writ large, it was a highly accurate description of a kind of lyric Frost had begun to write in the second half of the 1910s—reflective, often undramatic, a skeptical essay in verse on the scope and limits of a given common idea. It was a feature of his writing more profound when situated in the context of human drama, as with the subjects into which Frost thought poetry provided particular insight. These were areas in which Frost thought people had to intuit a belief in something before they knew enough about it to convince the world. In such cases the intuition of belief became a precondition for bearing out the belief. His examples were effectively "literature love religion and friendship"—the self-belief of a young man (he was speaking at Amherst, a men's college) who knew more about himself than he could show to the world, the belief in a new love or a new work of art, and the belief in God and nation as well, by which faith the believer brings into the world what they at first could take only on faith.

Frost knew well that these were matters not only for poetry. He thought that almost everyone attempted some such beliefs with effusions of feeling, which he called enthusiasm, whether for thinking of something in terms of another or for reaching to one's mouth with a spoon. Education by poetry involved enthusiasms such as these "tamed to metaphor," purifying sensibility by irradiating emotional beliefs with the intellect's prism.

VII.

One of the constant tensions in Frost's life was between his commitment to education and his ambivalence about school. He nonetheless spent the vast majority of his life involved with school in some way or another, close enough to his college employer to show off his conspicuous lack of scholarliness. Whatever else went into his scrupulous informality, it reflected a tension not only about his role as a teacher but within his very conception of the poetry he considered so important to education.

Frost was fond of saying that poetry was much more of life than of school. He did not mean this in terms of subject matter alone. He was inclined to call some imaginative people who wrote no poetry poets, a theme he extended to other domains about which he thought poetry was distinctly educative, saying repeatedly and in any number of ways that there was more poetry outside verse than in, more love outside marriage than in, more religion outside church than in. It was natural that anyone who believed such things would betray some misgivings about a life spent teaching verse in school.

In saying there was more poetry outside verse than in, Frost echoed

a conception of poetry articulated most famously by Shelley in his trea-
tise "A Defense of Poetry." Shelley wrote that "poetry" referred first and
foremost to any act of insight by the Imagination otherwise illegible
within a world of things, and only secondarily did "poetry" refer to such
works of Imagination embodied in writing. Such was Frost's conception of
poetry in schematic form. His conception differed from Shelley's in a way
that reflected a disagreement in fundamental philosophy (after *Twilight*)
with the Platonist Shelley about the faculty of Imagination, Frost believing with Aristotle that the Imagination lacked access to a realm of Ideal
forms and instead formed its ideas, or at least the overwhelming majority
of them, by inferences drawn from things in the world. Frost called this
means of inference "nature piety," seeing a debt to Aristotle in the final
couplet of Wordsworth's in "The Rainbow":

And I could wish my days to be
Bound each to each by natural piety.

Nature piety, per Frost, involves forming one's ideas according to faithful observation of nature, external and internal to the self. Such ideas
were not limited to physical nature—Aristotle, Wordsworth, and Frost
all drew ideas of divinity and the human soul—but were by their physical
mediation not amenable to the self-evidence afforded by direct penetration
of a realm of Ideal forms. One could form the right idea about spirit or
God with no way to know whether you know, involving one's thinking in
a general interplay of observation, extrapolation, and uncertainty in the
effort to say one thing in terms of another.

    If Frost rejected Shelley's theory of Imagination but believed with
Shelley that poetry as conventionally understood was a written species
in a broader genus of imaginative acts, which acts of the Imagination
did Frost think amounted to poetry? One can reconstruct an answer
from views Frost articulated in different writings. He thought poetry
consisted of sight and insight, sight meaning observation and insight an
idea that penetrated something plausibly true and nonobvious in nature

or in human nature. He also thought a poem was "the emotion of having a thought," an idea first experienced as a feeling and then believed
into being. If one calls such pregnant feeling "inspiration," it follows
that Frost considered poetry the inspired emotion of an insightful idea,
with the qualification from Frost's anti-Platonism that the source of the
inspiration and the truth of the insight are at best imperfectly and fal-
libly known.

This extended conception of poetry along with Frost's contention
that there was more poetry outside verse than in raises the question of
why Frost dedicated himself to verse anyway. One could pose the same
question about his commitment to marriage with more love outside marriage than in (as Shelley had thundered in *Epipsychidion*). An institution has
arisen for love, as for poetry, to regulate and sustain products of inspired
emotion. The institutions of marriage and verse are as stable as the passions of poets and lovers are light as the wind. One can infer that Frost
committed himself to marriage and verse as the best reliable way to create
and preserve the spiritual goods of poetry and love. These grounds of
Frost's dedication to verse mark a distinctive view of the relationship between institutions and human potential—an optimism about humanity's
extra-institutional potential in theory tempered by a practical pessimism
about the human capacity to realize its potential without the constraint
and support of extant institutions. Theoretical optimism on the matter
set Frost apart from conservatives; practical pessimism, Romantics. It is
small wonder that Frost never escaped his misgivings about his role in
institutionalized education and also that he never left for good.

VIII.

Frost was fond in later years of quoting a couplet of his:

It takes all sorts of in and outdoor schooling
To get adjusted to my kind of fooling.

He would not let on that he initially wrote the couplet from the perspective of God.

IX.

I was thinking the other day, I'm like an old man leaning on a stick.
I leaned on the poems that there's a chance a lot of people have
seen in the anthology.

—FROST, 1950

The way to read a poem in prose or verse is in the light of all the
other poems ever written.

—FROST, 1951

Frost was not unusual among teachers of poetry in mainly teaching verse from anthologies. He was, however, unusual in the depth of his love for anthologies. He did not regard them as an expedient used to accommodate his students' lack of time or initiative for reading a poet's complete work but as the likeliest way that anyone could learn a poet's best work. He even considered the anthology "the highest form of criticism," an eccentric claim he supported by holding a dim view of most actual critics.

Reviewers, in Frost's experience, taught poets nothing. He abstained from reviewing, citing the people he knew who would "scratch each other's backs, then . . . scratch each other's eyes"—"I would rather teach." But Frost thought teachers were not in the best position to perform the essential function of criticism, which was to say how much a poet's work had been inspired and insightful—had "fit into the nature of people." Teachers are paid to love their pupils' work as parents will naturally. Editors, the opposite of teachers, are paid to hate the work submitted to them, screening it for imperfections. Publishers are more or less the same, biased like

editors toward a safe and well-recognized name. Academic critics Frost
didn't even consider. A poet generally wanted public esteem but not to be
a passing taste. One wanted the verdict of time, a verdict Frost thought
rendered best by anthologists.

He liked to assign a project for students and other audiences alike:
go through a celebrated poet's work and see if you could find poems in it
better than those that had been anthologized. Nine out of ten times, he
thought, you could not. In effect, he treated the anthology as an institution of sophisticated general taste, and thought, for all its imperfections,
it was better than the alternatives.

Frost would tout *The Oxford Book of English Verse* with the slightest qualification. It could not surpass, it was but the "silver anthology," in comparison to Palgrave's *Golden Treasury*, which he once called "a pretty little
sonnet of a book."

X.

Robert Frost to John Erskine, president of the Poetry Society of America,
January 18, 1923:

> Such news reaches me from the great world as that common sense is
> now considered plebean and any sense at all only less so: the aristocrat
> will spurn both this season; an American poet living in England has
> made an Anthology of the Best Lines in Poetry. He has run the lines
> loosely together in a sort of narrative and copyrighted them so that
> anyone using them again will have to enclose them in double quotation
> marks thus: "'I say no harm and I mean no harm.'"

In the final months of 1922, the character of modern poetry changed. An
American poet living in England, T. S. Eliot, published a poem unlike any
before. *The Waste Land* was issued first in literary journals in England and
America in October and November, then in book form in America and
England in December and January, the book including pages of endnotes

appended to the poem by the author himself. Ezra Pound, the poem's ded-
icatee and its clandestine editor, called it, at nineteen pages, "the longest
poem in the Englisch langwidge," a modern epic whose scale encompassed
not a grand sequence of consequential events but an interpretive mystery
of novel form, ranging allusion, spiritual longing, and evocative power, a
poem long on scale measured not in number of lines but in meaningful
difficulty. The poem was heralded in the literary world as revolutionary,
an achievement in verse that, like Joyce's *Ulysses* in prose, could by its
difficulty evoke the unparalleled complexity of modern life and transfigure
the complacent sensibilities of an audience that had experienced modernity but lacked the imaginative forms to respond to it. Frost was far from
alone in thinking the poem was a sham.

Admirers of *The Waste Land* were impressed by the breadth and het-
erogeneity of the poem's allusions. In the most influential early piece of
writing on *The Waste Land*, published in the December issue of *The Dial*
after the poem's publication in the issue before, Edmund Wilson, an
eminent critic, noted that the "poem of little more than four hundred
lines . . . contains allusions to, parodies of, or quotations from" more
than thirty recondite sources he could name. Wilson praised the poem
for managing to take place "half in the real world . . . and half in a
haunted wilderness" and yet "not only upon these two planes" but "as
if throughout the whole of human history," a perspectival synthesis he
attributed to "Mr. Eliot's extraordinarily complex mind." Frost seems
to have paid more attention to a source unattributed in Eliot's notes
in which most of his allusions to English poetry could nonetheless be
found: Palgrave's *Golden Treasury*.

Frost wrote to Louis about *The Waste Land* in a tone of mock urgency
two days before Christmas:

> Dont go to Europe till I tell you something. It's about poetry. It should
> always be Beautiful and Dimned. I should advise you to attempt noth-
> ing further under the old rules. Let this be the last thing we take up
> when we meet, which should be next week.

Sending up the authority claimed on Eliot's behalf by his admirers, Frost alludes to the putative new rules for poetry, rendering all prior standards outmoded. Poetry "must always be Beautiful and Dimned"—a pun (as so often in the words between Frost and Untermeyer) on F. Scott Fitzgerald's recent novel, *The Beautiful and Damned*, "Dimned" implying damnation and the dimness of obscurity, a word whose application to *The Waste Land* would soon become a source of vexation for Frost. Continuing in a similar vein in a letter to his friend and erstwhile colleague George Whicher on New Year's Eve, Frost wrote flippantly, "I happen to have just read The Golden Bough," the fifteen-volume work of anthropology to which Eliot assigned a central place in his notes, Frost's flippancy mocking Eliot's manner of casually brandishing his erudition in all its formidability. Frost ended the letter with his first reference to the eponymous poem of his forthcoming book, *New Hampshire*.

Frost's impressions of *The Waste Land* would become public more quickly than he ever intended. He made the mistake of speaking freely to a newspaper columnist on his trip to New York City in early January, striking up a conversation with the journalist, Burton Rascoe, at a cocktail party and continuing the talk on a long walk to Grand Central Terminal, only to find himself quoted at length in the *New York Tribune* of January 14 with the following criticism of Eliot:

> "I don't like obscurity in poetry," he told me. "I don't think a thing has to be obvious before it is said, but it ought to be obvious when it is said. I like to read Eliot because it is fun to see the way he does things, but I am always glad it is his way and not mine."

Frost responded to the surprise publication with a letter drafted in rage. He charged Rascoe ("You little Rascol") with misleading, misquoting, misunderstanding him, the last on the grounds that his objection had been not to the "obscurity" of Eliot's poem but to its "obscuration," by which Frost seems to have distinguished the deliberate concealment of meaning (obscuration) from mere difficulty (as in obscurity). The distinction is rather hard to pin down owing to the obscurity (or whatever) of the examples Frost used to illustrate his meaning, chosen apparently as an example of deliberate concealment, which would serve the three rhetorical purposes of showing that Frost could play at Eliot's game, that such a game could be maddening and pointless, and that his reader, Rascoe, was indeed simple, a point on which Frost left no obscurity. Frost ended by marveling at Eliot's apparently taking "six years to derange less than six hundred lines of mixed verse," on Rascoe's (misleading) report, and by recommending that Rascoe promote the poetry of Marianne Moore instead. Frost never sent the letter, on Elinor's and then Louis's advice.

"You and Jean [Untermeyer's wife] think such wrath ill becomes me," Frost wrote on January 23. "I'm over it now anyway. We wont send the letter to Burton the rat," a pest Frost had chastised in the letter for not "perform[ing] face-forward like a skunk."

In another letter to Louis two weeks later, Frost shared a new plan. He would publish *New Hampshire* with the titular poem followed by a series of "explanatory poems" that he would call "Notes," a form eventually expanded to include a series of lyrics called "Grace Notes." When published in October, *New Hampshire: A Poem with Notes and Grace Notes* would invite comparison with another recent book to whose eponymous poem its author had conspicuously appended his own notes.

"New Hampshire" was unlike anything Frost had published before. His longest poem to date—413 lines, approaching Eliot's 434—"New Hampshire" was also his first poem published in a consistently loose meter, his first long poem without a clear dramatic narrative, his first poem full of slightly modified quotations and unconcealed references to other poetry. Frost's allusions of note include reference to Ahaz, a king of Judah who in 2 Kings sets up an altar to a false god in the woods, an act of unholy devotion like those throughout *The Waste Land*, Frost's description seeing the present through a continuous mythological past as Eliot does. Frost slightly deranges several lines from Matthew Arnold, the Victorian

poet and stentorian critic on whose grand example Eliot modeled himself, quoting Arnold in the beginning of his essay collection *The Sacred
Wood* (1920), the title referring to an ancient myth in which the man who
would be king cuts a bough in a sacred grove and waits therein to fend
off an assailant who might approach to engage him in combat, a situation like that in which the petrified and dendrophobic pseudo-Arnold of
"New Hampshire" seems to imagine himself, only to run from the woods.
These references seem to serve a pair of rhetorical purposes also served by
Frost's references in his draft of a letter to Rascoe—showing that Frost
can play at Eliot's game (here the game of freely revising a predecessor's
poem into a hopelessly ambiguous narrative) and showing by example the
kinds of petty frustrations to which that kind of game leads.

In light of these parallels, it seems fair to surmise that Frost composed
"New Hampshire" in the same spirit of reactive pique in which he wrote
his letter to Burton the rat, defending himself and obliquely mocking his
rival. Frost's first mention of *The Waste Land* (December 23) preceded his
first mention of "New Hampshire" (ca. December 31), in a letter also
mocking *The Waste Land*. That "New Hampshire" was inspired in the end
of December by Frost's need for a comeback, a kind of inspiration Frost
was eager to foster, is a theory hitherto unproposed by Frost's critics most
likely because it contradicts Frost's own account of the poem's composition. Yet his account, which involves a comeback of its own, is not only
implausible on its own terms but a story that draws a pointed contrast
Frost meant to draw between himself and his rival.

According to Frost, the whole of "New Hampshire" came to him
over the course of a long waking night in Vermont in July 1922, after
which he walked out into the morning light, only to feel that he was not
yet finished. In a state between sleep and waking, the words of an entirely
new little poem came into his mind: "Stopping by Woods on a Snowy
Evening." Here was a rarity—a night of not one but two inspirations, the
second defying exhaustion, bearing no easy resemblance to the first in
form or content, and begetting a poem he recognized quickly as one of

his best. "Stopping by Woods on a Snowy Evening" was, among other things, a triumph of form, as intricately wrought as "New Hampshire" was slack-jawed. He called the little poem "my best bid for remembrance" as early as May 1923.

Frost would tell a story for decades of having composed "Stopping by Woods" without interruption or revision. A manuscript exists with his revisions. The first surviving record of the poem is from Frost's trip to New York City in January 1923, in which he read the poem to his publisher.

The genesis of "New Hampshire" was also other than the story Frost told. "New Hampshire" begins with Frost in propria persona meeting "a lady from the South" who says something affronting to his sensibilities, and Frost in December had just returned from a long lecture tour partly in the South, his first, a trip in which Southerners said a number of things affronting to his sensibilities. Frost's first reference to the overnight composition of "New Hampshire," on February 5, 1923, refers to his fall lecture tour in the same breath: "my fourteen lectures in fourteen days and three hundred lines of blank verse between ten at night and noon the next day." Most importantly, there is no contemporaneous sign of "New Hampshire" conceived separately from its place in *New Hampshire*. The first mention of the poem in the record is also the first mention of the book, in Frost's letter to George Whicher from the last days of 1922. It is even hard to imagine the poem outside the context of the book, built as "New Hampshire" is around the set of allusions to the other poems in *New Hampshire* that Frost would call "Notes." If Frost's annotations were a response to *The Waste Land*, so were the passages written for annotation that make up much of "New Hampshire."

One is left to wonder why Frost dissembled. While it was not out of character for him to hide his sources or his targets, and he admitted to veiling his competitiveness with other poets living or dead, it was curiously self-defeating to publish a poem drawing a contrast between himself and another poet only to establish for the record that he could not have had that other poet in mind, all but guaranteeing his poem's misinterpretation.

Irrational as this might seem, it followed the psychological pattern of Frost's reaction to Rascoe, in which Frost felt threatened, threw himself into a reactive frenzy writing a comeback, and wanted afterward to hide his reaction, feeling ashamed. The sources of shame in each instance were presumably both Eliot's example and his own response, which he was furious with Rascoe for sharing. And his response in each case was a peculiar kind of satirizing that both showed his own prowess by imitation and mocked the form itself, hiding both the shame of inferiority and the shame of comparing himself to begin with. If the layers of subterfuge amounted to something less than entirely clear, Frost may have come to feel that the story of "Stopping by Woods" invited all the comparison he needed. It invited a contrast with Eliot rather like the contrast Frost would draw a decade later when he conspicuously "pretend[ed] an inspiration" for a poem he wrote out as Eliot read from his work to a small group at the St. Botolph Club in Boston.

In an essay from 1919 collected later in *The Sacred Wood*, Eliot attempted to turn the received idea of literary originality on its head. He argued that a writer's most original work was not that which deviated most from prior examples but rather the work that embodied the writer's tradition most deeply. Among the implications of "Tradition and the Individual Talent" was that it would make it respectable for a poet to have been influenced: "Immature poets imitate; mature poets steal." Eliot posited a radically conservative relation between the institution of literary tradition and the originality of individual artists, in contrast with the standard prevalent since the dawn of Romanticism in which an indebtedness to one's predecessors was seen as a blight on a poet's claim to original inspiration. Eliot would make a virtue of the reception of influence. Frost was less than persuaded. "You're obliged to make your own quotable lines," he said about *The Waste Land*, calling the form of the poem "scatteration." Frost guarded his borrowings jealously. He was private about his associations with ghosts and how much of his writing grew out of it. He never admitted that he felt so threatened by Eliot's theory of influence because of the extent to which it might expose influences Frost had consistently hidden, not least in the same principal source from which Eliot borrowed so liberally.

If Frost likely found something threatening in this use of *The Golden Treasury*, he certainly felt threatened by *The Waste Land* for embodying a standard of excellence other than that under which Frost had labored for decades. And what better contrast with the new rules than one's best bid for remembrance under the old rules? There could hardly be a clearer contrast to a poem Frost considered erudite, opaque, loose, and allusive than a simple, clear, short masterpiece of form that Frost said was inspired, the antithesis of borrowed. Frost would compete on Eliot's terms and then on his own. It is no wonder he attached the composition of "Stopping by Woods" to the story of composing "New Hampshire"—if he did not in fact compose that little poem set on the winter solstice then, too.

"New Hampshire" was the first extended statement of principles among Frost's published poems. More than any verse he had published since "The Tuft of Flowers," it sounded like a piece of oratory, though where that was dressed up to prove himself, "New Hampshire" was dressed down to prove a point. He meant to set himself apart from a kind of intellectual cosmopolitanism in various manifestations, such as the bohemian New York he knew chiefly through Untermeyer and Eliot's Arnoldian "intellectual throne." For all the differences between Eliot's traditionalist conservatism and the radicalism of Greenwich Village, they had in common the elitism of intellectual subcultures that would remake the broader culture in light of their own ideas. (Eliot's theory of literature at the time combined a conservatism about literary tradition with a Romantic optimism about the ability of art to refigure the sensibility of its audience.) Against this highfalutin crowd Frost played the rustic showing off his homely wonders, his argument pitched as a defense of New Hampshire that he can't take entirely seriously, his arguments undermined repeatedly by irrational pride as shown in his improbable refrain: "It never could have happened in New Hampshire." Frost's pretense of regional chauvinism is a cover for a defense of regional attachment and localist self-sufficiency of a particular kind. Its self-sufficiency was not really that of political economy but something like the geographic analogue of self-reliance, a state that offered more than enough to the souls of its denizens. Frost denied consistently that he was a regionalist, calling himself a realmist instead. "New Hampshire" made the case that the region sufficed for the realm. His little state on his testimony had produced some of the best characters he knew, such as "Bartlett of Raymond." Frost's New Hampshire had more than enough to offer the imagination, as his poems—his narrative notes and lyric grace notes—might demonstrate. His New Hampshire was a place unapologetically beloved unlike Eliot's halfway-phantasmagoric land laid waste, itself a realm not of spiritual plenitude but of spiritual drought.

Frost draws the Eliotic character in "New Hampshire" with a number of sharp, if oblique, points of caricature. Rushing into a grove of trees as if to do battle for cultural supremacy, talking in snatches of literary quotation, he flees, yelling, "Nature is cruel, man is sick of blood," a famous line of Matthew Arnold's about humanity's disharmony with nature, the Eliotic character's overreaction going to show how the projection of categorical ideas onto the world can lead someone of Eliot's bent to misunderstand the world in front of his nose. The most salient contrast with Frost is another brief quotation from Arnold's poetry (slightly misquoted like much of the borrowed verse in *The Waste Land*): the Eliotic character "took dejectedly / His seat upon the intellectual throne." It was Frost's charge that Eliot took it upon himself to reeducate his audience, which was against what Frost stood for in both art and education. Of these two eminent conduits of New England literary tradition, these two men who had spent formative years in and around Boston and Cambridge, one was a Brahmin and the other a schoolteacher, the one pronouncing on a world he meant to bring in line with his standards and the other cultivating individual initiative by force of example, the one writing for a cultural elite and the other trying to meet a broader public where they were.

XI.

He knew too well for any earthly use
The line where man leaves off and nature starts,
And never over-stepped it save in dreams.

—"NEW HAMPSHIRE"

Part of Frost's charge against the Eliotic character in "New Hampshire" is that he disfigures his judgment and even the character of his experience with excessive intellectualized analysis. Frost illustrates the point by taking the character to the edge of the wood, where he regards the line of trees with self-certain, disengaged abstraction, missing the forest for "The line where man leaves off and nature starts." The characterization implies that his is a graceless response to a simple situation whose nature his phrasing obscures, like someone horrified of a glass of red wine because of ritual transubstantiation. A similar situation recurs in the consummately graceful poem Frost said he wrote after finishing those last lines of "New Hampshire." An unnamed narrator stops by snowy woods. The dark woods, the *selva oscura* (or "forest obscure") in which Dante's Pilgrim finds himself midway along the journey of his life at the outset of the *Divine Comedy*, seem to mark one line where man leaves off. A disquieted horse seems to blur such a line. The woods exert a fascination beyond anything the narrator tries to describe, and yet in an almost dreamlike state he feels himself drawn homeward, moving along from the woods' edge where the character in "New Hampshire" fled.

Stopping by Woods on a Snowy Evening

Whose woods these are I think I know.
His house is in the village though;
He will not see me stopping here
To watch his woods fill up with snow.

My little horse must think it queer
To stop without a farmhouse near
Between the woods and frozen lake
The darkest evening of the year.

He gives his harness bells a shake
To ask if there is some mistake.
The only other sound's the sweep
Of easy wind and downy flake.

The woods are lovely, dark and deep,
But I have promises to keep,
And miles to go before I sleep,
And miles to go before I sleep.

Like Frost's other most famous and most anthologized poem, "The Road Not Taken," "Stopping by Woods" is a rare combination of naturalness and form. Its lines of almost perfectly regular iambic tetrameter fold into a perfectly regular rhyme scheme of augmented Dantean terza rima like that of a foreshortened canto—yet the dramatic force of the lines is to wear their staging lightly and seem to one's suspended disbelief spoken in pure spontaneity. Like the woods for the poem's protagonist, the poem has exerted a fascination for its interpreters beyond any explanation offered for it. Most famous—almost as much as the poem—is the reading later popularized on which the snowy woods represent the temptation to withdraw into death and the prospect of an afterlife, which the speaker entertains but comes to reject on the strength of his earthly commitments, his "promises to keep." Frost often gainsaid this interpretation when reading the poem to audiences, saying the tone of the ending was not that of someone forswearing suicide but that of someone saying, at the end of a pleasant dinner, "Well, I must be getting on." One can find something persuasive in both the overwrought interpretation and Frost's coy, defensive non-explanation, the former manifestly right to find the poem imbued with mortal stakes and unassuming sublimity between the encroaching darkness, lulling snow, and unarticulated strangeness in a world the speaker thinks he knows. As "The Road Not Taken" embodies the liminal state of the crossroads, "Stopping by Woods" embodies the liminal state of the threshold, a line the crossing of which is freighted with the prospect of profound transformation, a prospect accompanied by a fascination not without fear. By whatever name, under whatever aspect, crossroads and threshold are metaphors we live by. Their ubiquity in our unthinking usage helps to explain why Frost was right to say that nothing like a resolution to live underlies the tone of "Stopping by Woods." The threshold embodied in the poem does not formulate so neatly. Its dramatic force is in conjuring the sense of a depth of meaning so incongruous with the speaker's easy tone, an experience bound to surpass the meaning we can assign to it. In this modesty about how to make sense of a line of trees he finds himself in front of, in his unostentatious engagement and elegant simplicity, in the genuine wonder that any regular person might feel on a walk on the winter solstice in New Hampshire, Frost's speaker contrasts with Frost's figure of Eliot as neatly as a pair of rhyming words.

9.

ASPENS IN RAIN

I.

On a sunny Sunday morning in August 1931, Frost and Elinor were driven from Boulder, Colorado, down to Colorado Springs, picked up at their hotel by Edna Davis Romig, Frost's fellow teacher at the Summer Writers Conference in Boulder, and her son, who drove the group the hundred miles south.

The Frosts had come to Boulder in July, brought west by work and trouble. Marjorie, twenty-six, was tubercular and convalescing at a sanitarium in town. Her parents brought her on vacation to the mountain village of Evergreen, from which Frost wrote to Untermeyer in bemusement over the situation he found himself in. "Isnt it strange for me to be living away off like this," Frost asked. "Three weeks ago I was settled for a month but as if forever in the sand dunes of extreme Montauk. Such lengths our children drag us to. . . . I don't care if God doesnt care." Did God really not care? Untermeyer would have presumed that Frost did not actually presume to know, leaving his renunciation in a state of perfect ambiguity, as if he were halfway inclined to cast off the weight of the cares he knew he could not cast off.

Frost and Elinor had gone to Montauk, Long Island, to be with Lesley as she was hospitalized late in her pregnancy. She had since recovered and delivered a daughter, her second, after a long and painful ordeal. Yet for Elinor it was not these troubles or even Marjorie's that brought out a rare lamentation in a letter from Evergreen to her close friend Edith Fobes. The source of Elinor's distress was her daughter-in-law, Lillian, Carol's wife, who had lately been diagnosed with a case of tuberculosis that Elinor thought was far worse than her daughter's. "Marjorie doesn't seem as well as I had hoped to find her," wrote Elinor. "But she seems happy, and I know she will recover, if she cannot be considered already recovered." "With Lillian it is different," she wrote with something close to despair.

> I am afraid she may not live, and the great concern I feel for her, and for Carol and Prescott [their son], stretches my endurance almost to the breaking point. Why are we so unfortunate? I have worked so hard for my family all these years, and now everything seems tumbling around me. I do not lament this way to everyone, of course. I am too proud, and with Robert I have to keep cheerful, because I mustn't drag him down, but sometimes it seems to me that I cannot go on any longer. Probably I have overworked these last six months, and will feel stronger after we reach home.

The thought of Lillian's precarious state broke Elinor's composure as almost nothing ever did in her writing. She was otherwise reserved as usual, writing about the cool nights and the pines and spruces and the "view of Mt. Evans, 14000 ft high, from our porch." In his letter, Frost had been moved to lament the fruits of his life's work as Elinor had lamented hers, though in his case as a result of going through his own poems with Elinor and Marjorie to send Louis a list to publish in a forthcoming anthology. (Elinor's first choice was "My November Guest.") "Sometimes I almost cry I am afraid I am such a bad poet," Frost wrote after selecting his poems. "But tonight I don't care if God doesn't care."

Two weeks later, Frost and Elinor were riding down to Colorado Springs on the road east of the mountains. The point of their trip was to meet a young man Romig knew who had enrolled in the conference to work with Frost but, after contracting pleurisy, had been confined to bed. When they got to the room of the young man, Bill Campbell, Elinor sat at his bedside and they talked for some time. Romig asked Frost to read. He requested *The Oxford Book of English Verse*—"England's greatest monument," he called it—and read aloud. He read "The Hound of Heaven" and parts of the eighteenth-century poem "Song to David," an extended ecstatic ode of devotion to God and the fruits of creation, a poem rather like "The Ode to Joy." Frost read some parts more than once, almost chanting. "At length he said a few of his own poems," Romig recalled, "'Stopping by Woods' being the last."

On the drive home, Frost talked of any number of things—the seasons in Colorado, the cultivation of orchids by someone they knew. Elinor talked about Campbell. "I just can't get that young man out of my mind," she said. "He has such fine dignity." "He's so alone."

On another drive the four of them took back to Boulder, this time after dinner at a lodge in the mountains to the north, Marjorie sat in the back seat leaning on her mother's shoulder, asleep. She had urged the group to take the scenic route up despite her parents' protests that she would get tired. She had asked to see "the aspens in the rain." And now she slept.

"That's nonsense, Rob," said Elinor from the back seat after he had been talking awhile. Her husband had pronounced "that no great poetry had been written in dialect," to which Elinor rejoined, "Robert Burns wrote in dialect." Frost, who had brought up Burns at the conference as "one who knew how to play with sorrow," responded to Elinor's objection tentatively, saying, "You can't call the Scotch tongue dialect." Then he asked Romig's son how he knew "where to turn on these winding canyon roads."

II.

The preceding years of Frost's life had been marked by growing public success and private strain. These two plots with opposite arcs would seem to have little to do with each other, the accumulation of accolades and appointments, on the one hand, and the mounting challenges of family life, on the other, but public and private would come to affect each other profoundly under the threat to the social institution Frost believed in most, the family. As of August 1931, it would be years before these effects were apparent. What was clear at the time was that Frost's loved ones were in trouble while he was, by all appearances, flourishing.

New Hampshire brought Frost his first Pulitzer Prize. His Collected Poems of 1930 brought him his second, though the honor had eluded Frost's fifth original collection, West-Running Brook of 1928. Colleges and universities did not renounce Frost as a teacher when he renounced teaching at Amherst in early 1920 to write and farm in Vermont—not Franconia, New Hampshire, but an old stone house in South Shaftsbury, Vermont, where Frost had moved his family in the fall of 1919 for a complex of reasons involving the superior climate for farming, proximity to Amherst across the Massachusetts border, Frost's distaste for the touristic turn in Franconia, avoidance of a possible scandal involving sexual advances toward Irma later cast into a very different light, and a long-standing wish for a proper apple-tree orchard. (The Frosts, or at least Robert and Elinor, would still go north to the Fobes's guest cottage in Franconia for hay fever season beginning in 1925.) The first school to lure Frost from his apple trees was the University of Michigan, which offered him a job with almost no formal obligations, something almost unheard of at the time for universities. Frost would serve sequential annual contracts as writer in residence, often not in residence but off lecturing, from the fall of 1921 through the spring of 1923, when, with Meiklejohn fired by the board of trustees at Amherst after a resounding faculty vote to demand his resignation, and Stark Young having resigned in protest, the college recruited Frost once again. He was eager to go back east even with teaching obligations, which he undertook for two years before returning to Michigan on a permanent basis, which lasted a year before Amherst brought him back a second time, now with tenure, less teaching, and the substantial salary Frost had been earning at Michigan. He had established the three sources of income—publishing, teaching, and lecturing—that he would compare to the three legs of a stool, his economic foundation as well as his family's. They were not wealthy, but they were financially comfortable as Frost's reputation grew from literary prominence to something more like preeminence.

His eminence was a dubious blessing for his poetry itself. The years since "New Hampshire" had seen his poetry grow altogether more polished, its graces of form and felicities of phrase less obstructed than ever. It had grown clear enough to be largely understood by an audience hearing it for the first time, which meant that it lost much of what would appeal less to the crowd. The loss was chiefly in the richness of surface that came from grounding poems in observations of people and things as they actually were or of minds as they made sense of themselves and the world. Disengaged from the fact, the poems began to proceed from ideas instead of having their ideas emerge from the mess of experience. The change was neither total nor totally negative. At least three masterpieces of lyric poetry in those years, "Desert Places" and "Spring Pools" and "The Freedom of the Moon," were as rich in experience as anything in life, while his poetry begun in ideas achieved new depths of communicable profundity in lyrics such as "The Armful" and "The Door in the Dark," and in narratives such as "The Bear," an anti-rationalist riposte to Alexander Pope's *Essay on Man* that offers a nuanced parody of that monument of the Age of Reason in the form of a bear rocking back and forth on his "fundamental butt." Still other poems are brilliantly descriptive but exclusively so. (The greatest of these is the lyric "Atmosphere.") What the poems gain in immediacy, they lose in the singular kind of enchantment that had been the lifeblood of Frost's poetry ever since "Mowing." Their ideas exist in a world of their own rather than in partial tension with the multifarious world from which they are drawn. They are not enough immersed in the world to hint that their words could transcend it. In these signs of the public man holding forth to the crowd, one can see realized Frost's fear, expressed long ago to Untermeyer, that he had become his own salesman, taking to market the calf that was his dead self the poet. What had been a premonition in 1916, when Frost was only forty-two, had come to pass fifteen years later in the sense that his persona had largely come to overwhelm the person composing the poems. The private person would nonetheless be called back to the heights of poetry over the following years by trials in Frost's private life to which a persona could hardly do justice.

The troubles for Frost's family had been mounting for the last half-dozen years. The decades before had been, by their standards, a relative lull. After the losses of Elliott in 1900 and Elinor Bettina in June 1907, Frost and Elinor enjoyed the relative fortune of a life that was, if not untroubled, free of family tragedies until the mental breakdown of Jeanie, Frost's sister, in 1920, after which she was sent to an institution where she would remain for the rest of her life. The ill health that had plagued Frost and Elinor in childhood and youth, though never absent entirely from their lives, had been less prominent for most of the first two decades of the century, between the move to Derry in the fall of 1900 and Frost's protracted case of Spanish flu in the fall of 1918. The ensuing years saw their health problems worsen from mostly seasonal viruses and periodic struggles, often combinations of physical and emotional exhaustion that manifested in the psychosomatic tangle known then as nervous exhaustion or nervous prostration. Frost was seriously worried about Elinor by the spring of 1925, and not only because she had lately suffered a miscarriage after unintentionally getting pregnant again past the age of fifty. He worried that his life of socializing and lecturing was too much for her, as she worried consistently that it was too much for him. Each would worry more about the other as their family gave them all the more to worry about. Of concern was not only the proliferation of health crises among their children and daughter-in-law but their children's general welfare. It is hard to say whether the problem weighed especially on Elinor or seemed to because she expressed her concern more straightforwardly. Both were most likely so. Frost had a public life to worry about, whereas Elinor had devoted her considerable gifts over the preceding decades to nurturing a family that was not only close-knit in emotional and practical terms but geographically concentrated into her children's adulthood. Having no direct ties to any institution other than family, she raised a family of people involved in each other's lives to an unusual extent for the time, though it would have been less uncommon on a New England farm in the late nineteenth century. Yet by August 1931, the Frost parents and children, after living mostly near or with each other over the course of the parents' moves over the years, were dispersed.

Lesley, thirty-two, was in Montauk with her baby daughter, Lesley Lee, and her two-year-old, Elinor. She was not with her husband, Dwight Francis, from whom she had separated. She had married him quickly in the fall of 1928, only to learn, also rather quickly, that he was unstable emotionally—unable, in the psychological terms of the time, to control his own nerves. His mother blamed her for the divorce; she blamed his mother for him. Her parents supported her choice. She ran an independent bookstore in Pittsfield, Massachusetts, where she had once employed Marjorie. In the years after her brief stints as an undergraduate at Wellesley and Barnard and the University of Michigan—her education interrupted by a job helping to assemble airplanes in World War I—Lesley had, among other things, reviewed poetry, worked in publishing, and converted her store, the Open Book, into a traveling book caravan, which she also took on a tourist sailboat around the world. She was a small-business person and writer like both her father and his mother, at work on genre fiction as he had been at a similar stage in his own career. Lesley would soon become a teacher like her father and his mother as well, though her career was still a parentally worrisome picture of uncertainty as of August 1931. She had inherited many of her parents' values as well as her father's independence of mind and, with it, his pride.

Carol, Lesley's junior by three years, set out with Lillian and Prescott in early August for Southern California, where Lillian would receive treatment at elevation in the San Gabriel foothills. Lillian and Carol had lived for the better part of the last eight years at the Stone Cottage in South Shaftsbury, from which Frost and Elinor had moved to another farmhouse within walking distance, the Gully (so called), in 1929. Carol made a go of life as a farmer, harvesting apples, raising chickens, growing cherries. Carol was hardworking, good with his hands, and gifted with animals, but hardscrabble farming in New England had only gotten harder since his father had set out to do it in 1899. It did not help that Carol was often in poor health, like all the other children but Lesley. His parents worried that he, like Marjorie, had contracted the latent tuberculosis they worried his father might have contracted from his father before him. (The long and unpredictable latency of tuberculosis could make the experience of the illness ambiguous at every stage from diagnosis to the cadence of progression. It was a mystery one had to live with.) Carol had grown up to be tall, handsome, sensitive, and shy, and seems to have been almost entirely guileless. He was the small farmer his father never entirely was. He wrote poetry, too, but was under the impression that the measure of a poem was its avoidance of grammatical errors, a standard his work seldom met. In addition to interests in farming and poetry, he shared his father's attentiveness to physical detail, a certain stubbornness, playfulness, and ease with children. Elinor was distraught about his leaving for California ("I have always wanted to watch Carol a little on account of his lack of vigorous health, and he is very dear to me"), but Frost thought the move might be good for him. Elinor tried to take the separation philosophically: "Young people have to work out their own salvation." Carol thought he might apprentice as an electrician. Carol and family passed through Boulder on their drive west, and his parents followed them out in late August to help them get situated, returning east afterward by way of Boulder.

Irma, born in 1903 to Carol's 1902, is the Frost child of whose early

years the least record survives. She was a talented visual artist—talented
in painting, drawing, and sculpting—but did not pursue work outside
the home seriously as her siblings did. She and her husband, John Cone,
whom she married in 1926, had a son born in 1927, Jackie (sometimes
"Jacky"). They had moved first to John's parents' house in Kansas, but
Irma left with Jackie in short order, finding the situation intolerable. John
followed her east, tried poultry farming on eight acres near South Shaftsbury bought for them by his father-in-law, and then went back to school
at Massachusetts Agricultural College in Amherst before switching to
architecture, which he studied at Yale on a scholarship with the help of
his father-in-law. Irma was painfully embarrassed that her husband was
no more than a "goddam school boy." She was severe, high-strung, and
fastidious—nervous, as they said then as a psychological diagnosis and
not just a description of a mood. When Louis and Jean Untermeyer visited once in South Shaftsbury, Irma left the room, not wanting to share
the space with a "painted Jezebel" (Jean was wearing lipstick). Her father
had to coax Lesley to spend time with Irma in October 1920, when they
were both young in New York—Lesley, twenty-one, at Barnard, and Irma,
seventeen, at the Art Students League. Irma resembled no one in the family more than Jeanie, who was also nervous, severe, and sensitive about
matters of sex to the point of paranoid delusion. Jeanie and her brother
had little contact in the years before her outburst and hospitalization
in Maine, at which point Frost tried to care for her dutifully but with
no hint of fondness. He was more charitable in his assessment of Irma's
prickly qualities to a twenty-one-year-old Lesley, herself headstrong and
adventurous:

> Please take the way with her that will keep the peace. Remember that
> her strictness is part of her nature. Don't try to make her over. Some
> of it she will outgrow, but not all of it even by the time she is eighty. It
> has its beauty if you know how to look at it. When you find it a little
> agressive, you can disregard it.

John graduated from architecture school at Yale at the top of his class. Frost spent graduation day trying to calm Irma from crying out of shame.

Marjorie was both the youngest and the most prone to physical illness. After finishing high school in 1923 and working in a pair of bookstores, the second of which was the Open Book with Lesley, Marjorie fell ill at the end of 1925 with pneumonia and appendicitis. She would not work again for three years. Her symptoms were intermittent but persistent and mysterious. They did not prevent her from becoming "the best poet in the family" as of 1926, in her father's estimation. A doctor diagnosed her in early 1927 with nervous prostration, a variant of nervous exhaustion in which psychosomatic symptoms had badly progressed psychologically as well as somatically. She was often exhausted, beset by coughing fits, sleep deprived, restless, antisocial, melancholic to the point of desperation. She would not eat for days at a time. Her parents, with whom she lived in those years, habitually described her condition as a weight on their hearts. Her father was not sure about the diagnosis of nervous prostration— other nervous prostrates he knew "were set serious" while "Marj has her ironies and her grins"—but if he had a better diagnosis, he did not share it. Her condition improved in early 1928 when she spent two months at Johns Hopkins Hospital, where she was so taken with the nurses that she decided to become one herself. She still tended to tire easily when she returned to Johns Hopkins as a nursing student a year later, but she finished her first term at the top of her class. All the surviving evidence indicates that she was happy there before falling ill again at the end of 1930 and being taken by her mother to recover from tuberculosis at Mesa Vista Sanatorium in Boulder, to which her parents would return that summer. There was no cure for the tubercular—just the potential of rest. Frost wrote to a friend after Elinor's return from Boulder that "the tendency to tuberculosis has merely come out into the open," not specifying whether the "tendency" was Marjorie's or the whole family's. "We seem composed for the moment," he wrote.

III.

Edna Davis Romig received an unexpected guest on a Saturday evening in the winter of 1932. Marjorie had an announcement: she and Willard Fraser were engaged. The young man had proposed earlier that evening on a walk up Flagstaff Mountain, south of Boulder. Marjorie had his fraternity pin on her blouse.

Her recovery had been lucky and swift. Her doctors thought her condition had been physically promising since early 1931 but exacerbated by a nervous breakdown—dejection coinciding with her relapse into being ill as she had been for three years after two years of fragile recovery. Any role that her emotions might have played in her illness may have been counteracted by her meeting and falling in love with a dignified and earnest Montanan in his senior year at the University of Colorado. Willard was a man with "the beautiful ideals that I had feared no longer existed," she wrote to her parents in announcing the engagement. "Another real Victorian, papa," she wrote. They would marry once he found work to support them.

His search, sadly, took time. It was 1932. The engagement was more protracted than either expected, more than twice as long as their courtship, but Marjorie came to be grateful for the way they got to know each other in writing before they had to negotiate the mundane tensions of cohabitation. Still, it ached. She started a draft of a novel. She went out to California to stay with Carol and Lillian, but, not wanting to linger around tuberculosis too long, for reasons more psychological than physical, Marjorie moved back to Amherst and waited for Willard to join the Frosts for Christmas.

The vision that she sketched out to Willard of their future together was dreamy and definite. If the manner was the headlong rush of young love, the matter was a coherent set of ideals at once lofty and practical. Life would be hard, circumstances would change unpredictably, no one but them would fight for their happiness, but if they stayed devoted to each other in every part of mind and soul, then they could weather anything together. It was a kind of Stoical Romanticism—Romantic in placing sexual love at the heart of the good life to the point of transcendence, Stoical in grounding such an elevation not in passion or intimations of divinity but in the practical argument of insulation from external circumstance, replacing the Stoical individual, prototypically male, with the couple united in wedlock. It was a vision familiar to Victorian literature, as in the triumphal end of *In Memoriam*.

The job search persisted. Willard could not make it for Christmas. Marjorie felt the self-effacement of a grown child trading the freedoms of adult independence for the security of her parents' home, a contrast made all the more drastic by her "return to being 'Robert Frost's daughter,' pure and simple, once more." She compared her household to a nunnery; no one could doubt who was the Father.

After Willard got a job on a progressive newspaper in Helena, Montana, Marjorie moved west. They were married at Willard's parents' house in June 1933, an endless half-year after the Thanksgiving wedding for which they had planned. Marjorie carried a shower bouquet of rosebuds and sweet peas that fluttered, she thought, "like Aspen leaves in a gale." She proceeded to have the greatest stretch of writing of her lifetime, seemingly at her best as a poet, like her father, in the context of a stable relationship. She expected a child in March.

IV.

Frost and Elinor arrived in Billings on a Sunday morning in early April 1934. Willard had called them the Thursday before. Marjorie had not recovered from an illness in childbirth, he told them, and her condition seemed serious, so her parents took the train out to Montana, Elinor returning after her departure from Billings for Amherst a week before.

They were met by John and Margaret Bartlett, who had driven the five hundred miles up from their home in Boulder to meet them. John noticed Frost's composure and the way it seemed to calm the other family members present when Frost talked calmly about the dangers that Marjorie faced. Frost projected goodwill on Sunday morning toward the head maternity nurse whose negligence Frost suspected of causing his daughter's infection, even "plaster[ing]" the doctor, whom Frost also held responsible, "with pleasant remarks which I didn't feel" because "I thought Marjorie would want me to," although "Elinor looked as if she disapproved." They met with a second doctor, consulting on the case, whose facial expression gave them a sense of how bleak the prognosis really was. Frost told John. Elinor told Margaret. The parents of the mother hardly slept on Sunday night.

Yet Frost was excitable and voluble. He kept up a long and engaging monologue for much of the Bartletts' two days in Billings, partly to solace his family, John and Margaret thought, and partly to entertain guests. He talked of tramps, whom he respected, saying that there is "some of the nomad in all of us," as in the poets of Homer's time who barded around. Frost talked of Hoover and Roosevelt, socialism and the New Deal and American civilization, saying that the essence of American civilization—not only our laws but our people, the whole of our institutions and customs—was the freedom it gave people to pursue the ends they themselves wanted to pursue. This was in contrast to full socialism or to tribal life, which he thought had taboos far more binding than those in modern America. His thoughts about socialism were in partial agreement with Elinor in her bitter opposition to what she regarded as the socialist encroachments of the New Deal. He had wanted Roosevelt to win. She said she could sense his victory ahead of time and Frost teased her, calling her "Prophetess." He talked about the problem of finding what you wanted to do in life, how parents could not supply it for children. He wondered whether he exercised "a soft tyranny" in his family. He thought it was possible but said he had never had a problem with his children. He wondered about the men he knew who were better father figures to children other than their own. He said we all have our own souls and minds to save and could think of any number of times his own had hung on a thread and but for his own interventions would have snapped like his sister Jeanie's, who built a "protecting illusion" around herself and lost touch with reality. Frost talked about how his father always put off treating his own tuberculosis till it killed him, about the tensions in life between ideals and loyalties and between mercy and justice. He preferred loyalties to ideals and justice to mercy, but in each pair there was always a balance to strike. He preferred jotting down his thoughts to keeping a conventional diary. He was always misplacing his hat—a forgetfulness John thought was in character. He told John that he had noticed many stones in New England graveyards of women dying right after childbirth, the women often sick, he figured, with what Marjorie has now.

V.

Frost played a kind of toddler's game with Marjorie in the hospital. As of the first of May, it was the only way he had spoken to her for a week. Her fever reached 110 degrees, the highest the Mayo Clinic had ever recorded. Her father took his hand and pressed it against her, slowly saying, "You," and then pressed it against himself and said, "Me," repeating the game for days. She acknowledged the game through her delirium on May 1. "All the same," she said with a slight smile—and then, with a slight frown, "Always the same."

In the third week of Marjorie's illness, a third doctor in Billings recognized her misdiagnosis. She in fact had childbed fever, a life-threatening bacterial infection, avoidable but for negligent hygiene on the part of the hospital in Billings. More than a hundred people volunteered to donate blood to her, most of them young men around Willard's age. The transfusions from roughly a tenth of them, the ones who had survived scarlet fever and developed antibodies similar to the ones Marjorie needed, were likely what kept her alive for weeks. Frost thought he had never imagined such an outpouring of "kindness and friendship." After reading about a bacteriologist at the Mayo Clinic who had developed a new treatment for conditions like Marjorie's, Frost arranged to have her flown there in a small plane along with a doctor and nurse. He did not think they had reason to hope, but he said he had hope in his soul. He drove east through snowstorms with Willard and Elinor.

Elinor marveled at her daughter's "pure and steadfast soul," her "courage and nobility." Frost found her courage the hardest thing to bear in his awe of it, saying, "No death in war could more than match it for suffering and heroic endurance." Marjorie passed away on May 2. "The noblest of us all is dead," her father wrote.

Elinor took a measure of comfort in Frost's saying that Marjorie's character made her dying easier for herself, as the Stoics counseled. She acted to the end as if "her ruling passion must have been to be wise and good," an example, he said, that counted against the anti-Romantic theory that the virtues of character evaporate without the structures and strictures of civilization. Still, Frost thought that he and Elinor would never be the same.

"Poor darling child!" wrote Elinor a month after Marjorie's death, back in South Shaftsbury. "It seems too heartbreaking, that after [sic] achieved good health, and finding perfect happiness in life, she had to lose it all so soon." Elinor was not sure how she could go on with her life but reminded herself, as she had in the immediate aftermath, that her husband depended on her. She reminded herself yet again in another letter to Edith Fobes:

> She wanted to live so badly, and yet she was so brave and noble.
>
> The pathos of it was too terrible.
>
> I long to die myself and be relieved of the pain that I feel for her sake.
>
> Poor precious darling, to have to leave everything in such a cruel and unnecessary way. I cannot bear it, and yet I must bear it for the sake of the others here.

The others there included Willard in his desperate state and the baby girl whom he and Marjorie had named Robin.

VI.

Frost marveled that everything his daughter had said in her delirious last days was "of an almost straining loftiness"; that she had been entirely herself, "grim ironical and noble." Her tone was the subject of one of the elegies he wrote for her, in which she inserts herself in the last line with a distinctive tone as in their toddler's game. She has only one line, but she has the last word. An early, untitled draft shows the poet wondering just how to write her part:

> Some things are never clear.
> But thanks to a clearing rain,
> The weather is clear tonight.
> The mountains are brought up near,
> The stars are brought out bright.
> Your sweet ~~concessional~~ ironical strain
> Would come in like you here
> "So ~~we won't~~ dont say nothing is clear"

"Sweet concessional" or "sweet ironical"? He eventually settled on "Your old sweet-cynical strain" and called the poem "Voice Ways," presumably for the way someone's voice can come to mind unbidden and bring with it a residue of indefinable character, one thing that's never clear. In the eight short lines of the poem, most as simple as something one would say to a child, we are made to expect an unfolding presence and clarity, as if something else would be brought near like the mountains, clear like the stars. Yet as the last lines of the poem reveal her, they also reveal the poem as an elegy, the clarified memory of her also clarifying her as a memory. His slow, deliberate poem gives her form, only to have her fade into formlessness, his grief calling her clearly to mind before she floats away.

VII.

Frost built another elegy for his daughter from a favorite line of his from the first canto of *In Memoriam*, "Let darkness keep her raven gloss." Tennyson's line is a plea to hold on to the feeling of suffering in extremis because the emotion of absolute loss retains a memory of what has been lost. "Let Love clasp Grief lest both be drown'd," pleads the canto. "Let darkness keep her raven gloss." Frost alludes to the line in "They Were Welcome to Their Belief," a little fabular mystery about compassion, whose definition Frost had twisted slightly from "suffering with" in a bleak letter in June to "only partly dying with those who die." Frost's letter on compassion had dispelled the idea that the experience had taught him and Elinor a thing. One is left to wonder what good it was for, a mystery like that of "They Were Welcome to Their Belief":

> Grief may have thought it was grief.
> Care may have thought it was care.
> They were welcome to their belief,
> The overimportant pair.
>
> No, it took all the snows that clung
> To the low roof over his bed,
> Beginning when he was young,
> To induce the one snow on his head.
>
> But whenever the roof came white
> The head in the dark below
> Was a shade less the color of night
> A shade more the color of snow.

Grief may have thought it was grief.
Care may have thought it was care.
But neither one was the thief
Of his raven color of hair.

The poem sounds like another lullaby. It has a similar meter to "Voice Ways"—a lulling three stresses per line—and takes the form of a just-so story and a mystery. The first revelations in the case rule out a pair of suspects—grief and care, who may think themselves guilty of the crime. Neither of them were, though: it happened along with "the snows that clung / To the low roof over his bed." Just so do we partly die with the dead by compassion. Our choice is not whether to grieve or whether to care but whether to accept the inevitability of suffering with. The first revelation at the end of the poem is of what the mystery had been all along: the identity of the thief (a trope of fairy tales) "of his raven color of hair." We had not known that his hair was raven once upon a time. The isolation of what has been lost preserves it in memory. The second revelation of the ending is stranger. We might have thought the thief was just the passage of time, but no, it is the appearance of snow on the roof, and even this is what coincides with the theft and not the culprit directly. Any easy formulation of snow also fails: it is not a symbol of grief or of care. We are told of a force in life that makes the story's protagonist gradually grayer—gradually more like a shade descended, as Frost described in his letter on compassion ("The spirit is only somewhat subdued and deadened [by compassion] so that when we have to die in full ourselves we wont have quite so far to descend into the valley"). We readers of the poem do not learn why we slowly turn into shades. We might have thought the just-so story was told to explain something past a child's comprehension. We learn that it could be beyond ours.

Frost wrote a third poem out of his grief for Marjorie that, like "They Were Welcome to Their Belief" and "Voice Ways," explodes its supposed simplicity in its last lines. The poems all startle the reader out of complacencies about grief or the dilution of grief into general sentiments. All three of the poems reveal an aspect of a person with a measure of clarity in the very end, when we know we will never hear another word about them. The third poem, "Moon Compasses," is something like another version of "Voice Ways"—eight lines, an interval at night with a mountain and no rain, the poems building from haze to clarity about a person who fades away as soon as they emerge. In "Moon Compasses," though, the person is also being held, the lover a shade along with the beloved.

MOON COMPASSES

I stole forth dimly in the dripping pause
Between two downpours to see what there was.
And a masked moon had spread down compass rays
To a cone mountain in the midnight haze,
As if the final estimate were hers,
And as it measured in her calipers,
The mountain stood exalted in its place.
So love will take between the hands a face. . . .

There is a startling shift in the poem's last line away from a scene developed in the first seven lines, giving a tell about what may have preoccupied the speaker elsewhere in the poem. Between this hint at preoccupations and the medical vocabulary of calipers and mask, the poem is about as autobiographically revealing as Frost could be.

The pathos of the last line is the doubleness of the analogy, a figure not only of embracing but of taking measure. Love will take between the hands a face like moon compasses because it will shine its proverbial light on someone beloved, as if, for the person who loves her, she glowed. Love is not entirely chosen, love is personal and not general. Love will take between the hands a face like moon compasses also because love would use what instruments it has to take the measure of a person in its hands like calipers. What fine instruments for expressing love or bringing a child into the world. What rough tools for grasping at a human soul.

"Sorrow is no more sorrow than it was before it struck us," began Frost's letter on compassion to his friend and colleague Otto Manthey-Zorn:

> It didnt need to be made personal for us to get the idea. The principle remains the same. We've been having it borne in on us by the general experience all along the way that compassion means only partly dying with those who die. We may never laugh as well again, but we shall live to laugh. We shall rejoice, if never again to the point of elation. But I was long since non-elatable. The spirit is only somewhat subdued and deadened so that when we have to die in full ourselves we wont have quite so far to descend into the valley.

"Be cheerful about us," he concluded. "It isnt as if we hadnt had time to learn from prose and poetry the perilous terms we live and love on."

VIII.

> When I am sometimes unjustly praised I accept it as making up for the other times when I have been unjustly blamed. Such is comedy. The only other way to take injustice is the way of tragedy. There I maintain my mystery for no one to pluck the heart out of.
> —ROBERT FROST TO SIDNEY COX, 1932

In a curious parallel, Frost employed a figure much like that in the last line of "Moon Compasses" in a very different poem from the period, "Two Tramps in Mud Time." The figure in "Moon Compasses" is of Love trying to focus its gaze on someone beloved, Love seeing and po-

tentially failing to see. When Frost returns to the focus of love in the end
of "Two Tramps in Mud Time," he returns once more to *focus*—not as
a dead metaphor, a synonym for "concentration" or "attention," but as
bifocal alignment, an operation largely automatic unless, as in "Moon
Compasses," the object of perception is too close or too far away. Frost
uses the figure in "Two Tramps in Mud Time" as a declaration of nothing
less than his sense of purpose, arrived at by way of a conversation with
himself after a pair of tramps come upon him chopping wood and one
of them lingers to watch. Self-conscious at being observed, Frost takes,
or says he takes, the tramp's silent presence as an assertion: "He wanted
to take my job for pay." The tramp does not have to say a thing to call
to Frost's mind the moral claims of Roosevelt's welfare state and Frost's
vexed and meandering assessment of those claims, conciliatory until his
resounding rejection in the last stanza:

> Nothing on either side was said.
> They knew they had but to stay their stay
> And all their logic would fill my head:
> As that I had no right to play
> With what was another man's work for gain.
> My right might be love but theirs was need.
> And where the two exist in twain
> Theirs was the better right—agreed.
>
> But yield who will to their separation,
> My object in living is to unite
> My avocation and my vocation
> As my two eyes make one in sight.
> Only where love and need are one,
> And the work is play for mortal stakes,
> Is the deed ever really done
> For Heaven and the future's sakes.

This astonishing leap from narration to declaration of faith is less surprising in light of the poem's main antecedent, a poem in Frost's own oeuvre that sketches out a theology placing paramount importance on the choices of the individual soul. Frost had used the double-ballad form of "Two Tramps in Mud Time" before only in that earlier poem, "The Trial by Existence," from *A Boy's Will*, which is also eight stanzas long. One can see the later poem as an elaboration of the faith of the earlier, placing not only choice but a specific sense of purpose at the heart of moral and religious life. The earlier poem goes so far as to proclaim that our lives are partly constructed by choices we make before birth and are destined to forget as our souls reinhabit the world for a lifetime. The later poem elaborates that making such choices in our lifetimes constructs our sense of our lives as fundamentally as being able to see. The earlier poem is about bravery, the later about an ideal altogether more complex and beautiful, uniting love and need in work that is play, in the bravery of play no less playful for its mortal stakes, in stakes no less mortal for feeling like play. Every line is dense enough to warrant a talk of its own:

> Only where love and need are one,
> And the work is play for mortal stakes,
> Is the deed ever really done
> For Heaven and the future's sakes.

One could rightly complain, as many did when the poem was published in Frost's sixth book of previously uncollected poetry, *A Further Range*, in the wretched economy of 1936, that the poet has used his oration on an ideal sense of purpose to change the subject away from the two tramps in need of work and possibly bread. Why feel no love for helping the tramps as he would help his own family member in need? The questions would recur in various forms for the rest of Frost's life as he increasingly took up national politics in his poetry, an extension of subject matter acknowledged in the volume's dedication to Elinor. Frost's views of socialism and the welfare

state would change subtly over the years, and his discussions of the issues involved would often be far more nuanced and insightful in private
than in his editorializing verse. Curiously, the view of socialism implied
in "Two Tramps in Mud Time," an Emersonian rejection of charity tout
court, sounds less like Frost's own view as of April 1934 than that of Elinor
in her bitter opposition to the New Deal. Frost was solicitous of passing
tramps in practice and employed relatively poor farmhands consistently in
later years. This raises the prospect that the tendentious change of subject
in conclusion was aimed not at winning an argument but at reconciliation
with "Prophetess" Elinor.

Did Frost write the poem, which he published in early October 1934,
after Marjorie's death? The evidence is inconclusive but suggestive. In addition to sharing a kind of figure with "Moon Compasses," "Two Tramps
in Mud Time" retraces in crystallized form almost all the ground that
Frost covered in his casual monologues in Billings on April 8 and 9.
Roosevelt and socialism; mercy and justice; the tendency of people out
in the country to lose themselves in observation of the people they come
across; tramps, their rights and our obligations to them; the tension between loyalties and ideals, loyalties being what Plato would have called
Eros, or Love, which he thought should be sacrificed for the needs of
society in the interests of ideal Justice; the idea that the greatest freedom
American society could grant to the individual was the freedom to create
what they could for themselves and could only create for themselves; that
this striving could save their souls and their sanity, was "play for mortal
stakes," "for heaven and the future's sakes." And what of his difference in
perspective with Elinor? Frost in 1937 would call her the whole of the end
of this poem. The reconciliation extended beyond their coming to see as
one in the conclusion of the poem. By its declarations, the poem would
affirm the worth not only of his work but of hers in her striving to align
love and need, respectively nurture and practical care in Elinor's work on
behalf of her family. The play was for mortal stakes. It was for heaven as
well as the future she could see.

There is yet a more deeply biographical sense in which Elinor might be said to be the whole of the end of the poem. To the author of "Twilight" four decades before, Love had been everything. Need obtruded. The poet found means to evoke his old ideal within the constraints of the world as it was, drawing in the person to whom they were spoken so as to intimate a kind of transcendence he never presumed. In this sense were love and need one in his poetry measured for Elinor's ear.

10.

THE WIND AND THE RAIN

OR:
The Fretful Poet and the Porcupine

———

I.

Elinor told Edna Davis Romig in a letter about the book they were printing of Marjorie's poems. "We think they are lovely," wrote Elinor from
Miami in February 1936. "We are having the little book privately printed
now, but it may come out with a publisher's imprint later. I think it will."
She and her husband wanted to spare the volume, *Franconia*, from public
discussion for the time being.

Frost and Elinor were wintering in Florida for the second year in a
row. The trip in their first year, to Key West, had been intended merely
for climatic relief from the illnesses the two often suffered in northern
winters. It did not seem to help Elinor, who spent the winter of 1935
in ill health, though pleased that the climate did more for her husband.
His fortunes were worse in Miami the following winter, where Elinor
spent the better part of a month caring for him while unwell herself. The
two had chosen Miami partly for climate and partly for Frost's lecturing

engagement at the Winter Institute of Literature at the University of Miami, where Frost met an outspoken fellow lecturer who would play an outsize role in the next years of his life.

Bernard DeVoto, a leading essayist of his generation, had impressed Frost with his writing for years. DeVoto's attachment to Frost was altogether more than admiration. After beginning to spend time with Frost in January 1936, he wrote to a friend that he had just "spent an average of five hours a day with the greatest living American." "I go tearful whenever I talk about him, so I won't try here," DeVoto wrote before talking about him:

> Whatever are the profoundest and most searching adjectives, those are the adjectives to use on Frost. He talks along, moderately, aimlessly, quietly, rather slowly, and you listen and pretty soon you notice some sparks, then a glow, then a blaze, then the incandescence of the interior of a new star. He is the quintessence of everything I respect and even love in the American heritage.

Their ways of carrying themselves were a study in contrasts despite their similarities in temperament. Each had an instinctive sense of human evil, a bad temper, a thin skin, and a chronic predisposition toward fear. Frost could often hide his fears behind a mask of charm and calm that suited his large, handsome face. DeVoto, small and snout-nosed, tended to project verbal aggression and animal strength. His mouth, like his pen, was a sword.

In Florida with Frost, the sword was sheathed. "I am not an inordinately silent man," he recounted, "but I hold my peace so long as Robert Frost is willing to so much as grunt." If DeVoto's reverence was not cause enough for deference—not to mention Frost's being older than DeVoto by twenty-three years—there was the force of Frost's energy. After objecting to a lecture DeVoto had given on the writer Sinclair Lewis, Frost was possessed: "He couldn't sleep for the ensuing eighteen hours and was constantly driving over or phoning over to convey new rebuttals." "He was like the sound of a horse shoe on iron," wrote DeVoto. "He was superb."

DeVoto, an untenured teacher in the English department at Harvard like his best friend, Ted Morrison, was thrilled to learn that Frost would be there in the spring, having been chosen to give the school's Norton lectures, a prestigious appointment that had gone to T. S. Eliot a few years before. DeVoto literally jumped to his feet on hearing the news.

A few days after leaving Frost in Miami, DeVoto reported that his wife, Avis, and Kay Morrison were helping him to find the Frosts a place in Cambridge. Frost had known Ted and Kay Morrison slightly before. Through DeVoto, they became his unofficial hosts, volunteering their house for receptions to follow his talks. The lectures were a great public success, their audiences overflowing the larger lecture hall DeVoto had persuaded the president of Harvard to hold them in, as well as an occasion for Frost to make the case for his aesthetic standards as against those of Eliot and Pound. The latter caught word of one of Frost's public slights, hearing from one of the people whom DeVoto called "the Amalgamated Adorers of Ezra Pound," and sent Frost what he described as "a really dreadful letter of abuse from Pound in which he complains of my cheap witticisms at his expense." Frost thought of writing back to say, "My contribution was the witticisms: yours the shitticisms." As ever, Elinor stayed home for the lectures and waited anxiously to hear how they went.

Shortly thereafter, Frost published *A Further Range* with a new kind of dedication to Elinor:

To E. F.

for what it may mean to her that beyond the White Mountains were the Green; beyond both were the Rockies, the Sierras, and, in thought, the Andes and the Himalayas—range beyond range even into the realm of government and religion.

It was a public gesture of a private conciliation. Her reaction against the New Deal had grown only more extreme, occasioning debates between her and her husband that would grow famous in family lore. She helped to persuade her husband, previously more skeptical than opposed, into opposition, voting like her for the Republican Alf Landon in one of the two states Landon carried in 1936.

The heart of Frost's objection to the New Deal was that its pursuit of "social justice" conflated the distinct goods of mercy and justice. Whether individual or social, justice was properly a matter of reasoned deserts while mercy never was. The social justice of the New Deal amounted to mercy, illogical kindness, bestowed on its recipient regardless of qualification. Frost granted that people needed some balance of mercy and justice but thought the New Deal risked an overemphasis on mercy. Frost's New Dealer friends Jeannette and Bill Snow protested on the example of all the mercies in the New Testament, to which Frost rejoined that he preferred the justice of the Old Testament, calling himself an "Old Testament Christian." Frost's letter to Bill Snow on Milton's conception of mercy, as articulated by the God of *Paradise Lost*, would inspire Frost's most ambitious verse of the early 1940s. The sources of Elinor's politics have sadly not been so well preserved. She feared fiscal profligacy and centralized state power. She seems also to have shared the prominent argument for the primacy of justice over mercy on the grounds that people living under a system of justice developed virtues of self-reliance and forbearance that life inevitably demanded. It was a bleak and lonely picture of life. One wonders how much it captured her own.

Released in June to great commercial success, *A Further Range* was rather less successful with critics. Many critics at the time were left-wing or properly Marxist and had less than kind words for Frost's forays into the realm of government. The criticism stung even after Frost received his third Pulitzer Prize for the book in the spring of 1937, and Frost granted DeVoto permission to defend him in writing after going back and forth on DeVoto's request for several months. DeVoto's essay appeared at the end of the year, forcefully prosecuting on charges of "asininity" three writers who had criticized *A Further Range* on Marxist grounds. The poet they attacked for not serving the cause of labor was the only poet in America who had not only captured the actual lives of the working poor but embodied the dignity of their lives in his writing, showing their everyday experience worth the observation of genius without condescension in the form of mockery or pity. More importantly, the writers had missed the point in judging poetry according to preordained judgments about what poetry needed to be. It was as if they could not see past their theories to the poetry under their noses that constituted "the only major affirmation that modern American literature has made": an affirmation of "the worth of the individual's experience" and the "infrangible dignity" of every human life. When Elinor read DeVoto's essay to her husband in Gainesville, Florida, on December 29, he was elated, as he let his friend know:

> I said to Sidney Cox years ago that I was non-elatable. While I wasn't actually fishing I suppose I hoped he might see I wanted to be contradicted. . . . After hearing all you said in my favor today, I tried it at the wistfullest I could command on Elinor. "What a lie," she answered. "You can't talk in public or private without getting elated. You never write but from elation."

Sad occasion had brought the family to Gainesville for the winter of 1937–38. Already at risk for heart attacks owing to her underlying angina, Elinor had an emergency mastectomy in Springfield, Massachusetts, at the end of September. Frost was painfully worried after the operation but resolved to shield her from his worry. Whether he knew that she had shielded him from hers in the past is unclear. "She's a brave one," Frost told Lesley. "She's been too brave. I have no doubt she will figure out for herself the danger she is in. But we are going to shut our eyes to it by agreement with the doctors." Frost told his daughter that he "[felt] to blame for being alive." "I have had almost too much of her suffering in this world," Frost told Louis, adding, "She has been the unspoken half of everything I ever wrote, and both halves of many a thing from My

November Guest down to the last stanzas of Two Tramps in Mud Time."
Frost told another friend, "You know how to read poetry and can tell
whom my poetry is all about." "I shall be taking her south soon," Frost
wrote to Ted Morrison. "She needs a long long rest."

Frost was especially vulnerable in letters to Ted from Gainesville that
winter. Ted sent Frost a draft of a review he had written of the book
DeVoto had used to cudgel Frost's detractors, *Recognition of Robert Frost*, a
collection of critical appraisals, to which Frost responded by begging Ted
not to follow his best friend Bernard in speaking ill of those who spoke
ill of Frost. Frost did not want too much made of them, the avant-gardists
of Marxism or Modernism, but wanted to be assured that his detractors
were wrong. He asked Ted to say so even if he did not believe it. "Merely
for mercy's sake regard me as a fiction to be kept up for the few years I
have left to live," signing his letter, "Your agéd old friend."

Ted in response wrote to assure Frost of the absolute sincerity of his
praise, which was born of veneration:

> You have no need of asking those whom you honor by calling them
> friends to help you maintain a fiction or support a pretense. Especially
> me. If I have not shown in ways more important than words that I ven-
> erate you and your poems, I do not know what language I can pluck out
> of the ether to convince you now. I quote you in the classroom and in
> private interviews with my students; I have your picture in my college
> study and on my mantel here at home; I feel my instincts fortified when
> they lead me along paths that you have helped to define and vindicate.

Left unvoiced by Ted were his reservations about Frost's social behavior,
as shared with Kay after a visit of Frost's to Bread Loaf in 1936. Though
"charming as ever," Frost "snipes and scandals about" and "can't resist
sneering at Eliot." "But he loves us, and is a great man still," wrote Ted,
adding, "By us, I mean you and me." Ted returned the affection in the
end of his response to Frost in February 1938, asking whether he and Kay

could drive up to Amherst in the spring. Frost responded by saying that
he and Elinor would expect them, clarifying, too, that he had not worried
about Ted's estimation of him in his letter but had merely despaired of
himself:

> I was the one I was bothered about, not you. You'd miss your guess if
> you thought that just because I dont despair of the republic and the
> universe I dont despair sometimes of
>   Yours truly
>   R.F.

It was a letter of someone whose sadness and fear had already bred self-
disregard, the testimony of a very worried man.

II.

In the course of a lifetime, Frost had published only one straightforward
poem about love. "A Prayer in Spring," from *A Boy's Will*, prays for seizing
the day, "carpe diem," a convention Frost had also played on in "Flower-
Gathering." In the more accurate translation of Horace's phrase, "carpe
diem" meant plucking the day as if it were a flower, taking pleasure from
the day instead of dwelling on the future. The poem asks that this be so:

> Oh, give us pleasure in the flowers today;
> And give us not to think so far away
> As the uncertain harvest; keep us here
> All simply in the springing of the year.
>
> Oh, give us pleasure in the orchard white,
> Like nothing else by day, like ghosts by night;
> And make us happy in the happy bees,
> The swarm dilating round the perfect trees.

And make us happy in the darting bird
That suddenly above the bees is heard,
The meteor that thrusts in with needle bill,
And off a blossom in mid air stands still.

For this is love and nothing else is love,
The which it is reserved for God above
To sanctify to what far ends He will,
But which it only needs that we fulfill.

The poem is a simple prayer for simple pleasure. "Oh, give us pleasure," it repeats; "And make us happy," too. It rhapsodizes on the white cherry blossoms like those of the orchard in Derry, revealing a hummingbird that rushes down to a blossom and hovers off it in a rapture of movement and stasis, bringing us pleasure in the flowers that our minds hover off like the hummingbird. After arresting us with such pleasure, the poem draws the moral to trust in our pleasure, trusting that the love we feel is fulfillment of the unknown ends of God.

Frost's second straightforward poem about love was an antithesis of the first, mocking its calls for pleasure and happiness. He sent "Carpe Diem" to Untermeyer from Gainesville in the middle of April, three and a half weeks after Elinor passed away from a heart attack and five days before her funeral in Amherst. "Carpe Diem" laments the impossibility of what "A Prayer in Spring" had prayed for, seeing from a ghostly remove the quiet young lovers he and Elinor were in the twilight.

CARPE DIEM

Age saw two quiet children
Go loving by at twilight,
He knew not whether homeward

Or outward from the village
Or (chimes were ringing) churchward.
He waited (they were strangers)
Till they were out of hearing
To bid them both be happy.
"Be happy, happy, happy,
And seize the day of pleasure!"
The age-long theme is Age's.
'Twas Age imposed on poems
Their gather-roses burden,
To warn against the danger
That overtaken lovers,
From being overflooded
With happiness, should have it
And yet not know they have it.
But bid life seize the present?
It lives less in the present
Than in the future always,
And less in both together
Than in the past. The present
Is too much on the senses
Too crushing, too confusing,
Too present to imagine.

The funeral was on April 22 in Johnson Chapel, Amherst College, on a Friday afternoon. Flowers were arranged around the bronze urn holding Elinor's ashes, the floral arrangements made earlier that afternoon by a group of women, faculty wives, led by a pair of Elinor's old friends. The youngest woman there, Katherine Canfield, showed up late and noticed a problem: there were too many flowers to fit neatly onto the altar. The problem bred disagreement, sides emerged, and with everyone talking at once, Katherine retreated and took a seat in a pew halfway down the aisle. Suddenly a hush fell over the room, and Katherine turned toward the chapel entrance to see what everyone was looking at: Frost.

> His face was drawn and pale, and he looked as if he had had no sleep. He was completely absorbed in his mission, his head bent looking at something small he held in his cupped hands. In the silence, and without removing his hat, he walked steadily and quietly up the aisle until he reached the platform on which the urn was resting. So intent was he that he looked neither to the right or left and seemed unaware of the presence of the ladies, now transfixed by what they saw.
>
> Then he reached down and placed what he held next to the urn. From where I sat I could see that it was a tiny clump of flowers, hepaticas, I guessed. He paused there for a moment with head bowed. Then he turned and, as silently and steadily as he had entered, left the Chapel without having uttered a word.

III.

Elinor had collapsed on the stairs in the house they were renting in Gainesville. A doctor came to treat her heart attack, and she suffered another and another. Her husband paced outside their bedroom all night and waited for her to call him in.

It would haunt him for years that she did not ask him to see her on her deathbed. He seems not to have thought that she was most likely in no state to ask. Shock followed shock as Lesley yelled at him for renting a place where her mother had to walk upstairs to sleep. In her anger, she told her father that artists should not have children.

Frost fell sick from exhaustion and lay in bed for a week. To Elinor's friend Alma Elliott and her husband, Roy, Frost's friend and former colleague, Frost described Elinor in the momentous terms prefiguring "The Silken Tent":

Pretty nearly every one of my poems will be found to be about her if rightly read. But I must try to remember they were as much about her as she liked and permitted them to be. Without ever saying a word she set limits I must continue to observe. One remark like this and then no more forever.

To his friend Hervey Allen, Frost quoted two passages from Tennyson. One was an abject pair of lines from his and young Lesley's old favorite "Morte d'Arthur," the lines lamenting the loss of King Arthur, which meant the loss of Camelot, which meant to him the loss of a world. "And I the last go forth companionless / And the days darken round me." The other line: "Let darkness keep her raven gloss."

When Frost invited DeVoto to her memorial service, his invitation had the uncanny clarity of mind of someone looking over a cliff he's falling off. "I expect to have to go depths below depths in thinking before I catch myself and can say what I want to be while I last," he wrote.

I shall be all right in public, but I can't tell you how I am going to behave when I am alone. She could always be present to govern my loneliness without making me feel less alone. It is now running into more than a week longer than I was ever away from her since June 1895. You can see how I might have doubts of myself. . . .

I suppose love must always deceive. I'm afraid I deceived her a little in pretending for the sake of argument that I didn't think the world as bad a place as she did. My excuse was that I wanted to keep her a little happy for my own selfish pleasure.

It is as if for the sake of argument she had sacrificed her life to give me this terrible answer and really bring me down in sorrow.

True to his word, Frost was fine in public. He and Lesley hosted a reception after the service at the Manthey-Zorns' house, where Frost was staying instead of his own place in Amherst. Though the mood at the reception was more sociable than funereal, it could hardly hide that Frost was out of sorts. He was resigning from Amherst after a half-imagined slight from the president and was thinking of cutting ties with his publisher as well. Frost did not know where he would live. He thought he might move to some town in New England with Lesley, getting a house for her and her two daughters with a separate wing for himself, where they could share one meal a day. Then again, he also said that he and Lesley hardly got along. He thought she acted like a social climber and said she had no sense—and still he did not consider living permanently with Carol or Irma. He retold old stories of his life to his biographer, Robert Newdick, with himself in the role of layabout where he was usually hero, his despair projected back into the past.

Otto drove Frost down to Derry to make arrangements to scatter Elinor's ashes in Hyla Brook. The two walked to the stretch of woods on the farm through which the brook ran, and Frost went to speak to the owner to see about buying that small plot of land. The owner struck Frost as entirely too excited about the prospect of having a shrine with Elinor's name to attract passersby to his farm stand. Frost took the urn back to the Manthey-Zorns' and then to South Shaftsbury.

Frost sold his house in Amherst back to the college. After leaving Otto's house in some acrimony over what seems to have been another half-imagined slight, Frost moved for the time being to the Stone Cottage with Carol and his family. Frost could compose himself for public performance but felt an inner void in private unlike anything before in his life. He shied away from the slightest of memories, felt estranged from the slightest of feelings. "I don't know myself yet and wont for a long time, if I ever do," Frost wrote to Untermeyer in May, at a loss for himself.

Frost stayed in South Shaftsbury for June and July, save for short trips to the Bread Loaf School of English—separate from the Writers' Conference—and to Untermeyer's farmhouse in the Adirondacks. "I have nothing left but work and ambition," Frost told Newdick on July 20. "But

I sometimes doubt I have even those. I show no disposition to work and I have only ambition when it is summoned by an audience present to get me talking." Frost wrote to Ted on July 29 to announce his plans to talk at the Bread Loaf Conference, which Ted directed, in August. "So I told Kay when she looked in yesterday to cheer me up."

IV.

Kay Morrison, née Johnston, was born in 1898 in Nova Scotia, where her Scottish father, Robert, served his first ministry in the Episcopal Church. The family returned to Scotland after five years in Canada, the reverend serving among the poor in his home country before receiving a prominent rectorship in Philadelphia in 1910. His wife being an invalid, Kay, the eldest, learned to manage the household from a young age. She remained in the area for college, attending Bryn Mawr from 1917 until 1921, where she met Frost when her literary society, of which she was treasurer, brought him to campus. She went to Oxford after college for a year of postgraduate study, a rare opportunity for any American. Enduring the privilege of long hours with Chaucer and Langland, discouraged by her own efforts at literature, she thought of "a glorious subject for some sort of tragedy": "the picture of a person tortured by the awful knowledge that his ambition far surpassed his ability." The recipient of her melancholy idea in a transatlantic letter was a junior at Harvard College, the handsome and literary Theodore Morrison, who would work alongside her at *The Atlantic Monthly* in Boston after his graduation in 1923. They married in 1927. Ted celebrated her character in relation to his on the eve of their wedding, writing with characteristic affection and loftiness and the distinctive ardor of marital rhapsody:

> I look up to you as a fixed star—my own star—from my own eccentric and faulty orbit. I mean, my sweet, that you seem to me to have steadiness and strength and beauty of nature such as I cannot hope to have.

Ted's sense of his own deficiency was no affectation. He worried already that a lack of inner direction and talent would prevent him from striking an original note in poetry, confining him to the old poetic music with which he was guilelessly in love. Though his premonition would prove itself accurate, Ted nonetheless enjoyed a fine literary career. It was, however, far from a rich one. As a teacher of English at Harvard and, as of 1932, director of the Writers' Conference at Bread Loaf, Ted earned more social prominence than remuneration. Kay continued to read fiction manuscripts for *The Atlantic* well after the birth of their first child, Robert, or Bobby, in 1930, and for the publisher Little, Brown until the day before the birth of their second child, Anne, in 1937. Kay's reverend father had been concerned for her worldly circumstances as she started a family, wondering how Bobby's future schooling would be provided for when Bobby was only an infant. Yet the elder Robert was no longer there to worry when his granddaughter was born. He had passed away after a car crash, his second, in May 1935, two hours before Kay arrived on the SS *Europa* to see him. Obituaries remembered the honorary canon of Washington Cathedral for his depth of humor, his love of the outdoors, his disdain for the trappings of "piosity" as against genuine piety, his "deep sensitivity for mankind beneath a brusqueness that would at first deceive those lacking in perception." Ted recalled a depth of admiration so strong for his father-in-law that he had a hard time expressing it in person. "I had the greatest enthusiasm for his mind and will, and felt myself drawn to him, as I do men of strong and deep feeling." A friend of the family's told Kay that a colleague of her late father's had called him "a poet—a poet of the love of God."

The man who would go on to suspect Kay of an Oedipal attraction to another Robert, Bernard DeVoto, was surprised at Bread Loaf in 1938 by Kay's walks in the woods. DeVoto's surprise was compounded by jealousy. Exceedingly fond of his best friend's wife, he put into words an infatuation with Kay's graces of character shared by a number of men at Bread Loaf. "Loyal, tender, warm," he wrote, "she is food for the hungry, drink

for the thirsty, shelter for the nightbound & wandering." Though capable
of passionate judgment, "she accepts you utterly." And here she was going
off on long walks in the woods with Robert Frost.

Surprised as he was by the situation, DeVoto was more surprised
by Frost himself. He drove Frost out for a hike on the first night of
the conference, only to have the drive interrupted by a porcupine in the
headlights, incurring Frost's wrath. "Robert said, 'I hate those bastards!'
and got out and chased it, yelling for a club. . . . That study in black and
white of America's greatest poet running hellbent behind his shadow over
the boulders and among the rock-maples of the main ridge of the Green
Mountains, and yelling oaths at the porcupine and me should be in somebody's book."

In the days ahead, Frost behaved like a creature of impulse. He drank,
swore, condemned himself, condemned others, confessed his sins, betrayed
his needs, complained petulantly and lectured masterfully. He struck out
alone for Bread Loaf Mountain on a Sunday at the end of August, cursing
his old friend Herschel Brickell when he tried to set forth upon his track,
and then turned around and asked Herschel to drive him out to Irma's
house in Hanover, leaving the conference suddenly and prematurely, only
to quarrel with Irma, finding her house inhospitable, and ask Herschel
for a ride back to Bread Loaf the next day in time to give the last talk
of the summer. Frost explained, in his friend's paraphrase, "that he went
away as a woman to let people know how bad he felt about everything."
Frost had always managed to intimate the movements of a turbulent depth
below a calm surface, his personality acting, like his poetry, as "a veil between [himself] and the rawness of life." The veil was gone. His friends
feared for his sanity.

A great deal of myth has accrued to Frost's behavior that August. To
this day, one need only mention Frost's name at the Bread Loaf Inn to hear
how he brazenly opened a newspaper in the front row of a poetry reading by Archibald MacLeish, or lit a match during the reading, or set the
newspaper on fire and needed help putting it out. The episode turned tall

tale in part because his behavior was genuinely startling for someone from whom people expected composure, in part because it was the rare instance of Frost's acting abjectly in public. Most of the drama in Frost's life was private, and most of his inner conflicts, when made public, were measured. Naturally, the exception draws attention, raising the question of what lies behind the veil otherwise. So much would be revealed on that score in the remaining years of Frost's life that one can hardly understand his earlier life and writing without it. In point of fact, though, the drama has been substantially overblown insofar as MacLeish was concerned. Frost criticized a poem of MacLeish's in front of an audience after MacLeish was done reading, a breach of decorum and an awful strain on the nerves of Ted and DeVoto. MacLeish had praised literalness in poetry and then read a poem about an air raid on a village in which the women of the village, instead of hiding like the men, stretched out their skirts for the bombers to see from above. Frost asked if such a thing would literally happen. He must have asked cruelly and at length, or he would not have sent Ted out into the rain twice to collect himself and courted a "rebuke" from DeVoto (his word), but Frost was not bad enough to prevent MacLeish from sitting with Frost on a couch after the reading, each man with an arm around the young writer in between them, recent Amherst graduate Charles Foster, while DeVoto reclined at their feet. Frost confessed a grievance: other poets taking credit for the literal turn in Anglo-American poetry around 1910, which he thought was his doing. MacLeish assured Frost that everyone knew that. "I'm an old man," said Frost. "I want you to say it, to say it often. I want to be flattered." When MacLeish tried to make the conversation less personal, Frost said, "God-damn everything to hell so long as we're friends, Archie," after which Archie reassured him once again.

The other myth accruing to that summer at Bread Loaf was Frost's doing. It surrounds something DeVoto said to him in anger to the effect of, "You're a good poet, Robert, but you're a bad man." That DeVoto said something like that is likely, but that he said it with the finality Frost remembered is very much not. Frost would tell the story in later years as the break in their relationship, not mentioning, perhaps not remembering, that DeVoto and his family visited Frost days after parting at Bread Loaf and Frost tried to give DeVoto a house for his family to use seasonally. The houses were in Concord Corners, Vermont, a mountain hamlet twenty miles north of Franconia in which Frost and Elinor had acquired property only one year before, including a house on a hilltop overlooking a lake. Frost also wanted DeVoto to buy a house across the lake from his. DeVoto could afford to buy it, he wrote, "but I don't think I will."

Though DeVoto got along easily with Frost in Concord Corners, DeVoto felt a bad migraine that he attributed to guilt over having gotten mad at the man he saw as his "father image." Perhaps the pain was also the shattering of an idealization. The greatest living American seemed to have fallen from grace. "These are terrible days for people who reverence him," DeVoto wrote in early September, before visiting Frost. "He breaks down into about equal parts willful child, demanding child, jealous woman, and mere devil." "I feel," DeVoto wrote, "as though God had milled and bolted me." "Frost's demon is loosed."

V.

Writing to Kay from Concord Corners before the visit from DeVoto, Frost compared himself to an ocean. "I am," he wrote, "like an ocean that in its restlessness may have brought up every imaginable shape to the surface, but won't be satisfied till it brings up the sea serpent." The serpent to which Frost referred was a mysterious force he hoped was a creative impulse in embryo: "Let us pray the sea-serpent I feel so big with and about may prove to be a poetic drama." He had described himself of late as like a drowning man who sees his life before his eyes.

Frost had left Kay a few days before with the plan to move to Boston soon and employ her informally as amanuensis. Sad to be apart from her and Ted ("Tears in my heart when I left you people"), Frost imagined them in the house across the lake:

> I wish you were in the house I am looking at over there above the lake where it in turn looks at the White Mts across the lake. It's a place I have had in mind for you if you werent so bound to Chester [in Vermont].

"Since you wont have it as a loan," he wrote, "I am going to sell it to Benny."

"You two rescued me from a very dangerous self when you had the idea of keeping me for the whole session at Bread Loaf," Frost wrote. "I am still infinitely restless, but I came away from you as good as saved."

It was Frost's first week alone since Elinor's death. The week would bring confusion and mania, rage and gratitude, absolution and fear, serenity and elemental tumult. The wind cut like a knife on his hilltop even on the wind's stiller days. Frost proclaimed, "I am where the wind never ceases blowing 'Cloe and I are not sorry at all,'" alluding to an old line of verse about waywardness and the refusal of regret. Frost wrote an angry letter to Lesley and another retracting it the next day. He wrote a letter to Untermeyer in bafflement at how he had behaved since Elinor's death. "I've been crazy for the last six months," he wrote. "I havent known what I was doing." With the wind and his mind never ceasing, Frost resembled no one so much as King Lear.

Here he was, an old man wild with grief, afraid for his sanity, possessed by his memories. He had been puerile and labile, unable to contain himself in public with the dignity befitting his station. He was newly unaccommodated, with no family with whom he felt he could live. He had even followed Lear in going to his second-eldest daughter's (Irma's) and leaving after he took quick offense, and in getting angry with his eldest daughter (Lesley) and quickly retracting it. He was like Lear in the storm in the third act of the play, with Lear in beggar's clothes as Frost suggested he wear in his letter to Untermeyer. "Blow, winds," calls Lear in the second scene of act 3 as he calls forth the "hurricanoes" to rain on his head. Shortly afterward, his young Fool sings a song of "the wind and the rain" before making a prophecy. Frost would write a poem called "The Wind and the Rain" about prophetic songs by young poets fated to grow old with what they have foretold.

"The Wind and the Rain" is like nothing else in Frost's art. For him, it is naked. It is Frost in beggar's clothes in the storm, a confessional poem by a poet who confided but never confessed. Its form, likewise, is singularly raw by Frost's standards in the sense that its ideas are inscrutable from the poem itself, relying instead on a dense fabric of allusions to poems by himself and by others. As the veils of personality and form wore away, the veil of allusion held his thoughts together as it did through the worst of his grieving. The poem's ample precedents reveal a mind plagued no less by self-recrimination for its loss of self-knowledge, a man holding himself responsible for the suffering around him although confused about his own complex of feelings, therefore confused about what he can't help but feel, the measure of the commitments of his soul, which, thrown off, calls into doubt the relations in which his soul stands.

"The Wind and the Rain" consists of two numbered sections, the only such poem in Frost's oeuvre. Its numbering alludes formally to the poem that served as its formal model, Coleridge's incomparable "Dejection: An Ode," from 1802. The ode is, like Frost's poem, unsettling in its lyric composure on the subject of personal breakdown, and stirring in its mental drama of the interplay between inner and outer sources of energy, specifically water. The poems are both about habits of mind that lead to incapacities of feeling that distort creative powers that, once altered, strain the role imagination plays in bonds of love. The poems both end on hope for renewal by means of howling rain at night.

The first section of "The Wind and the Rain" recalls the youthful composition of a poem that has come to feel like a prophecy.

I

That far-off day the leaves in flight
Were letting in the colder light.
A season-ending wind there blew
That as it did the forest strew
I leaned on with a singing trust
And let it drive me deathward too.
With breaking step I stabbed the dust,
Yet did not much to shorten stride.
I sang of death—but had I known
The many deaths one must have died
Before he came to meet his own!
Oh, should a child be left unwarned
That any song in which he mourned
Would be as if he prophesied?
It were unworthy of the tongue
To let the half of life alone
And play the good without the ill.
And yet 'twould seem that what is sung
In happy sadness by the young
Fate has no choice but to fulfill.

With the season turning, wind blowing, leaves blown, and Frost on "that far-off day" letting the wind drive him "deathward," singing of death, Frost has conjured the scene of "My Butterfly." No butterfly is mentioned. In describing the scene but not letting us share in it, the recollection is the opposite of an elegy. Rather than preserving the interior without the exterior, Frost recalls himself as if from outside, estranged from himself as in "Carpe Diem." His tone of recollection is wistful but abstracted. He returns to the scene of inspiration to call its fruits into question. Was it worthwhile to play the ill with the good, to pursue a life of verse, if it meant "That any song in which he mourned / Would be as if he prophesied"?

Frost's sense of misgiving is easy to understand biographically. It shares the retrospective futility of "Carpe Diem" and of Frost's new life story as good-for-nothing. His misgiving is a variation on the attack of Lesley's that would trouble him for years, on the harm done by being an artist. Literarily, the misgiving is harder to formulate. Frost laments clearly enough that his writing has cost him the capacity for unadulterated emotion, lamented also in Coleridge's "Dejection." "And yet 'twould seem that what is sung / In happy sadness by the young / Fate has no choice but to fulfill": a habit of finding happiness in sadness would make him fated to insulate himself from true sadness. It was the only use of the word "fulfill" in Frost's poetry since "A Prayer in Spring," a prayer for pure emotion proportional to his love for his wife, which was what "Carpe Diem" said he had never fulfilled. The associations cohere as habits become character and character is fate, but Frost charges his style of mourning not merely with effects on himself but with the burden of prophecy. He seems to be looking for ways to blame himself and finding them in his old inspiration for "My Butterfly" and "Twilight," Shelley's "Ode to the West Wind" with its climactic prophecy. It was a return to the idealism of *Twilight* in a dark mirror, from which he prayed for a reprieve by means of rain.

II

Flowers in the desert heat
Contrive to bloom
On melted mountain water led by flume
To wet their feet.
But something in it still is incomplete.
Before I thought the wilted to exalt
With water I would see them water-bowed.
I would pick up all ocean less its salt,

And though it were as much as cloud could bear
Would load it on to cloud,
And rolling it inland on roller air,
Would empty it unsparing on the flower
That past its prime lost petals in the flood,
(Who cares but for the future of the bud?)
And all the more the mightier the shower
Would run in under it to get my share.
'Tis not enough on roots and in the mouth,
But give me water heavy on the head
In all the passion of a broken drouth.

And there is always more than should be said.

As strong is rain without as wine within,
As magical as sunlight on the skin.

I have been one no dwelling could contain
When there was rain;
But I must forth at dusk, my time of day,
To see to the unburdening of skies.
Rain was the tears adopted by my eyes
That have none left to stay.

In the symbolic world of the poem, rain is a relief from the writing of
poetry and, by extension, from the very act of imagination. Wind becomes
song via breath; to inspire is etymologically to breathe in; and to make a
poem is mythologically to pass the wind through the reeds. Rain in the
poem is distinct—inarticulate, inexpressive. Rain destroys and preserves,
as Frost makes a drama of in a sonnet hidden in the last fourteen lines
of the first stanza in the second section, from a deluge to "the passion of
a broken drouth" (a drought relieved for land and man). These poles of

destruction and sustenance draw a conspicuous contrast to Shelley's ode, the canonical Romantic ode to the wind's inspiration, and to Frost's old poem about his desire to join by imagination with his butterfly as Shelley does the wind. Frost's wish is not, like Shelley's, for an expansion of creative powers but for their cessation. This stands in contrast, too, with Coleridge's sonnet, which the last section of his ode comprises, Coleridge praying for the renewal of clear "passion" by means of renewed powers of imagination. Frost prays for "passion" without imagination. He wants a purity of feeling his art had made him incapable of.

And yet Frost's wish for imaginative vacancy—at dusk, after twilight—coexists with an altogether different climate of feeling characterized less by sorrow than by unrestraint. That countervailing mood, too, has a poetic source. "The wind and the rain" as a phrase appears twice in Shakespeare—in the Fool's song in *King Lear* and in the final passage of *Twelfth Night*, a favorite play of Frost's whose opening line he had mentioned in a talk in late August. The song in *Twelfth Night* rounds out a scene of two weddings and the betrayal of the Puritan Malvolio. Just so was Frost torn between elated relief and uneasiness in his feelings toward Kay. "The Wind and the Rain" alludes to the appearance of the phrase in both plays, as Frost alluded to different readings of the Song of Songs in "The Silken Tent" at about the same time.

In the absence of self-knowledge, Frost's dual allusion to Shakespeare points to two ways of guessing at himself. Was he Lear in abjection of loss or among the improbably bound in the end of *Twelfth Night*, unions leaving another man in cursed sorrow as Frost's surely would? Or did he find himself in both relations at once?

"The Wind and the Rain" carries the tones of both plays in its restless ocean of feelings. It has the slapdash exuberance of *Twelfth Night* and the elemental howling of Lear calling the heavens down on his own head. The feelings are balanced within a metrical composure like that of Coleridge's ode, the extremity of emotions balanced against an ostentatious restraint of expression until the form begins to break down at poem's end, its stray lines like bits of clay chipped off a finely glazed vessel. No pattern emerges. For once in Frost's verse, the form breaks. The lines alternate between Learian chagrin ("And there is always more than should be said," which was Cordelia's point to begin with) and the intoxication of the play named after the festival of Twelfth Night. After playing the good with the ill, Frost ends the poem in yet another perspective, the Coleridgean dejection he started from. He seems to make a simple prayer for clarity of feeling, sensation and emotion and expression all aligned in his adoption of tears from the rain. Yet the tense of his prayer is retrospective, implying in the slightest way that he had gotten what he called for. All it took was failing to stay his every tear until he had none left.

Frost set out for Boston on September 21. The train he boarded in Springfield was thrown off its route by a hurricane, later called the Great New England Hurricane, the region's largest storm in living memory.

II.

Blake's Picture

I.

As Frost was disavowing all interest in purely idealized love in the fall of 1938, he was proclaiming an idealized devotion to Kay with something like the same pen stroke. "I am yours in a very noble sense," he pledged to Kay from a midnight train bound for Columbus in October, his testament written within a day or two of disclaiming all such nobility to DeVoto. It was perhaps unsurprising that Frost's letter to Kay was redolent of language like that in "The Silken Tent," and was most likely sent with the poem attached. In its endless ambiguity of sacred and sexual love, the poem stands as a figure not only for Frost's roiling inner conflict of loyalties between his lost wife and his new beloved but, however unwittingly, for the factual ambiguity at the heart of his new relationship. Which part of Frost's self-contradiction was the truth?

The problem is deceptively hard to resolve. Frost's stories would be less than consistent between different confidants, and would often be told by intimation rather than outright assertion. Kay's testimony was often as ambiguous as Frost's. Much evidence has been lost on both sides, including the countless letters that Kay wrote to Frost and a great many that Frost wrote to Kay. She set different boundaries with Frost at different times, especially in the early years of their intimacy. One can read between the lines of Frost's letters to see her setting limits he chafed at without knowing what limits she set. Their conflicting testimonies would take different shapes across time, facts and motives are hard to sort out, and third parties would be something other than impartial witnesses to the drama that the present work will describe in due course. These caveats notwithstanding, there was one basic disagreement in the contested history: Did they or didn't they? He said yes and she said no.

The disagreement over the terms of their intimacy had different implications for different stages of the relationship. Her visit in the summer of 1938 was an act of solicitude on her account and, on his, a tryst. His urging her over the next couple of years to leave her husband was on his account an effort to bring their love into the open, like his efforts to persuade her to let him share his passion openly in letters. On his account, these were requests for transparency. On hers, they were signs of delusion, their love affair a fantasy Frost conceived in his depths of mental disequilibrium after Elinor's death. This was also what most people close to Frost seem to have made of the early years of the relationship. Louis told Frost in November 1938 how pleased he was that Kay was there for "friendship and affection"—and this from Frost's most regular confidant and someone for whom fornication and ribaldry were matters of both enthusiasm and habit. To a third party, Louis described Frost's attachment as a kind of psychopathology, a "complex" and an "unchecked wish to possess her, to make her his mother-mistress-nurse." Though threatened by the relationship, the worst DeVoto would believe for years was that it constituted "psychical adultery," Kay standing as "symbol of an impotent desire." It is worth taking seriously the theory that Frost was imagining things, just as it is worth trying to take Frost at his word.

Most surviving evidence readily fits either story. Consider a poem of

sexual persuasion Frost most likely wrote in the fall of 1938 and implausibly dated to his courtship of Elinor to obscure its obvious addressee. "The
Subverted Flower," initially "The Inverted Flower," was a poem about
what Frost called "frigidity in women," taking place between a girl and
her suitor. The suitor's entreaties are comically imposing, literally bestial,
making the girl afraid that the brute is set to pounce. The disproportion-
ate extent of her fear serves to imply that others in her position were being
similarly unreasonable even if they did not think they were. The poem
is not shy in its didactic import: the girl is cruel in her fear of the man's
"tender-headed flower" as he holds it out to her, the girl unable to see past
the distortions of "her own too meager heart." One can readily guess at
the heart for whose edification the poem was intended, but one can only
wonder whether it was intended for persuasion during a lull in sexual
intimacy or in the absence of it to begin with.

That Kay was the most important person in Frost's life in its last
quarter century is obvious. Less obvious is her importance to understanding his first sixty-four years, but one can hardly understand his life's first
two acts without accounting for her place in the third and final one. This
is because Frost's last act was full of testimony that potentially sheds light
on everything that precedes it—testimony by Kay more than anyone else,
in the form of a single confessional letter. Yet this account of her experience with Frost is, on inspection, as hard to pin down as her relationship
with Frost, which itself stands as a mystery within the broader mystery
of Frost's character and earlier life. Her letter would have profound implications for the person most responsible for telling the story of Frost's
life, who would become all too intimately involved with her and Frost's
relationship in Key West in the winter of 1940.

Frost in his third act was to his earlier life and work as apostle to
prophet, trying to make sense of himself. Having been largely private, he
was open. His Boswells proliferated. Having achieved almost everything
of significance that he would achieve in poetry, he continued trying to
articulate and refine the ideas that had been implicit in his earlier work.

Fruits of this effort were apparent not only in his didactic verse but in any number of lectures, letters, and private talks with the growing number of people whom Frost held in confidence and who thought to keep a record of Frost. This later Frost, who has had an incalculable influence on the Frost whom posterity remembers—this storyteller driven in the early years after his wife's death to extremes of grief and self-laceration and even to the edge of madness in the impression of people close to him—to what extent was the Frost who emerged in his later reflections and relationships a distortion of who he had been and to what extent a revelation of what he always thought was true?

II.

The first revelation after Elinor's death was also the most shocking: Lesley's condemnation of her father. That Frost's eldest daughter thought he should not have had children is testimony that stands to shed light on his earlier life if anything is. Frost felt all too acutely that her charge had truth in it, and it became a rueful touchstone for his own memories of his long life as father and husband. Yet one would be hard-pressed to find signs that she felt this way before the shock of her mother's passing. She and her father were, in some ways, unusually close, which may have been part of the problem.

By some unmeasurable admixture of emulation, education, and genes, Lesley was, like her father before her, an aspiring writer with a strong will, faith in her own sensibility, and, perhaps consequently, a hard time conforming to academic formality. The institutional study of literature was for each of them in their youth like an institutional church whose preoccupation with the hollow forms of ritual distracted from the substance of religion. Frost recognized their similarity, occasionally warning her not to take after his own youthful tendencies but mostly encouraging and guiding her with the principles of a lifetime spent at the edge of literary and educational institutions and social groups. The important thing, he told her, was to lead "a literary life . . . honestly and not in pretense." "Write, write," he urged, "for this is all there is."

The path of her life followed her father's closely—a hodgepodge of jobs through her twenties and into her thirties along with scattered journalism in a period of protracted apprenticeship. She, too, wrote genre fiction at this stage of her career, hers not poultry fiction but a detective novel called *Murder at Large*, published in 1932. ("Such grand writing," her father wrote on the proofs, along with "Intensities of imagined scene [you grew up on this]." His chief criticism was that the writing was too good for its genre.) When Lesley, with young children to feed, took a teaching job at Rockford College in Illinois in 1934, it was a more distinguished version of her father's starting work at Pinkerton to support his young family, though Lesley did benefit in her appointment from having for a college president the young Gordon Chalmers, who was, like his wife, Roberta, a close friend of her father's and his ardent admirer. Lesley at Rockford clashed with credential-proud professors as her father had at Pinkerton, leading her father to wonder how he and his mother and daughter had all ended up at the "ragged edge of the profession," teaching without proper degrees, employed by schools but "hang[ing] round them unwanted." This was the stage in Frost's career in which he overcame his detractors and distinguished himself first in teaching and then, spectacularly, in literature. Lesley would have to wait for success. Aside from whatever else might have caused the discrepancy, only one of the two spent that stretch of their respective careers caring for two children on their own—a different kind of problem for an artist having children.

A representative letter of the period is one that Lesley wrote to her father in the winter of 1935. She was grateful for his praise of an article she had written. She shared her accomplishments at the cultural center she ran. She was tired and lonely, and her nerves were frayed. "There's so much to talk about I'm bursting with it and letters don't seem to help much."

As she prepared to leave Rockford in 1936, her father proposed that they collaborate on a textbook. She planned to write his biography, too. In 1937, living with her daughters in Mexico—she was an inveterate traveler, especially to Spanish-speaking countries—Lesley wrote a preface to her father's poetry. He told her in September 1937 that he had yet to read it, not having "had the heart to hear my praises at a time when I feel to blame for being alive." He asked Lesley not to let on to her mother the danger she remained in after her operation, and to keep a brave face in keeping with her mother's bravery. They gathered in Gainesville. Elinor counted twenty-three cloudless days in February, with the dogwoods and azaleas in bloom.

If Frost had the slightest preconception before Elinor's death that Lesley harbored deep judgments against him, no evidence to this effect survives. Nor does any record survive of his judgments against her while her mother still lived. Perhaps their long-stifled thoughts were brought to the surface, or perhaps their feelings were disfigured in the suddenness of grief. Perhaps Lesley took out her frustration of the past several years over being the daughter not of any artist but of this artist under whose shadow she had to exist and to whose achievements she still owed her own opportunities, however resentfully. In any case, her charge stuck.

Frost began to keep a measure of separation from Lesley, for which he apparently overcompensated by being entirely too open in his letters to her. "You are late in overcoming your selfconsciousness in writing," he wrote to Lesley in an enthusiastic but uncharacteristically critical letter as she approached a new success in writing with a collection of children's stories that would soon be published with an introduction by Untermeyer. Frost spoke to the subtext of the creative aspirations she had harbored for decades: "You have me to get over."

On March 1, 1939, Frost fell into an extreme of emotion after chancing upon an old letter of Elinor's to Lesley from her first year at Wellesley. In thinking back on their old life together, he declared himself "a jester about sorrow," like the old king's Fool, in response to Elinor's unadorned sorrow:

> My, my, what sorrow runs through all she wrote to you children. No wonder something of it overcasts my poetry if read aright. No matter how humorous I am I am sad. I am a jester about sorrow. She colored my thinking from the first just as at the last she troubled my politics. It was no loss but a gain of course. She was not as original as I in thought but she dominated my art with the power of her character and nature. I wish I hadnt this woeful suspicion that toward the end she came to resent some thing in the life I had given her.

This last had been Lesley's devastating charge, coupled here with a terribly bleak account of Elinor's suffering. That, too, is a piece of retrospective testimony found nowhere in her lifetime. It would seem to take her apotheoses of grief as her normal state, as if she were Tennyson's Priestess of Sorrow. Yet it is what Frost remembered in his own bleakness of grief, a memory impossible to assess with any certainty given Elinor's privacy and the paucity of the record she left. He did not have her to contradict him in his overstatement, and neither do we.

Lesley was measured in her letters where her father was effusive. She found him in crisis hard to bear, exhausting and inexhaustible, and diagnosed him with a persecution complex. Still, she was disappointed on March 2 to learn that her father had come up from Florida through Washington, D.C., without stopping to see her for even a few hours. "With several things that need talking out rather than writing out I feel quite frustrated!" she wrote. "And I wanted to see how tan you were."

III.

One close observer of Frost's life was especially skeptical of the stories he began to tell about his past after Elinor's death. Yet Frost's relationship with this careful witness, Robert Newdick, the preeminent chronicler of his life to date, was at the point of dissolution in March 1939. This owed something to fate and something to Newdick's belief in him.

On his most recent visit with Newdick in Columbus, Ohio, Frost had written a fateful letter to DeVoto beginning, "Being out here with my faithful biographer inevitably puts me on the defense of my native badness." Frost had indeed spent his visit to Ohio retelling the story of his marriage with himself as the villain, as he had retold the story of his life after the funeral with special emphasis on his own failures and fecklessness. Despair would seem to have hardened to guilt. "I am a bad bad man," Frost wrote to DeVoto with reference to "changes coming over me this summer" and a love of imperfection on record "in To Earthward and indeed elsewhere for the discerning." Frost impressed upon DeVoto that his badness "may throw light on every page of my writing for what it is worth." Frost's faithful biographer was unpersuaded by this revisionist history, as he told Sidney Cox in November 1938, shortly after Frost left:

> Over and over he told me, with illustrative examples, with what he regarded as illustrative examples, what a "bad" fellow he'd been, how "unmoral" if not indeed "immoral." So I know he wants that streak made patent. . . . Yet I do think (and I'd like to know whether you agree) that right now, and since Elinor's death and L's [Lesley's] lambasting him, he's overly insistent on the shadows.

Frost's tales of his own villainy were not altogether consistent. He praised Elinor's mental strength and firmness in superlative terms ("Elinor's a fine mind. R never encountered a better: clear, hard, no compromise"), and yet he said he broke her resolve. He remembered Elinor's passionate approval of their friends Bill Snow and his wife, Jeannette, for standing for poetry rather than money but could not believe that she had come to this conviction on her own, even though this was among his clearest points about her on the record as he described her to Louis in 1917, saying, "She seems to have the same weakness I have for a life that goes rather poetically." Such was Newdick's impression, as he shared in a letter to Frost after Elinor passed away: that in the "unutterable closeness" of Frost's and Elinor's lives Newdick "saw with joy a realization of the ideal most dear to me in my own life." He considered Elinor the most important influence in Frost's life.

Frost came to harbor a number of doubts about Newdick after the trip to Columbus, prompting Frost to issue the other Robert a friendly but paradoxical warning:

> I'll never forget my visit with you—what I said to you and what you said to me. The point I tried to make was that I was a very hard person to make out if I am any judge of human nature. I might easily be most deceiving when most bent on telling the truth.

This was followed by a remark in March 1939 to the Roberts' mutual friend John Holmes that Frost thought he needed "a showdown" with Newdick. Frost worried that Newdick's tenure clock would force him to rush the biography, and worried, too, that sharing the personal experiences of a lifetime, the raw material of his poetry, would make them cease to be properly his.

Frost's concerns about Newdick hardly conjure the version of his biographer that Frost would remember after he passed away, a kind of academic sycophant possessed of no judgment. Some of Frost's problems with Newdick plausibly owed to the tension between the way Newdick saw him and the way Frost had come to see himself. Some problems, too, owed something to Newdick's self-presentation, which verged into adulation and obsequiousness. But Newdick was not undiscerning. He noticed a number of Frost's flaws about which he said nothing to Frost. Newdick persisted in his impression of Frost not because he lacked his own judgment but because he loved Frost for who he thought Frost was. It was something Frost would hardly suspect at the time, believing as he did that he had hardly been worthy of love.

As it happened, the story of Frost's life would be lodged in public memory before Newdick's papers were brought to the public. Frost learned of Newdick's death in early July 1939. "My God, Sir," wrote Newdick's colleague to Frost, "that book was his life. And he worshipped its subject. In his last delirium he talked constantly of Robert Frost—not the book, but the man."

Within days of hearing from Newdick's colleague, Frost invited another adulatory young scholar up to Ripton to advise him on Newdick's papers, which Newdick's widow, Marie, wanted to sell. On Marie's visit to Frost shortly thereafter, she told him that her husband's last words were Frost's name.

IV.

Into this context entered the young man who would be Frost's biographer. Though he had known Frost slightly before, their intimacy began after Frost had grown convinced of his own badness. Larry Thompson, starry-eyed after being called up to Ripton to advise Frost on how to handle Newdick's materials, was in no position to doubt what Frost told him about his love affair with the woman set to spend summers in the farmhouse downhill from his little cabin in Ripton. These contingencies of Larry's perspective would have a long afterlife.

Of less consequence was Larry's being in no position to appreciate just what Frost's discovery of Ted Morrison's poem in *The Atlantic* meant to him. Frost read the poem, "The Schism," as a testament to the sexlessness of Ted and Kay's marriage, which was a source of profound psychic relief, as Frost would tell Louis that fall:

> I was confronted with the paradox of overlapping loves; for which nothing in psychology seemed to me to provide. The poem in the Atlantic

resolved the puzzle. It proved that what couldn't be wasn't. And I was
over my craze.... And now it has come about that I owe my restoration
to selfrespect and confidence in my judgement of what would be going
on in the mind of a lady.

It was Frost's most direct account of his psychic turmoil in the year between falling in love with Kay and discovering Ted's poem. He loved Kay.
He was sure she loved him. He did not understand how someone could
be in love with two people at once. She could not still be in love with her
husband. She was not.

Frost called "The Schism" a scholar's poem while "To Earthward"
was a true love poem. It had been among Elinor's favorites. Frost would
not read it in public. One night that summer as Larry and Louis were
talking to Frost, Louis took to defending sexual explicitness in literature
and Frost demurred. He said that if anyone wanted to know how to work
sexual references into their writing, they should read "To Earthward."
Frost proceeded to read the poem with what Larry later recalled as "a
gorgeous crescendo of emotion. When he finished it, his eyes were full
of tears."

Frost returned to Boston in the fall and began his teaching appointment as Ralph Waldo Emerson Fellow at Harvard, a position arranged
by Frost's friends and funded by alumni. Frost's semester was cut short
by a medical condition, cystitis, which turned into something far more
serious over the holiday. The psychiatrist and sonneteer Merrill Moore, a
friend of Frost's in Cambridge, happened to call Frost one day and, hearing something off on the phone, went over to check on him, finding him
alone in a maddened state of pain so severe that he thought he might die.
Moore thought Frost might well have died had he not happened to call.
Once in the hospital, Frost merely needed a hemorrhoidectomy, a major
procedure if not a life-threatening one. Frost had a "gastro-enteric attack,"
Kay reported, "and went out of his head alone."

The Associated Press ran a short piece on January 12, 1940, with the headline "Poet Robert Frost Issues Own Bulletin from Hospital Bed." The bulletin read, "Mr. Frost is resting on his laurels after a legal operation at the hands of Dr. Henry Faxon." "I hear you are resting comfortably on your laurels," wrote Larry to Frost in early February. "When do you take off for Key West?" Larry asked, adding, "I'm r'aring to go."

V.

A month later, after Larry had gone down to Key West and come back with a very different impression of Frost, Kay answered Larry's urgent letter of advice on how to manage Frost's "truly pitiable dependence" on her. Her letter is far and away her most negative about Frost on the record. As her only surviving confession, it potentially stands to reveal not only what she suffered privately in her relationship with Frost but what anyone suffered in romantic intimacy with him. It may be a revelation of what Elinor had suffered in silence. Kay began her letter by responding to Larry's report on Frost's teeth.

She was less concerned than Larry about teeth as a cause of cystitis. She would nonetheless persuade Frost to go back to the doctor, assuaging his reluctance by telling him he could get a new set of dentures before he got his old teeth removed. It would help with the "fatigue, depression, and general irritability and a lot of rheumatism" that his bad teeth were causing him. Then she turned to the other part of Larry's letter.

Larry had warned her that her arrangement with Frost had the potential to ruin her marriage. He had puzzled over how she could possibly sustain her own life while managing a man absolutely dependent on her; warned that their "present course," if continued, could be ruinous "for him, emotionally and mentally; for you, socially, maritally"; advised her to see his dependence for what it is but not cave to it, which he clearly meant in sexual terms improper to name in a letter. He apologized for prying but professed the desire to help. She responded by speaking to the exceptional difficulty of her situation: "I feel you are the only person I have met who really gets the hang of Robert. Whether it is possible for Robert to live without complete control of a person I do not know."

She had gotten herself into the situation, she said, by trying to help Frost. "When he was alone and miserable I did what I have done consistently for ten years brought him from his solitude and kept him with us all and acted towards him as I had all my lfe# [*sic*] towrds [*sic*] all of you—and brought down an avalanche." The rushed syntax and assortment of typos may attest to her writing in extremis. Even so, her letter is notable for professing to agree with Larry's assessment of her arrangement with Frost while accounting for it in terms inconsistent with his winking characterization. "I have always tried to free him, to tide him over a hard time, recognizing the danger to him in his dependence," she wrote. "I have not been successful as you see."

The first problem she faced was logistical: Frost demanded more of her time than she could possibly give. "He demands more and more," she wrote, her tone consistently defensive, even apologetic, for wanting a modicum of time to herself. She notes that while she tried to write him every day in Florida, she could not send letters on Sundays. In this context, she took Larry into her confidence and shared the problem of Frost's growing control of her, careful at first lest he "misunderstand" her description as too much a criticism of Frost:

> You see I am being very frank with you because you will not misunderstand, because I feel you are the only person I have met who really gets the hang of Robert. Whether it is possible for Robert to live without complete control of a person I do not know. More and more he tells me what to think and say. That I do not mind because we agree on so many things and I am away part time to think as I like.

Hard as it is to understand an excuse for domination on the grounds that she can think for herself during the decreasing share of the week when she's not with him, the sentence is also in its small way a declaration of freedom, attesting that he may tell her what to think and say but she still has a mind of her own.

She had proposed limitations to which she doubted Frost would yield. She had tried to get Frost "to try going away for six months . . . because I fear the strain is killing him." She made note of Frost's mercurial temper, presently flaring at her "because he thinks I did not turn Lesley off him"—"I tried," she wrote, "but you have seen Lesley in action and there is no turning her off"—but she knew Frost would be settled by the next day, just strained. Her concern for herself came back to her worries for Frost.

"I have never talked to anyone about Robert and I have tried to avoid any talk at all," she told Larry, adding that she had said "a little to Louis butjust [sic] a little" and that he had missed her understatement. Kay had little intention of breaking her reticence again about her relationship with Frost:

> I am writing this once to you to answer your letter and probably will
> never bring the subject up again unless t [sic] there is something special
> to say or an answer to something from you. You have seen the misery
> and have a right to know a little about it.

"Your letter took a great weight off me," Larry replied. "Now that I've told you what I felt, after spending nearly three weeks with Robert, I shall have nothing more to say," he wrote before proffering more advice, this time that she stand up to Frost's domineering behavior with the power of her own deliberate silence, a "weapon he really doesn't know how to combat." Larry quoted "The Silken Tent" in calling for "ruthlessness that cuts down and through 'countless silken ties.'" It was Elinor's silences that had tormented Frost as he recalled them to Larry in Key West.

How much Kay's situation resembled Elinor's is hard to surmise. The answer depends partly on how much of Frost's need for control and attention was a feature of him in relationships and how much a feature of his pining to be in a relationship that was denied to him. The answer also partly depends on how much of Frost's behavior was a product of him in extremis and how much a product of him at his most intimate and vulnerable, assuming the situations were distinct. One is also left to wonder exactly how much emphasis to put on Kay's confession, which, while announcing its own singular honesty, was also written at an intensely difficult time and might not represent her normal state any more than anyone else's dark night of the soul is their truest for all that Sorrow makes it seem so. It is also entirely plausible her confession was the bare truth and her following letter guarded in its breezy politeness because she had pledged not to speak of the subject again and Larry had responded to her suffering by thanking her for taking a "great weight off" him. "Thank you for your letter" was the extent of her response to Larry's further advice aside from a note of vague optimism: "Robert is off on a new way of life and maybe we can hold this one. I am wiser and perhaps can do better." Kay was surprised to find Frost in good health, even embarrassed to have given the doctors cause for concern. She suspected Frost's lingering problems were mental.

VI.

By outward appearances, the relationship between Larry and Frost resumed its old footing in the spring of 1940. No longer was the biographer giving care to a subject with watering eyes because Kay had not written that day, or cajoling his Emersonian subject into proper self-reliance. Frost had passed through his hour of abjection, and Larry was no longer adviser and caregiver but once again a young man acting as Boswell by a great man's leave. Larry's air of authority passed as swiftly as Kay's vulnerability. Toward Frost, Larry's manner retained its effusiveness but lost its ebullience. His professions of affection were prompted less by sheer gladness as of old than by circumstantial convenience, as when Larry felt moved both to demonstrate his loyalty to Frost and to assert his independence from him in response to a note Frost had written asking Larry to be patient with him, tacitly slighting Larry with the comparison to the supposedly impatient Newdick.

Frost was brought to grief again in the fall. Carol, whose mental condition had long been precarious, learned in September that Lillian needed a hysterectomy. Carol grew frantic. Frost spent the first weekend of October with him in South Shaftsbury to do what he could, but Carol had retracted an old promise. He was dead within days of his father's departure.

Carol's preoccupation with suicide had an unusually clear point of inception. During Frost's final year of teaching at Pinkerton (1911–12), the family moved from the farm to the village, where they rented a unit in a house that they shared with a man, Lester Russell, who, having been caught embezzling money entrusted to him to invest, ended his life by drinking insecticide. In an effort to shelter the children, Frost and Elinor told them that the man's life had been "fulfilled," an old Quaker euphemism for dying. Word nonetheless spread at school that what the man had done was to kill himself. The association between fulfillment and suicide began to exert a strange fascination on young Carol's mind. He discussed it with his parents over the years and even brought it up on his wedding night in 1923, surprising Lillian by declaring that they might as well kill themselves after having been fulfilled. The fixation persisted, mostly without a credible threat of his acting on it. Lillian worried that he might take his life in his awful distress after Elinor's death. Two and a half years thereafter, Carol, paranoid enough about elaborate machinations for spying on him that he would wake Lillian to look in the cellar for evidence, learned of her need for a hysterectomy and wondered why he should continue to live if she could not have any more children. On his visit to the hospital after her procedure, he told her that he was no longer bound to his old promise not to take his own life. Lillian, recovering in the hospital in Pittsfield, got their son, Prescott, fifteen, to call Frost up to visit. Frost spent the weekend of October 5 trying to talk Carol down, only to learn what had happened in a call from Prescott in the early hours of October 9. Carol had shot himself in the kitchen.

For all of his father's pride in his work ethic, Carol suffered from the shame his father felt himself in the same stage of life for not having established himself in a career that could provide for his family. Unlike his father, Carol had Frost's example to go by, which meant he had his father's example to live with. That he lacked his father's genius is a painful understatement. His grasp of writing was poor enough that he could not recognize his own manifest inability to make a career of it as his father had. Frost's letters to Carol about his writing, while less effusive than his letters to Lesley about hers, were full of concrete praise and sincere advice on writing and work, the result of someone trying to make his son feel good about his writing and also feel good about the prospect of not writing for a living, all without giving the slightest condescension.

Lesley thought her father should set money aside to provide for her brother after Elinor's death. Frost thought it better to set him up with a straightforward enterprise that he could feel responsible for. Frost bought five acres of land in Coconut Grove, Miami, in 1940 with the intention of giving Carol the project of overseeing construction on the property and moving down there full time. Yet all that Frost tried seemed to fail. So it was with his last trip to see his son. He tried everything he could, from reasoning to humor, to make Carol feel better about himself and feel he had reason to live. Frost felt he had done the job until Carol, in parting, told him he always won in an argument. Carol had settled an argument with his father in Ann Arbor in the spring of 1922 by driving all the way east to Vermont, showing by deed that if he could not win the argument he could win the power struggle by running away.

"He had many fine qualities," Frost wrote to Lillian at the hospital. "He was devoted to work, he was fond of little children and animals he was idealistic truthful and brave. And he thought everything of you and his mother." Frost echoed some of these notes in a wrenching letter to Louis: "He was splendid with animals and little children. If only the

emphasis could have been put on those. He should have lived with horses."
To Louis, Frost confided the wish that he could have tried something else
to help Carol. To Lillian, Frost said there was nothing they could have
done. Frost told her that he had been "in a terrible state of wondering if
it wasnt my duty to have him examined by a mental doctor" but reassured
himself in retrospect that things were "better this way than a life in an
institution," the kind of life he had seen his sister suffer through. He asked
Lillian not to write anything about Carol to Irma. "You know how she
is—only a little less strange in the mind than Carol was."

VII.

Larry's revised impression of Frost had all but ossified, to judge from his
notes taken in Ripton in the summer of 1941. The notes reached a crescendo of moral disgust on a July evening after a boat ride on Lake Willoughby with Frost and Kay. Larry thought of Frost browbeating Hervey
Allen and Ted, "overbearingly ruthless in his argument," subduing Hervey
in "poundings of words," giving Ted no chance to talk and reveling in his
own dominance. It was "exactly as though he used words to box with,"
Larry wrote, "exactly" blurring the literal difference between rhetorical
and physical violence, hiding that the metaphor was a metaphor. Thinking
of Frost as abusive brought Larry to crescendo: "Nobody could be more
completely selfish than Frost. He is more thoroughly self centered than
any person I've ever known. And it has been his vice more than it has been
his virtue, I'm sure."

Larry had begun to assimilate the new things he learned about Frost
to his preconceptions rather than adjusting his judgments to fit new material. He would note Frost's extensive support of his children without saying a word against Frost's selfishness. When Frost went over the story of
his relationship with Elinor, Larry surmised that she had fallen out of love
with Rob after he dropped out of college and failed to establish himself
in a career, and that she had settled for Frost only on account of his force.

Frost was lazy, spoiled, selfish, and emotionally overpowering; that Elinor might have loved the man she spent her life with despite his having no stable job at twenty, as she herself maintained, seems not to have crossed Larry's mind at the time. "My, but there is the making of a fine novel, in matching two lives like hers and his, and in watching the inevitable tragedy develop from it," he wrote to himself, inevitability and tragedy set in his mind. Larry was outwardly deferential toward Frost and inwardly resentful of his own deference. He seems not to have wondered what Frost might have noticed.

To Larry's surprise, he found Kay in August looking "younger and happier than I've ever seen her." DeVoto shared Larry's impression but had a deeper sense of a demon beneath. Though Kay "was pleasanter to me than she has been for some years," DeVoto saw her as "strained, empty, and forever changed"—"one shattered soul in the center of all this." By which he meant the nexus of Frost's "evil." DeVoto meant the word literally. "I'm damned if I can look on him as tragic or damned, or even paranoid," wrote DeVoto. "He has just become what I didn't believe in when I was younger, an evil man, a man of great evil."

Among Frost's victims was Louis, piqued by Frost's placid response to Nazi aggression in Europe. Though it would be years before the Shoah became common knowledge, Hitler's attitude toward the Jews was no secret, and Untermeyer had already begun what would become a long-standing effort to rally support for the cause of his people. Frost's objection to American involvement in the war, on categorical grounds of anti-imperialism, lay underneath his tension with DeVoto that summer as well. DeVoto had given a talk one evening at Bread Loaf on Manifest Destiny, based on his latest book of nonfiction, a narrative history of westward expansion in 1846. Frost, in the audience, volunteered the comment "that he, I, and the Nazis all had the same notion about world domination and how right we were, since the future belonged to the U.S." Recognizing Frost's feigned agreement as a rhetorical trap, DeVoto countered by drawing Frost out to what he took to be the absurd position that America could let Russia and England lose the war so that America, relatively un-scathed, could emerge to dominate the world.

DeVoto found that he "rejoice[d]" in Frost's displays of "evil" for af-firming his premonitions of three years before. He attributed no motives to Frost other than variations on selfishness, such as his drives toward domination and fame. He charged Frost with "a sizable sum" of "lives he has ruined completely . . . and the greater sum of those he has warped and twisted"; held him responsible for "the family he destroyed and the wife he killed," whether from selfishness or from evil. Two such ruined lives were Ted's and Kay's, though DeVoto understood the affair not as a matter of sexual intrigue but as a corrosive psychological drama, Ted "castrat[ed]" by "psychical adultery" alone. DeVoto was under the impression that Ted did not comprehend the situation he found himself in. Ted struck De-Voto as rather naive: "He never sees a sexual motive till it's confessed in court and then tends to scout it as probably misunderstood." Ted was still oblivious a year later in DeVoto's estimation when, visiting DeVoto, he remarked incredulously that "some of the ugliest emotions man could feel turned up in the poetry of this genius." Ted had "The Subverted Flower" in mind. DeVoto had seen the poem first in the fall of 1938. Shortly after DeVoto had shown up at Bread Loaf in August 1938, Frost asked DeVoto to take a photograph of Kay for him, posing her in a stand of goldenrod that DeVoto later found in the poem:

> She was standing to the waist
> In goldenrod and brake,
> Her shining hair displaced.

VIII.

That Ted may well have told his friend less than he knew can be sur-mised from stories like the incident at Untermeyer's house in the fall of 1941, months before he brought up "The Subverted Flower" on his visit to DeVoto's. What exactly Ted knew—and believed and feared and denied—is a separate question.

Louis lived on a gentleman's farm at the edge of the Adirondacks, in Elizabethtown, about forty miles west of Ripton on the New York side of Lake Champlain. Larry, Frost, Ted, and Kay went to visit Louis and his wife, Esther, his third or fourth depending on your count. Larry learned of the problem when Esther came up to the swimming pool in tears to report that Robert had gotten terribly angry. Kay had taken him on a walk to talk him down. The men told Esther not to worry. Frost infused an air of tension into dinner, took a long postprandial walk with his sheepdog, Gillie, and returned to the group in the living room, where, as Louis played the piano and talked about music with Ted, Frost sat down and scowled demonstrably in Kay's direction. "Kay kept her eyes on her knitting," Larry wrote, "but she knew all that went on."

Eventually Frost left the room. Larry told Kay he might ask Frost if he wanted to go for a walk. Kay told Larry to tell Frost "to stop acting like a child." Larry found Frost upstairs in the room where Ted and Kay were set to sleep and "asked him what was the matter."

> He said in a tragic voice which might have curdled the blood if the words hadn't been ludicrous: "They're going to sleep in a double bed over there." And I said I guessed there wasn't anything he could do about that. Well there was. He wouldn't stay. How could a person devote his life to stimulating his imagination and then be expected to handle an image like that double bed as though it were nothing?

Frost resolved to leave that night. Larry said he would take him home. Frost changed his mind: he could not leave and let them share that double bed. Larry said he couldn't stop them. Frost said Larry could ask Esther to change the arrangement of beds. Larry couldn't do that. He could go down and talk it out with Kay. As soon as Larry got downstairs, Kay told him the plan: "She said she thought she and Ted would go home immediately.

She wanted me to take Frost off for a drive somewhere and keep him out of sight until they had gone."

At year's end, she told Larry that Frost had had a difficult autumn, "had been almost hysterical several times." She and Frost went to Ripton for Thanksgiving a day before the others to get the place ready, in the course of which Frost started a small fire near the garage that seemed to burn itself out. Frost and Kay began to walk toward another property of Frost's, only to see "a great cloud of smoke coming from the tall dry grass beside the garage." The wind swept up the flames, encircling the cabin. A number of trees burned in the adjoining national forest, but the fire spared the cabin in the end.

Frost had struck a match after finding some lesson books of Anne Morrison's that he found contemptibly simplistic. Anne, four years old at the time, later remembered the uncomfortable position of having to tell her teacher what had happened to her workbook. She did not want to get Frost in trouble.

IX.

Frost began his major work of the period with a burning Christmas tree. *A Masque of Reason*, a play that was Frost's fictional "Forty-third Chapter" to the forty-two-chapter book of Job, drafted by October 1942, begins with a tree like those in Frost's woods on fire in a desert oasis. The fire is a theophany, a manifestation of God. Job spies the flames and points them out to his wife.

It is unclear when Frost decided to write an oblique self-portrait as Job. The fire could well have been the proximate cause. Job 1:16 tells of fire and miraculous escape in a line Frost knew well enough to adapt into "Iris by Night"—"And I only am escaped alone to tell thee" in Job, "And I alone of us have lived to tell" in Frost's poem about his covenant with Thomas. Frost had more than fire to draw on for parallels between Job and himself. There was the disorientation and agony of the preceding

years, the physical affliction that felt like torment unto death, the unremit-
ting loss of family. Frost identified especially with Job's loss of his children, framing Job's central question about the meaning of his suffering in
the terms on which Lesley denounced him:

> It comes down to a doubt about the wisdom
> Of having children—after having had them,
> So there is nothing we can do about it
> But warn the children they perhaps should have none.

A writer other than Frost might have said he was desperate for meaning after effectively losing the most important ties in his life. Frost hid
his identification with Job under layers of plausible deniability, likewise hiding the identification of Job's wife with the woman who had
brought him into a new family. Frost admitted to confidants that Kay
had inspired the character but buried the fact in the play under a trail
of associations. Job's wife in the Bible is nameless and given all of one
line. Frost names her Thyatira and makes her a major character who
happens to identify as a prophetess notwithstanding the skepticism of
her husband. This was much like the situation of Jezebel, canonically
synonymous with false prophecy following Jesus's use of her name in ad-
dressing the iniquitous church of Thyatira. Scholars have long debated
about the identity of Jezebel of Thyatira, some identifying her with the
Jezebel of the Old Testament, wife of King Ahab, and some reading
"Jezebel" as a generic reference to the original Jezebel's type, influential
and sexually deviant.

    When Frost later explained the character of Thyatira to a group of
actors preparing a production of the masque at Bread Loaf, he had this to
say, describing her first, even before Job:

> She's the kind of person who says, "I don't care, I've done the best I
> could." A marked kind of character. A housewife full of having done

what she thought was right. She's a very marked character. She doesn't like a lot of talk about philosophy and that. She's easy to do—easy to put on that air. Takes care of her husband. Justice and things don't bother her too much. . . . How deep is her shallowness?

The woman Frost portrays is much like the woman DeVoto had described in rhapsodic terms—unassuming, unflappable, unfailingly loyal and brave. She does not give a second thought to confronting God's misbehavior. She lives by self-assured intuition rather than speculation on the limits of theological abstraction, her temperament one in which Job could find grounding, guidance, and strength in his thousand years of ruminating on his torments. Hers was not, however, a temperament like that of either Jezebel. Perhaps Frost chose the name because of an insinuated resemblance of Kay's situation to Jezebel's in transgressing the bounds of sexual mores. That his Job was married to Jezebel was an oblique form of confession, but his Thyatira's being so unlike Jezebel amounted to a defense of her, maybe even a prayer for the two of them.

Though Frost never said so, Thyatira's characterization seems to borrow something from Elinor as well as Kay. The composite nature of the character does not seem inspired as in "The Silken Tent," and suggests perhaps that Frost sometimes ran the two together in his mind. There were indeed substantial similarities between his two romantic relationships, no matter the stories he told. The two were guarded women capable of assertiveness and understated shrewdness, women on whose assistance, guidance, and faith he could practically rely as he addressed each relationship with a private height of romance, tempered as it sometimes was by his doubts about how much his beloved partook in the romance as well. Frost identified Thyatira with Kay to Larry in less lofty terms. "Of course she is Thyatira," he said. "She's the one who always falls asleep whenever I try to read anything to her." When Job says the same thing about her in the masque, God calls her beautiful.

Lost in the obliqueness of Frost's identification with his masque is

that it implies a very different story of his past than the one he had tended
to tell since the loss of Elinor. While Frost blamed himself for the suffering of his wife and his family, his masque claims an inability to ascribe
all suffering to human responsibility. The play was a theological antidote
to overpowering personal guilt. The guilt was inspiration for a work of
creative theology.

Though Frost got ahead of himself and tried to stage his Forty-third
Chapter on Broadway, it is less a work of art than a lecture delivered, like
most of Frost's talks and essays, with charm. Given its religious subject
matter, one can regard this charming lecture as a sermon in verse. Frost
said that his ambition for the work was to do what Milton had done in
the masque known as *Comus*, which goes a way toward explaining Frost's
otherwise puzzling titular description of his work as a masque, a theatri-
cal form otherwise associated mostly with the sort of elaborate courtly
pageantry that the story of *Comus* subverts. Like *Comus*, *A Masque of Reason*
treats the idea of divine justice by presenting the fate of a character distinguished for superlative virtue. Frost regarded *Comus* as the singularly
"great poem" of Puritanism, presumably for its synthesis of Stoical ethics
and Christian soteriology—a scheme in which virtue, known by reason,
gives one the best chance of flourishing as well as salvation. Milton would
proceed to integrate this scheme into biblical tradition with *Paradise Lost*,
which was, among other things, a story of why human reason is not the
flawless faculty it is for the hero of *Comus*, capable of guiding a reasoner
unerringly to moral certainties within a schema of divine reward and retribution. *A Masque of Reason* is an alternate story. In choosing Job rather
than Genesis as its foundational myth from the Old Testament, Frost's
masque traces the limits of moral reason to the devil's temptation of God
rather than his temptation of Eve.

The book of Job is the canonical story of inexplicable suffering. God
tortures His most faithful servant, Job, after the devil tempts God by
contending that Job's faith would waver under trial. Job's visitors attempt
consolation by trying to reconcile his suffering with divine justice, which

implies Job's responsibility, which succeeds in affronting Job rather than comforting him—"Oh, that committee!" says the Job of Frost's masque in derision. God manifests Himself to Job at the end of the book and offers the most notorious non-explanation in the Old Testament, accounting for His treatment of Job not by defending His actions but by describing the awesome extent of His power. In the absence of an explanation, Job submits, reconciling himself to his incomprehension of God's ways. Such is the last chapter of the book, the forty-second, after which Frost's Forty-third Chapter begins.

Unlike the God of the book of Job, Frost's God explains Himself. As in the book of Job, the explanation implies human incomprehension of God's ways. It generalizes Job's condition to the human condition. When at last called to account by Thyatira, God says that He tortured Job just to show off to the devil. This is the explanation awaited for millennia: God showing off to the devil. Job is understandably nonplussed:

'Twas human of You. I expected more
Than I could understand and what I get
Is almost less than I can understand.

God's revelation is the lack of any deeper explanation, revealing a world in which good can simply show off to evil and do ill in the process. It is not that Job cannot understand the divine dispensation of justice but that it lies beyond the scope of reason.

The masque is a work of apologetics not for Job's God but for the book of Job itself. As one of the Wisdom books in the Hebrew Bible along with Ecclesiastes and the Song of Songs, the book of Job is conventionally regarded as an exception to the canonical rule, a fairy tale meant to test the Bible's normative theology. Frost would make the theology of the book not exceptional but paradigmatic. Where Milton sets out in *Paradise Lost* to "justify the ways of God to men," Frost sets out to normalize the ways of a God free to act outside the strictures of justice. It is a world in which, as God tells Thyatira, "Your husband Job and I together / Found out the discipline man needed most / Was to learn his submission to unreason." More beguilingly, it is a world in which God thanks Job for His own moral freedom, turning the theology of *Paradise Lost* on its head. Human freedom led not to human fallenness but rather to the freedom of God. In turn, it is the very freedom permitting God to act out of accord with His covenant of justice that sets a limit to human reason in regard to the scheme of salvation—divine freedom and not human sin.

Frost's version of Milton's God, like that of William Blake, is capricious and neither omnipotent nor omniscient, lacking what Milton called "foreknowledge absolute." (Frost depicts God in the aspect of Blake's painting of Him based on *Paradise Lost* and mocks Milton's apologetics for the justice of his God from a stretch in the epic that exerted a perpetual hold on Frost's imagination.) The limitations to Frost's God can look terribly bleak insofar as they refuse consolation or meaning for the forces that can afflict someone with crippling pain and irredeemable loss. And yet a corollary of divine fallibility is that it lightens the blame on human fallibility, absolving it of some responsibility. The difficulty people have in saving their souls owes not only to their actions but to a profound lack of knowledge, as Job conveys in his sharpest lament in the masque, which generalizes a bewildering disorientation to the human condition:

> We don't know where we are, or who we are.
> We don't know one another; don't know You;
> Don't know what time it is. We don't know, don't we?
> Who says we don't? Who got up these misgivings?
> Oh, we know well enough to go ahead with.
> I mean we seem to know enough to act on.
> It comes down to a doubt about the wisdom
> Of having children—after having had them,
> So there is nothing we can do about it

But warn the children they perhaps should have none.
You could end this by simply coming out
And saying plainly and unequivocally
Whether there's any part of man immortal.
Yet You don't speak. . . .

12.

ROBERT FROST AT MIDNIGHT

I.

The strangest thing about the crises in Frost's life from 1942 to 1946 is that they failed to happen. The years were not entirely easy for him, not unfree from illness, painful conflict, and even troubling disturbances of mind. Yet none of these unfortunate events proved tragic or irremediable as they easily could have. It was not good fortune, exactly, but neither was it the trials of Job.

Frost's arrangement with Kay, whatever it was, proceeded without outward alteration. Frost grew only more involved in their family's life between Cambridge, to which he relocated from Boston in 1941, and the long summers in Ripton that the Morrisons spent in the Homer Noble farmhouse downhill from Frost's cabin. To Anne, Frost was a member of the family, adored like her father and unlike her mother, for whom she had more complicated feelings. Kay took care of Frost's practical affairs to such an extent that he called her more manager than secretary. She also managed periods in which Frost was difficult enough, even scary enough, that few could have faulted her for cutting ties. (The extent to which she felt free to cut the ties that bound them is a separate question.) For reasons

hard to reconstruct, Frost was especially off in the late summer and early
fall of 1945, which Kay described as five weeks of "*Hell.*" At one point
that summer, he began a strange, unnatural chant and took an axe into his
cabin, threatening to kill himself with it, a logistical implausibility but a
terrifying situation nonetheless, Frost going on like that until Kay repeated
her discomfort with the axe enough times for him to lay the weapon down.
Friends feared for his sanity. Kay stuck with him, as she had after Frost's
indiscreetness about their alleged indiscretions was made known to her in
1943.

Frost's loose talk reached her by a byzantine pathway of rumors and
partial misunderstandings that ensnared Larry and DeVoto both. In the
summer of 1942, DeVoto learned from a source in Princeton that Larry,
now serving the war effort as a naval historian, had picked up on an
emotional entanglement between Frost and Kay that was threatening to
strain Kay's marriage, as DeVoto had feared. "If Larry understands what
has happened, then anyone can understand," DeVoto wrote, "for he's a
reasonably intelligent young man but not gifted at what we call psychology." Unsure himself what to make of "the Morrison triangle," DeVoto
had occasion to ask Frost directly while the two overlapped for a few days
in Bloomington, Indiana, on lecture engagements in April 1943. DeVoto
asked if Frost was sleeping with Kay. On Frost's recollection, he said no
while reminding DeVoto that his response was what any gentleman would
say if asked such a question. It was a teasing answer for the suggestion that
his denial owed to propriety and not fact, and DeVoto had reached the
point where he could attribute only ulterior motives to Frost. DeVoto had
grown sure that Frost was driven by a passionate urge to dominate and
eventually consume him, a fear that was hardly assuaged when DeVoto
learned that Frost had told their hosts in Bloomington, at a dinner after
DeVoto had left, that DeVoto was under the care of a psychiatrist who
advised him not to associate with Frost because Frost was too dominant
for him, a rumor that sent DeVoto into conniptions of denial despite its
being substantially true and rather in evidence from his own paranoia.

DeVoto met with Kay and heard her side of the story. He came away trusting her partly and partly confused about the heart of Frost's story, which
was that he and Kay were, DeVoto wrote, "bound together in the world's
greatest love since Adam's time."

> Her basic theory is that Robert was crazy for four years but has been
> sane again for one year. Her basic assertion is that he was crazy when
> he conceived his version of the central situation. Whether he is crazy
> in maintaining that conception did not appear.

Kay was irate. She dispelled the rumors in letters to the relevant parties,
Larry and Earle Bernheimer, a collector of Frost's manuscripts who acted
also as a kind of patron. Kay characterized her role in Frost's life as a
provider of support, practical and emotional. She explained that Frost
might have gotten the wrong idea just from wearing her down until she
stopped protesting with him. She said she wanted to stay with her family
and that she "will not stand this sort of thing." She did not say whether
or not she loved Frost.

After meeting with Kay, DeVoto wrote Frost a curt and legalistic
letter that was effectively a cease and desist. ("Please see to it that I do
not have to act any farther in the matter than thus calling it to your attention.") Frost felt "injured and misunderstood"—he had brought up
DeVoto's psychiatric care in a spirit of bemusement that someone as gifted
as DeVoto would feel that Frost was too strong for him—but Frost apparently left his correction of the record unsent. DeVoto would reconsider
the episode several years later, after getting his experience into a rather
self-flattering roman à clef, and offer Frost a grand gesture of forgiveness
and reconciliation that lasted roughly two weeks before DeVoto grew suspicious of Frost's motives on spurious grounds and the two were estranged
once again.

Frost's friendship with Untermeyer suffered no dramatic breach in
the early 1940s, their tension lingering instead in a cold war of mutual

exasperation. In the nadir of their relationship in 1944, Frost wrote a letter from Ripton to his newly distant friend in Manhattan, his only letter that year to the person he had written to more than anyone over the past thirty years. The letter was a showy gesture of friendship, written in six long pages of blank verse. In substance, though, the verse epistle refused to conciliate, defending Frost's lack of involvement in the war effort on the grounds that he was not in the business of taking up causes and that his words would not do much, though he would take gun to Hitler if he could. Frost named Louis among the four people "whom I have to count on most," "Kay Lesley you and Larry":

One of my four you'll notice is a Jew—
No credit claimed for either him or me.

"Aw come on off your cosmic politics" was Frost's final appeal. Louis, of course, did not, even with Frost's report that Louis knew Frost better than anyone but Kay, as Kay said herself.

Strained as their friendship was, it was not bad enough in early 1943 to preclude Untermeyer from lobbying the Pulitzer board to give its prize to Frost's collection from 1942, *A Witness Tree*. The committee had decided to give it to a book by a less decorated author that they deemed less deserving on the merits; their decision was reversed on Louis's appeal. Frost won his fourth Pulitzer Prize in Poetry in May 1943, making him the first and still the only poet to win it so often. The book was not only decorated but well received in general with its balance of older and newer verse including a number of excellent poems about his loss and his new attachment, such as "The Silken Tent." The book's success was in keeping with Frost's practical affairs in the period. *A Masque of Reason* was received favorably upon release in 1945, though Frost felt that the book was insufficiently appreciated and understood, most glaringly in a review by his biographer in *The New York Times*, which Frost thought mistook the book for a critique of Christian orthodoxy when it was really a critique of rationalism. Frost's response was somewhat puzzling, effectively conflating orthodoxy with legitimacy, current normative standards for belief with his sense of well-justified beliefs within the greater Puritan tradition, a puzzle that resolves if one remembers that Frost thought the tradition effectively collapsed orthodoxy into legitimacy, setting that which you can't help but feel as the pure standard for normative belief. His objection puzzled his minister's son of a biographer in any case, giving ballast to the warning of a jealous Sidney Cox, jealous because he had wanted permission for decades to biographize Frost, warning now that Larry was "too much a product of the academic rolling and stamping mill to be able even briefly to fold himself to anything like your solid, protean shape" as far as matters of the spirit were concerned. "He cannot think in such paradoxes," Cox warned: "You must be on any particular day either solid or protean, and he will think his problem is to explain your inconsistency, instead of to grasp your flexible firmness of form." The alarm of Cox, who himself taught English at Dartmouth but in a conspicuously charismatic and anti-academic manner that took after Frost in every way but reserve, earned him a phone call from Frost telling him to stop being silly. Sidney and Larry could both write about him—though only one was official biographer.

The period also saw Frost move from his temporary position at Harvard to a permanent position at Dartmouth with generous terms and so few demands that Frost would just stay at the Hanover Inn during the handful of weeks each fall and spring when he was informally in residence. Frost was delighted to return on such terms to the school he had fled summarily a half-century before. He wrote a number of poems in the period that were good of their kind but did his best work in prose, as DeVoto had predicted he would, and in extemporaneous talks, some of which were revised into prose that captures the heart of his insights but only a sliver of their grace of presentation that set his ambiguities in legible form.

Frost's trials returned once again at the end of 1946 when Irma's mental condition, long perilous, took a turn for the worse.

II.

The event precipitating Irma's collapse unfolded in Ripton in August 1946. She and John, having already been separated for years, met on neutral ground in Ripton on August 21, 1946, to discuss the divorce that John wanted and that Irma, despite her unwillingness to live with John in the place where he had found a job (New York City), meant to resist or at least to delay. The rendezvous was news to her father. On being brought word by Kay on the morning of the twenty-first, Frost, abed in his nightgown, entered into a familiar kind of trance in which he began to chant, slowly, in a screeching, unnatural tone, about going away. Kay thought about throwing cold water on him or slapping him, but he emerged on his own, looking perfectly calm.

Frost met with John and went on to the Waybury Inn, where the two met with Irma. For unrecorded reasons, father and daughter had an awful confrontation that led to an enraged Frost walking off by himself. Perhaps he lost his patience with her refusal to agree to a divorce. He had granted John's appeal to him in May: "The thing ought to be ended and you ought to be free to get something out of life." Frost agreed not out of fondness for John, whom he knew to have been adulterous, but out of sympathy for John's grounds for divorce, which Frost thought best approximated in the terms of New Hampshire law by "extreme cruelty" or "treatment such as to injure health or endanger reason." The latter also obtained in her treatment of their younger son, Harold, age five, in whose case Frost suspected severe malnourishment and would soon fear worse.

Merrill Moore had begun warning Frost about Irma's sanity by the end of 1945. Though Frost had found her intolerable company since the summer after Elinor's death, calling her "baffling" to Lesley earlier in 1945, it is unclear how seriously he questioned her sanity before Moore did. Moore strengthened his diagnosis after Irma suffered a breakdown in front of company in Cambridge over the winter holidays at the start of 1947. "Any remark you could make would be an understatement about

Irma," wrote Kay after the episode. "It has been beyond belief." Moore told Frost that she needed to be taken to an institution immediately because people with her kind of dementia were at serious risk of committing violence, often killing the person they love most and then killing themselves. Shortly thereafter, she asked Moore for a pistol.

Frost and Kay spent the better part of a year, between the summer of 1946 and May 1947, trying to find a place for Irma to live. Frost eventually bought her a house in Acton, Massachusetts, west of Boston. She had gone through ten places to stay, unable to inhabit this or that boardinghouse or hotel out of suspicions of terrible danger or the host's scandalous drunkenness. Frost was driven to distraction, expressing his misery with the situation in his letters more than he had about anything other than Elinor's death. Yet, racked as he was, he was also reluctant to commit his daughter, as he wrote to Louis in the first hours of the new year 1947:

> Merrill is for having Irma brought to rest in an institution or at least under a guardian. I find it hard to end anyone's freedom to range to waste and to ruin. Take that away from anyone and what is there left? Let them run I say till they run afoul.

Yet Frost was well aware that her liberty to "run afoul" involved the liberty to run afoul of her young son, whom, as Frost wrote two weeks into the new year, "we are specially anxious for." Frost cut short his travels for the spring to be near Irma, whom he was still hardly willing to see. He tried to deflect the situation with bleak glib humor, as Larry paraphrased him in early February: "Now that Merrill Moore has predicted that her type always winds up in some spectacular violence, usually first killing the one most loved and then self, we must just sit back, Frost says, and wait to see whom she really loves most!"

By the middle of June, Frost began to draft a letter about Irma to her son Jackie, now nineteen years old. The letter would take Frost a month to dictate to Kay. By July, he and Kay began to make arrangements for potentially taking Irma in for treatment against her will, enlisting Moore and Rastus Hewitt, Frost's attorney and neighbor, for help. Frost proposed the plan to his grandson at last in a letter of July 17, saying that though he would support whatever Jackie and his father decided, his greatest fear was that Irma would hurt Harold. "This is a sorrowful business all around," Frost wrote.

The situation came to crisis on July 29. Kay learned of the emergency from Jackie, who said his frantic mother was claiming to be in danger of enslavement and forced prostitution. Kay kept the news from Frost. The next day, she got a call from Hewitt informing her that Irma had shown up in Cambridge in a bad state. He thought the time had come to take her away.

As it happened, July 30 was also the day when a pair of younger poets, great admirers of Frost's, Robert Lowell and Theodore Roethke, were set to arrive at Bread Loaf. Frost, not ready to see the two of them, was delighted to spend the afternoon picking blueberries with Larry, "poking around for only the biggest berries," as Larry recalled, "finding what he wanted, talking and singing to himself, and scolding birds that scolded him, for trespassing. I've never seen him in such a blissful mood." Frost did not want to go home. Evidently, Kay had told him the news about Irma and Frost had said nothing to his biographer. When Frost returned to the farm and Larry was out of earshot, Frost told Kay that she would have to take especially good care of him in the coming weeks or he would go crazy. He touched his finger to his head as he spoke.

III.

The day after Larry and Frost spent the afternoon picking berries to avoid Lowell and Roethke, the younger poets did a fine job getting lost on their own. Lowell chronicled the pilgrimage from Yaddo, a writers' colony a hundred-odd miles away in Saratoga Springs, under the heading of "Mishaps": "Forgot fag— . . . leave raincoat in car—bus station moved—miss bus—$100 taxi—champagne for lunch . . . —Ripton area dry for miles around—no one knows about Frost farm." Despite their predicament, they managed to call Kay, whom they informed of their whereabouts at the Middlebury Inn. When she went to get them later that evening with Ted and Frost, Lowell and Roethke were to be found enjoying a grand dinner over bottles of champagne.

Their visit proceeded apace: three nights of harmless misadventures and drunken good cheer, albeit more equivocal cheer for their hosts. They stayed in Frost's cabin their first night until four in the morning, leading Frost to grouse afterward to Larry that he wished they had not come. This may have been less on account of their keeping him up than their reading him poems of their own and soliciting comments. Frost read them the current draft of his second masque, *A Masque of Mercy*.

Frost complained about the monotony of their work afterward in private. He criticized their respective styles to them obliquely over lunch, saying some poets tip the bottle so far that it makes a glug-glug sound while others tip the bottle just so for a smooth pour, leaving their intensity understated. "You can't be unclear in an epigram," said Frost to their manifest delight. Confiding afterward to another friend who had shared the meal with them, Frost said, "I've got a devil in me."

Coincidentally or not, "a marvelous devil of a man" was Lowell's description of Frost after the visit. "In the process of having his mad daughter committed," Frost, in Lowell's recounting, made a version of his habitual bleak joke about Irma, shocking Roethke: "'I always said, let her run loose till she kills someone.' Seeing Roethke's face drop. 'I suppose I shouldn't talk that way, but . . .'"

IV.

Hewitt called again the day after Lowell and Roethke had left. Irma had shown up at Frost's house in Cambridge, where Lillian happened to be staying on a trip. Lillian was terrified to be alone with her. Frost had sent

John a telegram passing along Hewitt's and Moore's advice about Irma's commitment. John replied that he did not want to make the decision. Frost joined the Morrisons for dinner at the house of William Porter, a doctor friend of Frost's.

Porter had lately told Frost that some doctors had begun to recommend the occasional drinking of alcohol to relax people, like Frost, who were afflicted by nerves. Frost took the doctor's advice and enjoyed a number of cocktails over the course of the evening. In a jubilant state, he began to sing for his company, notably the ribald stanzas he had made up to "The Keeper of the Eddystone Light," an old ballad about a lighthouse keeper who fathers a series of children with a mermaid. Frost's stanzas included the following:

> She didn't mind doin' it
> On a bale of kelp
> But a pair of legs
> Would've been some help.

Frost was so pleased with the effects of the drink that on the way home he proclaimed that he might buy a whole case of liquor. Back at home, close to midnight, he went up to his cabin and, seeing the light in the barn, went down to find Kay, who had hidden from him, having had more than enough. Ted covered for her. Frost went back to his cabin, irate. Kay and Ted could hear Frost from their bedroom in the farmhouse a hundred yards away. He shouted, "God damn, god damn-damn, god damn-damn-damn," he took a hammer and smashed his new writing desk, he smashed dishes by throwing them from the kitchen out onto the porch, he paced around the cabin shouting, waking Kay repeatedly for hours. He went to bed at five in the morning and woke up at noon.

He and Kay drove to Cambridge two days later. Kay had asked Hewitt and Moore to commit Irma on their own, but neither wanted to be the one responsible. Moore had made arrangements with the State Hospital in Concord, New Hampshire, an institution in the state of her official residence that he held in high regard. Moore showed up at the door of Frost's house and told Irma that she needed the help of a good hospital. She refused. He said he would carry her off if he had to. She packed for two hours and walked out to the car, surprised to find her father in the back seat.

After Moore handled her admission in Concord, Frost went in to say goodbye. He told her that she had to do this to get Harold back, that she could leave as soon as she was well. She stuck out her tongue, thumbed her nose, said, "Get out of here."

Frost met an old friend and her husband in Harvard Square on the morning after parting from Irma in Concord. It was August 8. He and Kay would drive to Ripton later that day. Naturally, Frost's night had been sleepless. He and his old friend Sue Walcutt, a student of his at Michigan in the early 1920s, had lemonades with her husband as Frost unburdened himself about his daughter. Walcutt later remembered that in addition to all the talk about Irma, Frost made a pair of jokes, one about Catholics and another about the intermittently Catholic poetry of Robert Lowell, who had won the Pulitzer Prize that year for his second book, *Lord Weary's Castle*, which Frost had found monotonous in structure. Frost repeated the figure he had lately used to criticize the writing of Lowell and Roethke in front of their noses: "Some people, Mr. Frost said, know how to tip the bottle just right, but Robert Lowell always gets it at the wrong angle so that it goes 'Glug-glug-glug' and very little comes out."

V.

In the weeks after her mother's death, Irma took comfort in her father's plan to scatter Elinor's ashes. Irma had been surprised by how fully and clearly her grieving mind brought the Derry farm back to her, as she described the lost world to her father: "the quince hedge and finding a quince there and the way the sun shone on the front of the house and

down in the yard inside the hedge, and a great many other things particularly all the naughty things we did, like taking apples."

Seven and a half years later, in early 1946, Frost published a poem
taking the reader through a lost children's world of farmhouse and farm.
Addressed in the second person to an anonymous reader, the poem, "Directive," is spoken by an anonymous narrator whose spectral presence lays
out its plan—its directive—for you, the reader, within the lost world. The
terminus of the directive is a cedar tree, as in the grove where the family
picnicked, next to a brook, as in the presumptive resting place for Elinor's
ashes. Your journey proceeds from the present world of overgrown woods
obscuring the old apple trees and into an earlier world of objects cast in
the uncanny light of memory: "the children's house of make believe, /
Some shattered dishes underneath a pine, / The playthings in the playhouse of the children." The narrator directs you to mourn the loss of a
child's perspective that would magnify the significance of things as incon-
sequential in the world of adults as taking apples from a tree. "Weep for
what little things would make them glad."

Frost's Modernist readers praised the poem for its self-conscious ambiguities of addressee and narrator and its self-consciousness about the very act
of imagining its world. Yet this was also the style of *Twilight*, whose poems,
albeit in an older idiom, also take the reader on a self-consciously imaginary
journey whose purpose is ambiguously either the discovery of something
imagined or the very act of imagining together. In "Directive," the directive
through memory's kingdom has for its terminus "a broken drinking goblet
like the Grail" hidden under an arch at the base of the cedar. ("I stole the
goblet from the children's playhouse.") The goblet is the lone object in the
poem to exist in a liminal state between the world in which the poem is
spoken and the world of which it is spoken. Between two worlds, the goblet
features in the ambiguous promise of the poem's final two lines:

Here are your waters and your watering place.
Drink and be whole again beyond confusion.

Seeming to leap from the world of memory to the world of enchantment, the goblet offers a prospect like that of the Holy Grail in restoring lost life, making you "whole again," beyond confusion. This is the implicit promise of the lost but extant artifact toward which your journey through the poem is a quest. And yet the last line also admits of a reading on whose terms the lost world is recoverable only in memory. To be "whole again beyond confusion" could well mean just to be psychologically beyond the mental scatteration of confusion, just as Frost famously called a poem "a momentary stay against confusion." The journey into lost time might restore something in the psyche of the traveler, otherwise confused.

VI.

Decades after Lowell's visit to Bread Loaf, he recalled Frost's discussion of Irma in one of his sonnets. The poem was in one of Lowell's later manners that, by whatever stream of influences, poured smoothly in irregular blank verse. Playing as Frost had done on Coleridge's "Frost at Midnight," Lowell's sonnet "Robert Frost" describes a private conversation with Frost late at night when Frost had hid away the "great act" and was, as the poem implies, being himself:

> Robert Frost at midnight, the audience gone
> to vapor, the great act laid on the shelf in mothballs,
> his voice musical, raw and raw—he writes in the flyleaf:
> "Robert Lowell from Robert Frost, his friend in the art."
> "Sometimes I feel too full of myself," I say.
> And he, misunderstanding, "When I am low,
> I stray away. My son wasn't your kind. The night
> we told him Merrill Moore would come to treat him,
> he said, 'I'll kill him first.' One of my daughters thought things,
> knew every male she met was out to make her;
> the way she dresses, she couldn't make a whorehouse."

And I, "Sometimes I'm so happy I can't stand myself."
And he, "When I am too full of joy, I think
how little good my health did anyone near me."

One should take the quotations with a grain of salt owing to poetic license
and the passing of decades before composition. One should be even more
suspicious of the finer points of Lowell's insight into Frost's inner life. The
glib bleakness that Lowell evidently saw as a revelation of Frost's disabused
emotion was itself a way of Frost's to cope with things that he could hardly
bear directly—an act. Lowell, himself inclined toward abandon in private,
familiar with Frost in performance and in private and in print but not in
extremis, may not have surmised that Frost's private manner toward him
was not a confession but a looser kind of composure that nonetheless concealed the torrent of feelings Frost would let out, the night after Lowell
left Bread Loaf, in a drunken breakdown, having tilted the bottle rather
too steeply.

In Lowell's poem, Frost responds to reports of manic excitement with
bits of humor that, however sad, are also ways of guarding his own psyche
from either extreme of polar emotion, as well as reassurance that Lowell
was not constituted like the suicidal Carol. If Lowell mistook as mutual
confession a conversation that was more asymmetrical, this was partly
by Frost's devilish design—partly, too, a result of distinct preconceptions about human psychology that would make Frost consistently harder
to understand for the younger generations. Between them lay the long
shadow of Freud. Though inconsistently Freudian in many ways over the
years, Lowell maintained the central Freudian premise of the primacy
of confession in psychological welfare. Lowell also maintained, save in
passing awakenings to the Catholic faith, the modern psychological conception of the soul of which Freudianism was an example. It is a picture
of the soul as at base medical rather than spiritual, a picture in which
thinking of something called mental health in abstraction from spiritual
welfare is not only coherent but the most straightforward common sense.

Frost rejected this picture of the soul like other forms of Romanticism that posited human fulfillment in experience rather than in a spiritual condition potentially visible through the keyhole of experience. The world, thought Frost, was one in which everyone was tasked with saving their soul, a task that would never get easier. This led him to think about psychology in terms of value and agency as against medical diagnosis. Frost objected to the confessionalism of Freud and his followers on the grounds that it rested on a misleading metaphor about psychological aberration, which saw it as a wound that needs air to heal while Frost saw it as a septic system that needs sealing to clean itself. That Frost was less than consistently sealed in practice hardly changed his psycho-spiritual ideal. It was with such preconceptions that Frost responded to Lowell's reports of his own mental life, having come to know Lowell years before as a young man in psychological distress at the behest of his mother, Charlotte Lowell, an intimate of Merrill Moore's.

Writing to Frost in October 1940 shortly after his loss of Carol, Charlotte extended her sympathy as well as her gratitude for Frost's help with her son, then twenty-three, who would continue to long for Frost's presence in times of psychic duress. Institutionalized at Baldpate Hospital for a manic episode in 1949, Lowell was profoundly grateful after Frost took him up on his request for a visit. "Come, come again," Lowell wrote. "Your visit meant more than all the others," putting the point to other friends even more strongly: "I've seen my mother & father once, Frank Parker many times and Robert Frost once. Robert was worth all the others many times."

VII.

The masque that Frost read a draft of to Lowell and Roethke sometime after midnight on their first night at Bread Loaf is, like "Directive," about the uncertainty of salvation. Salvation is never described nor any doctrine of salvation subscribed to, but each work strains openly toward it, whatever it may be.

A Masque of Mercy rounds out the heart of Frost's theology from the earlier masque. It takes up, literally quoting, God's proclamation on mercy in His opening speech in book 3 of *Paradise Lost*—the same passage on the primacy of mercy that Frost had discussed in a letter to Bill Snow in January 1938:

> In Mercy and Justice both,
> Through Heav'n and Earth, so shall my glory excel,
> But Mercy first and last shall brightest shine.

In *A Masque of Mercy*, Frost elaborates and by all appearances endorses the scheme for "Mercy first and last" that he had outlined in his letter to Snow. Mercy first, because human imperfectibility renders us incapable of justifying our own salvation according to the standards of the Sermon on the Mount, with their insistence on inner purity as well as purity of action. The very possibility of salvation for unworthy creatures is a mercy. Any realization of the possibility in the final judgment would be mercy last, though such a mercy is the last thing from certain. Just as one cannot reason out an ultimate connection between desert and reward in one's lifetime, per *A Masque of Reason*, so one cannot forecast one's reward in the hereafter, per the latter of the masques.

The place of justice is unclear in a world that demands mercy, as *A Masque of Mercy* shows by its plot. Its protagonist, Jonah, is persuaded to embrace the primacy and ultimate arbitration of mercy rather than justice, thereupon venturing into a threshold toward God and being rejected, realizing in his dying lines that in abandoning justice for mercy entirely he had abandoned all that he was.

The masque falls shy of saying that acting as justly as one can is a necessary condition of one's salvation, though the condition is made to feel plausible. The masque is unequivocal, however, in its argument that just actions are insufficient, owing to the sheer impossibility of meeting the standards of the Sermon on the Mount. One needs must aim for something more capacious and less formal, less rational, than justice, an aim Frost thought of in the old Old Testament categories of offering and sacrifice. A character in Frost's masque proclaims in his final speech that the simple prayer that one's sacrifice be found acceptable in God's sight is the only prayer worth praying, an opinion on which Frost himself had delivered a sermon at his friend's synagogue toward the end of 1946:

> We have to stay afraid deep in our souls
> Our sacrifice, the best we have to offer,
> And not our worst nor second best, our best,
> Our very best, our lives laid down like Jonah's,
> Our lives laid down in war and peace, may not
> Be found acceptable in Heaven's sight.
> And that they may be is the only prayer
> Worth praying. May my sacrifice
> Be found acceptable in Heaven's sight.

VIII.

Professor Reginald Cook of Middlebury College, nicknamed Doc, sat with Frost in the latter's study in Cambridge one evening in December 1947, before Lesley, back in the country from Spain, returned to her father's house for the night.

Cook, a former Rhodes scholar, worried to Frost that he had perhaps been too secure to take risks. Frost encouraged him in response: "Everyone starts with the security he busts out from." The aphorism took the same form as another of Frost's that night: "Everyone is marked by his own craziness that he does not give way to." Frost went over Irma's condition with Cook, saying that Lesley had grown worried that the strain of insanity might show in her children. Cook tried to reassure Frost by telling him about the various fates of Emerson's brothers, ending with the consolation, "It all adds up," to which Frost shook his head. "It's just sad," he said. "That's all." Lesley got back at eleven o'clock. Cook went to bed. And yet he could not sleep for hours, hearing the voices of father and daughter carry from the next floor until 2:30 in the morning.

Frost, who had been merely miserable about Irma's commitment, grew conflicted about it after Lesley's visit in December. She and Lillian were convinced that Irma would be better served in a less formal setting. Moore reassured Frost, but Frost was not entirely convinced. On the day after Christmas, Frost struck a new note in describing Irma as "at once too insane to be out of an institution and too sane to be in one." Lesley could bear the situation for only so long. Three years after Irma entered the State Hospital, Lesley contrived to trick Irma's guardian, Hewitt, into releasing her from the hospital for a week's vacation, which Lesley used to enroll Irma at Creedmoor Hospital on Long Island, closer to her and Jackie.

His anger notwithstanding, Frost was pleased that Irma had a change of scene. "The hardest thing for me to think of was her days stretching ahead unrelieved by any adventure or hope of adventure such as anyone loose in the world may expect." He let himself entertain the thought that Irma might be well again after spending more time with her sister— "Goodness what a comforting hope"—but the comfort of hope faded when he recalled the ways in which she had been "crazy" for many years, citing her breakdown at John's graduation from architecture school nearly two decades before.

"I write you all this purposelessly," Frost told his daughter. "There is no attempt to excuse myself for anything that has become of any of you. Im not fishing for exhonoration. I can't help thinking back over the past."

After her relocation, Irma, who had been left in her new surroundings without understanding why she was there, continued to agitate for her release. She wanted to get out to a farm.

IX.

Larry returned to Ripton with his young family in June 1948, the start of their summer, to find a long letter awaiting him in the farmhouse Larry rented from Frost. Frost had written the letter a few days before. He had been going through his old clothes until he found a shirt he did not recognize as his own, in whose pocket was a list of questions Larry had taken with him on their last walk together in the summer of 1947. Frost's letter was his way of answering the questions Larry had written to ask Frost about his religion.

Larry wanted to know precisely what Frost believed and how his faith had changed over his lifetime. Frost responded with a long and charming series of associations, pronouncements, evasions, halfway-serious arguments, and halfhearted jokes, a comic witness responding to Larry's cross-examination. The subject was meandering even by Frost's standards, but the subtext was clear: Larry wanted answers and Frost did not have them. Larry wanted to explain Frost's religion in terms of clear doctrines adhered to or spurned. Frost made it clear with joke after joke that he either did not know or would not tell. Frost conveyed an irreverence as to all matters of dogma and ritual except the single worthy prayer of *A Masque of Mercy.*

In conversation about the letter soon afterward, Frost elaborated that he found most religious talk absurd—absurd to express ritual adoration or regular prayer to a God who had withdrawn. This echoed what Frost had told Doc Cook on June 1: he had no patience for the false certainty of all religious orthodoxy. He stood with Emerson against dogma itself and had "been moved to the pleasure of tears in reading the Ionian philosophers who challenged the authority and hierarchy of the gods." Yet Frost's meaning was less clear to Larry, who came away from their talk with the understanding that Frost's evasiveness owed itself to the vanity of not being wrong and the convenience of ambiguity. He did not consider the other interpretation, likewise plausible, that Frost out of reverence for a truth he did not think he could understand systematically would see reticence as a point of integrity in avoiding the unearned clarity of dogma. Nor did Larry consider that Frost, in writing to him "I doubt if I was ever religious in your sense of the word," doubtless meant the modern sense of "religious" as adherent to a distinct set of beliefs or practices, as against the more general, premodern sense of the word, denoting any cultivation of one's own relation to the divine however understood or imagined. To Larry's credit, Frost did not spell this out, perhaps reticent to draw the distinction so neatly. In any case, their conversation left Larry delighted. Frost had warned him not to pay too much attention to what he said because he would try to "throw dust" in Larry's eyes. Larry thought this acknowledgment by Frost of his own obfuscation was the greatest gesture of respect that Frost had ever shown him—a sign that Frost thought highly enough of him not to assume that Larry would trust whatever he said. Larry thought their relationship was on the best terms it had been on since they met.

13.

THE BRINK OF MYSTERY

I.

When Sidney Cox passed away suddenly in the winter of 1952, he left behind a manuscript on Frost that he had been working on for decades by one measure and by another all the days of his life. The book, *A Swinger of Birches*, bore the unmistakable aura of apostleship. "You probably felt as I did," Cox's widow, Alice, wrote to Frost, "that Sidney had substituted you for the God that his preacher forebears had worshipped, and the missionary spirit was rampant." Cox could write about Frost in no genre other than spiritual autobiography.

As apostle, Cox approached the mysteries of Frost's religion in a way that was the opposite of Larry the apostate. If, as Cox warned Frost in 1946, Larry could not give himself over to trying to apprehend the mysteries of Frost's heterodox ideas or even respect their existence as anything but a set of inconsistencies, Cox lent himself so deeply to the twists and turns of Frost's mind that he had no independent vantage from which to judge them. The result was intellectually unsatisfying but literarily splendid as a guide to the spiritual possibilities Cox found in Frost's writing and life. For example, in the titular chapter 5, "He Swings Birches," Cox provides a grand figure from Frost's poem "Birches," begun in 1913 and collected in *Mountain Interval*, for what he finds distinctive in Frost's way of thinking. To swing birches, as Cox has it, is to falsify no ambiguities in Frost's spiritual belief—not resting in one extreme or the other, not finding a middle ground, but swinging between ideas in the free play of imagination. In discussing the poem, Cox cites a story of Frost's perfectly apposite for the poem's straining toward a sense of transcendence within the realm of unmistakably worldly things. Cox's story is of Frost by the fireside wondering whether there might be some truth in the claim of monists, like Milton, who believed, in contrast to dualists like Frost, that the material and the spiritual are one:

> One evening before my fire he again considered the claims of monists. And finally he said, No, they never quite come to one. A great many things are like the flames there, in the fireplace. The outside margin on each side swings inward and upward, upward, almost to a point. It's as if they want to. Once in a great while the two sides of the blade of fire go so close to one that for an instant you aren't quite sure. But they lapse so quickly that you almost conclude you didn't see it one. And like all earthly things, they are two. Two here, with enough suggestion now and then of one to make the wishful say it is so now.

At the risk of pedantry, one could venture a slight textual criticism of Cox's otherwise thematically apposite title. Though the title is *A Swinger of Birches*, the speaker of "Birches," unnamed in the poem but with nothing to distinguish him from Frost, is not in fact a swinger of birches. He is someone who once was a swinger of birches and someone who dreams of being one again, a swinger in reminiscence and in dreamy aspiration. Calling him a swinger in the present tense is typical of Cox's book in seeing the spiritual potential in the ambiguous reality, a practice that in this case falsifies an ambiguity on which the whole poem turns.

That "Birches" rests throughout on an implicit and ambivalent

analogy between the act of swinging and the art of verse is evident less in
discrete passages taken alone than in the whole sweep of the poem:

> When I see birches bend to left and right
> Across the lines of straighter darker trees,
> I like to think some boy's been swinging them.
> But swinging doesn't bend them down to stay
> As ice-storms do. Often you must have seen them
> Loaded with ice a sunny winter morning
> After a rain. They click upon themselves
> As the breeze rises, and turn many-colored
> As the stir cracks and crazes their enamel.
> Soon the sun's warmth makes them shed crystal shells
> Shattering and avalanching on the snow-crust—
> Such heaps of broken glass to sweep away
> You'd think the inner dome of heaven had fallen.
> They are dragged to the withered bracken by the load,
> And they seem not to break; though once they are bowed
> So low for long, they never right themselves:
> You may see their trunks arching in the woods
> Years afterwards, trailing their leaves on the ground
> Like girls on hands and knees that throw their hair
> Before them over their heads to dry in the sun.
> But I was going to say when Truth broke in
> With all her matter-of-fact about the ice-storm
> I should prefer to have some boy bend them
> As he went out and in to fetch the cows—
> Some boy too far from town to learn baseball,
> Whose only play was what he found himself,
> Summer or winter, and could play alone.
> One by one he subdued his father's trees
> By riding them down over and over again
> Until he took the stiffness out of them,

And not one but hung limp, not one was left
For him to conquer. He learned all there was
To learn about not launching out too soon
And so not carrying the tree away
Clear to the ground. He always kept his poise
To the top branches, climbing carefully
With the same pains you use to fill a cup
Up to the brim, and even above the brim.
Then he flung outward, feet first, with a swish,
Kicking his way down through the air to the ground.
So was I once myself a swinger of birches.
And so I dream of going back to be.
It's when I'm weary of considerations,
And life is too much like a pathless wood
Where your face burns and tickles with the cobwebs
Broken across it, and one eye is weeping
From a twig's having lashed across it open.
I'd like to get away from earth awhile
And then come back to it and begin over.
May no fate willfully misunderstand me
And half grant what I wish and snatch me away
Not to return. Earth's the right place for love:
I don't know where it's likely to go better.
I'd like to go by climbing a birch tree,
And climb black branches up a snow-white trunk
Toward heaven, till the tree could bear no more,
But dipped its top and set me down again.
That would be good both going and coming back.
One could do worse than be a swinger of birches.

The poem recalls and slowly reconstructs the climb and descent that con-
stitutes swinging a birch, the deliberate path upward and the graceful
swing down as the weight of your body bends a high, thin part of the tree

toward the earth. The poet imagines the climb as if it took him out of earthly life, only to set him back down in the world. The poem climbs slowly and almost imperceptibly from associations concrete, physical, and temporal to those immaterial, ethereal, and outside the normal course of time, from the material toward a spiritual realm. The climb is eased by the exquisite gracefulness of the lines, Frost's greatest achievement in versification for the play of sentence sounds against a regular meter, lines in which the tone moves by increments from a charmed recollection to a wistfulness whose longing overtakes the speaker's reserve. These movements of emotion, tone, and associations take the reader with the poet on the final imagined swing at the end of the poem as the poem itself strains toward the transcendence that the poet yearns for in the swing. And then the ending brings the reader and the poet back to earth, to the quotidian, to the point of view from which the climb is not a felt reality, as in a vision, but a mere possibility, thought of with reserve once again. Hovering over the end is a question like that at the end of Keats's rhapsodic "Ode to a Nightingale": "Was it a vision, or a waking dream?" As in, does the poet of "Birches" intuit the spiritual or merely long for it in dreamy aspiration? Is he a swinger of birches?

This ambivalence is as representative of Frost's thinking as anything else in this representative poem. For all that Frost imagined a spiritual realm behind a material surface, he also held the misgiving that what seemed like spirit was no more than matter in disguise. That Frost so often asserted his belief in the spirit says in part that he felt the need to assert it in company. The spiritual ideal of the self is constantly beset by the possible intrusion of evil or the baser drives of psychological impulse in the intimate doubt of the poems. Doc Cook insightfully called Frost's dual vision of spiritual and material aspects of the world "stereoscopic" for the process by which distinct images combine to form a continuous whole.

Another way to see the poet's ambivalence about his spiritual insight in "Birches" is to note how dissimilar the act of swinging birches really

is to the art of writing a poem. One doubts that the boy climbing trees
in the woods has much of a penchant for spiritual longing. In fact it is
partly the boy's lack of self-consciousness that makes his play a figure
for the spiritual experience of which the poet fondly dreams. One can
hardly miss the tension in finding a dream of transcendence in a wish
for regression. This tension is, as it happens, as old as the genre in which
"Birches" slyly participates, that of pastoral, in which the self-conscious
artist composing the poem affects a stylized identification with mower
and herdsman, supposedly primitive artists with a profound and spontaneous connection to their natural surroundings. To write pastorally is
not to believe yourself primitive, but it often is to evoke what you believe
primitive artists can. In English poetry since Wordsworth, the early stages
of life have readily served as a substitute for the supposedly early stages of
civilization. The boy whom Frost imagines riding tree after tree does so
on his way to fetch the cows, making him a kind of cowherd after the
shepherds and goatherds of pastoral convention. Frost had said that the
poems of *North of Boston*—the poems he once called "New England Eclogues," in whose style "Birches" is written—had been inspired not only
by the pastoral *Eclogues* of the Roman Virgil but by their Greek source in
the *Idylls* of Theocritus. Frost's image of birches bent by human weight
down to the ground finds an echo in the harvest festival at the end of
Theocritus's famous Idyll 7, in which the trees also seem to bestow a
grace on the people around them:

> Apples and pears rolled all around us, enclosing
> Our bodies with plenty; branches reached to the ground,
> Bent with the weight of plums.

It was the idyll in which Theocritus introduced a herdsman poet with a
most distinguished afterlife: the goatherd Lycidas.

Milton borrowed the name and, roughly, the character for his eponymous pastoral elegy written for an acquaintance in 1637. "Lycidas"

enjoyed a superlative reputation in the time of Frost's youth. One critic memorably called it "the high-water mark of English Poesy" in 1879. Frost called it "the height of poetry" and "the greatest poem of them all." He claimed to have recited the whole poem to himself on the summit of Mount Lafayette. When asked once by Doc Cook where he got his theory of vocal tones, Frost exclaimed, "'Lycidas!'" before "quot[ing] a dozen lines with the vocal images in them." Frost only ever made a similar claim for the sonnets of Shakespeare. Writing to Frost in 1928 about his third elegy for Thomas, "A Soldier," Cox reminded Frost "what you said to me about Lycidas: the sound alone, if I could not hear the words, would make me worth more to myself and would give me a moment so perfect I could almost call it absolutely perfect." It is an astonishing thing for Frost to have said. Nowhere else in the record does he talk about a poem in language so close to that of spiritual clarification and a sense of tran-scendence. The sound without the words would make him worth more to himself. It would give him a moment he could almost say was absolutely perfect.

Though "Lycidas" is dense with allusions and learned to the point of ostentation, Frost was struck by the sense of a voice speaking out to him in his encounter with the poem in Palgrave. He found the poem "almost colloquial." It gave him "something to do with every sentence," he said, "something to do in tones and dramatic shading." Milton's every sentence was as Frost would want his sentence sounds to be in his poems: at once directly meaningful and distinctly embodied by an implicit perspective of character. Frost said he found something new in the poem whenever he read it after having known it for sixty years. Frost found a characteristically homely figure for the bounty of meanings that continually dawn on the reader after a slight delay: popcorn.

> Every single line pops like popcorn. Turns white on you. The delay, the beauty of one word. You get it in three people chiefly . . . Shakespeare, Milton, and Keats, and almost in Tennyson by derivation. Keats wrote

this very way in "On First Looking into Chapman's Homer" and in "Ode to a Nightingale."

Perhaps Frost had in mind those deep veins of meaning when he said of the poem that "in every sentence there is something that *is* something." It was a claim on the cliff's edge of mysticism, perfectly suiting Frost's sense of the poem.

Setting mysticism aside (or keeping it in mind), one can notice the similarity between the experience of reading "Birches" and that of "Lycidas" as Frost describes it. Each of the poems affixes an exquisite range of emotional tones to a regular meter. Each is pentameter, though "Birches" in blank verse and "Lycidas" irregularly rhymed with the occasional foreshortened trimeter line of the ode, an effect Frost manages in his own way. The lines in each poem have the rather amorphous but arresting effect of letting their meanings dawn on the reader with a slight delay, the kernels of meaning never disclosing themselves quite the same way twice. Impressionistically, the sentences in each of the poems give the sense of a lingering meaning apprehended but never comprehended entirely— something that *is* something. There is a striking resemblance between the felt experiences of the superficially dissimilar components of the two poems, the height of Frost's achievement with vocal tones and the poem from which Frost said he got his theory of them. If Frost's poem is the far more colloquial, that was also what he heard in "Lycidas," alongside an intimation of transcendence conjured by the very art of the poem.

The issue of transcendence is the subject of Milton's pastoral as well as Frost's, a prospect figured in each case by a pastorally stylized poem within a poem. Milton's pastoral poet is a classical "herdsman" who sings along to his rustic wind instrument. Frost's cowherd swings rather than sings, climbing black branches up the white trunk of a birch, while Milton's shepherd lets the wind blow through the black holes along the trunk of his oaten flute. The wind makes itself felt in the first line of "Birches": "When I see birches bend to left and right." Archetypally, the wind figures in "Lycidas" both as an instance of the destructive power of the natural world and as the manifestation of an invisible divinity within the material realm. It is this sense of enchantment for which the poems both yearn as recompense (Milton's word) for their respective losses, Milton's for Lycidas the lost youth and Frost's for his lost state of youth, each hoping to revive that enchantment by the connection their respective primitive poets bore toward a natural order not indifferent to them. The transcendence figured in both poems has a distinctive cosmology both Christian and polytheistically Greek, one in which the divine is not only on a separate plane of existence but literally above the human realm. So it is that the tree Frost imagines bringing him up *"toward* heaven" carries a sense of an ascent in degree that also elevates him in kind, just like the wind that carries Lycidas aloft into a presiding spirit at the end of that poem.

The speakers in each poem undergo emotional progressions in a number of similar stages. A brief introductory frame is followed by a depiction of destruction and loss, a recollection of a harmonic past, and a vision for a future in which the present loss is transcended, the enchanted harmony of the past raised to spiritual salvation. The poems each end with a short coda pulling the reader away from the vision. In structural terms, the great difference between the poems is that "Birches" lacks the long and incomparable theo-mythological interlude between the recollection in "Lycidas" and the vision of transcendence, greatly condensing disparate parts of the poem as Frost did when writing his own versions of other poets' longer verse, as with Wordsworth's ode in "Nothing Gold Can Stay." The interlude accounts for the missing lines in the parallel outline below. The overlapping sections of the poems are unsurprisingly also the passages in which the language of "Birches" resounds most often with the language of "Lycidas."

I. FRAME

"BIRCHES" 1–4

Speaker introduces himself by
reference to trees beheld by
him

"LYCIDAS" 1–5

Speaker introduces himself by
reference to trees beheld by him

II. DESTRUCTION DEPICTED

"BIRCHES" 5–16

Extended description of birches
brought low by ice storms, never
to be righted again

"LYCIDAS" 6–22

Extended description of Lycidas
drowned

III. RECOLLECTION OF HARMONIC PAST

"BIRCHES" 17–37

Speaker describes a swinger of
birches, as he himself was as a
boy

"LYCIDAS" 23–44

Speaker describes himself and
Lycidas together in youth

IV. VISION OF RECOMPENSE

"BIRCHES" 38–53

Speaker envisions swinging a
birch as a way to get away
from earth "And then come
back to it and begin over."

"LYCIDAS" 165–85

Speaker envisions Lycidas
transformed into the presiding
spirit of the shore, "sunk low, but
mounted high."

V. CODA

"BIRCHES" 54–55

"LYCIDAS" 186–93

The codas to the respective poems, though both brief and discontinuous
with the visions preceding them, are something like opposites. The coda
to "Birches," abrupt at only two lines, is almost jarringly understated, as
if its very tone were letting the reader down from the ascent and back to

the disenchanted world in which the poem began. The coda to "Lycidas"
is among the most sublime passages in English literature, disclosing that
the poem had been spoken thus far by a pastoral character, an "uncouth
swain," and amplifying the preceding spiritual vision in a prismatic array
of images on a scale simultaneously human and as wide as the horizon
and then as wide as earth, as if the pastoral poet were one with the whole.
Frost's understatement leaves the reader cut off from this grandeur, left to
long for it inchoately or maybe never think of such spiritual confidence
at all.

   Both poems envision transcendence in terms of ascent and descent mediated by a nature no longer indifferent. The spirit of Lycidas is stretched
into the air above the shore: "So Lycidas sunk low, but mounted high."
Frost's birches in the storm from section 2 are brought perpetually low.
His vision of transcendence inverts the motion of Lycidas, mounting high
and being set down again, in a vision not of transcending the world but of
knowing transcendence possible in this world. It is a vision that, like Milton's, adds a Christian sense of the penetration of spirit into matter to a
previously pagan image of harmonious existence with a reciprocal natural
world. Milton's principal image of natural harmony from the third section of his poem was, as is only fitting, trees moving in harmony with the
primitive poet. The willows with their low-hanging branches moved their
leaves to Lycidas's song while he and the primitive poet in their younger
days dallied as they went out to fetch their flocks:

   The willows, and the hazel copses green,
   Shall now no more be seen,
   Fanning their joyous leaves to thy soft lays (sec. 3, lines 42–44)

If this sounds rather far afield from "When I see birches bend to left and
right," Frost may well have wanted it that way. He had a habit of covering
the tracks of his influences, all the more so the deeper the influence. In
this case, writing "Birches" in a register far simpler than that of "Lyci-

das" was itself an engagement with the tradition of which "Lycidas" was part, Milton's learned poem being an imitation not of Theocritus but of Virgil's learned imitation of Theocritus, who actually imitated something of the manner of the folk poetry of his day. Whether or not Frost had this in mind, it is of the essence of his poem that its manner of presenting theology is the opposite of Milton's in "Lycidas." Milton's manner is dense, grand, and visionary, befitting both his temperament and his epoch. He had doubt enough to fear that there was no consolation to be had after death and no way to be certain of the presence of the soul, but faith enough to quell his doubt with a resounding declaration of belief. Frost's manner could hardly be more different on the subject. It has no theology, allusiveness, density, or formality of any kind. Its religion is almost entirely implicit. It asserts no transcendence. It offers no grand affirmation in response to spiritual disquiet. What it offers instead is a story set within the bounds of the material world of the wish for something beyond it. Milton envisions, Frost dreams, but in a dream that brings one to an experience so nearly perfect that one might well wonder if the waking dream was a vision. One could surely do worse than Frost pacing around his yard in Beaconsfield, four miles from where Milton wrote *Paradise Lost*, thinking of birches back home.

II.

Among Frost's oldest and oddest convictions was a belief in some version of the transmigration of souls. Following a passage in Schopenhauer, itself following a passage at the end of Plato's *Republic*, Frost in the year of his graduation from high school, 1892, began to draft a poem about Plato's Myth of Er, in which a human spirit chooses its life before its entrance into the realm of material life. Having chosen its course in the poem, "The Trial by Existence," the spirit is bound to matter until the onset of death. Yet the binding to matter also blinds the spirit to the memory of its whole prior existence. Some such version of the myth stayed with Frost his whole life, the belief that people were spirits, or wills, entangled in matter but that the presence of spirit could not be known directly. Spirit had rather to be inferred under conditions of uncertainty. Frost said as much in his last major piece of prose, "The Constant Symbol," from 1946, in which he described poetry as in every instance a symbol "of the will braving alien entanglements," a constant symbol of spirit investing itself in matter and managing to carry out its intention without being lost amid the contingent pulls of its material. Poetry was in the abstract always a figure for spirit attempting to retain its integrity as embodied in the material world. In other words, poetry was a figure for life as Frost thought we experienced it, in the ambiguous space between that which we determine and that which is determined for us, between will and impulse, soul and body, love and need. It was no accident that his figure for the clear manifestation of spirit was often that of water on the edge of clarity, as in the pools of snowmelt destined to vanish in "Spring Pools," a dialogue of self and soul, or the pasture spring he's going out to clean.

Frost was fond of saying that poetry and religion and even science meet in excelsis, which translates literally as "the highest" but which he also spoke of as "glory," as in the glory of God. He invokes this range of meanings in his description of "Birches" as "play in excelsis," a climb upward as a figure for reaching beyond. Frost also described poetry as "play on the brink of mystery." It was a charmed description of his lyric poetry at its most arresting as well as the poetry of his precursors that he was moved to make into his own. "Play on the brink of mystery" evokes play in the abstract and the concrete at once, as in playing on an idea and playing up in a tree, tree and idea each on the brink of mystery. The phrase captures the constant action of the constant symbol at the edge of commonsensical material existence and the life of the spirit. It is the boy in "Birches" in his solitary play "climbing carefully / With the same pains you use to fill a cup / Up to the brim, and even above the brim" until his cup runneth over. It is the figure made by "The Pasture" of love that transports the listener as it invites them, an intimacy at the edge of the listener's will.

"Play on the brink of mystery" encompasses the figure in "The Free-dom of the Moon" of the poetic imagination either grandly unconstrained or unconsciously channeling the origin myths of the Christian tradition; the figure in "The Silken Tent" of the loose bonds of erotic love enmeshed with the binding of souls after death; the figure in "Hyla Brook" of the spiritual imperative and cascade of practical doubts involved in following the maxim "We love the things we love for what they are." No less is "Two Tramps in Mud Time" play on the brink of mystery for setting the very ideal that "Only where love and need are one, / And the work is play for mortal stakes, / Is the deed ever really done / For heaven and the future's sakes," for spirit and self, or "Directive" for the renewal of spirit through the restoration of memory, an act whose being of the imagination need not, might not, make its conclusions merely imaginary. That is a question for every instance of the constant symbol, for every lyric of Frost's heretofore considered in the present work: the extent to which what has been imagined has been invented and to what extent revealed, as in the entrance of God's spirit into matter in the shining image of "The Freedom of the Moon." Frost's paradigmatic response was Horatio's line for its inarticulably fine shades of ambivalent faith—"So have I heard and do in part believe it." How else to take "They would not find me changed from him they knew—/ Only more sure of all I thought was true"? "And I—/ I took the one less traveled by, / And that has made all the difference"? "Yet some say Love by being thrall / And simply staying possesses all / In several beauty that Thought fares far / To find fused in another star"? "We love the things we love for what they are"?

14.

The Heart of Any Religion

————

I.

Anne Morrison had boys at the house when she got the call from the hospital. How old was she, they asked. Seventeen. Was there an adult they could speak to? It was about her brother. Anne rang the bell to call Frost and her mother down from his cabin and her father down from his, where he worked on his writing alone. The boys had the good sense to get lost. Anne didn't know what she was going to say.

It was the day before New Year's Eve 1954. The family had gone up to Ripton for Christmas vacation. Anne's older brother, Bobby, had gotten married two days before, driving north afterward for a honeymoon in the ski town of Stowe. He had gotten out of the car, leaving his wife, Barbara, inside as he removed the chains from their tires when another car, driven by a sixteen-year-old boy, skidded. Bobby was dead within hours.

Frost kept quiet when he heard the news despite his obvious distress. Anne took his silence as a way to be supportive, presumably because she thought he didn't want to distract from their grieving with his. Her mother's composure struck her as something else entirely. Years later, Anne could remember only one thing her mother told her after Bobby's death. It was on the drive to the funeral. Her mother said, "We do not cry at funerals."

Anne could sense the depth of her mother's fear even as the self-stifling left her aghast. She was especially angry at her mother for not supporting Ted in his grieving. Anne may well have been swayed in her perspective by a letter Bobby had sent her from college, warning his little sister about the unkind aspects of their mother hiding under a pleasant exterior. Anne felt that her brother, whom she greatly looked up to, was trying to protect her. The letter resurfaced one evening when Anne and her father were talking, her father reminiscing about how much Bobby had loved Kay, to which Anne responded, with an impulse she later saw as tinged with revenge toward her mother, by saying that Bobby did write this letter to her. She handed her father the letter, which he tore up after reading.

His destroying the letter was a shock to her, a betrayal. Though she still loved and admired her father profoundly, never again could she trust him entirely. Part of her surprise was the evident fact that he could get rid of something so easily.

II.

As a child, Anne often ran a high fever. It was her father in her recollection who would sit with her in her feverish state. Anne would babble about fairies or other creatures in a local pond; her father would remember every detail. She remembered him as inveterately thoughtful and generous; as reserved and genteel but affectionate with her; as a beautiful man and a "saint."

Anne remembered feeling that she never wanted to be like her mother even before she was old enough to know what it was she wanted to avoid. Her mother was neither affectionate nor nurturing as Anne remembered her. Although Anne later wondered whether to attribute the lack of such impulses to her mother's early experiences accompanying her father on parish calls to poor areas in Scotland with children in horrifying conditions, in which people would hold sick babies by the feet over running gas in unlit fireplaces in a vain attempt at healing their croup, that was not how she, as a young person, understood her mother's emotional unavailability. Anne marveled at the extent of her mother's intimacies outside the family: her mother meant so much to so many people but just not to her.

Anne thought her mother was preoccupied with appearances, "a great one for the fixings." Her mother trusted in the little rules of formal education, and Anne had no respect for little rules in any walk of life. This standard by which Anne would judge her mother owed something to the standards that her mother set for her, pressuring her daughter in Cambridge to grow up to become a scholar. Even at the tony Cambridge School of Weston, Anne "felt like a bit of a freak" for having been brought up to think so much for herself. But this was Frost's influence, too.

There was a summer in high school when she discovered the existentialists and would walk up in the evenings to Frost's cabin to talk existentialism. He persuaded her not to become one. She was among the people for whom his style of teaching worked in encouraging her to take ownership of the material she cared about so that she could get up her own ideas about it. In this and in her disdain for little school rules getting in the way of the idea she was after, "the big prize" as she called it, she inherited Frost's values in contrast to what she felt her mother practiced and thought her mother believed.

During a time when Anne had a sick horse that needed medicine poured in its throat at midnight every night, Frost would join Anne in the barn every midnight. He joined her because, as she learned from her mother (who had learned it from Frost), he would have been afraid to be alone in the barn at that hour. It summed up her relationship with Frost for her that he would do this and also not tell her why. Generally speaking, she felt that her relationship with Frost was full of play. "He never had anyone to play with, I don't think," she recalled, excepting herself by implication.

Nothing was said to Anne in the household about the mysterious terms of the arrangement that had obtained between Frost and her mother since Anne was young enough for Frost to hold her on his knee. She had the thought half a century after Frost's death that she didn't tend to think of Frost as attached to other people, even though she knew abstractly that he was, and did not "know anything about Frost before we had him." "He was ours."

Her earliest sustained memory of the strangeness came from a car ride. Anne, ten or so at the time, sat in the back while her parents and Frost sat on the bench seat in the front, Ted driving with his arm around Kay, and Frost, to Kay's right, with his arm around her as well. That the memory might be less than entirely accurate makes it no less emblematic of Anne's point of view as she grew up with the strangeness. She had grown aware by high school of the shadow at the heart of the family's atypical arrangement. The precipitous event in her sense of the relationship was on a Saturday night in the summer of 1953 or 1954, when Anne was sixteen or seventeen. Stafford Dragon, Frost's bibulous hired man, was predictably drunk. He told Anne that he knew Frost and her mother were sleeping together. She made what she saw in retrospect as the mistake of asking how he knew, and he said he looked in the window.

Anne thought the ugly truth of the situation was that her mother got more "flash" from Frost than Ted could give her, putting Ted in a position Anne never knew why he put up with. Anne did, however, take it as a given that her mother loved Frost.

III.

Once on a summer evening toward the end of the decade, the Morrisons' dinner was disrupted by the sound of a gunshot outside the farmhouse. Frost, hard of hearing by then, got a sense of the disruption from the looks on Ted's and Kay's faces. Anne's first husband, Chisholm Gentry, or Chis, went outside to find Stafford firing his pistol into the air and brandishing a pint of vodka in his other hand. Stafford was animated by the sense that Kay was being mistreated, that Ted was not good enough to her, that she was a fine woman who deserved better. Chis asked for a drink from his pint, hoping to stop him from getting any more drunk, only to discover that the bottle was not full of vodka but a cheap white wine.

Chis was sure that he spotted a fraud. He knew Stafford's prodigious drinking habits well enough to know that Stafford would never lose control of himself on the strength of something as weak as that wine. The wine's transposition into the vodka bottle was a sign that Stafford was acting drunker than he was to say what he couldn't get away with saying sober. It was a way to mark his territory, thought Chis, "like a dog pissing on a tree."

Chis took the display as a sign that Stafford and Kay were sleeping together. All it shows on that score, however, is that Stafford was besotted with her, which everyone around them already knew, Anne included. Rumors nonetheless persisted. Almost surely, the rumors say more about the rumormongers than the subjects, seeing in a hint of unbound female sexuality the Whore of Babylon, a creature dominated by sexual impulse. One can say much the same about the other sexual rumors trailing Kay around Bread Loaf. Anne was privy to whispers about her mother and Larry as well as her mother and Benny DeVoto. Neither case was remotely substantiated, and either would have required a psychologically unthinkable level of risk not only from Kay but from the men putatively involved, the biographer who would risk losing it all with his subject, the best friend of Ted for whom Frost's purely emotional intrusion on the friendship was an act of psychic devastation. It is true that DeVoto once had a crush on her of sorts, but so did any number of men moved by her charms, as he said himself. The pattern of rumors about Kay attests to the fear that would magnify the destructive effects of female sexual power. The rumors were also surely a reflection of the tendency for tall tales to grow where satisfying explanations are scarce, as with the arrangement at the heart of Kay's professional life.

One can also infer from Chis's story that Stafford was an imperfectly reliable witness when behaving drunkenly and talking about Kay.

IV.

When Larry showed up in Ripton in the beginning of August 1957, he found Kay and Ted picnicking with some of her relatives on the lawn of the Homer Noble Farm. She asked Larry to stop by soon for a talk, requesting that he come sometime when Stafford wasn't around. The reason, she explained, was that Stafford had gotten the idea that she and Larry had slept together on Larry's last night in Ripton the summer before. Larry took the misapprehension as a consequence of Kay's flattery: "She has always tried to butter Stafford up in ways which Stafford takes as 'intimacies,' and he has misinterpreted her butter-ups as justification for his subsequent jealousies." Larry thought it was a "nice variant on the D. H. Lawrence formula of relationships between the caretaker and the 'lady,'" one in which the relationship existed only in the caretaker's mind.

Though Kay and Larry shared a private breakfast a few days later, their most revealing conversation of the summer was at a cocktail party later in the month. Kay went up to Larry with a problem. She was concerned about the references to her and Frost that might be in the archives of Benny DeVoto, sold the year before to Stanford, a year after he passed away. She said Frost had misled people about their relationship, giving people a sense of intimacies that were not there and a rupture in her and Ted's marriage that was not there either. Larry, too, had once misunderstood, warning her in a letter not to leave her marriage for Frost. On the present matter, Larry tried to assuage her concern, "remind[ing] her that I had already told Frost, repeatedly, that whatever I said about Kay and Frost would be subject to Kay's revision and censorship; that I considered this a matter of good taste to avoid offense of Kay or Ted or Anne, and she could count on me." Kay took Larry's reassurances well before adding a reminder of her own, saying, "I'm his literary executor, you know," as Larry was all too aware.

She had no need to fear, Larry thought: he meant what he said about leaving whatever he wrote about her and Frost to her judgment. Larry thought that her dishonesty made her fearfully suspect dishonesty in others. In this case, she was hardly far off, as it was with a dissembling much like dishonesty that Larry listened to her explain the prevailing misunderstandings about her and Frost while "wondering what she would say if I told her Frost had asked me three times, while we were together in England, if I couldn't 'leave something in escrow,' about his love-affairs with Kay, and about the fact that Kay had really saved his life." She was doing her best as a censor whom Frost was doing his best to subvert.

The trip to England, with an interlude in Ireland, had lasted a month between May and June. Frost received honorary degrees from Oxford, Cambridge, and University College Dublin in a grand tour that afforded him some of the highest distinction possible in Anglophone literature. Larry went along partly to do things like arrange for Frost's breakfast in his hotel room and ration Frost's sleeping pills, per doctor's orders, incurring Frost's wrath. On the trip, Frost's insistence on Larry's leaving a record of his and Kay's secret was reminiscent of Frost's lament the year before about how hard it had been on Kay and him to keep their love hidden for the last eighteen years, in response to which Larry thought "she must have had some kind of love for him, to survive all the punishment he has given her."

Those eighteen years had also begotten a three-way conflict of interests among poet, biographer, and manager. The terms of the conflict had recently been brought toward the surface: Frost with the power to disclose or withhold parts of his life story and the authorization to tell it, and Larry with the power to write it as he chose except, of course, as Kay exercised her power to censor what she disapproved of in his telling. The parties to the conflict had begun to show their hands, with Frost urging exposure of a story Kay intended to suppress, and Larry pledging suppression to Kay and subversion to Frost. Frost was torn between placating Kay and dignifying what he believed to be their love, Kay between keeping up appearances and placating Frost.

On a long drive with Larry at the end of the summer, Frost proposed that Larry write not one book about him but two, a less than candid one that Kay would permit as well as a candid shorter book, requiring no per-

missions and therefore subject to no oversight from the executrix. Frost
hoped, Larry wrote, that the shorter book would be written "with the
intent to do honor to both people, caught in an awkward situation, and
acting as honorably and as nobly as love would permit them to act." Curiously enough, Frost's insistence that Larry set the story straight in writing did not compel him to begin the process himself even so much as to
authorize the second book in writing. Indiscreet as Frost was in discussing
the subject with his confidants, his written accounts never crossed the
bright line beyond which insinuation passed into assertion. Even Frost's
pornographic poems with arch implications about himself and Kay—the
work perforce circulating privately or in oral tradition, as when Frost
said a pair to Larry as he drove—were no more clearly testimonial than
"Entree," a ribald comedy in six short lines of verse. Frost's greatest
achievement in the frivolous genre of bawdry, "Entree" is spoken in the
anonymous first person to an anonymous "you," a man reminiscing to
a woman about their old tryst. Frost brings his old powers of compact
drama to this lark of a poem, raising both narrative tension and shock
value with the outlandish end rhymes that close each of three couplets.
The first couplet concludes by revealing that the title is meant anatomi-
cally. The second reveals that the speaker, having noticed his addressee's
initial flinch upon entrée, attributed it at the time to his own generous
endowment, setting up the final couplet:

> But you in quick riposte
> Advised me not to boast

Whether she based her advice on factuality or mere propriety is the question on which the scene turns, an ambiguity of less consequence for the
reader than for her interlocutor.

When poet and biographer returned to Frost's cabin, he copied out
part of a manuscript poem, "Kitty Hawk," and inscribed it for Larry. It
was Larry's last day with Frost for the summer. "So the Ripton diary ends
for 1957," wrote Larry. "Add this to the trip to England in 1957, with

Frost, and it brings him and me to the most intimate relationship we have so far established." But Larry's enthusiasm was no match for his fatalism. "I suppose it can't last," he continued. "We both still suspect each other of certain inadequacies of friendship."

V.

In retrospect, the inadequacies of which poet and biographer suspected each other at the time are something less than certain. This ambiguity would prove consequential because of the extent to which Larry, the chronicler of their friendship, came to misremember its earlier texture. One can nonetheless follow the contours of their relationship over the previous decade even if its innermost heart is opaque.

Though the Thompsons spent every summer in Ripton from 1946 through 1954, a number of those years are short on notes. The incidents between Larry and Frost that Larry saw fit to record tended to involve peaks and troughs of the relationship, heights of intimacy and praise or the strain of rebukes and misgivings. Peaks and troughs were both on display in the summer of 1953, which at the time seemed to Larry "the summer in which I have been on terms of intimacy with Frost, greater than at any time since we were in Key West together." Frost was concerned that in his biography Larry might attribute some of his own thoughts to Frost by mistake, and continue to discount the importance of fear as the beginning of wisdom and, with it, religion. As Larry nodded along to Frost's airing of concerns while Larry packed his last things to leave Ripton at summer's end, he felt like nodding off, which Frost may have noticed in frustration before giving Larry a long cold look as the two parted ways for the summer. Larry pretended not to notice but did not pretend to understand:

> As we shook hands, I looked him square in the eyes and found to my surprise that he was looking, not only square into my eyes, but hard, in a way I couldn't understand but didn't like. I smiled, and didn't flinch my gaze. So we stared, for a second, and so we parted.

"I had hoped that some of the tensions of the past might be buried," Larry wrote after their parting. "But now I know that the tensions will never stay buried, and that Kay Morrison will keep them operative, even if nobody else does." Thus end his notes for the summer on that damning accusation. Writing for himself, he chose not to clarify the charge. Contextual evidence suggests that Larry was upset with Kay over raising the rent for the farmhouse of Frost's that the Thompsons stayed in, and that Kay's problems with Larry were twofold: she feared what Frost had told him about her and resented the loss of a certain quality of his attention after his marriage, finding him, as he later reflected, altogether less "charming." The pieces fit together if she thought his marriage made him less sensible to her charms as well, giving her, who wielded influence through charm, all the more reason to fear what he knew.

Kay's tensions with Larry obtruded most directly on the biography in the summer of 1954. At least Larry thought it was her wishes behind a startling proposal Frost made after the two men shared a "very pleasant" lunch in a town west of Ripton on a rainy day in July. "Wasn't it possible," Frost asked, "that I had been working so hard and so long on Frost that I was actually sick of the whole thing? Wouldn't I be pleased if he gave me the chance to set out from under the whole load, and turn to something else?"

The curious thing about Frost's proposal is that he was hardly trying to push Larry away in general. Frost had lately offered Larry suggestions about the biography, and earlier on the day of their lunch had asked Larry whether he might buy the Euber farm the Thompsons had rented from him for years. It was not Frost's first time proposing the sale, nor was it Larry's first time rejecting it on grounds of affordability. Larry responded to Frost's suggestion about the biography with an impassioned speech, to which "Frost said that was all very nice, but that I knew too much. I had been with him in Elizabethtown, the night he had come closer to murdering than he had ever come at any other time." This was the point at which Larry surmised that Kay had asked Frost to make the request. Larry responded to Frost by sharing a plan to assuage the concerns that Frost

might share with Kay: "I wanted it understood between him and her and
me that if she saw anything in the book which she thought should not be
there, I'd be perfectly willing to take it out." "He may think I am inadequate, incapable, as biographer," Larry reflected, "and maybe I am. But
at least he now has my word that I shall not be writing a book filled with
petty and personal stuff which would be offensive to him and others."

On matters regarding Frost's estimation of Larry's adequacy in discussing his work, Larry was exquisitely sensitive. He would remember a
discussion of Frost's poetry that he and Frost filmed for NBC in early
1955 as shambolic, a "public humiliation" of him at the hands of an angry
Frost. Had Larry brought himself to watch the recording, he might have
noticed Frost restraining himself as Larry tried to provoke him by expli-
cating his poem in front of him, even saying to Frost, "Now I've broken
it down so I've made you unhappy, I hope." Larry said on camera that he
had "a way of measuring" his different responses to a poem before and
after analyzing it—"but it might be a way of measuring my stupidity."

Larry's insecurity about his authority on Frost's work helps to frame
the most dramatic conflict among him, Frost, and Kay in those years,
which stretched from early 1956 through the summer of 1960. The protracted contretemps was a tale of rivalry and, for Larry, of treachery. A
longtime acquaintance and admirer of Frost's, Elizabeth Shepley Sergeant,
had appealed to Larry for help with the biographical context for a book
she presented to him as an appreciation of Frost's poetry, only to use the
substantial research he shared for a book she sold as a proper biography to Al Edwards, Larry's and Frost's editor at Holt. Larry was furious
with Sergeant for years before his fury extended to Kay and Frost as well
sometime between the spring of 1958 and the summer of 1959. Larry
had come to believe that Kay and Frost had actively betrayed him and
then pretended that their sins of commission were no more than lapses
in oversight. Though he left no record of specific betrayals, he most likely
caught wind of the extensive help Frost and Kay provided Sergeant, hardly
a secret among the close associates of Frost's with whom Larry was often

in contact. For Frost's and Kay's part, there is no reason to doubt their good faith in telling Larry that they did not think her book posed any threat to him, a view Larry himself came to grant when he read it after it was published in 1960 and even wrote a gracious review of it. Still, he had been disregarded. Word even reached him on his short visit to Ripton in the summer of 1959 that Frost had lately taken to blaming Larry for letting his guard down with Sergeant. It was not the first time Larry saw Frost criticizing someone he had wronged to avoid feeling guilt for the wrong, a sign nonetheless that Frost felt some guilt to deny.

Was Kay wrong, then, to ascribe Larry's reaction to jealousy? Not entirely. For all that his indignation proved to be righteous, it was magnified throughout by the acute vulnerability and fearful possessiveness that characterize jealousy as distinguished from envy. His jealous fear made their thoughtlessness out to be malice, a reaction he saw not as a sign of his own vulnerability but as an external threat. Such things had happened other times as well. Larry's reactions were politic in each instance, hiding the depth of his feelings for the sake of comity. Yet the price of buried rage was its entrenchment, leaving mute anger and compensatory detachment where there had been intimacy. Frost wrote to Larry about the Sergeant affair in a placating letter whose generosity was visible only to the kind of sympathetic eye that Larry's resentment had largely left shut. "We have sized each other up without disillusionment," Frost's letter read. "One or other of us will fathom me sooner or later."

VI.

Late in the evening of Larry's last night in Ripton in August 1959, Frost raised the problem of his biography in a way he never had with Larry before:

> What I had to realize, he said, was that his way of going after knowledge constituted his idiom: and his way was to think of things in terms of uncertainties; issues which could not be resolved; issues which had

two sides to them, so that they worked as "struts" to hold different things apart. Knowledge of truth was impossible, but knowledge of opposed ways of looking at one and the same thing was something. He said that particular attention should be paid (by his biographers) to this line: "I would be taken as never having rebelled." He said that I was a rebel, and I was a fighter. I like to rebel, liked to fight. So I would have a tendency to read into Frost my own story of rebellion. That would be a mistake.

Larry took Frost to be making an argument for his own open-mindedness. Larry fought the idea in his notes. "Well shit," he wrote. "We're back to another one of those precious Frost postures or myths which are important because they reveal the way he wishes people would 'take' him. He would not be taken for the narrow minded and prejudiced sonofabitch he is. . . . I just sat and listened."

As Frost walked Larry downhill from the cabin toward his car, Frost wondered what his old, unself-conscious letters might reveal about his motives. The problem, Larry said, is that they would reveal, at most, motives at a particular time. The difficulty of biography, even the impossibility of it, was, Larry said, to gather and reveal the interaction of contradictory motives—to show the range of motives over a lifetime. Frost liked that way of framing the problem. "He remembered," Larry wrote, "that someone had said to him, after they had talked for a while, I NEVER BEFORE HEARD SO MANY CONTRADICTIONS THAT MAKE SENSE," to which Larry responded in his notes, "There it is."

Implicit in the constant symbol is a constant mystery of motives. To render the nature of human motivation ambiguous between forces admitting of spiritual and material explanation, Frost had to embed at least a pair of perspectives as if by struts in a poem. This balance of perspectives represented Frost at both his most modest and his most insightful, in lyric or narrative or letters or life. Yet by 1959 it had been nearly two decades since he last consistently made his contradictions make sense in verse, leaning instead on poems that tended to entertain or to pronounce with something like the conviction that Larry saw him using to shut down an argument. It was these private displays of domineering narrow-mindedness that Larry felt marked the real Frost underneath the precious postures, having been witness to many such displays over the prior two decades. But what if Larry had grown too close to Frost to take his measure? What account could he give of Frost's life after growing cynical about Frost's every motive and dismissive of Frost's understanding of human psychology and the spiritual tradition to which it belonged? There was hardly anything as important to that tradition as a faith in the potential integrity of personal ideals. To hold yourself to such an ideal is to live with the painful sense of having often fallen short after trying, a pain in which Frost took a mysterious pleasure. Yet for Larry to see such ideals—open-mindedness, for one—only from the perspective of cynical doubt was to not see the trying at all.

VII.

Frost, always one to repeat himself, spent a good deal of his later years doing just that. In his public appearances, held in a semi-regular circulation corresponding roughly to the school year, he said a number of the same poems to his audiences night after night. These readings, so called, were a partly improvisational performance like the informal talks with which he would begin, one-sided conversations that most often returned, if not quite verbatim, to familiar themes that helped to frame the poems he then began to say, dropping here and there back into raffish commentary after, say, "The Road Not Taken," "Stopping by Woods on a Snowy Evening." The poet Randall Jarrell, Frost's great critic among Lowell's generation of poets, saw Frost's opening monologues as a kind of singular extempore free verse that was, in Frost's deafness, his way to connect with the world.

Jarrell exaggerates. Frost was never so deaf, and had social connection enough with all his friends who hosted him on tour, not to mention his friends at Bread Loaf in the summer, in South Miami in the heart of winter, at Amherst (to which Frost moved from Dartmouth in 1949 with almost no obligations of instruction and residence), and in Cambridge when he wasn't off talking somewhere. Still, Frost did call his appearances before "town and gown audiences" the great pleasure of his later years, and his monologues really are best understood as something like free verse. Free verse is relatively informal poetry. Poetry for Frost was the experience of the dawning of an idea, among other things. Frost's introductions and asides were old ideas entertained as if they were new until every so often something dawned on him to make them new again.

The poetry he wrote increasingly resembled the kind of poetry he talked. This is illustrated well by a poem he said in public countless times in those years, "Choose Something Like a Star," from 1943. As he once told a crowd, the poem was a prayer for himself. Almost every poem he ever wrote had at least a line that saved his life for a moment, he once told a crowd in a meaningful variation on an idea he had written before. There can be little doubt which lines in "Choose Something Like a Star" meant most to Frost even for those who did not hear him point the lines out in talk after talk. In this obviousness the poem is unlike the best of his work, in which every line is integral to a form more profound than any one of its parts. The obviousness is like that of his talks, in which much material serves to frame an insight crystallized. Some of what is lost in subtlety is gained in immediate force, as in this poem about finding something constant to look up to in an inconstant world:

O Star (the fairest one in sight),
We grant your loftiness the right
To some obscurity of cloud—
It will not do to say of night,
Since dark is what brings out your light.
Some mystery becomes the proud.

But to be wholly taciturn
In your reserve is not allowed.
Say something to us we can learn
By heart and when alone repeat.
Say something! And it says, 'I burn.'
But say with what degree of heat.
Talk Fahrenheit, talk Centigrade.
Use language we can comprehend.
Tell us what elements you blend.
It gives us strangely little aid,
But does tell something in the end.
And steadfast as Keats' Eremite,
Not even stooping from its sphere,
It asks a little of us here.
It asks of us a certain height,
So when at times the mob is swayed
To carry praise or blame too far,
We may choose something like a star
To stay our minds on and be staid.

Besides the ending, the line to which Frost said he owed his life was "Some mystery becomes the proud." The line was his way to reconcile himself to the poetry of Eliot and Pound. "You don't know what I went through for that," he once told an audience with the kind of animus that sometimes discomposed his public reserve. "Years of trying to bear some of my fellow poets . . . I didn't know what they were talking about."

Staid is the last thing one could call another of Frost's favorite poems to say to an audience, also a prayer, consisting entirely of a rhymed couplet. Frost would intone its first line and pick up his pace for the punch line:

Forgive, O Lord, my little jokes on Thee
And I'll forgive Thy great big one on me.

On a given night, the crowd laughs uproariously and Frost says he always wonders what the poem *releases* in them, so excited his gravelly voice starts to crack.

VIII.

Misunderstandings between Frost and Larry aside, a new phase in their relationship commenced with a trip they took to Israel and Greece in March 1961, arranged by the State Department. Having "got[ten] along so very well" with Frost on their travels, Larry softened in his descriptions of the old man. His newfound sympathy doubtless owed something to his having provided care on the trip for Frost in the vulnerable state of which Larry was increasingly aware. His care would be required again a year later, as Larry learned from a hectic Kay when she called to inform him that Frost, down in Florida, was possibly dying of pneumonia, having gotten himself sick by what Larry called "an accumulations [*sic*] of typically Frostian rages and tensions which clustered a bit too thick." Kay flew down in the morning. Larry would relieve her, if Frost recovered, on March 3.

Among Frost's preemptive goodbyes was a message for Larry, relayed by Kay: Larry was wrong to think he had had religion, lost it, and found it again. He had always been religious. The subject recurred rather often in the two and a half weeks Larry spent at Frost's place in South Miami. Larry was reminded that there was "more religion outside the church than in," and Frost returned to a favorite theme of recent years to the effect that the Bible tells us not only to love thy neighbor as thyself but to hate thy neighbor as thyself because to love something greater than ourselves is to hate the part of ourselves beyond our power to transcend. "It's only when we hate ourselves and our shortcomings that we can love and need God."

Frost, feeling stricken by chest pain at the end of a long night of talking, told Larry that he would have to go easier on him in the future. Larry let it be known that he was in fact exhausted by all the talking. Larry's companion, weeks shy of his eighty-eighth birthday, kept his younger

guest up too late to write notes at the end of the night a few times in the
course of the trip. It was plausibly not a coincidence that Frost observed
on their way to the train back up the coast that life has two basic needs—
sustenance to keep us alive, and attention to keep us from suffering too
much. Frost was deep in an explanation of the arrangement of poems in
his forthcoming book, *In the Clearing,* when Larry began letting on that his
stop was approaching, first subtly and then less so. Larry said that he'd
see Frost at his birthday party, that he thought the visit had been one
of their best. Frost reacted impassively. To Larry's final, anxious "To be
continued," Frost said, flatly, "Yeah." Larry stepped out onto the platform
at about the last possible second, chagrined at the inconsiderate relentless-
ness of Frost's monologuing, and feeling "the great sense of relief I always
experience when I get out from under Frost's commanding and demanding presence." Larry waited on the platform to watch Frost's cabin pass
by, and, when it did, was surprised to find the curtains already drawn.

Larry seems to have meant what he told Frost about the visit. For
all his inner reservations and frustrations, the two were getting along.
Frost wanted even more of Larry's time than Larry wanted to give. Frost
might well have sensed it. Regardless, the evidence suggests that he saw
their relationship differently. "Furthering friendship in Florida" was the
way Frost inscribed *In the Clearing* as a parting gift. The gift made Larry
feel less than appreciated for having helped out Frost for two weeks at
his own expense. The implication was that Larry felt he was there as
a matter of work on Frost's behalf when not at work on the biography,
while Frost, for all that Larry did in the garden, had wanted him there
as a friend.

One can only wonder what feelings from their parting lingered
for Frost when the two saw each other a week afterward at the party for
Frost's eighty-eighth birthday. Larry saw Frost for only a moment on
the evening of the stately affair at the Pan American Union in Washington, D.C., in which Kay, too, received a long round of applause for
her support of Frost's work. Visiting Frost in his hotel room the next

morning, Larry praised the party and Frost belittled it. Frost brought up
a newly published volume of critical essays about him beginning with an
excerpt from the study Larry had been working on when Frost appointed
him biographer, *Fire and Ice*, published in 1942. Larry's book, Frost said,
was referred to in the new volume as the best work on Frost. "He said,"
Larry wrote, "that might be what the professors thought, but that actually
I came first only because I had been the first to make the mistake of trying
to pigeonhole Frost, in ways acceptable to the academic dump of learning." Larry took Frost to be venting on account of his bad mood, precipitated, Larry knew, by Kay's having drunk too much the evening before.
"So I just smiled at him, and at the glare he kept turning my way while
he walked around the room as though he were looking for something."
Lesley and the grandchildren walked in. Larry left amid the commotion
without saying goodbye.

They saw each other briefly three more times. Once was a tense day
in Ripton in August, during which Larry had a passing moment of conspicuous jealousy after learning that Frost had chosen someone else to go
to Russia with him on a trip of cultural diplomacy in the fall. Frost got
word that the choice had upset him, Kay said, and Frost was distressed.
After treating Larry gruffly at dinner, Frost wrote him a consolatory letter
explaining that he wanted people around him on the trip who were "not
too critically intent on who and what I am" because he "didn't want to be
made too self conscious in this momentous expedition." Larry noted the
pretense of Frost's asking, "Who's told you that I was afraid that I had
hurt you by not bringing you with me to Russia" in a letter dictated to
Kay, which went on at some length to describe Frost's plans for the mis-
sion undertaken at President Kennedy's behest, including one request that
Frost would ask "the great Kruschev [*sic*]" to grant him. After returning
from Russia, Frost asked again if Larry was mad at him when they saw
each other at Trinity College in Connecticut, where Frost had praised
Larry anonymously by telling the audience that he had a friend in the
crowd who had distinguished himself among academics for having his

doctoral thesis picked up by a trade publisher. As to his anger, Larry demurred. He and Frost never saw each other again. The closest Larry came to emotion in his account of Frost's death that winter was to write, in response to the honor of a consolatory cable sent by Premier Khrushchev to Frost's family, "It was an impressive climax to an impressive life."

15.

The Agitated Heart

I.

The poet was publicly mourned in superlative terms. Bill Snow told the press that "Frost contributed more to poetry in America than anyone who has ever lived." Louis was slightly more tempered in the praise he offered to the Associated Press, calling Frost "unquestionably one of America's three great poets—the other two being Walt Whitman and Emily Dickinson—and I am not sure but that time will judge him to be the best of the three." Louis added that "a combination of what I call levity and gravity" characterized the attitude toward life of "my oldest and closest friend."

Many private notes of mourning found their way to Kay. One friend of Frost's shared her admiration for Kay's "staunch support and care of this lonely genius all these years," declaring that Kay was for Frost "his real family, his chief mainstay," and "his real daughter."

A public memorial service was planned for mid-February at Amherst, before which was a small, private funeral for family and close friends in Appleton Chapel at Harvard. It was held on the afternoon of January 31, an urn of flowers sitting on a table front and center with a laurel wreath next to the urn. While "nobody seemed to go to pieces during the service," Larry observed, "the women knew how to respond, at the end, and all came out starry-eyed or blowing into handkerchieves." The solemnity of the occasion prompted Larry to add, "I did wish Huck Finn could have been there"—a wish to have Frost, like Huck, hiding in the rafters and laughing at the solemnity of his own funeral, or just a passing wish that Frost had followed Huck in faking his own death before Larry walked out with the rest of the mourners into the snowy afternoon.

II.

It fell to Larry and Chis to bring the flowers from the chapel to the nurses who had cared for Frost at Peter Bent Brigham Hospital. Frost's room, Larry noticed, was a corner room on the highest floor, with a long view over Boston. Larry returned to the gathering at Kay and Ted's house to learn, happily, that Louis had already left. Louis was planning to publish, with Holt, a volume of Frost's letters to him, which, as it happened, Al Edwards brought up with Larry at the Morrisons' house. Edwards was relieved to hear Larry say that he didn't mind Louis's book coming out before his planned *Selected Letters* and that he would even help Louis with his volume. Larry planned to let his selections prepare readers of his biography to be disillusioned about the "mythic image" of Frost. "The letters would astound people who thought they knew Frost," Larry wrote to himself. "I could sit back and say, 'Look, Ma: no hands.'"

Larry evidently did not suspect that his rival in publishing Frost's letters shared his intention to shatter the icon. What struck him about Untermeyer's book was not the editorial tenor but a series of unacknowledged edits of primary sources that offended his scholarly integrity, bowdlerizing for which he held responsible an editor at Holt, Stanley Burnshaw, who would earn Larry's enmity in the course of their working together on *Selected Letters*. Unflattering as a number of Louis's published comments were, they were nothing like the notes he left on the cutting-room floor. "After a Visit with R.F. at Ripton, September 20–21, 1960," as drafted, records Frost "aged pathetically" and increasingly degenerative, an old story for a poet who, "more than most authors . . . sometimes wavers on the thin line between genius and insanity." Louis's judgment was a humorless paraphrase of a note Frost had written playfully about the two of them in 1915, the first year of their friendship: "You and I are not clever, Louis: we are cunning, one with the cunning of race the other with the cunning of insanity." Frost's Jewish friend might have felt less than entirely in on the joke.

Perhaps Louis's assessment of Frost's sanity bore on his account of Frost's relationship with Kay. Unlike Larry, who never doubted the basic aspects of Frost's side of the story, Louis seems genuinely not to have known what to believe, as he wrote after visiting Frost in September 1960, concluding, "It is impossible for me to determine the full truth."

> It is obvious that Robert was in love with Kay as soon as she began to take care of him. Moreover he told several people—Lawrance Thompson, Bernard de Voto, William Sloan, and myself—sometimes by innuendo, sometimes explicitly—that Kay reciprocated his feeling. . . . "Absurd," said Kay when she heard this. "I told him that I would not consider marrying him if I were single." . . .
>
> Whatever she felt twenty years ago, I get the impression that she no longer has any illusions about Robert's kindness, or the quality of his care for her. "He is not only the most selfish man I know, but [also] the cruelest." What makes her furious and what she fears most is that Robert might persuade people to believe that he was her lover. His insistence on this takes the form of humiliating her husband and injuring her.

Louis hedged about the relationship yet again in a letter Larry requested for the record:

There's not much to add to what we said about Robert's averred relations to (and with) Kay. He hoped that you and I would, somehow, somewhere, tell "the real story." He wanted me, Horatio-like, to justify him as a man, to report him and his "cause right to the unsatisfied."

If Louis was Horatio bidden to tell Frost's story, then Frost by implication was Hamlet in his ambiguous sanity about an emotionally overwhelming part of his life. Other sources on the subject of Frost's averred relations with Kay were more forthcoming to Larry but hardly more helpful in determining the truth.

Frost once described Louis as a friend who, having been married six or seven times, had been loyal to him through it all, which was most important. Many observers of their relationship were hard-pressed to say where friendship ended and self-interest began. If there is no end to guessing what the two really were to each other, there was probably no end for them, too. The friendship of performers in whatever medium is liable to be a performance, and the two of them were indeed more cunning than most.

Kay and Ted shared their sense of the friendship with Cook on a visit of his to the farmhouse in September 1963, shortly after the letters' release. For all that Frost's affection for Louis was real, they thought his self-presentation had been calculated and less than sincere in almost half a century of letters to Louis. Cook was puzzled by their impression.

Cook had been surprised to read in a reminiscence about Frost that he had harbored a "mean streak." Kay responded, "Well, he was sweet-tempered to Anne." It was, in context, rather faint praise. "I have seen Robert treat Gillie, his Border collie, and the horses, too, with terrible meanness," said Kay. "In one of his moods I had to throw a pail of water over his head to bring him to his senses," she added, "and I've seen him flop on the floor and beat his head against it."

Ted proceeded to quote a particularly evocative description by Frost of how he felt in periods of mental disturbance: "You know what my mind is like? Take a cup of clear water and drop one pill in and it becomes a cloudy green tumidity." The figure is familiar. It is the pasture spring before the water clears. It is the troubled waters of what Frost saw as both mind and soul, sensitive enough for the smallest thing to muddy all the water in the vessel.

Cook asked about the present situation with Frost's biographer. "Oh, he's a different Larry," said Kay. "He doesn't feel the tension he did while Frost was still alive. He's taking it all in stride now, and he's made his peace with Elizabeth Shepley Sergeant."

III.

Larry had not made his peace with Elizabeth Shepley Sergeant. Neither had he begun to forgive Kay herself. He had, in fact, written the following to himself just a week before Cook's visit to the Homer Noble Farm: "Kay has always been willing to sacrifice her most dearly beloved, for personal gain. How like Frost in that regard. No wonder they loved and hated each other." In keeping with this cynicism, Larry thought Kay had lately been nice to him because "she thinks she can get me to state the story in a way which will bring to her a lasting honor and glory." Yet her powers of censorship did not extend to authorial insinuation. Though Larry had to "cover up the facts" of her and Frost's relationship "by telling half-truths," as he wrote to himself, he trusted that the facts would come out in due course. Meantime, he was free to frame the story, beginning with *Selected Letters* in 1964, in a way that would "settle a few scores between Kay Morrison and me": "One of my weaknesses is that a large part of my concern is vengeance on that bitch."

Kay did not act like someone who hated Larry in return when she hosted him twice for dinner in the summer of 1964. At the second dinner, she confided something about Frost that Larry had never heard before. Frost had told her, she said, that he slept in his mother's bedroom from the time his father died until he left for Dartmouth. Larry had studied Frost for the better part of a lifetime, only to learn this from the third woman on whom Frost depended. The other revelation of the visit came from Ted after a pair of characteristically strong cocktails. Ted said something harsh about Frost that even Larry questioned, giving rise to what Larry called "a funny expression on [Ted's] face." "He said, almost apologetically, 'Well, let's face it: I didn't like him.' Kay changed the subject."

One can only wonder what exactly the same man had been thinking when he said to Kay, as the couple hosted an old friend of Frost's and theirs, Ed Lathem, a young and devoted archival librarian at Dartmouth, for another bibulous dinner shortly after Frost's death, "Now you must remember that Larry Thompson must have access to all the information—all—that nothing must be held back," to which Kay answered, "Yes, Larry will have access to all the information."

Larry had recently gained access to information that was perhaps the most shocking in the whole of his research. His sources were the gossipy parents of Prescott Frost's wife, Phyllis, Donald and Marie Gordon, whose purchase of the Euber farm Frost had tried to forestall by offering it to Larry. The Gordons told Larry that in their years of serving as caretakers of Frost's pair of cottages on his property in South Miami, after one of Kay's visits, Donald discovered a used "condrum," or condom, next to one of the beds. Setting aside the question of the Gordons' credibility on the subject—they had disliked Kay profoundly for years and passed along other false and sensationally damning gossip about her—any condrum they did indeed find could well have had a provenance other than what they suspected. It is technically possible that Frost and Kay, were they sleeping together, were still using birth control as Kay approached fifty in 1948, the first winter when the Gordons acted as caretakers; and possible that Kay, though scrupulous to keep up appearances, was careless enough to leave evidence of fornication in a room she knew the Gordons would be cleaning. Or, in a possible turn of events only a touch more distasteful, Frost could have deliberately planted the evidence in a bid for their relations to be acknowledged, just as he had faked a raucous party, also singlehandedly, on New Year's 1947, for the impression he thought it would make on Kay. (It is also perhaps worthy of note that Frost wrote privately in his later years of "my love of . . . squandering fluid lust.") The idea of planting a condrum is outlandish and crude, but how out of character? And how much more outlandish than the alternatives?

The information most important to Larry as he polished the first volume of the biography came from an unrelated book of psychology. Having turned in a completed draft of volume I, *The Early Years*, in August 1965, Larry picked up *Neurosis and Human Growth*, by Karen Horney, a post-Freudian psychoanalyst, in October, only to find that this work by the distinguished theorist was practically his book in abstract terms. "Stop press," he wrote. "If it had mentioned Frost on every page it couldn't have come closer to giving a psychological framework to what I've been trying to say in the first volume of the biography."

The parts of Horney's book that Larry annotated—which he did extensively, rhapsodically, and cathartically—trace the growth of a neurotic's mind. Neurosis begins with a child's inability to cope with the stress of his environment and consequent inability to cope with himself as he actually is in the world. The neurotic child imagines an idealized self free from all humiliating imperfections—a perfect version of himself, supreme in the ways he fears himself inadequate. Alienated from his real self, the neurotic child identifies himself with his imaginary ideal, denying any genuine self-knowledge that would shatter his myth of himself. (On this point, Larry noted Frost's habit of equating self-knowledge and masturbation with a joke, which he would make after ensuring no ladies were present, about achieving solitary knowledge in the biblical sense. Frost's preferred ideal was that of being true to oneself.) The neurotic adult, having identified himself with his fantasy of himself, is driven to sustain the identification by bringing it about to the best of his ability. What is achieved by the neurotic's quest for glory is not genuine self-confidence but a fragile and neurotic pride, unable to admit its imperfections, alternately self-deceived and self-hating. The subject of self-hatred made Larry think of Frost's conception of the hatred of self as the foundation of religion. Larry saw nothing of Frost in the chapter titled "The Self-Effacing Solution: The Appeal of Love" but much in the chapter on "morbid dependency."

The biographer had found a unified theory for explaining his subject in terms of need rather than love. His diagnosis released a groundswell of anger that settled into a reaction that had been absent in Larry's writing about Frost for years: sympathy. The less Frost could control his neurosis, the less Larry could blame him for acting neurotically. Larry copied out a relevant sentence of Horney's, "When we realize how deeply he is caught within the machinery of his pride system, when we realize the efforts he must make not to be crushed by his self-hate, we see him as a harrassed [*sic*] human being, struggling for survival," a sentence Larry described as "tremendously important to me as biographer of Frost." Larry rewrote a variant of the sentence in all caps at the end of his notes, the later version adding "PITY" to sympathy.

Just so did pity emerge as a salient part of the biographer's relationship toward his subject. It was not hatred, but neither was it respect, depending as it did on seeing Frost as a victim of circumstance rather than the author of his own life. Pity renders it all the less plausible to see Frost's mental life as in any instance insightful rather than symptomatic.

What of the poetry Frost wrote about the vexed and intricate relationship between self and ideals? Their reconciliation was the master theme of *A Boy's Will*. The way of the Youth, like the way of the Soul in *In Memoriam* before it and Dante's *Commedia* before that, is among other things the very sublimation of emotion toward a higher sense of purpose that Horney describes as a constructive adaptation for neurotics. Larry recognized the parallel between poetic themes and neurotic conflicts by the time he came to write the introduction to the manuscript he had finished, transposing his reading of Horney onto the story of Frost's life in outline. Frost's poems, Larry wrote, were "orderly ways of dealing with dangerous conflicts he found operative within himself or between himself and others," poems "used . . . either as tools or as weapons for actually trying to bring under control and resolve those conflicts which he viewed as being so dangerous that they might otherwise engulf and destroy him." If Frost's reactions to the world were symptoms of psychosis, the function of his art was personally therapeutic or symptomatic as well. Larry had reasoned his way into a perspective that would have been barely conceivable to the convert to Frost's poetry of four decades before, one in which he didn't sincerely consider the prospect that Frost had achieved not only mental order with his poems but something larger than himself.

The problem was implicit in "The Freedom of the Moon." The poet who boasted of moving the moon as he pleased was either Romantic or lunatic, possessed of grand imaginative powers he boasted of figuratively or deluded into thinking that he had the literal powers he boasted of. The paths of the moon in either case followed the paths of the Magi in different versions of the Nativity, a story of divinity's entry into matter, suggesting that the poet could be reaching beyond himself, whether he knew it or not, to all the wonder that followed—though not according to the disciple tasked with writing Frost's life.

IV.

There are three narrative confabulations, or tall tales, in Larry's biography—one in each volume. Each concerns his subject's relationship with the opposite sex. With the exception of a certain relationship about which Larry felt he had no choice but to dissemble, beginning his third volume with a more chaste encounter between Frost and Kay in the summer of 1938 than Larry believed it to have been, one can charitably read the tall tales as his efforts to dramatize what he thought was true of Frost's mind but did not actually know. And each is a marvelous story. The first, in volume I, tells of Frost's trip to the Great Dismal Swamp in 1894 as an effort to throw his life away to punish Elinor for refusing to see him at her college, where male visitors were not allowed. But Frost was never sure why he went off on that adventure, saying weeks afterward that he had "been out of time a little while" and sixty-eight years later, "I suppose it was all nothing but my young way of having the blues." The second tall tale, in volume 2, takes the reader with Frost as he walked the grounds of the old farm in Derry in the spring of 1938 in an effort to decide if he should carry out Elinor's wish that her ashes be scattered in Hyla Brook. The pathos of the story is exquisite. The reader walks with Frost through the old terrain of his poetry, seeing what Frost sees and remembering something of what he remembers, the overgrown alders of the present and the footpath out to Hyla Brook as the family walked it when the path and the family were intact. The reader follows the steps of Frost's vexed decision not to honor Elinor's wish. Yet Larry, who cited unspecified talks with Frost as evidence for the chapter, learned only after Frost's death, in February 1963, that Frost had not scattered Elinor's ashes in Derry. The story is a fiction in all but its outline.

There are no further discrete and detectable lies in the books. The tall tales are emblematic, however, of a recurrent falseness in authorial perspective that would recount the events of Frost's past and say what Frost had been thinking or feeling at the time with more authority than Frost had claimed himself. It is the perspectival equivalent of a just-so story, its error the replacement of uncertainty with diagnostic confidence. Larry knew that this was a familiar pitfall for biographers—he said as much to Frost in 1959—yet he fell into it with the certainty of his sense of the poet's psychology. Though the pitfall was familiar, it was devastating in a book about someone whose great subject was the constant ambiguity of motives. Such was also the great subject of Frost's perpetual recounting of his life—his old impulses and motives and thoughts that were a constant mystery to him. The variations were not lost on Larry, who began his introduction to the first volume with a sentence that deserves to be famous: "Robert Frost was so fascinated by the story of his life that he never tired of retelling it." Yet the very next sentence undermined the first with the premise that the resulting variations in Frost's recollections were a matter of Frost's deceptions or delusions and not of his uncertainties as well, a premise representative of the biography on the whole. The premise would cast a long shadow. Far more consequential than Larry's small handful of fabrications or even his judgment of Frost's character was the distorting effect of telling the story of Frost's life with the constant ambiguity of motives obscured, making it as hard for the reader to see what might be of value in Frost's life and writing as it was for the biographer.

V.

"We all loved Larry," Anne recalled of herself and her parents. They had high hopes for the biography that were, as she recalled, disappointed when he first read a part of his manuscript to a group of them gathered together. However tinged it might have been with disappointment, her father's response to reading the whole manuscript of volume I, *The Early Years*, was to be galvanized into writing a substantial essay of his own on the relationship between Frost's life and his poetry. Ted respected Larry's judgment enough to ask him for comments on a draft of the essay, to be called "The Agitated Heart."

"Whose heart?" one could reasonably ask, though the essay leaves no doubt that Frost's is intended, quickly explaining its thesis in reference to the poem from which its title is quoted, "Revelation," from *A Boy's Will*:

We make ourselves a place apart
    Behind light words that tease and flout,
But oh, the agitated heart
    Till someone really find us out.

'Tis pity if the case require
    (Or so we say) that in the end

We speak the literal to inspire
The understanding of a friend.

But so with all, from babes that play
At hide-and-seek to God afar,
So all who hide too well away
Must speak and tell us where they are.

What the poem revealed, Ted thought, was a fundamental tension in Frost's writing and life. "Frost wanted to be found out—by the right people in the right way." He wanted desperately to be recognized but wanted just as badly to set the terms on which people recognized him. It was a precarious balance to strike, risking collapse from an imaginative identification with Frost into something closer to idolatry, a situation in which a reader or friend could understand Frost only by following his indirections of speech in precisely the way Frost intended them.

Ted defended a partly biographical approach to Frost, noting that Frost would keep something in his pocket when he talked to a crowd to remind himself that he was the same person in public as he was in private—after Elinor died, Ted noted, a thorn. Clearly, Ted shared something of the way Larry felt about Frost, calling Frost in his essay egotistical, petty, and sometimes impetuous, "a great man who also contained a small man." Ted's difference in perspective with Larry, whether Ted saw it or not, was that only one of them still beheld the great man. The depth of Ted's respect is as manifest as his criticism in his writing that Frost's character was made up of paradoxes, "pairs of opposites, both of which were true of him at the same time," a dynamic psychological tension Ted captured exquisitely with the metaphor of a gyroscopic spinning top:

He surely made on thousands who heard his readings an impression
of magnificent sanity, a sanity as firmly grounded as a granite slab, yet

in private his complicated balance, as complicated as the motions of a gyroscopic top, could be so disturbed as barely to recover its perilous equilibrium. Each side of the paradox, each of the opposites, was true.

Ted's framework for making sense of Frost's mind was open to both sides of the paradox in a way that Larry's framework was not. A neurotic manifesting his symptoms is just a neurotic. A person driven to achieve a wide-ranging communion of minds along the lines of the painstakingly careful ways he chose to make sense of the world is a person driven toward a genuine good for all that he is liable to trip over himself. The divergence in frameworks roughly tracks the divergence between Freudian and Adlerian psychology, the former explaining motivation in terms of ineluctable inner forces and the latter in terms of irreducible ends to which people are drawn. But Ted was not much for psychology, and Freud and Adler were merely modern participants in an old debate about human motivation—whether one could explain it in terms of passions or interests, or also needed to account for values that were not themselves explicable in terms of passions or interests. The question was the constant ambiguity in one of its manifestations. Frost had faith in Ted's answer, rejoining to anyone who called him an escapist that he was a pursuitist, writing also, in a late companion piece to "Into My Own" describing himself in the third person, "His life is a pursuit of a pursuit forever."

Ted had given a tribute to Frost at a commemorative ceremony in August 1964. He recounted that since 1939 Frost and the Morrisons had shared the Homer Noble Farm as a kind of "joint summer family," with Kay having taken a role as "Mr. Frost's secretary and much more than secretary." Her duties, Ted explained, encompassed all manner of practical help as well as serving as spiritual counselor, for which he praised his wife's "success in this delicate and arduous enterprise."

Ted ended his speech with a reading of "Choose Something Like a

Star." The poem came to mind for Larry in his reading of Horney as an instance of Frost's placating himself with his fantasies. Ted, who had used the same figure of a fixed star to describe his bride-to-be in a letter to her years before Frost wrote his poem, said at the end of his speech he was sorry that Frost was not there to read the poem he alone could write in the voice he alone could bring to it.

VI.

Roberta Teale Swartz Chalmers to Larry Thompson, December 30, 1968, a year and a half before the publication of volume 2:

> Larry, I hope you'll let me see anything I've said, if you happen to wish to use it. I'm deeply concerned about the biography, and your entire success with vols. II and III—and I don't underestimate this terrific task and confrontation with the Old Man of the Sea—not RF, but the truth one tries to lay hold of. Vol. I dismayed me in some ways, because—well, I can best express it by saying that too many persons who did not (or did) know I knew you, kept raising the question, "What has he got against Frost?" or "What did Frost do to *him?*"

No record survives of any women other than Roberta—or, as she called herself, Rob—to whom Frost was so casually revealing. It seems that he did not know what to make of his friendship with this woman he had known for four decades, she having been introduced to Frost after winning an essay contest at Mount Holyoke with a piece about him when she was only nineteen. Frost once called her and her husband, Gordon, surrogate children, but he treated her like his mother. She harbored no illusions about Frost's capacity for pettiness and unwarranted anger, calling Frost's jealousies "Othello-like" in his gullible suspicion of his friends' motives. She said the psychic cost to Gordon had been awful. But what others experienced as flaws, she experienced as vulnerabilities. Frost sweated so much in the months after Elinor's death, Rob said, that he had to change his underwear three times a day. Frost "was the only person I ever knew," she said, "who had the spirit and stamina to confront and conquer what could have become, and likely was, a nervous breakdown." Frost's prevailing against long psychic odds was, in other words, heroic. She saw Frost as not only Lear and Job but Proteus, the proverbial Old Man of the Sea, "and I do not mean that he wore masks (not that cliche again) but actually changed his shape for reasons of 1. curiosity & finding out, 2. not letting others get a vanquishing grasp on him, and 3. privacy and freedom." It was a finer (and more flattering) metaphor for the beguiling range of Frost's mind than he ever thought of himself. It was also an exculpatory way to make sense of Frost's evasiveness and mercurial nature, facets of what she saw as his personal, artistic, and even spiritual freedom. The last meant more to her in Frost's thinking than anything else. "His endurance of the mystery we must all manage to endure, was exemplary," she wrote. "He was the most irrevocably and radically religious person I have ever known."

Larry acknowledged her brilliant understanding of Frost early in their correspondence, which began after the publication of *Selected Letters* in 1964. "Your letter and its wonderful postscripts," wrote Larry, "go deeper into Frost's complicated personality than any letter I've ever received from anyone else." "Bless you," he wrote, "for understanding so much about the great and complicated man we both loved." He had not written that way about Frost in two decades. Perhaps, if only for the moment, he meant it.

Though Rob objected to Larry's portrayal of a number of people close to Frost, especially his depiction of Elinor as dour and withdrawn, Rob's deepest divergence from *The Early Years* was a judgment of character hard to disentangle from her and Larry's divergence in religious perspective. Namely, she thought Frost was good. This followed from thinking that Frost's sense of the good was legitimate. Her perspective is clearest in light of an apparent digression she wrote out by hand in a postscript. "I haven't anything against the Hippies & Yippies & young rioters," she wrote—it was, again, the end of 1968, the apogee of Sixties Romanticism. "Our generation (esp. by way of Freud & Dewey) has so cheated them"—by which she meant the disaffected and spiritually searching young—"of incentive & aspiration, & made the surface of the earth like the surface of the moon to them—footprints going nowhere in grey sand." Freud and Dewey, Dewey whom Frost and Larry had spied on the beach all those years ago in Key West, had each been influential in their way in troubling traditional ideas of the pursuit of genuine good, Freud's analysis by severing motivation from a sense of the good and Dewey's by severing the good from a foundation in truth (other than the truth of pragmatic usefulness). Rob's was a moral world in which decisions could not be explained away as the result of unconscious forces, and moral judgments could not all be explained away as judgments of usefulness. As against a generation taught categorically to distrust their motivations and the grounds of their moral convictions, she thought of the world as a place for the human will to struggle to do good rather than evil. Such were the terms on which she judged Frost's life, though "beset" by "darkness," "not the least was the pain he caused others and knew he caused," "a great victory . . . a victory of human will." Though Frost was never so confident about his success, he emphatically shared her sense of the world as a trial. "You believe," she told Larry, "that to conceive of this life as a journey toward personal victory over his special faults—each man a prince—is insanity, perhaps inherited from one's mother's insanity. I can only say that I've never known ANYONE who 'hungered & thirsted after righteousness' so much as R.F. For this much hunger, we could forgive him all."

VII.

By and large, the critics liked the first volume of the biography as they had
liked *Selected Letters* before it. The book was also well received by two of the
three Frosts whose opinions survive. Though Lillian objected to some of
the less than complimentary portrayals in the book, Phyllis and Prescott
were grateful for it. In contrast, a man who had once thought of himself
as Frost's surrogate son felt "that the reading of the book gave me a deep
sense of loss, such as I experienced when my boyhood home was taken
over by strangers." So wrote the man, Wade Van Dore, to Larry.

> My sadness is mainly that your Frost seems quite a different person
> from my Frost. I realized many years ago that he was some kind of
> a rascal. But the way you handle your material that word seems too
> happy and likeable a term for your use.

Wade, who had spent a good deal of time with Frost in the two decades
following his pilgrimage to meet the poet, his greatest hero other than
Thoreau, in 1925, wondered why *The Early Years* "seems to make [Frost] out
a very dark, brooding, troubled sort of person." Wade had a conjecture:
"It almost seems that spending so much of your time—life—on getting material for the biography, you began to resent your subject." Wade
said he would empathize if Larry had felt that way. He himself declined
Frost's offer of full-time employment in the early 1940s in order to keep
a measure of distance from someone he did not want to come to resent.
While he did not hold Larry's approach against him, he worried that
Larry had failed to appreciate the tremendous risks involved in what he
was doing:

> It is your right to do what you please just as much as it was Frost's right
> to do what he did to get ahead in the world. Only in this case I'm fear-
> ful there may be a sizable backlash. At this moment think of all the red

faces there must be on those who feel unable to challenge your verdict. They may even begin to blame you for their having been taken in! I hope you have enough fortitude to withstand all the resentment that may be aimed at you. I hope you never get to feel buried beneath all this, and I also hope your book doesn't begin a mass movement toward the silent burial of Frost as a poet.

VIII.

The burial foretold began on August 9, 1970, on the front page of *The New York Times Book Review*, the interring article a review of Larry's newly released second volume by a young critic named Helen Vendler. There were other words printed against *The Years of Triumph* and many in its favor as well. The book would win a Pulitzer Prize in May—a triumph by any sensible measure. There were, however, no words of praise or blame for the book other than Vendler's that distilled the general impression that Larry had given of Frost into a new image that would persist in the cultural imagination for decades. She encapsulated the mass of often unsettling evidence that Larry had presented about Frost into a single, haunting word: "monster."

The word stuck. This is not to say that her judgment has been universally, or even generally, accepted. Its detractors came to call it "the monster myth." Any number of books about Frost in the ensuing half century have been said by some critics to definitively refute the monster myth until another book came along to definitively refute it again. The myth would seem to haunt Frost's memory as a perpetual possibility, a premonition of some malign force hidden within the charming human form. It is as if the constant ambiguity animating the poems had been transposed into a singular question about the nature of Frost's character, making the poetry seem to so many readers as if it might just be the product of an abnormal psychology rather than the insights of a sensitive nature to which your nature may well correspond. This was Larry's premise, not Vendler's, yet her following Larry's evidence to its apparent conclusion transfigured his portrait into the stuff of myth. What the portrait loses in translation is the distinction between a psychosis that invites sympathy and even pity and a monstrosity that invites neither. Lesley wrote as much in a shocked letter to the *Times*. For all its harshness of judgment, the myth is curiously also more faithful to Frost than the portrait in a pair of important respects. The portrait is a diagnosis, which implies explanation, while monstrosity implies that which defies explanation, as Frost did. The myth of monstrosity also preserves a supernatural dimension to Frost's character if only in an attenuated, negative, and figurative way. It is often said that the myth owes its resonance to being the opposite of another popular image of Frost. But hidden monstrosity is the opposite not of saintliness or wisdom but of the almost indefinable quality Gwendolyn Brooks tells of in "Of Robert Frost," that of his very face intimating a sense of hidden spirit common to us all. The one guise conceals something more than human, the other something less. The guises are rather like Love and Thought in "Bond and Free," Love Platonic or creaturely, Thought transcendent or Satanic. The modern imagination could perhaps come no closer to fearing the work of the devil in one's innermost thoughts than to suppose that another person might be a monster.

In contrast to the myth it happened to spawn, Vendler's review was itself a straightforward argument against Frost's moral character as Thompson had presented it in volume 2. Her case rested on a handful of judgments drawn from the stories told in the biography: that Frost's egotism was beyond the pale, that he was insensate toward Carol, that he was self-protective to the point of paranoia, and most important that he was responsible for the tragic outcomes of the people around him. If Frost had left "behind him a wake of destroyed human lives," the implication was that he had destroyed them. The hard question of the responsibility Frost bore for any avoidable suffering on the part of the people around him, especially Carol and Lesley, is a question one could ask of any parent and their children. Anne's understanding of

Frost's culpability was something like the opposite of Larry's, remembering him as "very intense and very loving and very unfortunate in his family life."

Larry's depiction of Elinor's emotional remove from her husband and of his general culpability owes less to the facts of his life than to the distortions of his guilt and his grief after she passed away. It is ostensibly such expressions of her father's paranoiac self-doubt that Lesley called "the kind of lies my father was telling" Thompson, lies she wrote to the *Book Review* to express her incredulity that Thompson had really believed. Larry thought her letter was nonsense—she had not even read the biography—but it is perfectly coherent if less than perfectly consistent with other things she had said on the subject. Had her letter not been edited down before its publication, it would have been the first public accusation of Larry's "betrayal" of Frost:

> I find myself speechless at the moment, with the shock of surprise at what appears to be a book written by one who hated my father, instead of loved him, as his family, and thousands upon thousands of Americans, and hundreds of true friends, did. [I had no knowledge of the betrayal, by author and publishers, that was being arranged behind my back.] I guess my father never realized, or believed, that Thompson believed the kind of lies my father was telling him. My father's chief trouble was his closeness to the razor's edge of insanity—with a persecution complex involved, and which his family + most particularly my mother, saved him from. We may have suffered deep scars in the process, but we suffered them willingly since love was the first consideration. It was all part of protecting a creative genius from his own worst enemy, doubt of himself. We knew, even when he wasn't sure, that he was the greatest poet, one of the greatest minds and hearts that our country has ever known. Far from being a "disastrous" family life it was a splendid one. Struck too often by tragedy—but tragedy is something else again from evil.

Though Larry may not have felt responsible for the charge of evil she rebuts at the end, he had left it open for readers to infer by describing Frost diagnostically without revealing the diagnosis, telling an often tragic life story without drawing the bounds he saw to Frost's agency in what he saw as actual psychosis. The monster was his unwitting creation.

IX.

When the Pulitzer Prize was announced in May 1971, Kay imagined Larry's detractors complaining "about that incomprehensible decision of that badly chosen committee!"

She and Ted had done their part to edit Larry's manuscript, chiefly by encouraging him to judge Frost less harshly. After hosting Larry for a discussion of the manuscript over a few days in Ripton in August 1969, Kay reported to Ed Lathem, by then Larry's friend and editorial collaborator on a pair of ancillary volumes of Frost material, that Ted and Lathem had by joint effort persuaded Larry to "stop bearing down on R.F.," noting that Larry "even admits he had been relieving himself of his own aggressions!"

Larry maintained in public that he had tried "to offer a balanced portrait of an extremely complicated poet and personality." There was an irreconcilable conflict between the selfishness of artists and the moral obligations of human beings, Larry said, noting that Frost himself tended to think that great writers tended not to be great men. Larry was rather more dispirited in private, as in a pair of letters to Wally Stegner and his wife, Mary, in early 1971. To Mary he confessed that his reviewers had bred "a secret feeling of self-doubt over whether he [had] miserably failed to do what he tried to do just as honestly and fairly as he could." To Wally, who had also written to Larry supportively, Larry wrote of his fears for his final volume on the grounds "that too much of what must be said in the third volume must be written between the lines." Larry was so afraid of having to "write a dishonest third volume" that, as he told Wally, "there are even times when I hope I am 'called home.'"

X.

Ed Lathem apologized separately to Kay and to Larry's widow, Janet, for having been unable to see them after Larry's memorial service in June 1973. The librarian had been "utterly overcome by the occasion" marking the loss of his friend and collaborator. Kay told Lathem, "I've been as shattered as you were."

The problem had begun in August 1971, four months after Larry's sixty-fifth birthday and three months after his award of the Pulitzer Prize. Larry had an unexpected stroke from a cerebral hemorrhage, only to be "saved from death I suppose," he recalled in February 1972, "by a brain operation." Larry improved over the course of the winter, but the situation had worsened by May. His doctors discovered a malignant and inoperable tumor in his brain, which they told Janet about, who told Kay before she told Larry himself. Kay shared her reaction with Lathem in June: "May the Lord have mercy on us all. I can't bear it."

Larry bore his diagnosis by resolving to bring the book to completion in the time he had left. His student Roy Winnick signed on to write what Larry would carefully outline. Roy, a graduate student of Larry's in his mid-twenties, had no particular interest in Frost. He took on the project for the professor to whom he felt a great loyalty, moving into the Thompson household to make collaboration easier as Larry's health declined. Larry passed away on April 15, 1973.

Among the challenges Roy inherited was the one whose difficulty had made Larry halfway wish to be called home. Under perceived threat of Kay's censorship, Larry, who had intended to treat her relationship with Frost seriously but not literally, walked Roy privately through his approach of description by insinuation. Naturally, Kay was worried. "I am sure I'm going to suffer when this volume comes out," Kay told Lathem in the fall of 1973. She had read drafts of some early chapters and concluded that "there (I'm afraid) may be *many*, many, objections from K.M." Yet none of her direct intercessions approached the force of her husband's rebuke after reading the revised manuscript in the fall of 1975. The "chief and indeed all-important problem," Ted told Roy, is "the way you deal with Frost's relation to Kay."

> It seems to me the main biographical fact is that in his desperation after Elinor's death he tried to pry her away from her husband and children and persuade her to marry him, that she firmly rejected this plea, and that he accepted her rejection, I've no doubt with chagrin as well as disappointment, because he was not a man who easily accepted the thwarting of his wishes. You keep coming back to this theme, I think melodramatizing it, exaggerating it and making it appear that Frost kept up a sort of lovesick knocking at the door that puts him in the light of an aggrieved adolescent rather than the man he was.

Roy's treatment of the case was less biographical history, Ted thought, than "romantic fiction." While Ted granted that Roy may have gotten his ideas from Larry, he argued that neither Larry in general nor Frost in the wildness of his grief was a reliable source on the subject:

> I sadly suspect that your interpretation comes from Larry's notes in great part, but on this particular theme, great as was our affection for Larry, I suspect he was led by some of his own propensities to romanticize out of all reason and proportion.

The truth of Ted's case hinges on a basic ambiguity: What exactly was "Frost's relation to Kay" that Roy had tried to present? The whole point of insinuation is to hint without saying exactly. To the extent that the relation was a matter of Frost's feelings alone, Roy had, like Larry, ample evidence to draw on, no matter what the book cited. The situation was different if relation meant relationship. To the extent that it did, Ted's arguments hold. Save a dubious pair of secondhand reports, Larry built his whole case on the testimony of a single witness whose credibility he undermined in the opening sentences of his biography, especially insofar as Frost spoke as witness to the events of his own life. Larry was especially struck by Frost's ability to sustain the fiction for decades that the woman who would become his wife had been engaged to another man in college. If Frost's emotional imagination could convince him to misremember such a fact pertaining to the first woman he loved, how far did it lead him astray from the facts of the second?

XI.

The Morrisons' fears were realized and Wade's prophecy fulfilled yet again in the review of *The Later Years* in *The New York Times* of January 16, 1977. The reviewer, David Bromwich, then a graduate student in English, wrote that to Kay Morrison, "by Frost's own account, we owe the mixed blessing of his longevity." That Frost's literal survival was a mixed blessing was among the kinder things Bromwich had to say about Frost as a person. Bromwich repeatedly calls Frost "bad," as DeVoto is said to have said, but what Bromwich is really describing is evil.

His case rests primarily on an echo of Vendler's charge that Frost had been unfeeling toward his children—in response, in this case, to Carol's suicide and Irma's psychosis. In the letter Kay wrote to the *Times*, she showed the baselessness of Bromwich's argument about Frost's attitude toward Carol and attested from personal experience to the pains Frost took to avoid committing Irma, relenting only on medical authority that she posed a danger to her young son. The dominant tone in her letter was a mixture of incredulity and moral indignation. She marveled at Bromwich's capacity to miss Frost's "vulnerabilities" and consequently portray him as a "prodigy of evil."

Can Mr. Bromwich really believe in the non-human monster he has
put forward as Robert Frost? Does Mr. Bromwich know suffering and
self-reproach when he sees them? Does he mistake the darkness of sorrow for the darkness of settled moral obliquity? It is amazing that even
one who feels repelled by Frost the man should review his life without
once mentioning the overwhelming tragedy in it, the death of his wife
Elinor and its effect on him.

Her case is free of false notes, yet it hardly represents the balance
of how she felt about Frost. What she omits in frustration and fear, she
emphasizes in sympathy. One could say the same of her book, *Robert
Frost: A Pictorial Chronicle*, published to unfortunately little notice in 1974.
Here, however, the disproportion in emphasis crossed over at times into
dishonesty. Describing Frost in his wild summer of 1938, she writes that
"he laced his conversation with innuendos of sexual exploits that were
utterly foreign to his nature"—though, in all fairness, innuendos were
more in character for him than exploits. Notwithstanding such mischar-
acterizations, Larry's description to Roy of the book as a whitewashing
was grossly overstated. It was meant as a corrective by a woman who saw
in Frost's vulnerability something other than a cause of psychological or
moral pathology. She had, after all, worked for the better part of her adult
life in a constant effort, with necessarily inconstant success, to save him
from his worst impulses. She mentions in her opening paragraph Frost's
"many threats to punish those opposing his wishes by making them sorry
for his death," only to cast this unfortunate habit in a more sympathetic
light than Larry had in his overtone of Frost's vindictive triumphs. To
Kay, Frost's threats were "an evidence of that deeply hidden sense of insecurity that dogged him to the end of his life, even in his final days of
triumph." She could have said the same of the biographer to whom she
dedicated her book.

It was only a matter of time before a host of Frost's defenders regis-
tered further differences with Larry. Wade both predicted the trend and

led the charge, a warrior-prophet. The seminal book of this kind was a work of great critical insight by a man who had known Frost as a young English professor at Amherst, William Pritchard, whose *Frost: A Literary Life Reconsidered*, in 1984, persuaded Vendler herself to change her mind about trusting Larry's account of Frost's life. Ted observed that "the reconsideration," which he generally praised, "is aimed in good part, though not exclusively, at Larry."

The reconsideration was followed two years later by something more like a bludgeoning. *Robert Frost Himself*, by Stanley Burnshaw, old enemy of Larry's at Holt, briefly told the story of Frost's relationship with Thompson in a way that stood to discredit Larry almost entirely. Burnshaw's Larry thinks Frost is a "monster"—Burnshaw cites a secondhand source misleadingly—and Burnshaw's Larry sets out to undermine Frost by portraying him as such. Though Burnshaw did not use the word, the implication was obvious and influential: Larry's biography had been a betrayal.

Having not reviewed Larry's files himself, Ted could not tell precisely where Burnshaw went wrong. He could not know that the relationship between biographer and poet was far more intimate and variable than the relationship Burnshaw portrayed, for better and for worse, and on nothing like the timeline Burnshaw gave; that the story showed Larry's books to be a sincere attempt to understand a flawed man rather than a malicious attempt to undermine him; that Larry was truthful on all but a handful of matters of fact; that the deepest gap between Frost and Larry was philosophical; that Larry's harsh diagnosis of Frost's psychology was just a more systematic explanation of what other people close to Frost had observed, and that it was in Larry's case not a point of attack but an attempt at sympathy. Ted was not in a position to know the above. He did, however, have the sense that something in Burnshaw's story was wrong. For all his gratitude that the book had "demolishe[d] once and for all the 'myth' of Frost as a 'monster,' putting the Vendlers and Bromwiches in their place for good," Ted was troubled by the way the book treated Larry.

"It's as though in ridding the record of one monster Burnshaw had sub-stituted another." While Ted found himself "puzzled and astonished" by Burnshaw's quotation of Larry's notes, which "seem[ed] to reveal strains in Larry's mind and temperament I hadn't encountered or suspected," Ted nonetheless felt his old friend had been wronged. "Can any blow be struck in Larry's defense, and how?" he asked Lathem. His only idea was to leave a letter in the archive on the chance that some researcher might come across it and take note.

16.

MYRTLES AND ROSES

I.

On June 8, 1957, a clement Saturday in London two weeks into the month Larry spent with Frost in England and Ireland on the trip Larry saw as the long swell behind the last high-water mark of their friendship, Larry, with the Saturday to himself, walked from his hotel to Hyde Park with the intention of taking the afternoon sun. At the edge of the park, however, was a crowd overlooking a vast field. The people were watching a tournament of sheepdogs. The sheepdog trials, so called, held Larry's attention for some time as he watched the dog athletes make sport of herding small flocks of sheep in spectacular fashion at the command of their shepherds. Larry hoped to bring Frost back to see the dogs. Sure enough, he returned with Frost on Monday morning and found Frost no less rapt than he had been despite having seen trials before in America. Where Larry took note of the form that the competition took, Frost made note of the dogs' personalities, every one of them, as he said, distinct—the alert dogs, the nervous dogs, the dogs that crawled toward the sheep on their bellies, the dogs that looked back at their shepherd to try to make out what he'd said.

Frost's first triumph of the trip had been a talk on their first evening together in England. His first medical scare was a pain in his chest the next evening. Thus was established a pattern of public luster and private vulnerability. Larry felt sure that Frost did not recognize the pains he took to support him. Larry was wrong. Frost did acknowledge all of Larry's help, just not to Larry. "I suppose Larry is having to work more than I foresaw," Frost wrote to Kay. "Much as I feared the prospect I did realize ahead how much help I was going to need." Frost plausibly said as little as he did to Larry out of shame for needing all the help, as shown by Frost's tantrum of Learian indignation upon learning that Larry had attempted to ration his supply of sleeping pills on doctor's orders. If Frost felt controlled and deceived and demeaned—as well as chagrined when Larry dissuaded him from talking on Puritanism at the University of Cambridge—Larry felt terrified by what he had seen the pills do to Frost. So it was that when Larry went on to watch Frost receive his high honor from Oxford University, made all the higher by being in a ceremony only for Frost, Larry "couldn't help but feel a sense of amazement over the change between the way he now looked and the way he had looked, only a bit more than twenty-four hours earlier, drooling that soft egg all over the bed." Larry watched Frost smile at the part of the Latin tribute that praised "his features which reflect the genius of the poet, the sturdiness of the farmer, and the peace of old age." Frost went on to give the best reading of his that Larry had ever seen. "Watching the procession," Larry later recalled to himself, "I saw no harm in taking a bit of credit to myself for having gotten Frost there all in one piece."

Larry expressed a similar pride in a letter to Frost days after their return to America. Feeling exhausted and let down after all the excitement, Larry imagined that Frost felt all the more so after having been "the ball-carrier, in play after play," and Larry "only the water-boy." Apt as the metaphor was, it was nothing close to a charming metaphor of Larry's relayed to Frost secondhand in a letter from a man whom the two heard singing in Dublin toward the end of the trip:

I should like to have the name and address of the man who was with
you. . . . He said he was attached to Princeton, and that he was here as
your "sheep-dog."

The metaphor is a fitting last word on their profound and turbulent
friendship. There is dignity in the sheepdog. There is a profound understanding of their master's commands. Granting the lack of equality in the
sheepdog's lot, the metaphor, like the whole trip that inspired it, points to
terms of understanding, however uneasy, on which a genuine friendship
might have been salvaged between the two men. As in so many lyrics of
Frost's, the depth of the metaphor owes to its ambiguity, pointing in this
case to a question Larry had long asked himself in so many words. If he
was accompanying Frost as his sheepdog, how much was Frost Larry's
shepherd and how much his sheep?

II.

Stricken with pneumonia in Florida in February 1962, on what he thought
was his deathbed, Frost thought, as he had after Elinor's death in Florida,
of some old lines of Poe's. The lines that came to him this time, from Poe's
lyric "For Annie," were of a soul's freeing itself from considerations in its
last hours, in particular "Its old agitations / Of myrtles and roses," that
is, of honors and love. Frost went on, after recovering, to talk about the
lines in his talks for the rest of the year, discussing them in his very last
weeks of public performances.

Myrtles and roses were emphatically Frost's agitations in England,
from which he wrote letter after letter to Kay with longing and playful
affection. "My very dear if mistaken love," he called Kay, her error being
that she did not come to England, "the mistake of our lives." "I end as I
began," he ended one letter, "at the mercy of your mere looks."

Of all the myrtles bestowed on Frost in England, the one that meant
most to him was the least institutional—a toast Eliot gave in his honor at

a formal dinner in London. The rivalry had begun to ebb as early as 1947, when Eliot called on Frost in Cambridge, Massachusetts, on a visit to his country of origin. His visit made Frost more warmly disposed toward Eliot, if not inclined to stop making jokes at his expense, told often and not only in private. Frost poked fun at Eliot's self-importance and aversion to physicality, saying we knew that Eliot had achieved orgasm at least once because "they've got one of his condrums in the Harvard Collection." Frost rejected Eliot's idea that a complex age called for complexity in art, an idea he likened to the absurd call for confusion in art in a confused age, and drew a contrast implicitly between his own writing for an audience like Jesus's, people who could become as children, as against Eliot's crowd of "scribes and Pharisees," the soulless sophisticates whom Jesus rebuked. He and Eliot both played, he said, but "I like to play at a level where I don't play humility or rapture," the difference crystallized in Frost's joke that he played euchre while Eliot played Eucharist.

One has to think a lot of someone to spend so much time defending the ways one differs from him, and Frost shared his admiration for Eliot's achievement in a letter to Eliot announcing his trip to England. "You have been a great poet in my reading," Frost wrote. The compliment was more than reciprocated.

In Eliot's climactic toast, he called Frost "the most eminent, the most distinguished . . . Anglo-American poet now living." Eliot paused before deciding on "Anglo-American" as the proper adjective for Frost, charming the crowd by ostentatiously including himself in the comparison. Frost's localism was universal, Eliot said, listing alongside "the relation of Dante to Florence, of Shakespeare to Warwickshire, of Goethe to the Rhineland" "the relation of Robert Frost to New England." Frost took a long pause after Eliot finished, then said, "There's nobody living in either country that I'd rather hear that from."

III.

It took Frost a long moment before he continued. He confessed, uncharacteristically, to being somewhat overwhelmed, and then began a characteristic twenty minutes of talking followed by twenty minutes of saying his poems. The talk revolved around the two countries, his own and the one he said he went to out of a Romantic admiration for *The Golden Treasury*. His reading, so called, began with a poem of his called "The Gift Outright," which he said was about the Revolutionary War, lest the subtext be lost. He added graciously that the poem had been written on his long-held assumption that almost all conflicts, wars included, were conflicts not between good and bad but between good and good. Frost was fond of quoting on the subject the great Victorian poet George Meredith: "In tragic life, God wot, / No villain need be!"

Frost had teased Eliot in his letter for "leaving America behind too far and Ezra not far enough." Eliot picked up the latter theme in his toast, saying it was in his own early years in London, beginning after the outbreak of war in August 1914, that he first heard of Frost, from Pound, who spoke of Frost "with great enthusiasm." In his toast, Eliot wondered how his own writing might have turned out differently if Pound had told Eliot to read Frost at the time as Pound urged other reading on him. He could hardly have known that Frost had at the same time been worried that this new, young protégé of Pound's had begun to displace him in the inconstant favor of the Poetical Boss.

In Frost's response to Eliot's toast, he described his and Eliot's responses to Pound's early influence in the language of "The Road Not Taken." "It's interesting that both of us came out of the same road," said Frost, referring in fact to a literal road. "Was it at 6 Church Walk that you first saw Ezra?" Frost asked. (It was not.) "I took it one way, Mr. Eliot took it another way," Frost continued, knowing how way leads on to way. There is the slightest hint in Frost's discussion that his was the road less traveled by, though the real question at issue was freedom from excessive influence, the subject of "Etienne de la Boéce." Eliot "took Ezra in charge," Frost

said, drawing a contrast with himself. The fine shades of this possible
slight were plausibly lost on the audience as it laughed loudly at Frost's play
on the word "charge," an allusion to Pound's internment at St. Elizabeths
Hospital in Washington, D.C., where the poet had for years been held as
mentally unfit to stand trial for treasonous radio broadcasts conducted
on behalf of fascist Italy during his decades-long residence in the country.
Hence, "He took Ezra in charge, and [Ezra] still hasn't been charged." "I'm
trying to do something about it," Frost added, "for old sake's sake."

What Frost alluded to was the role he intended to play in the movement
afoot among Ezra's old friends, Eliot included, to secure his release. Frost's
description of the plan in the first-person singular would be habitual and
not entirely misleading. The scheme was neither his idea nor mostly his
doing, but in April 1958, Frost's statement on behalf of Pound, prepared
with the help of a government attorney, carried the day in court.

Frost's successful lobbying was both a reflection of his growing eminence and a boon to it. He had begun to see himself as a Washington
big shot, a role he would inhabit as consultant in poetry to the Library
of Congress, then the anti-monarchic name for the role otherwise known
as poet laureate, which Frost would endow with a newfound distinction
in the American context. His appointment was announced in late May.

In the weeks after the case had closed, Frost objected to calls by
Pound's friends to set up a recording of his poems in the Library of Congress. Frost said he would do no such thing as consultant in poetry, not
wanting Pound to think he had been exonerated rather than shown mercy.
For his part, Pound had written Frost the following letter of gratitude in
early April, on "Easter mourn," as Frost was working on the case:

R.F.

Thanks for your kind endeavours.

Of course I shd/ like a little serious conversation . but then one
can't get everything.

Yours

Ez P.

Frost made no reply. Pound was released on May 7. On June 19, eleven days before he set sail for Italy, he wrote Frost a letter that read in entirety,

> RF.
>> I hear tell how as yu don't open yr mail.
>> yrs
>> EP.

On disembarking three weeks later in Naples, Pound gave the old fascist salute.

IV.

"Dear Mr. Frost," wrote Senator John Fitzgerald Kennedy on April 11, 1959, "I just want to send you a note to let you know how gratifying it was to be remembered by you on the occasion of your 85th birthday." Sending "my own very warmest greetings," numbering himself by implication among Frost's "admirers," the senator also echoed the context in which Frost had spoken of him at a press conference in New York on Frost's eighty-fifth birthday two weeks before, a defense of New England. "I do," the senator guaranteed the poet, "share entirely your view that the New England heritage is not a fading page but that it has continuing vitality and a distinctive future."

Frost's mention of Kennedy at his press conference came about when a reporter asked if Frost thought New England was in decay. In response, Frost predicted that both the next secretary of state and the next president would be from Boston. Asked to clarify whom he meant with regard to the presidency, Frost told the gaggle of reporters to figure it out for themselves. Pressed again, Frost said, "It's a Puritan named Kennedy."

For decades, Frost had thought of Catholics not as a Christian sect to which Puritans were especially opposed, as they were historically, but as a sect of Christianity that especially embodied the values of Puritanism.

"There are plenty of good Puritans in the Catholic Church—more there than anywhere else," he wrote to himself in a notebook in the late 1930s. Frost saw Puritanism in Kennedy's *Profiles in Courage* (1956), a book whose vignettes of exceptional heroism Frost thought were possible only as every man depicted "reaches and makes the 'Divine' a part of himself."

In another session with reporters on April 21, Frost walked back his prediction with a belabored neutrality, claiming to speak as neither Democrat nor Republican. For whatever reason, he was saying less than he felt, judging from his delight at the news of Kennedy's victory on the second Tuesday of November 1960. Writing to Kay from Stanford University, Frost imagined her staying up "gloating over the returns." "It is a bigger Victory than you may think," Frost wrote, adjuring her to "always remember I was among first in the country to see Boston Puritanism restored in the Presidency of a Boston Irish Catholic." In the rush of victory, Frost thought it marked an end to the need for sectarian difference, even an end to the Reformation, as the force of Protestantism had "saved the Church."

Frost opined in his letter to Kay that his prophecy had by rights earned him an invitation to the victory dinner at the Vatican. The invitation actually forthcoming was by the president-elect: Would Frost read a poem at his inauguration? No such reading had happened before. "I MAY NOT BE EQUAL TO IT," Frost told Kennedy by telegram a day after the request, "BUT I CAN ACCEPT IT FOR MY CAUSE—THE ARTS, POETRY, NOW FOR THE FIRST TIME TAKEN INTO THE AFFAIRS OF STATESMEN." "I AM GLAD THE INVITATION PLEASES YOUR FAMILY," Frost continued. "IT WILL PLEASE MY FAMILY TO THE FOURTH GENERATION AND MY FAMILY OF FRIENDS AND WERE THEY LIVING IT WOULD HAVE PLEASED INORDINATELY THE KIND OF GROVER CLEVELAND DEMOCRATS I HAD FOR PARENTS." Easy to miss in the thrill is a formulation new for Frost in the record, his "family of friends." Striking that his new pinnacle of fame should make him think of the phrase.

V.

After Frost failed to read through the glare of sunlight on the podium the
poem he had written in the last few days specifically for the presidential
inauguration at which he was presently reading, his eyes failing him for
two minutes in the most public moment of his life before he took the hat
held over his manuscript by Vice President Johnson and made the crowd
laugh with a joke under his breath, Frost drew applause by saying he was
just going to recite the poem for which his new poem had been written
as a preface: "The Gift Outright." Written in roughly 1935, the poem
was one of Frost's last truly great lyric poems, an inversion of Romantic
nationalism underneath an almost identical aspect:

> The land was ours before we were the land's.
> She was our land more than a hundred years
> Before we were her people. She was ours
> In Massachusetts, in Virginia,
> But we were England's, still colonials,
> Possessing what we still were unpossessed by,
> Possessed by what we now no more possessed.
> Something we were withholding made us weak
> Until we found out that it was ourselves
> We were withholding from our land of living,
> And forthwith found salvation in surrender.
> Such as we were we gave ourselves outright
> (The deed of gift was many deeds of war)
> To the land vaguely realizing westward,
> But still unstoried, artless, unenhanced,
> Such as she was, such as she would become.

Where Romantic nationalisms depend on the intuited right of a people
to land, their occupation of which supposedly confers or reveals a set

of putatively national virtues, "The Gift Outright" inverts every one of
these relations. The poem recasts a right to the land as a debt to the land
that imposes a duty in the realization of which is forged a national character. "The land was ours before we were the land's," the poem begins.
We became a nation in giving ourselves to it outright—an origin myth
fundamentally opposed to the Romantic nationalisms ascendant in Europe at the time of the poem's composition in the mid-1930s, a myth of
a nation brought into being not by advantage of blood or soil or divine
dispensation but by the exercise of duty, described with a variation on
the phrase Frost had used to describe the sacrifice made by the widow in
"The Black Cottage" for the sake of the American creed. Such was the
duty the founders expressed. "The Gift Outright" is an origin myth of
creedal nationalism with all the grandeur and mystique of Romantically
nationalist myths.

The poem does not mention the creed. It mentions "deeds of war."
That our "deed of gift" comprised deeds of bellicosity rather than generosity seems ironic to the point of rueful sarcasm. Taken plainly, this
triumphalism about American belligerence sounds like the most egregious
kind of history written by the victors, a smug and self-satisfied pretense
like the idea of the Thanksgiving holiday to which the young Frost's "Sachem of the Clouds" had responded with outraged sarcasm, "'Thanks!'
I hear their cities thanking that my race is low in death." It is just such a
colonialist arrogance, crystallized in the proclaimed deed of gift consisting of deeds that seem the opposite of gifts, that runs through "The Gift
Outright" in its climax, which sees the land "realizing" to settler colonists
as if it had been unreal before settlement, the land "unstoried, artless,
unenhanced" as if its prior inhabitants had no stories or art or ways to
shape the land, as if the land stood only to be enhanced and in no ways
disfigured by western expansion. Many readers have taken this uncriti-
cal nationalism, opposed in every point to Frost's own judgment, as the
perspective of the poem. It sits in tension with his own description of the
poem as a history of the Revolutionary War as the beginning of the end of
global colonialism. One can square the perspectives by seeing the presence

of triumphalism as a comment on the temptation of nationalist sentiment to glorify the nation in its every aspect. Frost indulges this tendency
of Romantic nationalism to refashion it into the critical nationalism of
the American creed. Recall that only deeds of war are mentioned in the
poem, not the creed. The omission lets the reader ask what the soldiers
in the wars gave their lives for—not only the war launched by colonists
in Massachusetts and Virginia alike, but the war cast here as a necessary
continuation of the former, in which Massachusetts and Virginia found
themselves on opposite sides.

To the American creed, the poem offers an allusion more elaborate than that to the widow in "The Black Cottage," calling up a battle
mentioned in Frost's earlier poem. In describing the land "still unstoried,
artless, unenhanced," Frost recalled a formulation from the most famous
speech in American history, another set of three negations of distinct human powers to make meaning in light of what has already been done to
the land by those who gave their lives for America. Thus did President
Lincoln, in honoring the fallen at Gettysburg, proclaim "we can not
dedicate—we can not consecrate—we cannot hallow, this ground" because
"the brave men, living and dead, who struggled here, have consecrated it,
far above our poor power to add or detract." It was the speech in which
he rededicated the war effort to the nationalism of the American creed,
describing the country at inception as "a new nation, conceived in Liberty, and dedicated to the proposition that all men are created equal" and
describing the sacrifice of the Union dead as that of "those who here gave
their lives that that nation might live."

Frost brings in Lincoln's presence by allusion at the point when the
myth of the land begins to break down. The land, which had elsewhere in
the poem been a solid and literal thing, is said in the poem's antepenultimate line to have been "vaguely realizing westward," as if it had not merely
manifested itself to earlier Americans but been a potential in the hazy
process of realization. The land stands to be realized by the expression of
words. "Unstoried, artless, unenhanced," it will, the sequence implies, see
enhancement not by the work of hands only but by stories elevated to art.

The logic of Frost's three negations about imagination working ineffably on the land parallels the logic of Lincoln's three negations about the same thing. To dedicate is to tell a story that consecration draws into a ritual for sacredness whose aim is realized in hallowing, which is enhancement by divine blessing. Whether the enhancements of the land have been such or just the enhancements of stories we tell of ourselves as a nation is a question left by Frost in perfect irresolution. "The Gift Outright" ends in uncertainty about how much the country has come to meet the ideal of self-determination on which it was founded, adapted by Lincoln into the American creed. Lincoln concluded, like Frost, with uncertainty, charging those among the living at Gettysburg to dedicate their lives to the soldiers' unfinished cause. Yet Frost would sometimes alter the phrase "would become" in writing out or reading "The Gift Outright." When he reached the line at the inauguration, he added, after "such as she would become," "*has* become, and for this occasion let me change that to 'what she will become.'" It was a grander pronouncement without the poem's doubt about how much we have achieved of our national purpose and how much of it we will go on to achieve. The gesture came at the expense of the doubt that was the very moral force of the poem.

Frost's mood was dour after the performance. He felt that it revealed him in his dotage. After a nap, however, he revived his energy enough to charm a number of well-wishers that evening from his box at the inaugural ball. His performance on the biggest stage of his life had, as the stories in the press would soon reveal, made him into an icon. His reading was also not lost on one Harriet Carter of Andover, Massachusetts, who wrote to tell him how proud she had been made to have spoken along with him at their graduation threescore and nine years before:

Dear Robert,

You cannot imagine how distinguished I feel when I tell my friends that Robert Frost—"The Poet of the Inauguration" was a classmate of mine, and that at our graduation we each had a place on the same program. Was not your subject "A Monument to Afterthought Unveiled"?

VI.

After the crowd-shy Rob Frost elocuted to the graduating Lawrence High School class of 1892 his abstruse valedictory speech, "A Monument to After-Thought Unveiled," his poem was sung in praise of such after-thoughts. This poem written for his first formal performance, "Class Hymn," bore more than a passing resemblance to Emerson's august "Concord Hymn," written to be sung fifty-five summers before at the dedication of the Battle Monument in Concord, Massachusetts, marking the start of the Revolutionary War. Frost's hymn, like Emerson's, takes place by a quiet stream with a simple bridge reaching over it, by which is laid down a stone (or stones) in a kind of sacred ritual drawing past and future together. "If Emerson had left us nothing else," Frost wrote in 1959, "he would be remembered longer than the Washington Monument for the monument at Concord that he glorified with lines surpassing any other ever written about soldiers." The poem was more monumentalizing than the most substantial monument in the country.

Among Frost's other favorite poems of Emerson's was a poem written to be sung on July 4 twenty years after the singing of "Concord Hymn." The later poem, known colloquially as the "Concord Ode," meant most to Frost for the last two lines of its last quatrain, about the immutable freedom of the human spirit, a pair of lines with which he thought all his thinking about freedom had begun:

> For He that worketh high and wise,
>   Nor pauses in his plan,
> Will take the sun out of the skies
>   Ere freedom out of man.

The lines describe a freedom so fundamental that no circumstance can circumscribe it, a freedom resting not on worldly contingency but on something close enough to divine necessity that the world would be un-recognizable and uninhabitable without it, a freedom of the soul essential to what it was to be human. The "Concord Ode" retells the story of our national founding as an effort to bring about on earth a government and a people devoted to the universal freedom of the will. This endeavor, heroic and holy, is in Emerson's retelling the work both of hands and of divinity, or in his terms the over-soul as it worked in humanity and outside it in the very land and seas and air. Whatever Frost thought of the rest of the poem, he objected strongly to the first half of the last quatrain, which recasts the whole story before it as the work of a methodical and orderly God. Frost was convinced that Emerson had the insight of his last two lines about human freedom before thinking up a preceding pair of lines about a foreordained divine order to round out awkwardly the quatrain.

As well as anything in Emerson's writing, the "Concord Ode" illustrates the inspiring and troubling legacy of the Concord Sage. In the political foment leading up to the Civil War, the "Concord Ode" was not only a work of abolitionism but a condemnation of any compromise with slavery as standing in contradiction to the fundamental freedom that was both reason for and cause of the nation's existence. This identification of America with a recognition of a universal human capacity conferring dignity regardless of circumstance brought an untold number of Americans to the abolitionist cause and gave untold more a sense of sacred meaning in their fight for the Union. Yet in positing a nation dedicated to the universal recognition of an aspect of divinity in all people, Emerson also posited a particular divine dispensation to the people by whom it was the over-soul's plan to bring such a nation about. Emerson identified such a people as "Saxon" by the pseudoscientific racial genealogy of whiteness that he tragically did much to bring about:

> The men are ripe of Saxon kind
>   To build an equal state,—
> To take the statute from the mind,
>   And make of duty fate.

One is left with the paradox of a putatively superior race divinely favored to promulgate equality. Such was the consequence of Emerson's boundless spiritual imagination, which lent a divine imprimatur to prejudice and principle alike, dignifying chauvinism along with egalitarianism, a chauvinism that was in his later years both regional and racial, New Englandist and Saxonist.

Frost's own late career saw a deviation that mirrored Emerson's own—an attempt to dignify racial chauvinism by a claim to divine favor. Like so many in the New England cultural tradition, Frost had largely inherited Emerson's prejudices along with his principles. Yet it was an inheritance tempered by Frost's own principles, among which was a refusal to identify qualities of soul with those of demography, disclaiming regionalism for realmism. Frost's Pilgrims, imagined in an uncollected occasional poem as spirits conveying weary travelers of all races to America's shores, stand for the realization of an idea in a state that could encompass any race without perversion of the idea. Their meaning is not regional but Puritan, a devotion to principle rather than a Romantic heresy of seeing divinity in the people who happened to act on the principle, Romantic in its purport to discover transcendence outside the realm of the relation between God and the individual soul. Though Frost rejected Emerson's Romantic New Englandism even as he kept Emerson's Puritanism, Frost replicated in his late career Emerson's own late capitulation to a belief in the providential arc of white civilization. Emerson's providential chauvinism was, for instance, everywhere in Frost's late long poem "Kitty Hawk," which saw human civilization as the adventure of spirit into matter, having in aggregate taken place in an arc west-northwest, from Israel to Greece to Rome to France to England to New England. Frost in his later years was an integrationist in principle as ever, an integrationist in practice once or twice, and a pessimist about the prospect of racial equality like the minister in "The Black Cottage" in his wretched worldliness about the American creed.

Frost's collapse into Emerson's New Englandism was part of a broader shift in his imagination that had been underway for some time. The change began in 1938. It involved a general dissolution of adaptations Frost had made to the Romanticism with which he began. Lending credence to a Romantic regionalism was one instance among many of his later verse assuming transcendence that would have been tempered by a thoroughgoing doubt in almost every poem between "Flower-Gathering" and "The Silken Tent." A measured sense of transcendence touched all things in the best of his poetry like intimations of gold in nature's first green. This reserve, in which the grace of things was seldom overstated, amounted to an extended figure the poetry made of finding beauty in things as they were. It was a vision of the world around him "in several beauty," the world as seen by Love in "Bond and Free"—a fitting perspective for someone who wrote as his own epitaph, "I had a lover's quarrel with the world." Yet Frost's art also needed another kind of love. One can infer as much from the example of his last quarter century. In moving away from the Romanticism of "Twilight" to take the measure of his love as she was, Frost evidently depended on the bond to sustain his achievements of style. His later complexities of style rested no less on the attachment. A human love that might intimate the divine as in "A Prayer in Spring," as in the Song of Songs, it was a bulwark against both loneliness and spiritual dread, two longings to which Romanticism offers hope of solace. It was a relation encapsulated by Frost's elegy for Elinor that was the last of his great poems, the silken tent a figure for the gossamer lightness and looseness of the bond of love by which he was attached "to everything on earth the compass round," a bond of his spirit that let his spirit feel free. In theory, Frost could have generalized from this attachment to other imagined intimacies and achieved the same heights of style. As it happened, his poetry all but died with Elinor. A bond like his and hers is what Frost demonstrably also needed from the new beloved also addressed in "The Silken Tent," and what, to judge by the pains he took over the years to substantiate the relationship in carnal terms and glorify it in Romantic terms, he never had with Kay.

VII.

On a walk with friends in Ripton in the fall of 1962, Frost recalled how the lines of Poe's from "For Annie" had come to him as he lay on what he thought was his deathbed that winter in Florida. "I never thought of it," said Frost, "till I nearly lay dead down in Florida and the doctor told me not to worry and I said I've had enough of the—never said it before— old agitations of myrtles and roses." Frost thought of the line as a way to express an acceptance of death while maintaining reserve. "That takes up everything without your turning yourself inside out and everything," he said. "You just say that's all you've had, agitations of fame and—love and fame, you know. Ask me no more." This last line was said in a tone somewhere between defiance and petulance, making Frost, but not his friends, laugh.

Though myrtles had not ceased to accrue to him, neither had their agitations. Frost could hardly stop talking about the honor of having gone to Soviet Russia and met with Premier Khrushchev. Yet all the distinction was nonetheless a strain on him both for what it was and for what it was not. Recalling his earlier sickness in Florida to Doc Cook in June of that summer, Frost said it had begun with his sense of chagrin at people who had let on that he owed his recent successes to his popularity and, by implication, not the achievements with which his popularity had been earned. When Cook brought up "the honors John Kennedy's administration had showered on him," Frost deprecated them by historical contrast, saying "that when Longfellow visited the Senate accompanied by Sumner [Senator Charles Sumner of Massachusetts], it recessed and gathered around him." Even the exhilarating meeting with Khrushchev would prove cause for grief, as Frost, exhausted after the long flight back from Moscow, told reporters on the tarmac that the Soviet premier had called America "too liberal to fight," a slight mischaracterization that, unlike Frost's usual teasing of liberal irresolution, had real implications for Cold War diplomacy, precipitating a good deal of concerned speculation and agitating President Kennedy enough not to reach out to Frost again in his lifetime. It was plausibly not unrelated that Frost went on to dictate on his actual deathbed, four months after his return from Russia, the beginnings of a poem about a king who has all his prophets executed as merely "common commentators" save a single true prophet with the power to tell the king's dreams.

An agitation of another kind of love arose on Frost's walk in Ripton when his friend Mark Van Doren saw a swallow. Van Doren called the bird in flight "the bow flying away with the arrow," quoting a line that Frost had cited for decades in talks about feats of association in writing. Frost would leave the line's author anonymous. This time, as Van Doren started to share his esteem for the image, Frost interrupted him to reveal that it was Lesley's from "when she was a little girl." "Oh, you didn't tell me that," said an impressed Van Doren. "No, I didn't," said Frost. "And Edward Thomas liked that so much he just said, 'You don't mind if I put that in one of my poems?'" Frost grew suddenly wistful. "Lesley should have gone on," he said.

> She had all that in her somewhere. I don't know. She scattered herself in all sorts of ways. She could've written novels. She ought to have just buckled down. She wasn't patient enough or else she just felt that it wouldn't happen twice in the same family.

"That's the way I have her—that it comes that way to her," Frost added mumblingly, trailing off in a rare inarticulate moment.

If Frost never understood why his daughter was not a greater success as a writer, neither did he understand why the two were not closer. Nor, it seems, did Lesley, whose Manichaean accounts of her childhood, either implausibly dark or just as outrageously saccharine, might best be understood as signs of deeply unresolved feeling. That the relationship came into crisis with Elinor's death may well explain a good deal, to the extent that the collapse of their bond was explicable by anything but raw grief and mischance. If the family was unusually close, Elinor's death may well have broken the ties that had held back any latent resentment on Lesley's part. Three weeks after Lesley's charge about artists and children, Frost wrote his short note to Hervey Allen, quoting the first canto of *In Memoriam* ("Let darkness keep her raven gloss") as well as an abject pair of lines from "Morte d'Arthur," which read, "And I the last go forth companionless And the days darken round me." Arresting enough on their own as a lament about consignment to solitude, the lines are all the more powerful in the context of Sir Bedivere's lament for the loss of King Arthur, which meant the loss of Camelot, which meant to him the loss of a world:

> But now the whole Round Table is dissolved
> Which was an image of the mighty world;
> And I, the last, go forth companionless,
> And the days darken round me, and the years,
> Among new men, strange faces, other minds.

Was it by chance that Frost went on in "Directive" to put the broken Arthurian grail in the children's playhouse?

Frost's letter to Hervey echoes Bedivere's lament for a domestic world that was a figure for the mighty world at large. Such had been the world of the farm, the world where Lesley's school was walking off into the woods with her father. Even when the children belatedly joined formal school, there was little in the way of other institutions under whose influence the children might fall. As eldest, Lesley had even less formal school growing up than her siblings and, it seems, even more of her father's attention. With such influences, without much in the way of other influences, how could she not have wanted to be a writer? However unwittingly, Frost put his daughter in a position where she couldn't but want to be something hard to achieve for anyone and especially hard for someone in his shadow. Even if his belief in her was genuine and the advantages he provided were real, there was a sense in which he had set her up for a kind of failure despite his best efforts and even by virtue of those very efforts on the part of an artist with children. In tragic life, no villain need be.

Frost's behavior in the wake of Elinor's death—his wildness, his guilt in his grief, the loosing of his demon—makes it harder to see that in losing her he effectively lost a family. In turn, his sexual bluster and general fixation on the erotic aspect of his relationship with Kay obscure that in making arrangements with her, whatever they were, he gained a kind of family again. Kay, who thought that Frost had done his children a disservice by not exposing them to more formal schooling, he not understanding that not everyone could teach themselves as well or as quickly as he taught himself, sent her daughter to fine schools even when Anne would rather have been with her horse. Anne did not resent Frost. So it was that it fell to her to keep him company in his last weeks in his hospital room overlooking Boston in January 1963, first along with her mother and then, when her exhausted mother left for a weekend away with her father, alone.

VIII.

Between the two cantos in the end of *In Memoriam* reimagined by Frost in "Into My Own," a pair of poems constituting the imaginative climax of the sequence, the perspective of the speaker is utterly transformed from the earthly quotidian into spiritual rapture. "There rolls the deep where grew the tree," the second canto begins, beholding earth as flux from the vantage of timelessness. The point of this ecstatic transformation, the point of the whole sequence of poems, is to find and hold a perspective from which the friend the poet mourned has not been lost, dwelling "in my spirit," per the speaker—into his own:

> But in my spirit will I dwell,
>   And dream my dream, and hold it true;
>   For tho' my lips may breathe adieu,
> I cannot think the thing farewell.

Though much of the story of the king and the prophets that Frost
dictated to Anne in his final days in the hospital is less a poem than a
sketch of a poem, a couple of lines scan in regular iambic pentameter.
The first describes the king after ordering the death of all the false
prophets: "And there he sat alone and dreamed his dream." The second
line, the last in the sketch, describes the true prophet, who can, unlike
the false, share in the king's dream. "If you're a prophet not just a com-
mentator on the news," says the king, "You dream the only dream there
is to dream." One can only wonder if Frost had in mind the true dream
of Tennyson's rapture in his own description of a true dream of spiritual perception breaking through to another soul. Tennyson's passage
had once meant enough to Frost to transmute into the end of "Into My
Own" about those who might miss him someday: "They would not find
me changed from him they knew— / Only more sure of all I thought
was true."

In his final days, Frost found himself possessed by a new quality of
spirit. His was not the dramatic transformation of Tennyson's speaker,
but it was substantial, mysterious, liberating. "The new freedom is hard
to report or transcribe," Anne noted on Frost's description. He implored
her not to exaggerate the change and, as she wrote, "fall over the line
into sentimentality." He was "freed from a certain kind of reticence,"
she wrote, and in this spirit welcomed Ezra Pound's daughter, Mary de
Rachewiltz, who visited Frost on Sunday, January 27, to thank him on the
part of the family. Frost was beside himself with gratitude and gracious-
ness, calling Pound "a wonder—all sorts of person." "Politics make too
much difference to both of us," said Frost. "Love is all. Romantic love—as
in stories and poems. I tremble with it." Frost dreamily told Anne of "all
differences forgotten" between him and the man he once considered a false
prophet, "everything forgotten but romantic part of past."

Since his admission to the hospital in early December, Frost's condition had grown quickly worse, improved, and then worsened again with
a series of blood clots in his lungs. He had hardly walked or drunk water

since the first week of January. When Frost's doctor called on him on the morning of the twenty-eighth, Frost said, with no hint of sorrow, "I'm going to die tonight."

He kept his true prophecy from Anne. On the twenty-eighth, he continued recounting the old story of his acquaintance with Pound. He dictated notes for the poem. The king, it turns out, dreamed a "great dream for all people" like the dream Christ died for, about what Anne set down as the "difficulty between mercy & discipline." Frost tended, of course, to describe the conflict not as between mercy and discipline but as between mercy and justice, as in the letter to Roy and Alma Elliott that he dictated to Anne later on the twenty-eighth. "I was just saying today how Christ posed himself the whole problem and died for it," Frost dictated: "How can we be just in a world that needs mercy and merciful in a world that needs justice. We study and study the four biographies of him and are left still somewhat puzzled in our daily lives."

Anne went home for the night. She called the nurse attending to Frost in the evening, who, on the phone, did not have to repeat Frost's response to Anne's question about how he was, because Anne heard his answer in the background herself: "FINE. HOW'S IT GOING WITH HER?" The nurse, Laurel Earle, would later recall that Frost seemed to take "pleasure and comfort in having Anne to himself that last afternoon." After Anne left, Earle spoke to Frost about Kay's kindness to the hospital staff. Frost said in response that Kay "carries a heavy load of responsibility for me" and that Anne thought of him as her grandfather. He had told Anne as she was caring for him that he and Kay liked to pretend she was their daughter.

Frost's condition was steady, but he was not taking fluids. He asked for his sleeping medication early and slept for an hour and a half. Nurse Earle, a New Englander, tried to hold Frost's attention with stories about people she knew from Vermont. Frost, though responsive, grew restless. The night nurse relieved Earle at eleven. The doctor was called at 1:30 a.m. and failed to resuscitate the patient. Anne called Larry and said, "It's all over." At 4:00 a.m., Stafford called Doc Cook, who lay in bed for three hours before rising to a bright and cold morning.

So dawn goes down to day.

We love the things we love for what they are.

NOTES

ABBREVIATIONS

ACL: Amherst College Archives and Special Collections
CPPP: *Robert Frost: Collected Poems, Prose, and Plays*
DCL: Rauner Special Collections, Dartmouth College
EY: Thompson, *Robert Frost: The Early Years, 1874–1915*
JL: Jones Library Special Collections
Letters: *The Letters of Robert Frost*, vols. 1–3
LOC: Library of Congress Manuscript Division
LY: Thompson and Winnick, *Robert Frost: The Later Years, 1938–1963*
MCL: Middlebury College Special Collections
RFLU: *The Letters of Robert Frost to Louis Untermeyer*
RFSC: *Robert Frost and Sidney Cox: Forty Years of Friendship*
SL: *Selected Letters of Robert Frost*
VCL: University of Virginia Library Special Collections
YT: Thompson, *Robert Frost: The Years of Triumph, 1915–1938*

ABBREVIATED NAMES

Elinor Frost: EF
Edward Thomas: ET
Kay Morrison: KM
Lawrance Thompson: LT
Lesley Frost (later Lesley Frost Francis and then Lesley Frost Ballantine): LF
Louis Untermeyer: LU
Robert Frost: RF

EPIGRAPH

vii *"The way to a poem"*: Draft of "The Prerequisites," Notebook 31, DCL 1178, box 16.

vii *"We shall often find"*: "Tradition and the Individual Talent," *The Sacred Wood: Essays on Poetry and Criticism* 48 (London: Methuen & Co., 1920).

vii *"When I am sometimes"*: RF to Sidney Cox, 1932. *Letters*, 3:251–52.

vii *"I knock on wood"*: RF to Walter Prichard Eaton, May 26, 1915. *Letters*, 1:301.

I. THE FREEDOM OF THE MOON

3 *the first time he saw:* LT offered somewhat varying accounts of the story over the years. Precedence on matters of fact is given herein to the most nearly contemporaneous version, that in LT's introduction to "Notes on Conversations" (box 5), written on July 21, 1962. Other details are drawn from a typescript LT wrote in preparation for a lecture to be called "Some Adventures of a Frost Biographer" at Ripon College on Oct. 5, 1970 (VCL, 10044-A, box 18), and from the recorded audio of a variant of the lecture called "Some Adventures of a Robert Frost Biographer" (DCL 590, box 3).

3 *had seen him perform:* LT, "Notes on Conversations," July 21, 1962. LT in this late recollection misdates RF's earlier reading to January or February 1926. RF's reading at Memorial Chapel is announced for the evening of May 1, 1925 in *The Wesleyan Argus* of the same day, and alluded to in *The Wesleyan Argus* of April 12, 1926, which recalls the impression made by "his visit here a year ago" with no mention of a subsequent visit. LT remembered having been late to see RF because his date was delayed in getting to campus for the winter dance, which might have in fact been the spring dance held that night (May 1, 1925).

3 *It showed the beauty:* CPPP, 224.

5 *he had not wanted to write:* LT, "Notes on Conversations," July 21, 1962.

5 *The appointment that Thompson:* LT, "Some Adventures of a Robert Frost Biographer," DCL 590, box 3.

5 *Frost had invited Thompson:* RF to LT, July 17, 1939, VCL 10044, box 1.

5 *Thompson had written Frost:* LT to RF, June 20, 1939, DCL 1178, box 11.

5 *Thompson was well-qualified:* LT, "Notes on Conversations," July 21, 1962.

5 *Yet what Thompson learned:* LT, "Notes on Conversations," July 21, 1962.

6 *disliked the man on the spot:* LT, "Notes on Conversations," July 21, 1962—though the animus seems to have been nonreciprocal, as Newdick made note of an "especially good [talk]" with LT later that evening. *Newdick's Season of Frost*, 331.

6 *"I am told his mind":* RF to LT, July 17, 1939, VCL 10044, box 1. RF borrowed the phrase "his last delirium" from a letter he had received earlier that week from a colleague of Newdick's: "My God, Sir, that book was his life. And he worshipped

its subject. In his last delirium he talked constantly of Robert Frost—not the book, but the man" (DCL 1178, box 8).

6 *he thought of a plan:* LT, "Notes on Conversations," July 21, 1962.

6 *Frost asked for a name:* LT's various accounts of the conversation are inconsistent on minor details. His introduction to "Notes" of 1962 has him mentioning Mark Van Doren instead of his brother Carl, for instance, and makes no mention of middle age as a putative criterion, though it is mentioned in other accounts. Where inconsistencies arise, precedence is given to LT's most nearly contemporaneous account, a letter from 1947: LT to KM, ca. early 1947 on internal evidence, DCL 1178, box 11.

6 *as Thompson told the story:* LT, "Some Adventures of a Robert Frost Biographer," DCL 590, box 3.

6–7 *had told Frost in letters:* LT to RF, ca. 1936, DCL 1178, box 11; LT to RF, April 19, 1938, DCL 1178, box 11.

7 *"I said I wanted to":* LT, "Notes on Conversations," Aug. 12, 1939, box 5.

7 *"that which I timidly hoped":* LT to RF, ca. Aug. 5, 1939, DCL 1178, box 11.

7 *"You are the best loved poet":* Sloane to RF, Dec. 19, 1939, DCL 1178, box 10.

8 *"It can be elfin":* Cox, *Robert Frost*, 23.

8 *"one of the best things":* Stegner, memo to Secretary of the Interior Stewart Udall on "Proposed Robert Frost Shrine at Ripton, Vermont," Oct. 20, 1961, DCL 1178, box 11.

9 *"Of Robert Frost":* Included in *A Friendly Visit: Poems for Robert Frost, Chapbook Number Five by the Beloit Poetry Journal* (1957).

9 *Frost introduced his collected work:* CPPP, 3. First published as a prefatory poem to *North of Boston* in 1914, "The Pasture" prefaced various collected editions of RF's poetry beginning with his *Collected Poems* of 1930, an editorial choice for which RF disclaimed responsibility late in life, rather dubiously crediting his publishers for thinking to use the poem in the way he himself had used it in *North of Boston*. See "Government by Disagreement," a recording of a talk given by RF on March 30, 1959, LM0011, ACL 00181.

10 *a love poem unlike any other:* A former student of RF's at Amherst recalled his saying of "The Pasture" something to the effect that "there is a poem about love that's new in treatment and effect. You won't find anything in the whole range of English poetry just like that." Quoted in E. A. Richards, "Two Memoirs of Frost," *Touchstone* (March 1945): 20.

11 *"My first reaction is one":* LT, "Notes on Conversations," Aug. 12, 1939, box 5.

11 *an easy test of literary interpretation:* LT, "Notes on Conversations," July 21, 1962; "The Schism," *Atlantic Monthly*, Sept. 1939.

13 *just bought a house:* LT, "Notes on Conversations," July 21, 1962.

13 *150 acres:* A handwritten note by KM, ca. 1960, breaks down the property into twenty-five cultivated acres, twenty-five of pasture, and a hundred of forest.

13 *Frost told Thompson how he had paced:* LT, "Notes on Conversations," Feb. 18–19, 1940, box 5.

14 *"I am practically walking on air":* LT to KM, Jan. 11, 1940, DCL 1178, box 11.

14 *"GETTING SERIOUS":* LT, "Notes on Conversations," Feb. 22, 1940, box 5.

14 *"If I don't hear from her":* LT to KM, ca. early March 1940 on internal evidence, VCL 10044, box 1.

14 *Frost's long talks with Thompson:* LT, "Notes on Conversations," Feb. 17–March 2, 1940, box 5.

15 *"I am having the time of my life":* LT to KM, Feb. 20, 1940, on internal evidence, VCL 10044, box 1.

15 *"a mixture of strangeness and intimacy":* LT, "Notes on Conversations," Feb. 19, 1940, box 5.

15 *"We have gotten past":* LT, "Notes on Conversations," Feb. 19, 1940.

15 *Frost's moody "ups and downs":* LT to KM, Feb. 20, 1940, on internal evidence, VCL 10044, box 1.

15 *"Lucky he doesn't know":* LT, "Notes on Conversations," Feb. 24, 1940, box 5.

16 *"The real trouble":* LT to KM, ca. early March 1940 on internal evidence, VCL 10044, box 1.

16 *To Frost he made the argument:* LT to RF, ca. early March 1940 on internal evidence, DCL 1178, box 11.

16 *"kind of sadism which you know so well":* LT to KM, April 12, 1940, VCL 10044, box 1.

17 *Kay assured him:* KM to LT, April 16, 1940, VCL 10044, box 4.

17 *in the midst of consolation or flattery:* LT to RF, ca. Oct. 1940; LT to RF, Dec. 4, 1940; LT to RF, March 18, 1942, DCL 1178, box 11.

22 *"The Song of Songs is hard":* "The Constant Symbol," in *CPPP*, 786.

23 *"It was almost in spite":* LT, "Notes on Conversations," Feb. 18, 1940, box 5.

23 *"the unspoken half of everything":* RF to LU, Oct. 4, 1937, in *RFLU*, 295–96.

23 *"Pretty nearly every one of my poems":* RF to Alma and Roy Elliott, April 13, 1938, ACL 00181, box 6.

23 *"The Silken Tent":* CPPP, 302.

24 *house not made with hands:* Biblical quotations throughout are from the King James Version, the Bible with which RF was most familiar.

24 *"I almost dropped my false teeth":* LT, "Notes on Conversations," Dec. 26, 1963, box 6.

24 *Lesley continued to remember:* KM to LT, March 29, 1965, VCL 10044-A, box 14. LF also quotes the poem apropos of her parents' relationship in her foreword to an edition of Frost family letters published in 1972: *Family Letters of Robert and Elinor Frost*, xi.

24 *"I was thrust out":* RF to LU, Nov. 28, 1938, in *RFLU*, 313–14.

25 *"In Praise of Your Poise":* VCL 6261, box 1.

25 *the first book of poetry: Selections from the Poetry of Robert Herrick, with Drawings by Edwin A. Abbey* (New York: Harper & Brothers, 1882). For confirmation that this was

the specific volume, see, for example, RF to LT, ca. early March 1942, VCL 10044-A, box 11. For testimony that this was the first book of poetry RF read, see "Verbatim," a series of notes by Reginald Cook, July 2, 1949: "Hadn't read until about twelve and the first book was an elaborately got-up edition of Herrick." RF omitted the book in other chronologies of his early reading, for whatever reason, though he does attest elsewhere to having been fascinated by Herrick, if only by name, from the early age, seven or eight, at which the volume caught his eye. Common sense urges that the young RF did at least peruse this book that exerted such fascination, his boyish aversion to reading notwithstanding (and despite self-mythologizing claims to the contrary, as in RF to LU, Nov. 7, 1917, in *Letters*, 1:586–89). His mother probably read the volume to him as well, given the depth of RF's knowledge of Herrick, his mother's esteem for the work, and her propensity for reading poetry aloud to the children.

26   *"The Need of Being Versed in Country Things"*: CPPP, 223.

26   *"All Revelation"*: CPPP, 302.

26   *read alternately as courtship:* The interpretive controversy was a commonplace with which RF would have been long familiar. He spoke of it directly late in life, opining that no matter how much the poem also bears on religion in general, it remains a sheer "luxuriance in love." RF at Hebrew Union College, April 2, 1960, recording, ACL 00181.

27   *"The Wind and the Rain":* See chap. 10 for further discussion.

2. AND BE THE MEASURE

28   *offered to St. Lawrence University student:* The account given of RF's surprise visit to EF follows in outline the received version in the biographical record, derived from LT (*EY*, 173–76). LT cites as his source a private conversation with Clifton Waller Barrett, a prolific collector of RF's books and manuscripts, who in turn claimed to have heard the story from RF himself. This citation of secondhand testimony at once understates and overstates the strength of LT's evidence for the pivotal story—understates, for instance, the extent to which RF had also told him the story, more than once, in broad outline, including the trip and the new suit and the peremptory dismissal. Barrett's contribution to the story was the role of *Twilight*, about which RF was evasive with LT and inconsistent in other accounts, possibly from motive and doubtless from lingering psychic distress. No credible alternative to Barrett's testimony has emerged to explain when and why RF gave EF her copy of *Twilight* and destroyed his own. That notwithstanding, his testimony could hardly have licensed LT to write, as thirdhand witness, that Elinor in receiving *Twilight* from RF "took it from him as casually as if it had been the morning paper"—but LT's embellishment on the details need not detract from reliability on the basics, about which Barrett could have challenged LT upon publication had he thought himself misrepresented.

28 *met in the fall of 1891:* EF to Edna Davis Romig, Feb. 4, 1935, VCL 10044-A, box 15.

29 *Rob insisted that the honor:* For slightly different accounts of the conversation, especially regarding whether RF protested the head of school's suggestion on grounds of loyalty toward EF or petulance toward the head of school for the suggestion, see LT, "Notes on Conversations," Feb. 21, 1940, and June 8, 1946, box 5, and Sergeant, Notes on conversations with RF, 1956.

29 *as scholars that their classmates:* Quotations from former classmates are from Item 12 in the appendixes to *Newdick's Season of Frost,* the letters written from 1937 to 1938.

30 *contraction of typhoid fever:* LT, "Notes on Conversations," June 8, 1946, box 5. Typhoid was epidemic in Lawrence in 1890.

30 *Elinor gave him love poems:* LT, "Notes on Conversations," June 8, 1946. On RF's account, the poems, which he at first mistook for EF's, had been written by her sister. In *EY,* LT also attributes to RF a "jealous [admiration]" of the poetry EF was herself writing at the time, on the strength of two sources: EF's wish, expressed in a letter to Edna Davis Romig of March 12, 1935, that Romig not mention in response the single poem EF had recalled publishing in the *Bulletin;* and private conversations of his with old friends of the Frosts, Alma and Roy Elliott, in which they "expressed to LT their conviction that RF conveyed to Mrs. Frost, at the time of their marriage, his feeling that 'one artist in the family . . . is enough.'" Yet an expression of conviction, so called, is a surmise, not an observation, and one couple's surmise about the inner life of another is especially prone to distortion. The Elliotts seem to have inferred RF's discouragement of EF's painting from her having given it up soon after marriage, but soon after marriage is also when she started raising children, and the Elliotts noticed the painting because it was displayed in the Frosts' house. LT took the Elliotts' conjecture literally and badly distorted RF's record of support for the artistic pursuits of the rest of his family, which was in fact profound, as discussed in subsequent chapters. This leaves open the mystery of EF's reticence about her old poetry. It is possible that some of it had been inspired by romantic sentiments that preceded RF, which fits the timing if one accepts LT's conjectural identification of her poems with a pair pseudonymously published in fall issues of the *Bulletin* (from "An Infinite Longing": "It is not strange we find / *The craving to be loved* / *That was in the Infinite Mind*"). It is even more probable that EF would have worried that RF would have been troubled by the prospect of another romantic attachment of hers, as was his unfortunate wont.

30 *His first gift to her:* EF to Edna Davis Romig, Feb. 4, 1935, VCL 10044-A, box 15.

30 *Her essay, published in the Lawrence High School Bulletin:* Quoted in *EY,* 125–26.

31 *gone to the baggage car:* Cook, "Verbatim," June 1, 1949.

31 *a wife who devoted herself:* Undated recording, ca. Oct. 1962, LM0451, ACL 00181.

31   *She considered apprenticing Rob:* Newdick's notes on a visit with the Frosts, Sept. 1–3, 1937, published as Item 18 in the appendixes to *Newdick's Season of Frost.*

31   *an offer to stay on and teach:* LT, "Notes on Conversations," June 6, 1946, box 5.

31   *a population that was almost half foreign-born:* About 46 percent as of 1890, per demographic statistics in Donald Cole, *Immigrant City: Lawrence, Massachusetts, 1845–1921* (Chapel Hill: University of North Carolina Press, 1963), 209.

32   *a group of unusually gifted:* RF's conversation with Mark Van Doren and Fred Adams, ca. Oct. 1962, recording, LM0191, ACL 00181.

32   *Their instruction was so scholarly:* RF's talk to a graduate seminar on April 2, 1959, recording, LM0008, ACL 00181.

32   *especially Caesar, Cicero, Virgil, Homer:* Newdick's notes on a visit with the Frosts, Sept. 1–3, 1937, published as Item 18 in the appendixes to *Newdick's Season of Frost.* See also *Newdick's Season of Frost,* 24: "He often said that his happiest hours as a high school student were those he spent reading the *Iliad* with Miss Ada Lear."

32   *he began to read books on his own:* See, for example, RF to Jack Gallishaw, ca. Dec. 1922, in *Letters,* 2:283.

32   *His early enthusiasms:* For Hughes, Cooper, Porter, and Poe, see EF to Edna Davis Romig, Feb. 4, 1935, VCL 10044-A, box 15. For Scott, see, for example, Newdick's notes on conversations with RF from Oct. 1938, published as Item 30 in the appendixes to *Newdick's Season of Frost.* For Longfellow and abolitionist Whittier, see a recording of RF from March 25, 1958, LM0212, ACL 00181.

32   *probably read most often:* RF read the book "several times" around 1890, per EF to Edna Davis Romig, Feb. 4, 1935, VCL 10044-A, box 15. The inscription to the book, in RF's hand of the early 1890s, is *Queen Mab,* 2:69–76 (Robert Frost Library, NYU). RF wrote:

> Approached the overhanging battlement.—
> Below lay stretched the universe.
> There, far as the remotest line
> That bounds imagination's flight
> Countless and unending orbs
> In mazy motion intermingled,
> Yet still fulfilled immutably
>   Eternal Nature's law.
>   Shelley.

32   *" '92 Milton students":* Lawrence High School *Bulletin,* Oct. 1891.

33   *"Conversation as a Force in Life":* Lawrence High School *Bulletin,* June 1892.

33   *mortal fear of the crowd:* See, for example, LT, "Notes on Conversations," Feb. 28, 1940 (box 5), in which RF recalled having been sick for several days after the speech.

33 *Rob had wanted Elinor to attend:* EY, 133.

33 *floating together on the Merrimack:* Susan Holmes to RF, July 7, 1949, DCL 1178, box 6.

33 *Rob read Elinor Shelley's* Epipsychidion: EY, 136–37. LT cites no source, but the poem fits contextually, being the best source in Shelley for what RF called his Shelleyan view of marriage at the time of his exchange of rings with EF, recalled in LT, "Notes on Conversations," Aug. 20, 1942, box 5.

33 *They exchanged rings before summer's end:* LT, "Notes on Conversations," Aug. 31, 1941, box 5.

34 *"knights and dragons and prancing steed":* Holmes to RF, July 7, 1949, DCL 1178, box 6.

34 *owed something to Tennyson's* Idylls of the King: Holmes to LT, March 17, 1964, VCL 10044-A, box 13.

34 *perpetual hijinks and war games:* RF offered especially extensive recollections in a recorded interview with Edward Connery Lathem on Dec. 2, 1958, DCL 1178, box 38.

34 *he wanted to "do the telling":* See, for example, RF's recorded speech to Amherst parents at Johnson Chapel on Oct. 18, 1958 (LM0081, ACL 00181).

34 *his classmates were perplexed:* See, for example, Cook, "Verbatim," July 13, 1948.

34 *he had shared a bedroom:* LT, "Notes on Conversations," Sept. 15, 1964, box 6.

35 *asked for an itemized accounting:* RF's grandfather requested he report every ten cents spent on a can of kerosene for lamplight; RF reported many expenses as kerosene. RF's "Great Issues" lecture at Dartmouth, March 28, 1957, recording, DCL 12, box 11512.

35 *the closest thing to a contemporaneous account:* RF to Dean LeBaron Russell Briggs, Sept. 18, 1897, Records of the Dean of Harvard College, 1889–1995, Houghton Library.

35 *always a bit of a mystery:* RF implied as much in citing as his reason for leaving nothing more than a general feeling of wasting his time. "America's Great Poet Revels in Beauties of Old Vermont," Boston Traveler, April 11, 1921.

35 *different kind of "rough boys":* "Left Dartmouth to come home and take my mother's room in the grammar school at Methuen, Massachusetts. She had been having a hard time with some rough boys. I was feeling pretty rough myself from hazing and all that at college." RF to LU, Feb. 21, 1950, in RFLU, 354–58.

35 *Rob had recourse to them:* See, for example, Sergeant, Notes on conversations with RF, Aug. 2, 1949.

35 *Rob urged her to leave college:* LT, "Notes on Conversations," June 8, 1946, box 5.

36 *under threat from other men:* RF's retrospective sense of EF's wavering attachment to him in those years would be one of his most tortured memories. It was also highly dubious, appearing nowhere in the record before the somewhat dissociative months after the loss of EF and his newfound attachment to KM (in Newdick's notes on conversations with RF from Oct. 1938). RF told LT repeatedly that

EF had been engaged to her classmate Lorenzo Dow Case, who had this to write to EF in 1938 after the two had lost touch for decades: "Do you recollect telling me about the youth to whom you were then engaged? I do, for you told me of your love of him, your faith in him, and your deep confidence that he would later be known as a poet of distinction. And how wonderfully he has justified your faith in him." Case recalled "how immensely I admired your brilliant mind" and asked for her husband's autograph. Case to EF, Jan. 3, 1938, DCL 1178, box 2.

36 *Elinor thought they would burden their families:* EF attempted to correct the record as early as 1924, when she told someone writing about RF that, in contrast to the impression RF had given, "The fact was I said again and again I was willing to leave college and be married as soon as he was earning enough money to rent one room somewhere, but that I couldn't consent to be a burden to our parents." EF to Dorothy Bromley, Dec. 27, 1924, VCL 6261, box 9.

36 *lacked the slightest dramatic inflection:* Though RF told the story on many occasions, he made special note of the reader's dramatic insensibility in a conversation with LT on Sept. 1, 1956. LT, "Notes on Conversations," box 5.

36 *"read Shakespeare's thunders to the heavy machinery":* Edgar Gilbert to Robert Newdick, Dec. 31, 1937, published as Item 19 in the appendixes to *Newdick's Season of Frost.*

37 *"If I could meet that poem again":* Quoted in Beverly M. Bowie, "New England, a Modern Pilgrim's Pride," *National Geographic,* June 1955.

37 *not only enthralling but literally inspiring:* As Doc Cook recorded in "Verbatim" on May 2, 1957, RF "told us that there weren't many prominent echoes in his early poems but that we might find some echo of Thompson's 'Hound of Heaven' in 'My Butterfly.' He had been reading the former at the time he wrote his poem." This admission of direct influence—a rarity for RF, even as regarded "My Butterfly"—incidentally helps to date his discovery of "The Hound of Heaven," elsewhere muddled, to sometime in the winter of 1893–94, before the composition of "My Butterfly" but after the publication of Thompson's *Poems,* in London, in Dec. 1893 (publication month given in Paul van K. Thomson, *Francis Thompson: A Critical Biography* [New York: Nelson, 1961], 108).

37 *locking the door to the kitchen:* RF, interview by Lathem, Dec. 2, 1958. In the version of the story published by Elizabeth Shepley Sergeant, with RF's tacit approval, in *Robert Frost* (34), his sister Jeanie is banging on the door to get in until RF has finished writing. RF did not include that detail often, however, for instance telling Lathem only that there was once a time when he had locked himself in the kitchen and forced his sister, "poor thing," to bang in the outer door. What a psychologically convulsive memory, accurate or not, of your career-begetting inspiration as a time when your sister, whom fate or grace would never save, was left out angry in the cold.

38 *an issue with a poem on the front page:* "Seaward," by Richard Hovey, in the issue of Nov. 17, 1892. See, for example, Sergeant, Notes on conversations with RF, 1955.

38 *she had just discovered a poet:* A former member of the editorial staff recalled the discovery fifty-three years later. Hamilton Holt to RF, Feb. 5, 1947, DCL 1178, box 6.

38 *"Thine emulous fond flowers":* The quotation is from the original manuscript (JL Series 7).

38 *"The memory of your note":* RF to William Hayes Ward, March 28, 1894, in *Letters,* 1:27–28.

40 *"the technique of sincerity":* RF to Harriet Moody, March 7, 1917, in *Letters,* 1:539.

40 *"Since last I wrote":* RF to Susan Hayes Ward, June 10, 1894, in *Letters,* 1:32–33.

40 *"My thanks unlimited!":* RF to Susan Hayes Ward, April 22, 1894, in *Letters,* 1:28–32.

40–41 *also included in* Twilight: All quotations from *Twilight* are from the MS in JL Series 3.

41 *a self-conscious attempt to write:* LT, "Notes on Conversations," Feb. 23, 1940, box 5.

42 *generally making a pain of himself:* EY, 169–75.

43 *Elinor did agree to finish school:* LT dates EF's decision about graduating early to the summer of 1894 (*EY,* 171) but gives no citation. Though the dating is plausible, the archival record shows only that EF made the decision sometime between April 1893 and Oct. 1894, per excerpts of the student paper shared in a letter from EF's former classmate Owen D. Young to LT on Oct. 30, 1946, VCL 10044-A, box 17.

43 *There, on November 6, he boarded a ship:* Election Day, on which RF repeatedly said he had set sail.

43 *walking through the fabled stretch:* Transcription of RF's retelling of the story on March 3, 1961, sent in a letter from Arthur Palmer Hudson to KM, April 4, 1961, DCL 1178, box 6.

43 *A saloonkeeper who had met Frost:* RF mentioned the line of work of his new benefactor in many versions of the story, for example, Newdick's conversations with RF, April 21–25, 1938, published as Item 21 in the appendixes to *Newdick's Season of Frost.*

43 *looked into hiring Frost:* RF was inconsistent about how close he came to being hired by either, but he mentioned the efforts of the principal with far more consistency.

43 *"tramp's jungle":* RF to Jean Gould, Dec. 13, 1962, DCL 1178, box 5. The brakeman's robbery was a story told to Newdick, as well as to LT in "Notes on Conversations," Feb. 29, 1940, box 5.

44 *a famous moral reformer:* Newdick's Season of Frost, 50.

44 *a job at a grocery store:* LT, "Notes on Conversations," March 5, 1962, box 6.

44 *"eaten by alligators or bitten by snakes":* Holmes to RF, July 7, 1949, DCL 1178, box 6.

44 *"The occasion is, or was":* RF to Susan Hayes Ward, Dec. 4, 1894, in *Letters,* 1:34–35.

45 *"It has some secret of genius":* Maurice Thompson to William Hayes Ward, Nov. 10, 1894, VCL 6538, box 18.

46 *"Twilight," Frost would later recall:* RF to Earle Bernheimer, Oct. 16, 1947, VCL 6261, box 5.

47 *half a decade after the turbulence:* The source for dating most of RF's early published verse that is best, because most nearly contemporaneous, is a copy of his 1930

Collected Poems in which RF penciled in dates at the request of the poet and critic Genevieve Taggard (cited hereafter as Taggard, *CP*, JL). Unfortunately, RF changed his mind in short order and asked Taggard to erase all but ten of the dates he had written—but, fortunately, the erasures still bear marks of indentation, most of which are, at least with the help of digital technology, legible. The date he gave for "Flower-Gathering" was 1899. This appears to conflict with an inscription RF made in a copy of his first book, given to Edward Connery Lathem on Aug. 9, 1957, in which RF wrote "Allenstown N.H.," which would date the poem to the summer of 1896 (VCL 10044-A, box 20). But twenty-seven years had elapsed since the first dating, and RF plausibly just mistook the scene of the poem for the site of composition. "Flower-Gathering" is substantially more like RF's poetry of 1900 than anything he wrote as early as 1896. *CPPP*, 22.

48   *"Waiting: Afield at Dusk"*: *CPPP*, 23.

50   *the anthology Frost knew best:* No book would matter more to RF's poetry than *The Golden Treasury*, which RF most likely picked up in a bookstore during his semester at Dartmouth (RF wrote that he "had just got hold of the book" as of fall 1892, in RF to Susan Hayes Ward, Oct. 29, 1906, *Letters*, 1:48–49). RF inconsistently dated his first looking into *The Golden Treasury*, saying decades later that he had it in high school (but avoided anthologies for a time given his teachers' deprecations of the genre), and that he saw it first in 1890 after noticing a reference to it in Emerson's introduction to his anthology *Parnassus* (recording, talk at Cornell University, April 20, 1950, LM00229, ACL 00181; Cook, "Verbatim," July 17, 1950). Precedence is granted to the much earlier account, in which RF bought the book at Dartmouth, though one can partly reconcile them by supposing that RF heard of *The Golden Treasury* in 1890, perhaps browsing it at the library, but, staying away from anthologies for a time, did not obtain his own copy until the fall of 1892.

　　　　The Golden Treasury in RF's lifetime went through many editions of which RF owned many, making it hard to say with certainty which edition he read most in his formative years. However, the balance of evidence suggests that he first read, and then knew best, the original, 1861 edition rather than the expanded edition of 1891. RF casually spoke of the book as from 1861, and in a talk at the Bread Loaf School of English on July 4, 1960, RF wondered at the absence from *The Golden Treasury* of "Song to David," by Christopher Smart, which in fact was in the 1891 edition (in abbreviated form) but not in the earlier (Cook, "Verbatim"). References in the text to *The Golden Treasury* are thus to the edition of 1861. *The Golden Treasury of the Best Songs and Lyrical Poems in the English Language*, selected and arranged with notes by Francis Turner Palgrave (Cambridge and London: Macmillan and Co., 1861).

52   *"The Figure a Poem Makes"*: *CPPP*, 776.

52   *"a carefully measured amount"*: Notebook 17, ca. 1929, DCL 1178, box 16.

52   *"What more is needed to measure"*: Notebook 7, ca. 1911, DCL 1178, box 16.

3. THE SWEETEST DREAM

54 *a windy afternoon:* RF told the story often but not always with the atmospheric
details shared in his recounting to an audience at New York University on March
23, 1956 (LM0013, ACL 00181).

54 *he knew he would never want:* See, for example, Gardner Jackson, "I Will Teach Only
When I Have Something to Tell," *Boston Globe*, Nov. 23, 1924.

54 *one of the first books:* EF to Edna Davis Romig, Feb. 4, 1935, VCL 10044-A, box
15. LT cites the same source but claims not only what EF writes, which is that
RF read the book in the year before writing "La Noche Triste," but that RF read
the book, and others, in the summer between his freshman and sophomore years
of high school, LT's inference presumably being that RF would have been too
busy to read books at home during the school year (*EY*, 84). Yet LT's own notes
on conversations suggest that RF may well have read the book in his sophomore
year, as evinced by RF's recollection of his reading habits from that year with
special emphasis on Cortés: "By his sophomore year, Frost had developed an
insatiable hunger for reading books. Now 14 years old, he had been spared the
traditional method of getting to know books, and had no idea how to go for
authors. So he started with subjects. If he heard some reference to Cortey [*sic*], he
looked up Cortey [*sic*] in the library catalogue" (LT, "Notes on Conversations,"
June 24, 1946, box 5). This suggests that the book was fresh in mind when RF
made the Cortés story his own, as was "The Hound of Heaven" before the composition of "My Butterfly."

54 *History of the Conquest of Mexico:* First published in 1843, in three volumes.
The part RF retells is bk. 5, chap. 3.

54 *"La Noche Triste":* CPPP, 485–88.

55 A Century of Dishonor: RF recalled reading Jackson's book before writing "La
Noche Triste" in a recorded interview with Lathem on Dec. 2, 1958.

55 *a Native chief's scorn:* "The Sachem of the Clouds (a Thanksgiving Legend)," in
CPPP, 494.

55 *His second poem:* "Song of the Wave," in *CPPP*, 489.

55 *another poem from high school:* "A Dream of Julius Caesar," in *CPPP*, 490.

56 *"An Unhistoric Spot":* CPPP, 500.

56 *a peaceful tribe in a secret canyon:* Munson, *Robert Frost*, 28.

56 *fantasized in high school:* RF, recorded interview with Lathem, Dec. 2, 1958.

57 *the man whose gravestone:* Sergeant, Notes on conversations with RF, 1956.

57 *dog chain:* Bartlett, Notes on conversations with RF, Aug. 8–9, 1934, VCL 10044-
A, box 19.

57 *years after his father died:* LT, "Notes on Conversations," June 28, 1951, box 5.

57 *might have lived to be a senator:* Sergeant, Notes on conversations with RF, early spring
1956.

58 *threw it into the fireplace:* LT, "Notes on Conversations," Aug. 29, 1956, box 5.

58 *substantially embellished:* Hart, *Life of Robert Frost*, 23–24.
58 *blaming the race:* RF's annotation on MS of Elizabeth Shepley Sergeant's *Robert Frost: The Trial by Existence*, 1959, VCL 6538, box 1.
58 *swimming out into the bay:* LT, "Notes on Conversations," July 28, 1941, box 5.
58 *had hated his own father:* Bartlett, Notes on conversations with RF, Aug. 8–9, 1934.
58 *a rope ladder he made:* LT, "Notes on Conversations," May 31, 1946, box 5.
58 *fled south from Lawrence:* LT, "Notes on Conversations," June 6, 1946, box 5.
58 *refused to take a cent from his father:* Bartlett, Notes on conversations with RF, Aug. 8–9, 1934.
58 *"Some of my ancestors":* RF's "Great Issues" lecture at Dartmouth, May 19, 1953, recording, DCL 12, box 11512.
58 *prowess at cards:* "Notes on Conversations," Sept. 3, 1941, VCL 10044, box 5.
58 *second or third in his class:* Sergeant, Notes on conversations with RF, Aug. 1955.
59 *an attempt to blackmail her:* LT, "Notes on Conversations," June 6, 1946.
59 *an old pupil of theirs:* Elizabeth Beckwish to RF, 1915, DCL 1178, box 1.
59 *a newsroom whose windows were shot:* LT, "Notes on Conversations," July 28, 1941, box 5.
60 *a theory to which Will and Belle both subscribed:* RF's annotation on MS of Sergeant's *Robert Frost: The Trial by Existence*, 1959.
60 *Rob was often quite sick:* LT, "Notes on Conversations," June 10, 1947, box 5.
60 *Levy's saloon:* Sergeant, Notes on conversations with RF, Dec. 11, 1954.
60 *Father and son would see the cows killed:* See, for example, Cook, "Verbatim," June 3, 1959, in which RF, with reference to a pair of younger poets who wrote with candor and drama about their troubled psyches and families of origin (Robert Lowell and Delmore Schwartz), called his early trips to the slaughterhouse "a terror equal to any they could invent."
60 *refighting the battles:* LT, "Notes on Conversations," June 6, 1946.
60 *seven sections:* Cook, "Verbatim," Sept. 27, 1947.
61 *saw the rows of stenographers:* LT, "Notes on Conversations," May 31, 1946, box 5.
61 *"did what I could":* RF to LU, Nov. 14, 1916, in *Letters*, 1:504–5.
61 *importunate and impatient:* Sergeant, Notes on conversations with RF, early spring 1956.
61 *told the story of his father:* LT, "Notes on Conversations," June 30, 1951, box 5.
61 *lost a dime on an errand:* LT, "Notes on Conversations," June 1, 1946, box 5.
61 *running out into the street:* LT, "Notes on Conversations," Feb. 21, 1940, box 5.
61 *pleading from Columbus:* Belle Moodie Frost to William Prescott Frost Jr., Nov. 1, 1876, VCL 6261, box 5.
61 *mixed with love:* LT, "Notes on Conversations," June 30, 1951.
61 *said his father had been inscrutable:* Sergeant, Notes on conversations with RF, Aug. 1955.
61 *"I thought his ghost followed us":* Jeanie Frost to RF, ca. early 1920s on internal evidence, VCL 10044, box 1.

62 *afraid to move:* LT, "Notes on Conversations," June 30, 1951.

62 *Rob and Jeanie were off playing:* LT, "Notes on Conversations," May 25, 1946, box 5.

62 *in the streets after dark:* Bartlett, Notes on conversations with RF, Aug. 8–9, 1934.

62 *"A great teacher":* The first two quotations in this paragraph were sent, ca. Jan. 17, 1960, from a typescript, by Clara Searle Painter, of an article eventually published as "Mrs. Frost's Private School" in *Mount Holyoke Alumnae Quarterly* (Winter 1963). The following quotations are from letters: Susan Nash to LT, n.d., VCL 10044-A, box 14; Susan Holmes to LT, July 5, 1964, VCL 10044-A, box 13; Carl Burrell to Edna Davis Romig, March 5, 1935, VCL 10044-A, box 9.

62 *"delightful sense of humor":* Susan Nash to LT, n.d., VCL 10044-A, box 14.

62 *"In her Sunday-school class":* Susan Holmes to LT, March 17, 1964, VCL 10044-A, box 13.

63 *the "joyous time":* Susan Holmes to RF, July 7, 1949, DCL 1178, box 6.

63 *"Auld Lang Syne":* Susan Holmes to LT, March 17, 1964.

63 *"My mother was very fond":* Quoted in "America's Great Poet Revels in Beauties of Old Vermont."

63 *a natural teacher and the inspiration:* RF's conversation with Van Doren and Adams, ca. Oct. 1962, recording.

63 *Poe, Shelley, and Keats:* RF's talk to a graduate seminar on April 2, 1959, recording, LM0008, ACL 00181.

63 *the lesson her son learned:* RF, interview by Randall Jarrell, May 19, 1959, recording, LM0007, ACL 00181.

63 *reading Emerson again:* RF's talk to American Academy of Arts and Sciences, Oct. 8, 1958, recording, LM0156, ACL 00181.

64 *"second sight":* LT, "Notes on Conversations," June 10, 1947.

64 *caught the eye of her young son:* RF to LT, ca. early March 1942, VCL 10044-A, box 11.

64 *must have been too proud:* LT to Jean Moodie Walker Rau, Oct. 17, 1965, VCL 10044-A, box 14.

64 *thinking that the country was at risk:* RF quoted in *Newdick's Season of Frost,* 19.

64 *"Some people cant resist tragedy":* RF to LF, ca. mid-1932 on internal evidence, VCL 6261, box 1. *Letters* 3 dates the letter more confidently to early fall 1932, ahead of LF's finalization of her divorce on Nov. 1 of that year.

64 *"Romantic":* LT, "Notes on Conversations," June 30, 1951.

64 *Frost wrote to Susan Hayes Ward:* RF to Ward, Dec. 27, 1896, in *Letters,* 1:41.

65 *a friend of the family's:* RF's talk to a graduate seminar on April 2, 1959, recording, LM0008, ACL 00181. On that occasion and on others, RF remembered thinking that the fight would make him have to leave town, but made light of it in the retelling. "He said I hit him, and the judge looked at me and I said, 'It looks as if I did,'" said RF to the audible amusement of a press conference at the Library of Congress, May 21, 1958, recording, LM0076, ACL 00181.

65 *The word stuck with Frost:* LT, "Notes on Conversations," Feb. 18, 1940, box 5.

65 *"Flower-Gathering"*: See note to *half a decade after this turbulence*, in chap. 2, sec. 7.

65 *"to the exclusion I fear"*: RF to Susan Hayes Ward, Aug. 15, 1896, in *Letters*, 1:40.

65 *occurred to him while reading Tacitus*: LT and Newdick have similar versions of the story in their notes, for example, Newdick's notes on a visit with the Frosts, Sept. 1–3, 1937, published as Item 18 in the appendixes to *Newdick's Season of Frost*. LT tells the story with some additional details in *EY*, 230, with Elinor bathing baby Elliott as RF shared his idea and reacting with an impassiveness that RF would find wounding. These details are curious because neither the bath nor her reaction is in the versions of the story recorded in LT's "Notes on Conversations," Feb. 26, 1940, and June 8, 1946. It is possible that LT simply misremembered or confabulated, and also distinctly possible that RF told the story to LT in a more negative light, after Elinor's death, than he told it before her death to Newdick, who noted Elinor's encouragement of RF's plan in the draft of his biography (59).

65 *Frost pleaded his case*: RF to LeBaron Russell Briggs, Sept. 11, 1897, Records of the Dean of Harvard College, 1889–1995, Houghton Library. The scholarly edition of RF's letters from Harvard University Press, praiseworthy in all other ways, lamentably omits the spelling errors RF made as he commended his own intellect to the dean. *Letters*, 1:42–43.

66 *as well as his Greek model Theocritus*: Interview at Trinity College, Oct. 12, 1962, recording, ACL 00181, LM0454.

66 *the instructor would later recall*: Alfred D. Sheffield to Robert Newdick, April 24, 1939, quoted in Item 31 in the appendixes to *Newdick's Season of Frost*.

66 *the teacher from whom he learned most*: See, for example, a talk at the Bread Loaf School of English, July 4, 1960, collected in Cook, "Verbatim."

66 *Belle worried*: Susan Holmes to LT, March 17, 1964, VCL 10044-A, box 13.

66 *piqued Frost's moral indignation*: See note to *"how Frost might have actually felt,"* in chap. 5, sec. 6.

66 *Frost's strident criticisms*: RF's rejection of Santayana's notion of true and false illusions took many forms over the years, one of which, as argued in chapter 5, took the form of his poem "The Black Cottage." Another rejection appeared in a letter to LT half a century after RF had taken Santayana's class ("The last pop of poppycock was for Santaanna [*sic*] to say, 'true illusion and false illusion that is all there is to choose between'" [RF to LT, June 12, 1948, in *SL*, 529–32]). Santayana so inflamed RF that he called the literary philosopher "the enemy of my spirit," though the relationship was outwardly cordial enough for RF to call on Santayana as late as 1912 (respectively, VCL 10044-A, box 14; Cook, "Verbatim," Oct. 3, 1959).

66 *one of the best in his life*: RF, conversation with Harvard professor Reuben Brower and students, March 25, 1958, recording, ACL 00181, LM0149.

66 *suggested a move to the country*: LT, "Notes on Conversations," June 6, 1946, and Aug. 29, 1956, box 5. Some uncertainty surrounds the timing of RF's doctor telling him to rusticate in more ways than one. There might have been two distinct doc-

tor's visits in 1898 as well as the following spring, as LT claims in *EY* (250), but he offers no citation and the relevant passages in "Notes on Conversations" tell of only one visit.

66 *the strain of living alone:* Newdick's *Season of Frost*, 69.

67 *other familiar agita:* Newdick's *Season of Frost*, 69; RF, conversation with Brower and students, March 25, 1958, recording.

67 *the dean of men attesting:* LeBaron Russell Briggs to RF, March 31, 1899, note, VCL 6261, box 5.

67 *a plan to do as his doctor prescribed: EY*, 251–52.

67 *keeping hens in his parents' yard:* EF to Edna Davis Romig, ca. winter 1935 on internal evidence, VCL 10044-A, box 15.

68 *far more unwell than her son:* LT, "Notes on Conversations," June 6, 1946, Feb. 20, 1946, box 5.

68 *his grandmother's brown eyes:* Susan Holmes to LT, March 17, 1964, VCL 10044-A, box 13. LT has the eyes as blue (*EY*, 223); maybe they darkened after infancy.

68 *The doctor recommended no urgent treatment:* The account of Elliott's illness and death is that told to LT on June 6, 1946, in "Notes on Conversations" (box 5). Another version recounted by LT, on Feb. 27, 1941, refers to Belle's doctor (not quoting RF directly) as a homeopath and claims that he prescribed homeopathic pills for the boy. It is hard to overstate how much hinges on the distinction, because if Belle's doctor was a homeopath, then RF and EF would have had good reason not to defer to him and, in light of what happened, all the more reason to hold their deference against themselves. One cannot rule this possibility out, but the evidence preponderates against it. For one, the line between reputable doctors and quacks was much thinner in 1899 than it would become. Pharmacological standards were so loose that it would not have been at all unusual for a normal doctor to prescribe nonstandard medication. So the doctor prescribing homeopathic pills could have been a normal doctor with a penchant for homeopathy rather than a homeopath. This is also consistent with the context of the notes from Feb. 27, 1941, which are unusually error-ridden, mistaking the house of the appointment and referring to both the doctor and Elliott as "her." So, LT might have misheard, misremembered, or simply inferred that any doctor with homeopathic pills was a homeopath. This raises two all-important questions of context. If RF regarded his mother's doctor as a quack, why would he consult the doctor at all? And if RF placed his trust in an obviously illegitimate doctor, would he not have blamed himself lastingly and not just in the reactive, passing way the record suggests? RF cursed God after the death; he did not hold himself responsible after the shock had subsided. This is all consistent with his having gotten bad advice from a doctor who was not obviously bad but who, with the unconcern RF mentioned in his other account of the story, gave the child some pills not to treat the case but to alleviate symptoms in a case that did not need to be treated.

Yet one cannot entirely rule out the alternative, on which RF made the negligent decision, knew it, and could never live it down so much as to confess it to anyone who would go on to leave a record, including, possibly, himself.

68 *He blamed himself:* Victor Reichert attested to RF's self-recrimination in an interview with Jay Parini, quoted in *Robert Frost*, 68. RF's curse of God recorded by LT in "Notes on Conversations," June 6, 1946, VCL 10044, box 5.

68 *Elinor renounced her belief:* LT, "Notes on Conversations," Dec. 13, 1963, box 6. Her disbelief was relatively short-lived, to judge from her professed belief in immortality as of 1915, as relayed in Cox, "Walks and Talks with Robert Frost," 30.

68 *Frost responded with a poem:* LT dates the composition of the poem circumstantially, but persuasively, to the aftermath of Elliott's death (*EY*, 546–47). Even if the poem was not written in immediate response—although that seems probable to judge by its style—it was assuredly written after Elliott's death rather than before, as "Stars" drew inspiration from another poem about cosmic disappointment after a loss (see herein chap. 4, sec. 5).

68 *"Stars":* CPPP, 19.

70 *Frost's copy in use:* Robert Frost Library, NYU. Inside the book is written, in what appears to be KM's hand, "R.F. cherished this book because his first son, Eliot, scribbled in it." No title page of the book is visible.

71 *"Mowing":* CPPP, 26. Dating derived from Taggard's edition of RF's 1930 *Collected Poems*, in which RF appears to write "1901" before crossing out the 1 and writing in another 0. Plausibly he couldn't remember, three decades later, whether he had written the poem toward the end of 1900 or in the spring of the following year, once mowing had begun again in earnest (Taggard, *CP*, JL). His other recollections are consistent with the above, having written for Lathem "Derry N H" and for Sergeant "First talk-song I was ever aware of," dating the poem before the inflorescence of talk-songs to follow (VCL 10044-A, box 20; VCL 6538, box 1).

71 *"one of the keys to all my life":* RF speaking at Boston University, Oct. 30, 1958, recording, LM0163, ACL 00181.

72 *"The highest minds of the world":* "The Poet," published originally in Emerson's *Essays: Second Series* (1844).

74 *"Christabel":* Jeffrey Meyers noted the echo of Coleridge's "bright green snake" in "Mowing" in *Robert Frost*, 363. Other echoes cluster around the selfsame scene of dream interpretation in the ballad—a line ending "on the ground" (in "Mowing," "to the ground"), an elf and a fairy "That always finds, and never seeks" (in "Mowing," "easy gold at the hand of fay or elf"). Much could be said of the inspiration provided for "Mowing" by "Christabel," a ballad about what goes wrong in a family; about an absent parent; about the interpretation of a certain kind of dream, the child abandoned by the parent's Romantic sentimentality born of regret and the wish to avoid dishonor. The scene of "Christabel" echoed so richly in "Mowing" is of the child attempting a less sentimental, less regretful interpretation of a dreamlike experience than its interpretation by the parent figure alluded to.

RF cited "Christabel" as a precedent in notes written for a speech he would give in Cincinnati in Oct. 1938. About poetic meter, RF wrote, "All that matters is that a definite number of accents should be observed per line. The number of unaccented syllables between the accented is any you choose to make it. There is plenty of precedent in Gerard Manley Hopkins and the ballads and Crysta-bel [*sic*]" (DCL 1178, box 19; date derived from Item 30 in the appendixes to *Newdick's Season of Frost*). RF's metrical description corresponds precisely to the meter of "Mowing," highly irregular for his verse, with anything from ten to thirteen syllables in each of fourteen five-stress lines.

74   *"Revolutions": The Golden Treasury* (1861), 18–19. "Carpe Diem" appears on pp. 16–17.

75   *one can call make-believe:* The elaboration of the term "make-believe" in the present work draws on RF's marvelously rich formulation that "poetry plays perilously close between truth and make believe, so that it might not be extravagant to give it the name true make believe—or making believe what is actually true" (prose fragment, ca. March 1938, DCL 1178, box 19). See also RF to R. P. T. Coffin, ca. March 7, 1938 (*SL*, 467).

75   *"Choice of Society":* MS, Huntington Library HM 7656. Dating derived from Tag-gard's edition of RF's 1930 *Collected Poems*, in which RF wrote "1900" next to the version of the poem published, with minor revisions, as "The Vantage Point" in *A Boy's Will*. RF appended a note to the fair copy of "Choice of Society" sent to Susan Hayes Ward that serves as a hint to the kind of persona employed: "Comment: Not quite honest."

75   *Sonnet 66:* "The World's Way," in *The Golden Treasury* (1861), 39.

4. NOT FIND ME CHANGED

80   *The first poem of* A Boy's Will: *CPPP*, 15. Epigraphs for most poems in *A Boy's Will* appeared in the table of contents in the initial publication but were dropped from most subsequent editions. RF would later claim to have written the de-scriptions "to make the poems look more connected than they were" (Lathem annotations, VCL 10044-A, box 20). His intentions notwithstanding, the impli-cation of disconnectedness between the poems is belied by the argument in this chapter. Dating of "Into My Own" is derived from Taggard's 1930 *CP* (Taggard, *CP*, JL). Robert Newdick cites the inception of the poem rather prettily to the schoolroom RF presided over in the spring of 1894, the children working at their desks as the teacher looked at the trees through the window and wrote (*Newdick's Season of Frost*, 43–44). Even if one doubts that those students ever worked at their desks, it is eminently plausible, even likely, that RF held for years the seed of the poem about the long thoughts of youth before writing it out in a polished draft.

81   *once parodied by Alexander Pope:* In "An Essay on Criticism," lines 350–51.

81   *Shakespeare's famous sonnet:* "True Love," in *The Golden Treasury* (1861), 15.

83 *"Ghost House"*: CPPP, 15–16. Dating derived from Taggard's 1930 *CP* (Taggard *CP*, JL).

86 *"I died for beauty, but was scarce"*: First published in Dickinson's *Poems* (first series), 1890, as poem 10 in sec. 4 ("Time and Eternity"). As critics have long noted, Dickinson's poem also responds to a response to Keats's ode by Elizabeth Barrett Browning in "A Vision of Poets": "these were poets true, / Who died for Beauty, as martyrs do / For Truth—the ends being scarcely two." Browning's allusion to Keats does not relate to RF's in any special way.

87 *"afraid I deceived her a little"*: RF to Bernard DeVoto, April 12, 1938, in *SL*, 470.

87 *"My November Guest"*: CPPP, 16–17. Dating derived from Taggard's 1930 *CP* ("1903") and RF's earlier, if vaguer, report ("about 1900"). Taggard, *CP*, JL; RF to Charles Franc Goddard, Feb. 1, 1917, in *Letters*, 1:527–28.

90 In Memoriam: It is unclear which edition, or editions, of Tennyson's works RF knew best. In the portion of RF's library preserved at NYU, there is no edition of Tennyson's works from before 1899, by which time RF was long familiar with Tennyson. As nothing of substance hinges on the bibliographical details, quotations are taken from the 1899 edition, *The Poetic and Dramatic Works of Alfred, Lord Tennyson, Household Ed.* (Cambridge, Mass.: The Riverside Press). Cantos in the end of *In Memoriam* have variant numbering in some other editions.

91 *Each of the first nine poems*: In reverse numerical order, "To the Thawing Wind," "Wind and Window Flower," "Storm Fear," "Stars," "A Late Walk," "Love and a Question," "My November Guest," "Ghost House," "Into My Own," in CPPP, 15–21.

92 *"The Record of a Phase"*: RF to Mark Antony DeWolfe Howe, ca. Nov.–Dec. 1912 on internal evidence, in *Letters*, 1:83.

94 *poems of attachments*: Respectively, CPPP, 15, 15–16, 16–17, 19, 22, 23–24, 26, 26.

5. OTHER FAR

99 *"changing works"*: RF to Gorham Munson, ca. June 18, 1927, DCL 1178, box 8: "I got acquainted with my neighbors when we 'changed works,' mostly in haying time."

99 *prose writings for widely read poultry journals*: See *Collected Prose*, 35–73.

99 *wondered what was so strange*: "As I would write and have my poems returned, I would ask myself three questions. Are my poems too bad to be published? Are they too good? Or are they just too strange?

"If I admitted the first I would get discouraged, and I couldn't be discouraged. If I said they were too good I would get conceited. I could never do that. So I always just agreed that they were too strange." RF as quoted in "America's Great Poet Revels in Beauties of Old Vermont."

99 *"with a view to a volume some day"*: RF to Susan Hayes Ward, Jan. 15, 1901, in *Letters*, 1:44.

100   *"Loving children (which is teaching)"*: Notebook 7, ca. 1911, DCL 1178, box 16.

100   *"playing school"*: LF, Oct. 4, 1906. Her journals from Derry are reproduced photographically in LF, *New Hampshire's Child*, from which all journal quotations are taken.

101   *"i like snake mouth"*: LF, *New Hampshire's Child*, June 6, 1906.

101   *"About War"*: LF, *New Hampshire's Child*, June 1, 1906.

101   *"our war game"*: LF, *New Hampshire's Child*, Aug. 6, 1907.

102   *"Poems are very pretty sometimes"*: LF, *New Hampshire's Child*, most likely ca. Jan. 22, 1907. The entry, undated, appears between entries dated Jan. 21, 1905, and Jan. 23, 1905, which themselves appear between entries dated to Jan. 1907. The Jan. 26, 1907, entry on Wordsworth implies that she was writing about him at the time, and the 1905 entries are out of sequence.

102   *"I like Wordsworth's poems"*: LF, *New Hampshire's Child*, Jan. 26, 1907. "The Daffodils" refers to Wordsworth's poem beginning "I wander'd lonely as a cloud," sometimes called "Daffodils" but called "The Daffodils" by Palgrave and seven-year-old LF ("the dafidils"), among others.

102   *a later story*: LF, *New Hampshire's Child*, April 15, 1908.

102   *"journeys On The Farm"*: LF, *New Hampshire's Child*, April 9, 1908.

103   *"Hyla Brook"*: CPPP, 115–16. Dating derived from Taggard's 1930 *CP*. RF elsewhere dated the composition of the poem inconsistently to 1912 and to the period on the Derry farm, which was EF's recollection as well. One can reconcile the various dates by positing that RF began the poem in 1904, on the farm, only to finish it to his satisfaction eight years later.

106   The Rime of the Ancient Mariner: Quotations are taken from the poem as published in *The Oxford Book of English Verse* (1900), which RF knew in Derry. It is unclear which edition of Coleridge's poems RF knew best.

106   *"Somebody did something wrong"*: LF, *New Hampshire's Child*, April 15, 1908.

106   *"in the land of mist and snow"*: See, from "Hyla Brook," "That shouted in the mist a month ago, / Like ghost of sleigh-bells in a ghost of snow." In another sign that RF knew this part of *Rime* well, he quoted part of a line from it, "Like a pawing horse let go," in a letter to Sidney Cox with a poem in it that also alludes to the *Rime*. RF to Cox, Dec. 26, 1912, DCL 1178, box 3. See p. 158.

108   *letter in verse*: VCL 6261, box 2. Dating of the verse letter is derived partly from internal evidence—the winter, the financial concern—and partly from a clue in RF's Coleridgean marginal gloss about his finances, "Inelastic currency as much to blame as anything," the phrase "inelastic currency" having been popularized (relatively speaking) after the eminent banker Jacob Schiff blamed the inelastic United States dollar for the instability of financial conditions in a well-publicized speech to the Chamber of Commerce on Jan. 5, 1906. RF's gloss sounds like the kind of thing newspapers were printing after the speech—"Bankers Agree That Inelastic Currency Is Perilous," for example, was a subheadline in *The New York Times* on Jan. 6, 1906.

Notes

421

109 *His story:* LT, "Notes on Conversations," June 18, 1946, box 5.

109–10 *"The Tuft of Flowers":* CPPP, 30–31. Also published in *The Derry Enterprise*, March 9, 1906.

110 *his first recorded account:* RF to John Bartlett, Feb. 26, 1913, VCL 6261, box 5.

110 *he granted again decades later:* On March 12, 1931, RF told an audience that "The Tuft of Flowers" was "the only poem I ever wrote for an occasion" (ACL 00181, box 2).

112 *A number of Frost's former students:* Quotations from former students are from a series of letters solicited in 1968 by Martha B. Pushee (VCL 10044-A, box 15).

115 *"The Lost Leader":* RF alluded to the poem even more directly in "The Lost Follower," in CPPP, 325–26.

116 *Gettysburg Address:* The text quoted is from the Bliss copy of the address, one of six extant variants. None of the minor discrepancies between versions bear on arguments herein about RF's knowledge of the address.

117 *published in* The Derry News: Two days before the publication of "The Lost Faith," RF's thematically similar poem "The Later Minstrel," an encomium to Longfellow written to order for his centennial, had been sung in chapel at Pinkerton to the tune of the hymn "As Pants the Hart for Cooling Streams" (Donald S. Learnard to Martha B. Pushee, June 18, 1968, VCL 10044-A, box 15). It is one of the only instances in RF's poetry in which he drew clearly on the poetic structure of the hymn, and was, perhaps relatedly, a composition he often denied over the years with great implausibility.

117 *thinking an editor might want to time it:* Sergeant, Notes on conversations with RF, Nov. 9, 1955.

117 *"The Black Cottage":* CPPP, 59–62.

117 *"an everyday level of diction":* RF to Thomas Bird Mosher, July 17, 1913, in *Letters*, 1:132. In drawing attention to the language "even Wordsworth" kept above, RF draws a contrast between the ambition declared in the "Preface to *Lyrical Ballads*" and the diction Wordsworth actually used in his poems.

117 *The draft that survives:* MS, Huntington Library HM 7656.

117 *Frost dated the draft:* RF to Robert Newdick, Jan. 18, 1938, VCL 6261, box 6. In the same letter, RF also recalls having written the unrhymed revision of "The Black Cottage" in the same years—a version of a claim he made regularly about three narrative poems from *North of Boston*, telling an acquaintance in 1917, for example, "The Death of the Hired Man, The Black Cottage and The Housekeeper belong to 1905. Nearly all the others in North of Boston were written in England between 1911 and 1913" (RF to Charles Franc Goddard, Feb. 1, 1917, in *Letters*, 1:528). Setting aside that RF was not yet in England in 1911, his account strains credulity for a number of reasons, among them that, as published, the three poems whose composition RF dates to the mid-aughts are shockingly different in style from everything RF is known to have written in that period. It also strains credulity that RF would have discovered this style, which he later knew to be transformative, and then not written any other poems in the style for half a dozen

years. His account has all the trappings of a retrospective myth of inspiration, in which the innovation in style was simply something that came to him rather than something he had to work for, something RF later admitted offhand in a letter to LU that also establishes the antecedence of "The Black Cottage" relative to the other two eclogues putatively written in the mid-aughts: "The first of the eclogues (really too much action in them for true eclogues) was The Black Cottage. I had trouble enough getting it the way I wanted it and no success in getting it published." RF to LU, Feb. 27, 1950, LOC MSS84950, box 3.

118   *"Ruth: Or the Influences of Nature": The Golden Treasury* (1861), 277–83.

120   *how Frost might have actually felt:* As if "The Lost Faith" were not evidence enough of RF's views at the time about the American creed, he discussed his feelings about the minister on many other occasions. Each discussion is suggestive; together they reveal his hidden target.

RF all but declared his disagreement with the minister in a letter of 1914: "Sometime we *must* discuss that minister and his creed. I make it a rule not to take any~~body's side~~ 'character's' side in any thing I write. So I am not bound to defend the minister you understand" (RF to Cox, Oct. 4, 1914, DCL 1178, box 3). Forty-four years later, RF paused his reading of the poem to an audience after the minister says, of Jefferson's words, "Of course the easy way / Is to decide it simply isn't true. / It may not be. I heard a fellow say so," at which point RF inserted, with a sneer, "He was one of my teachers—but never mind that." RF at Webster Hall, Nov. 19, 1958, phonotape recording, DCL 1238.

Though RF does not identify the teacher, he criticized precisely one former teacher elsewhere on similar grounds. George Santayana advocated a theory compatible with the minister's conception of truth, in phrasing reminiscent of the minister's vagueness. On Frost's interpretation, Santayana argued that there were no religious or spiritual truths, only illusions, which could be more or less true for people in different historical periods. In a commencement address at Oberlin in 1937, Frost mocked what he saw as the sophistry of Santayana's talk of "true and false illusions," which led to Santayana's aestheticism as an ersatz religion, making Santayana a kind of minister lacking in reverence (elsewhere called by RF "high priest of Beauty is Truth" [Cook, "Verbatim," summer 1928]): "You can get out a theory that meanings go out of things. You can call it disillusionment. You can get disillusionment of a phrase, such as 'fearing God,' and 'equality.' And then you can form a religion, like George Santayana. He lets you see that there is nothing but illusion, and it can just as well be one kind as another. . . . You grow to be a sad person." "What Became of New England," June 8, 1937, typescript by Robert Newdick, VCL 6261, box 2.

In the same commencement address, Frost recalled with contempt a nameless someone in his student days at Harvard mocking the idea that we were created free and equal. One is put in mind, not for the last time, of RF's tendency to use poems, consciously or not, as comebacks to things that had been bothering him a long time, as he admitted in conversation at Harvard in 1958 a few minutes after talking about his old days as a student of Santayana's:

> Every little while that's what poetry is to me—I get something off my mind that has been bothering me a long time, or that somebody's bothered me with. . . . Sometimes I don't realize I'd been dealing with something that somebody had bothered me with. I answer him behind his back long afterward. He doesn't know that he's bothered me to that point. It's myself I'm saying it for, really. Clearing it up. (RF, conversation with Brower and students, March 25, 1958, recording)

None of this is to identify the minister entirely with Santayana. More plausibly, the character was a composite—part fiction, of course, and part Reverend Wolcott, who consistently meant to help RF but whom RF regarded as pompous and inclined to sententious pronouncements of received wisdom, like the minister in the poem.

123 *respective contributions to* Lyrical Ballads: *Lyrical Ballads* does not survive in what remains of RF's library, but RF was demonstrably familiar with the book and in particular the editions of 1800 and later with Wordsworth's famous preface. RF knew Wordsworth deeply and knew the better poems of Coleridge no less well, although he was sometimes evasive on the subject. In any case, no one of RF's literary background would have been unfamiliar with the book that, more than any other, inaugurated Romanticism in English poetry. RF also plausibly knew that "Christabel," so important for "Mowing," was intended by Coleridge for *Lyrical Ballads* (and left out at Wordsworth's suggestion).

123 *"being occupied with the idealizing part"*: Notebook 7, ca. 1911, DCL 1178, box 16.

6. THE TRAVELER AND THE ROAD

125 *Bartlett could remember the rest:* Bartlett to Gorham Munson, April 30, 1927, VCL 6261, box 6.

126 *questioning the scholarly footnote:* LT, "Notes on Conversations," Aug. 29, 1956, box 5.

127 *the distinctive Irish wit:* RF would honor the laconic wit of his old friend, as well as his wife, with a versified story of them, "The Cow's in the Corn: A One-Act Irish Play in Rhyme." The diminutive play, which RF never collected, was written, he said, "in memory of his great friends the John Lynches on the South Road out of Bethlehem." Note by Edward Connery Lathem, VCL 10044-A, box 20.

128 *Cox disagreed with the protesters:* RFSC, 9.

128–29 *Frost would cast some doubt:* RF to Cox, Nov. 10, 1928, and Aug. 8, 1942, DCL 1178, box 3.

129 *"After the walk"*: "Walks and Talks with Robert Frost," I, a manuscript Cox left unpublished in the wake of RF's stern disapproval.

129   *Their memories:* Quotations from former students are from a series of letters solicited in 1968 by Martha B. Pushee (VCL 10044-A, box 15).

130   *dashingly, inconsistently, and rather implausibly:* No coin flip is mentioned in relatively early accounts of the decision—for example, the *Dearborn Independent,* July 29, 1922, or Munson's early biography *Robert Frost,* 58–59. One of Munson's sources, none other than John Bartlett, recalled that RF had planned on Vancouver before settling on England, believing also that he had the next few years to make his name in literature (Bartlett to Munson, April 30, 1927, VCL 6261, box 6). The flip of a coin makes for a good, serendipitous story, and RF was ever keen to make his strategic acts of literary ambition look like serendipity.

130   *an unpublished poem about selling his farm:* CPPP, 519.

132   *Cox's pilgrimage up to Franconia:* Recounted in Cox's series of diaristic letters to his sister and parents from Aug. 1915, reprinted in *RFSC,* 77–94.

134   *sent Cox from England:* RF to Cox, July 10, 1913, DCL 1178, box 3. On the manuscript, "Plymouth N.H." is written in the bottom left.

135   *editorial selection in* Parnassus: RF recalled reading the book as early as 1890, around the time he began to write (and read) poetry. Cook, "Verbatim," July 17, 1950.

136   *"little room":* RF may have adapted the phrase from the subtitle of *Our Place Among Infinities:* "A Series of Essays, Contrasting Our Little Abode in Space and Time with the Infinities Around Us."

137   *We are in something:* Quotations follow Satan's escape from hell, flight through the heavens to earth, and fateful entrance into Eden before his capture as he tempts Eve asleep in her "narrow room." These scenes span the second half of book 2 through the end of book 4 of *Paradise Lost,* a portion of the epic RF would draw on repeatedly in his poetry over the years. A partial list includes:

- "For Once, Then, Something": Like "Bond and Free," a poem from the 1910s (ca. 1917) that drew together the perspectives of Satan and the first two humans in Genesis to tell a representative but conflicted story about human knowledge and belief. "For Once, Then, Something" balances a pair of optical epiphanies, Satan's in his surprisal by Sin directly before the flight out of hell echoed in "Bond and Free" (compare Milton's "Thyself in me thy perfect image viewing" and RF's "Me myself in the summer heaven godlike") and Eve's falling in love with the gorgeous creature she beholds in the water, herself, a scene from book 4 also echoed in "Bond and Free" as Satan spies on Adam and Eve. *CPPP,* 208. (See p. 138.)

- "Desert Places": A poem from the early 1930s that echoes Satan's flight in darkness, toward earth, at the end of book 2. Satan encounters a void much like that described in "Desert Places"—"A vast vacuity: all unawares," the phrasing echoed in RF's line "The loneliness includes me unawares," the lines scanning identically and nearly rhyming internally (*CPPP,* 269). It is one of only two uses of "unawares" in all of Milton's epic, just as another signal word in Frost's poem, "lonely," appeared in one of two instances in *Paradise Lost* shortly beforehand in Satan's speech before his interstellar flight. That speech, addressed to Sin and Death, is in response to the speech of Sin's on which Frost drew in "For Once, Then, Something."

- "Birches": RF's simile, "Such heaps of broken glass to sweep away / You'd think the inner dome of heaven had fallen," is phrased rather like a simile of Milton's for the stormy sound of Satan's descent through the darkness of hell at the end of book 2 of *Paradise Lost*: "Nor was his ear less peal'd / With noises loud and ruinous (to compare / Great things with small) . . . / than if this frame / Of heav'n were falling." *CPPP*, 117.

- "Fire and Ice": A poem of 1919 that speaks with unsettling composure about the end of the world, recalling the scene in book 2 of *Paradise Lost* when groups of fallen angels debate with unsettling composure some of the deepest problems in philosophy and theology, "Fix'd fate, free will, foreknowledge absolute." Their discourse follows Satan's grand resolution to ascend to God's new world and bring about the end of man, and their discourse precedes a description of the cyclical torture of these fallen souls, every one of them brought in perpetuity "From beds of raging fire to starve in ice." *CPPP*, 204.

- *A Masque of Reason*: In this later work, Satan's only lines refer to the opening speech of book 3 of *Paradise Lost*, inspiration for RF's subsequent *Masque of Mercy* as well. *CPPP*, 386.

One suspects that this stretch of the epic stuck so deeply in RF's imagination in no small part because in them are the main appearances of the archangel Uriel, a spiritual alter ego for RF on the basis of Emerson's "Uriel," which RF called, in *A Masque of Reason*, "the greatest Western poem yet." *CPPP*, 383.

RF tended to downplay his esteem for *Paradise Lost* and, by implication, its influence on his own work, his denial in proportion to his debt. Quotations from Milton are from an edition RF was actively reading in the late 1890s, to judge from scribbles made on the second page of book 5 that resemble the scribbles Elliott made in RF's copy of *Representative Men* (Robert Frost Library, NYU; see [note *Frost's copy in use*]). *English Poems by John Milton*, ed. R. C. Browne (Oxford: Clarendon Press, 1897). A couple of Milton's archaisms have been modernized herein.

137 *The version Frost would publish: CPPP*, 116–17.

139 *"The Definition of Love"*: One cannot infer from the record where or when RF first encountered this famous poem. Though RF did not discuss the poem as much as some others of Marvell's, he alludes to it in a draft of a poem about Love in a notebook from the 1950s: "She is the cause that doth them bind" (like Marvell's "Therefore the love which us doth bind"). Notebook 40, DCL 1178, box 16.

141 *letters Frost wrote to Cox:* The letters, from Dec. 26, 1912, through Feb. 2, 1915, are reprinted in *RFSC*, 22–62, though better transcribed in *Letters*, I. Originals in DCL 1178, box 3.

144   *"the sound of sense":* RF to Bartlett, July 4, 1913, *Letters,* 1:121–24.

145   *saving their integrity:* RF's signal formulation of this was in his letter to "The Amherst Student," ca. March 21, 1935: "Whatever progress may be taken to mean, it
can't mean making the world any easier a place in which to save your soul—or if
you dislike hearing your soul mentioned in open meeting, say your decency, your
integrity." *Letters,* 3:519–21.

145   *Aristotelian in a general sense:* In other words, RF agreed with Aristotle, in contrast
to Plato, that our knowledge of natural things was derived first by observation
from experience rather than deduction from innate knowledge. As far as the spirit
was concerned, RF also believed, with Plato as well as Aristotle, that knowledge
of natural things could yield knowledge of essences. Hence his belief that what
we know of ourselves, as spirits, is from observation—"All is observation of
nature (human nature included) consciously or unconsciously." This belief did
not imply that he thought we knew much of ourselves, that he thought ours was
anything other than a world in which much must be taken on faith—a world in
which we're left, as he said, to "[guess] at ourselves." Quotations respectively from
Notebook 31, DCL 1178, box 16, and Cook, "Verbatim," July 2, 1956.

Though RF might have encountered the ideas of Aristotle earlier, he was certainly exposed to them in his philosophy textbook at Harvard, Alfred Weber's
History of Philosophy (1896). It was perhaps no coincidence that the timing of that
exposure preceded the dawning of his mature poetry with "Flower-Gathering," with
its conflict between ideas inferred from experience as against the old Platonism of
"Twilight." The record is too sparse to warrant strong conclusions about the effects
of Aristotle on RF's poetry—though the way RF was wont to formulate advice
about the primacy of observation over theory, "You can't back up into poetry from
Aristotle," suggests that he might have once tried. As for poetry in general, however,
RF credited to Aristotle the whole enterprise of what RF referred to as nature
poetry but described so as to encompass the qualities RF valued in all poetry. RF
expounded this idea in a pair of draft essays in a notebook, ca. 1948, on the phrase
"natural piety" from a poem of Wordsworth's often entitled "The Rainbow":

> Ever since I began to see the relation of Aristotle to Plato I have had a
> growing suspicion that it is even worse than Aristotle said when he said we
> must respect not only the a priori but equally the a posteriori: what comes
> up is as important as what comes down. Plato would have it that nothing
> down here below but is an imperfect copy of the ideal idea above. Aristotle
> broke that when he turned to study nature with the same respect reverence
> piety that he used in thinking the thoughts Plato believed nature derived
> from. One day in my reading it was revealed to me that what Wordsworth
> meant by "days bound each to each by natural piety was" . . . nature piety.
> In above way he had been taken (by me perhaps by nobody else) as mean-
> ing a religious piety that was natural for all of us to feel. He was talking
> an Aristotelian philosophy contrary to the Platonic. Maybe Rousseau set

him in the right way. But Aristotle should have set us all long ago. I have a growing suspicion that might line me up in disloyalty to the humanists that nothing comes down from above but what has so long since come up from below that we have forgotten its origin. All is observation of nature (human nature included) consciously or unconsciously made by our eyes and minds developed from the ground up. We notice facts of nature— that's all we do. (Notebook 31, DCL 1178, box 16; "You can't back up" quoted in Item 30 in the appendixes to *Newdick's Season of Frost*; for "The Rainbow," see herein chap. 5, sec. 2, chap. 7, sec. 9, and chap. 8, sec. 7.)

See also note to *"nature piety"* in chap. 8, sec. 7.

145 *his insight and his sight:* See, for example, RF to Cox, Jan. 2, 1915, *Letters*, 1:240.

145 *similar to some of James's formulations:* See, for example, sec. 4 of William James's "Will to Believe," in *The Will to Believe, and Other Essays in Popular Philosophy* (New York, London, and Bombay: Longmans Green and Co., 1897): "The thesis I defend is, briefly stated, this: *Our passional nature not only lawfully may, but must, decide an option between propositions, whenever it is a genuine option that cannot by its nature be decided on intellectual grounds.*"

146 *believing the future in:* RF used the phrase in "Education by Poetry: A Meditative Monologue" (1931), in *Collected Prose*, 102–11. His inspiration in James's work was "The Will to Believe." RF might also have drawn inspiration from Emerson's poem "Fate," about the will to believe in so many words. It concludes,

For the prevision is allied
Unto the thing so signified;
Or say, the foresight that awaits
Is the same Genius that creates.

146 *Frost was not a Jamesian pragmatist:* The case for RF's pragmatism has been influentially, and brilliantly, made by Richard Poirier, esp. in *Robert Frost: The Work of Knowing*.

146 *written in French in one of his notebooks:* RF has the phrase as "Que sais je." Notebook 8, ca. 1912–15, VCL 6261.

147 *"The Road Not Taken":* CPPP, 103.

147 *On Frost's recollection:* See, for example, Cook, "Verbatim," Aug. 26, 1961; Aug. 4, 1951; Aug. 19, 1953; as well as LT, "Notes on Conversations," April 11–13, 1947, box 5.

147 *"Etienne de la Boéce":* The version quoted in the text is that of the 1847 edition of Emerson's *Poems*, identical to the version in the 1896 Household edition of the *Poems* but for the first word of the line "That the poor is wealthy grown," which begins "Till" in 1896. Both editions survive in RF's library, and RF might well have known both versions of the poem. The earlier is used on the grounds that RF knew Emerson's poems long before 1896.

149 *"Circles":* Published in *Essays: First Series* (1841). RF's lightly marked-up edition of 1892 survives. Robert Frost Library, NYU.

149 *a pair of essays:* "The Will to Believe" and "The Dilemma of Determinism," both collected in *The Will to Believe, and Other Essays in Popular Philosophy.*

149 *terms too poetical:* Cook, "Verbatim," Aug. 26, 1961; Aug. 4, 1951; Aug. 19, 1953.

150 *Emerson's ending:* Though Montaigne in "Of Friendship" cites a pair of Cicero's famous works on the subject, a passage from a work of Cicero's not primarily on friendship best encapsulates the classical ideal of friendship to which Emerson responds in "Etienne de la Boéce." From *On Duties*:

> Nothing, moreover, is more conducive to love and intimacy than compatibility of character in good men; for when two people have the same ideals and the same tastes, it is a natural consequence that each loves the other as himself; and the result is, as Pythagoras requires of ideal friendship, that several are united in one. (*On Duties*, bk. I, sec. 17, trans. Walter Miller and published in the Loeb Classical Library)

Emerson's poem effectively follows this passage, first rejecting the attempt of his friend to follow him (and thereby to approximate his ideals and tastes), then offering a vision of a surpassing instant in which his friend could witness his sense of the ideal and *seem* to unite the two in one. (They *are* united in Cicero's source on ideal friendship, Pythagoras.) Emerson's "man's and lover's part" is much like Cicero's, and his final symbols, the traveler and the road and the errand, are all Pythagorean. As for RF, he believed until his last days that no people, or nations, would ever want quite the same thing. RF in Ripton, Vt., Oct. 1962, recording, LM0255, ACL 00181.

150 *car commercials:* As noted on p. 1 of David Orr's fine *Road Not Taken.*

150 *eventually challenged:* For a characteristically incisive version of the ironic reading, see William Pritchard, *Frost*, 125–28.

7. THE CURIOUS COVENANT

154 *"Iris by Night":* CPPP, 288.

154 *"Iris all hues":* Paradise Lost, bk. 4, line 696—a scene alluded to in "Bond and Free." See note to *We are in something*, in chap. 6, sec.4.

154 *Robert Herrick's "The Rainbow: Or Curious Covenant":* Selections from the Poetry of Robert Herrick, 114. "The Bracelet to Julia" appears on the same page.

155 *always telling people:* See, for example, RF to Benjamin Miller, Dec. 20, 1921, in *Letters*, 2:212–13.

156 *"the only brother I ever had":* RF to Edward Garnett, April 29, 1917, in *Letters*, 1:552–53.

157 *an uncanny range of similarities:* For general facts of ET's biography, see esp. Jean Moorcroft Wilson, *From Adlestrop to Arras: A Biography* (New York: Bloomsbury, 2015); Matthew Hollis, *Now All Roads Lead to France: The Last Years of Edward Thomas*

(London: Faber & Faber, 2011); R. George Thomas, *Edward Thomas: A Portrait* (Oxford: Clarendon Press, 1985).

157 *a product of the spirit:* ET says so exquisitely in a discussion of the poet John Clare: "Poetry. . . . is the utterance of the human spirit when it is in touch with a world to which the affairs of 'this world' are parochial." *Feminine Influence on the Poets* (London: Martin Secker, 1910), 86–87.

157 *a pagan of sorts:* ET refused in general to identify with a religion his passionate and spiritual love of nature (Wilson, *From Adlestrop to Arras*, 39). But in the absence of the metaphysics or soteriology of any organized religion, his passion and spiritualism rendered him effectively a modern pagan, a designation he embraced in a party game one evening in the spring of 1914, ranking himself 9 out of 10 in paganism and 1 out of 10 in Christianity. That he designed the game to render paganism a positive quality and Christianity a negative is telling as well. (Ranking reproduced as "Edward's Chart of His Friends" between pp. 70 and 71 of Eleanor Farjeon, *Edward Thomas: The Last Four Years* (London: Oxford University Press, 1958).

158 *a Christmas letter:* ET to Gordon Bottomley, "Christmas-time," in *Letters from Edward Thomas to Gordon Bottomley* (London: Oxford University Press, 1968), 226–27.

158 *his first letter to Cox:* RF to Cox, Dec. 26, 1912, *Letters*, 1:81–83.

158 *as Elinor wrote:* EF to Mrs. John Lynch, Oct. 25, 1912, DCL 1178, box 12.

158 *Carol looked out of his porthole:* Notebook titled "An Important Year" with contributions by all four Frost children, written in Beaconsfield, 1913, "Dedicated To Papa & Mamma" (VCL 6261, box 2).

158–59 *"the people who in the wars":* "An Important Year," VCL 6261, box 2.

159 *"feeling greatly excited":* EF to Mrs. John Lynch, Oct. 25, 1912.

159 *a week of "theatre":* EF to Alice Brown, Oct. 25, 1912, VCL 6261, box 5.

159 *a confessional letter:* RF to Susan Hayes Ward, Sept. 15, 1912, in *Letters*, 1:69–70. EF also noted their proximity to the site where Milton wrote *Paradise Lost* in her letter to Alice Brown of Oct. 25, 1912.

159 *a tempting letter to Cox:* RF to Cox, July 10, 1913, *Letters*, 1:126–27. Confessing to secrecy about the sources of his writing, RF used the example of Tennyson: "You give your case away as Tennyson did his when he confessed that wherever he wrote King Arthur he had in mind Prince Albert. He spoiled the Idyls [*Idylls of the King*] for the present generation (I mean our own) and perhaps for all generations to come. And yet the poems are neither better nor worse for the confession. You must not disillusion your admirers with the tale of your sources and processes. That is the gospel according to me." "Not that I bother much to live up to it," RF continued. Who could have caught a trace of secrecy?

160 *he said at the time:* RF to Thomas Bird Mosher, Nov. 19, 1912, in *Letters*, 1:73–75 (the observation that RF may have been drawn to a note prefacing *Poems* is owed to a footnote in that volume). Though RF did not name Henley in his letter to Mosher, RF often mentioned Henley in later versions of the story. He most likely ran the name Nutt by the columnist, as he said in a late interview: "I was the one that

proposed the name 'David Nutt' because of the poems of Henley that they'd printed and that I'd seen in America—a fine couple of volumes, I think. So I asked him what he thought of that" (RF, ca. Oct. 1962, recording, LM0387, ACL 00181). RF told the same story to Ray Nash in 1945 (Notecard in VCL 10044-A, Notecard box 2).

160 *"safe mediocrity":* RF to Harry Alvin Brown, Jan. 7, 1913, in *Letters,* 1:85.

160 *Frost would later apologize:* RF to F. S. Flint, Jan. 21, 1913, in *Letters,* 1:89.

161 *sending Frost a calling card:* Flint to RF, Jan. 30, 1913, DCL 1178, box 4.

161 *Frost referred to him:* RF to Bartlett, March 11, 1913, DCL 1178, box 4; RF to Silver, May 7, 1913, in *Letters,* 1:97, 105.

161 *"Someone says he looks":* RF to Silver, May 7, 1913, in *Letters,* 1:105.

161 *"that great intellect abloom in hair":* RF to Flint, July 6, 1913, in *Letters,* 1:124.

161 *sometimes adding:* For example, in conversation with Cook on Sept. 19, 1951. "Verbatim."

162 *Pound told Frost to call on T. E. Hulme:* LT, "Notes on Conversations," Aug. 24, 1956, box 5.

162 *Thomas Stearns Eliot:* Eliot, toast in honor of RF, June 11, 1957, DCL 1178, box 37.

162 *"a man in some dream":* RF to Silver, May 7, 1913, in *Letters,* 1:105.

162 *"Yates is a kite":* Notebook 29, ca. 1937–42, DCL 1178, box 16.

162 *a letter to Bartlett:* RF to Bartlett, March 11, 1913, in *Letters,* 1:97.

163 *Pound "has found me":* RF to Bartlett, March 11, 1913.

164 *Frost sent one to Bartlett:* RF to Bartlett, ca. June 16, 1913, in *Letters,* 1:110–13.

164 *"He had a finger":* RF to Flint, June 24, 1913, in *Letters,* 1:115–16.

164 *"Poets Are Born Not Made":* RF to Flint, fall 1913, in *Letters,* 1:158–59.

165 *"A Poetical Boss":* Notebook 11, ca. 1919, DCL 1178, box 16.

165 *another piece of vers libre: Letters,* 1:117–18.

167 *Having first seen Pound:* Review of *Personae* in *English Review,* June 1909, republished in *A Language Not to Be Betrayed: Selected Prose of Edward Thomas* (New York: Persea Books, 1981), 118.

167 *Thomas came to see him:* Review of *Exultations of Ezra Pound* in *Daily Chronicle,* Nov. 1909, republished in *Language Not to Be Betrayed,* 120.

167 *As Pound would praise Frost:* Review of *A Boy's Will* in *Poetry,* May 1913.

167 *"are subdued to his spirit":* Review of *Personae* in *English Review,* June 1909, republished in *Language Not to Be Betrayed,* 118.

167 *"the old miracle that cannot be defined":* Review of *Personae* in *Daily Chronicle,* June 7, 1909, republished in *Language Not to Be Betrayed,* 117. ET regretted his praise of Pound by June 8, 1909, the day after his praise of *Personae* appeared in the *Daily Chronicle.* ET to Walter de la Mare, June 8, 1909, in *Poet to Poet: Edward Thomas's Letters to Walter de la Mare* (Seren: Bridgend, 2012), 65–67.

167 *Frost wrote to Flint:* RF to Flint, Oct. 10, 1913, in *Letters,* 1:144.

168 *"possible for the modern mind":* Pater quoted in ET, *Walter Pater: A Critical Study* (London: Martin Secker, 1913), 56.

169 *Thomas had declared belief:* ET to de la Mare, Feb. 19, 1908, in *Edward Thomas's Letters to Walter de la Mare,* 45–47.

170 *the response of the spirit:* ET, *Feminine Influence on the Poets*, 86–87.

170 *"I go about the world":* ET to Bottomley, Feb. 26, 1908, in *Letters from Edward Thomas to Gordon Bottomley*, 157–60.

170 *a dull flat shore:* ET to Eleanor Farjeon, Oct. 1913, reproduced in Farjeon, *Edward Thomas*, 41.

170 *at the edge of life:* ET to Bottomley, March 30, 1908, in *Letters from Edward Thomas to Gordon Bottomley*, 160–62.

170 *only by spiritual means:* ET to de la Mare, Nov. 19, 1911, in *Edward Thomas's Letters to Walter de la Mare*, 114–16.

170 *By the end of 1912:* ET to Bottomley, Sept. 1, 1912, in *Letters from Edward Thomas to Gordon Bottomley*, 222–23.

170 *"ember" and "September":* ET to de la Mare, ca. Sept. 1913, in *Edward Thomas's Letters to Walter de la Mare*, 166.

170 *Frost wrote to an old friend:* RF to Gertrude McQuesten, ca. Oct. 20, 1913, in *Letters*, 1:148–51.

172 *"We are on a lane":* RF to Cox, May 18, 1914, DCL 1178, box 3.

172 *Elinor wrote to her cousin:* EF to Leona Harvey, ca. June 20, 1914, in *SL*, 126–27.

173 *"This England":* Republished in *Language Not to Be Betrayed*, 268–71.

173 *"like the first that ever was":* ET to Eleanor Farjeon, May 22, 1915, in Farjeon, *Edward Thomas*, 141.

173 *"taking to verse":* ET to RF, May 19, 1914, in *Elected Friends*, 10.

173 *"a book on speech and literature":* ET to RF, May 19, 1914, in *Elected Friends*, 10.

174 *three separate reviews:* Republished in *Language Not to Be Betrayed*, 125–31.

174 *"When you are in England":* Notebook 8, ca. 1912–15, DCL 1178, box 16.

175 *Farjeon was awestruck:* Farjeon, *Edward Thomas*, 90.

175 *"the Cretan Labyrinth":* Farjeon, *Edward Thomas*, 239.

175 *Thomas's account to Helen:* ET to Helen Thomas, Oct. 11, 1914, quoted in Wilson, *From Adlestrop to Arras*, 282.

177 *"no matter what road he took":* Cook, "Verbatim," Aug. 19, 1953.

177 *Frost got only as far:* Cook, "Verbatim," Aug. 19, 1953. Though RF did not always share this detail, this version of events is all the more credible for making the composition of the poem seem less inspired, less altogether poetical, than in RF's other accounts.

177 *The poem's subject:* ET to RF, June 13, 1915, in *Elected Friends*, 61–64.

177 *lacking the faith of a "believer":* ET to RF, May 15, 1915, in *Elected Friends*, 67.

177 *"in the king's uniform":* ET to RF, July 22, 1915, in *Elected Friends*, 82.

177 *"I wish I could explain":* ET to RF, July 14, 1915, in *Elected Friends*, 81.

177 *"try & forgive me everything":* ET to RF, July 22, 1915, in *Elected Friends*, 82.

177 *"All belief is one":* RF to ET, July 31, 1915, in *Elected Friends*, 86–87.

177 *Thomas's poems about Frost:* All of ET's poems are quoted from *Edward Thomas: The Annotated Collected Poems*, ed. Edna Longley (Tarset, Northumberland: Bloodaxe Books, 2008).

178 *"Not to Keep":* CPPP, 212–13.

179   *tradition of Puritanism:* RF's reception of Puritanism was a matter of cultural continu-
      ity (partly imagined, as with all such inheritance); affinity with heroic examples such
      as Cromwell and Milton; and distillation of general principles never exhaustively
      defined by RF but explicated throughout the present work. It was not a matter of
      adherence to the specific articles of faith or moral strictures of the historical Puri-
      tans. RF's description of "New England character" was, as quoted by a friend, "the
      residue of Cromwell and Milton"—a figure encompassing the customs, values,
      and principles inherited in the once-Puritan civilization by these heroes, to RF, of
      political freedom and poetic imagination (Charles Foster to RF, March 21, 1959,
      DCL 1178, box 4). RF's most pointed affront to his Puritan forbears was probably
      his declaration that God was a "God of waste," turning on its head the grave injunc-
      tion against waste that had been justified by the doctrine that God was in all things
      purposeful (LT, "Notes on Conversations," June 29, 1952).

179   *"To E. T.":* CPPP, 205.

181   *the famous elegy to which Frost's poem alludes:* Catullus 101.

182   *"A Soldier," which he said was about Thomas:* CPPP, 240; Cook, "Verbatim," June 30, 1950.

182   *"the bravest and best and dearest man":* RF to Helen Thomas, April 27, 1917, in *Letters,*
      1:550.

182   *"more beautiful":* RF to Edward Bliss Read, May 24, 1917, in *Letters,* 1:557.

182   *"the only brother I ever had":* RF to Edward Garnett, April 29, 1917, in *Letters,* 1:552.

182   *"I never had, I never shall have":* RF to Amy Lowell, Oct. 22, 1917, in *Letters,* 1:581.

182   *Frost wrote to the editor:* RF to Wilbur Cross, Nov. 22, 1917, in *Letters,* 1:592.

182   *"[Thomas's] concern to the last":* RF to Amy Lowell, Oct. 22, 1917, in *Letters,* 1:581.

182   *"Nothing Gold Can Stay":* CPPP, 206.

184   *The Immortality Ode:* "Ode on Intimations of Immortality from Recollections of
      Early Childhood" appeared in *The Golden Treasury* (1861), 301–306.

185   *"To Daffodils": Selections from the Poetry of Robert Herrick,* 23. RF would have encoun-
      tered the poem in the book as "To Daffadills," with other antiquated spelling that
      has been modernized herein.

186   *preceded by a little poem of Wordsworth's:* Golden Treasury (1861), 301. The poem, often
      called "The Rainbow," also preceded the Immortality Ode in *The Golden Treasury*
      of 1861 (as well as in other subsequent editions). For RF on "The Rainbow," see
      note to *Aristotelian in a general sense,* in chap. 6, sec 5. See also note to *"nature piety"* in
      chap. 8, sec. 7.

8. THE LINE WHERE MAN LEAVES OFF

187   *chanced upon an unfamiliar magazine:* Amy Lowell's review appeared in the Feb. 20,
      1915, issue of the magazine. That no mention of the review appeared on the
      cover, and that "The Death of the Hired Man" had been mentioned on the cover
      of the issue two weeks before, suggest that the poet might possibly have been
      tipped off before he just happened to walk up to the very magazine issue that
      would do much to launch his reputation in his own country. Though RF's ver-

sions of the story varied slightly, a representative one is from a press conference on CBS News after his eighty-eighth birthday: "I came ashore to find my first book was published here on George Washington's birthday. And I went on a side street with my children from the boat to find a new magazine called *The New Republic* that Walter Lippmann was on, to find that that had a review of a book that I didn't know was out in America, namely *North of Boston*" (March 29, 1962, recording, LM0027, ACL 00181).

188   *"the imagining ear"*: Republished from the notes of George H. Browne, RF's host, in *CPPP*, 687–89. RF's talk was on May 10, 1915.

188   *mountain fastness:* RF to Franklin P. Rice, June 17, 1915, in *Letters*, 1:319.

189   *lament in May 1916:* RF to LU, May 4, 1916, in *Letters*, 1:440.

189   *Tennyson's famous lament in "Ulysses":* As late as Nov. 1960, RF thought he knew much of the poem by heart. RF to Lord Ancaster, Nov. 1, 1960, DCL 1178, box 1.

189   *what begins in felicity:* RF, interview by Jarrell, May 19, 1959.

190   *"A Servant to Servants":* CPPP, 65–69.

191   *"Paul's Wife":* CPPP, 178–82.

191   *"Elinor has never been":* RF to LU, Nov. 7, 1917, in *Letters*, 1:586–89.

191   *"about the kind of person":* Annotation by RF in March 1925 of a copy of *New Hampshire* owned by Elizabeth Shepley Sergeant, Bryn Mawr Archives.

192   *"The Song of Wandering Aengus":* RF was surprised to learn from Yeats that the poem, whose inspiration seemed so fluent to RF, had taken "nine hours of sweating blood and chewing pencils." RF at Bread Loaf, Aug. 1953, as recalled by LT in "Notes on Conversations," box 5.

193   *"how I fell in love":* RF to LU, June 8, 1915, in *Letters*, 1:312–13.

193   *"To Earthward":* CPPP, 209–10.

193   *"A Day of Sunshine":* As published in *The Complete Poetical Works of Henry Wadsworth Longfellow* (Boston: Houghton, Mifflin, 1893), which RF had in his library.

193   *Yankee Romantic:* "Yankee Romantic" was a draft title of LT's biography eventually published as *Young Longfellow.*

197   *when touch and not resistance was enough:* It is apposite, if indiscreet, to cite the following passage from a notecard of LT's: "When Frost was first beginning to discover the power of his own sexual drive, while he was courting Elinor White, he told me that his love-making got so hot that he went off in his pants." VCL 10044-A, Notecard box 1.

197   *"Christmas Trees":* Transcribed in *Letters*, 1:404–407.

197   *Frost sent the poem to Louis:* RF to LU, Dec. 22, 1915, in *Letters*, 1:407.

197   *the poem, lightly revised:* CPPP, 103–105.

198   *His appointment was announced:* Alexander Meiklejohn to RF, Dec. 16, 1916, DCL 1178, box 7.

198   *"I've been up to my ears":* RF to Henry Meigs, May 24, 1917, in *Letters*, 1:556.

199   *As cited, Frost's intolerance:* From a student, RF heard that Young was conducting clandestine "undressing parties," which RF reported to Meiklejohn. LT, "Notes on Conversations," Jan. 1, 1944, box 5.

199   *"What is it? The Greek vices?"*: William Meredith's notes on conversations with RF, Nov. 1, 1960, VCL 10044-A, box 4. Recalling the interaction to Meredith, RF said, "Of course he can come to me, to my house, but I can't recommend him anywhere." The friend in question was Ned Spofford, arrested along with his colleague on the Smith College faculty Newton Arvin. See Barry Werth, *The Scarlet Professor: Newton Arvin, a Literary Life Shattered by Scandal.*

199   *"the conflict now on"*: RF to LF, May 10, 1919, in *Letters*, 1:679–80.

200   *"to leave teaching"*: RF to William Constable Breed, Feb. 2, 1920, in *Letters*, 1:729–30.

200   *"by luck he hits his mouth"*: Virginia Proctor, "Robert Frost Farewell Talk at the Writers' Conference, Bread Loaf, 1941," VCL 10044, box 4.

201   *"Miss Pains"*: Notebook 7, ca. 1911, DCL 1178, box 16. Other representative pedagogues include Miss Gurgle, the pure enthusiast, who can hug five to six books at once.

201   *"when others get the idea"*: Notebook 38, DCL 1178, box 16.

201   he warned not to *"cultivate shame"*: Notebook 6, 1912, and earlier, reproduced as Appendix E in *Newdick's Season of Frost*.

201   *"lack of initiative"*: "Caveat Poeta," in *CPPP*, 830.

202   poetry and Puritanism: "What Became of New England," June 8, 1937, typescript by Robert Newdick, VCL 6261, box 2. "The whole function of poetry is the renewal of words," RF said, and had this to say on the renewal of words in Puritanism:

> And the thing New England gave most to America was the thing I am talking about: a stubborn clinging to meaning,—to purify words until they meant again what they should mean. Puritanism had that meaning entirely: a purifying of words and a renewal of words and a renewal of meaning. That's what brought the Puritans to America, and that's what kept them believing: they saw that there was a meaning that was becoming elusive.

202   *"Education by Poetry"*: CPPP, 717–28.

202   more systematic treatment in recent years: See esp. Douglas Hofstadter and Emmanuel Sander, *Surfaces and Essences: Analogy as the Fuel and Fire of Thinking*, and George Lakoff and Mark Johnson's contemporary classic *Metaphors We Live By*, whose title echoes a couple of passages in "Education by Poetry" nearly verbatim: "These are slighter metaphors than the ones we live by"; "Let's take two or three more of the metaphors now in use to live by."

203   *"saying one thing in terms of another"*: "The Constant Symbol," in *CPPP*, 786–91.

204   more of life than of school: For example, "We dont want much school even when we are young, that is to say, we want a great deal more of life than of school. . . . Literature—I dont know where literature comes in, if it comes in at all. It is ever so much more of life anyway than of school." RF to Cox, June 24, 1915, in *Letters*, 1:320.

204 *more poetry outside verse than in:* See, for example, RF's conversation with Van Doren and Adams, ca. Oct. 1962, recording. RF clarified on this occasion that though he believed there was more poetry outside verse than in, "I belong to the institution of verse. That's my most conservative thing."

205 *a disagreement in fundamental philosophy:* Though RF never laid out his disagreement with Shelley explicitly, he took a resurgent interest in both Shelley and anti-Platonism in the late summer of 1938, followed shortly thereafter by the closest thing he ever wrote to a prose defense of poetry, "The Figure a Poem Makes," a non-Platonic account of inspiration's embodiment in all poetry worthy of the name. Years earlier, in the beginning of his lecture career, RF sketched out a mock critique of Shelley's philosophizing, and eventual drowning, that one wishes RF would have actually given:

> Query, if what Shelley meant by Prometheus wasn't the philosophizing poet. Shelley himself. The world's gain could he have stood fate off for one year. Two years. Five years. Ten years. Futility of speculation. Distance between speculation and insight. Shelley's mistake in developing a system. . . . How he could have saved himself. (See Drummond: You cant get drowned on Lake Champlain so long as you stay on shore.) (RF to LU, May 24, 1916, in *Letters*, 1:452–53.)

205 *"nature piety":* See *Aristotelian in a general sense,* in chap. 6, sec 5., and note to *preceded by a little poem of Wordsworth's,* in chap. 7, sec. 9.

206 *"the emotion of having a thought":* "The Constant Symbol," in *CPPP*, 786–91. RF used "thought" and "idea" interchangeably in this context, for example in a discussion about "The Constant Symbol" after publication. LT, "Notes on Conversations," Sept. 3, 1946, box 5.

206 *"It takes all sorts":* CPPP, 478.

207 *from the perspective of God:* DCL 1178, box 19. The couplet appears, with minor variations, in an unpublished draft of a late (perhaps mid-1950s) didactic-comic poem about a discussion with God, who explains the need to keep up with His "evanescent" metaphors to retain an intimation of divine purpose.

207 *"I was thinking the other day":* RF at the Museum of Modern Art, New York, Dec. 1950, recording, LM0021, ACL 00181.

207 *"The way to read a poem":* "Poetry and School," *Atlantic Monthly*, June 1951. Frost offered various formulations of the idea, of which one is the first epigraph to the present work.

207 *"the highest form of criticism":* On May 5, 1939, in Lawrence, Massachusetts, RF gave a talk titled "The Anthology as the Highest Form of Criticism" (VCL 6261). Quotations in this section are from the talk unless otherwise cited.

207 *"scratch each other's backs":* RF at College of Wooster, May 18, 1962, quoted in the *Wooster Alumni Bulletin* of June 1962. VCL 10044-A, box 4.

208 *"a pretty little sonnet of a book"*: RF at the Bread Loaf School, July 27, 1960. Cook, "Verbatim."

208 *"Such news reaches me"*: Letters, 2:300.

209 *"the longest poem in the Englisch langwidge"*: The Letters of T. S. Eliot, vol. I, 1898–1922 (New Haven & London: Yale University Press, 2011), 626.

209 *most of his allusions to English poetry:* Counted by Murray Prosky in "Lamb, Palgrave, and the Elizabethans in T. S. Eliot's *The Waste Land,*" *Studies in Humanities* 2 (Fall–Winter 1970–71): 11.

209 *"Dont go to Europe"*: RF to LU, Dec. 23, 1922, in Letters, 2:300.

210 *"I happen to have just read"*: RF to Whicher, Dec. 31, 1922, in Letters, 2:291–94.

210 *a letter drafted in rage:* RF to Rascoe (unsent), Jan. 20, 1923, in Letters, 2:301–305.

211 *"You and Jean"*: RF to LU, Jan. 23, 1923, in Letters, 2:307.

211 *In another letter to Louis:* RF to LU, Feb. 5, 1923, in Letters, 2:310–12.

211 *"New Hampshire"*: CPPP, 151–62.

212 *a kind of inspiration:* RF discussed recognizing literary moments in the comebacks that occurred to his students as early as March 18, 1916, in a talk to teachers at the Boston Public Library. VCL 10044-A, box 19.

212 *a comeback of its own:* RF said he conceived of the poem, a rambling verse speech (of sorts) in praise of the state, in response to "These United States," a series of articles in *The Nation* begun in the spring of 1922 treating each state in turn by a different writer. RF objected to the articles, he said, for their socialistic snobbery in finding fault with state after state for its commerce, spurring him to satirize the attitude in a talk at a Rotary Club in Michigan in early summer and, wanting to elaborate further, set his ideas down in verse in July. RF's satire would unapologetically celebrate the commercial situation of his state, fortunately nonexistent in New Hampshire, per "New Hampshire." The hole in this story (noted by LT in *YT*, 592) is that none of the five essays in *The Nation* that RF might have seen before leaving Michigan in June—on Kansas, Maryland, Mississippi, Vermont, and New Jersey—remotely fit his description of what he purported to satirize. Some of the other essays published later that year in the series better meet his description, especially "Iowa: A Mortgaged Eldorado," from the issue of Dec. 13, 1922.

212 *"Stopping by Woods on a Snowy Evening"*: CPPP, 207.

213 *"my best bid for remembrance"*: RF to LU, May 2, 1923, in Letters, 2:339.

213 *A manuscript exists with his revisions:* JCL, Series I. LT discussed RF's "extremely inconsistent" accounts of composing "Stopping by Woods on a Snowy Evening" in *YT*, 596–98, and *EY*, 595–97.

213 *The first surviving record of the poem:* On a letter RF sent to Lincoln MacVeagh, his publisher, on March 16, 1923, MacVeagh wrote in the margin, "[RF read "Stopping by Woods"] to me in MS in my apartment on Waverly Place," which RF visited in early January. Letters, 2: 324.

213 *things affronting to his sensibilities:* RF complains of such affronts in his first surviving letter after the trip. RF to Lincoln MacVeagh, Nov. 28, 1922, in Letters, 2:281–82.

213   *Frost's first reference:* RF to LU, Feb. 5, 1923, in *Letters,* 2:311. In the passage quoted, RF is referring to his recent exertions: "I'm on a tear."

213   *The first mention of the poem:* RF to Whicher, ca. Dec. 31, 1922, in *Letters,* 2:293.

213   *allusions to the other poems:* RF's account would be less implausible if he had written "New Hampshire" before the other poems he would call "Notes," first conceiving the book as a whole before its constituent parts, and only later choosing to present the unified whole by means of annotation. RF hinted at such a chronology in a discussion of "New Hampshire" in 1958, saying he drew on "New Hampshire" as inspiration for a few other poems in the book (April 21, 1958, recording, LM0035, ACL 00181). Yet, with at least ten of thirteen "Notes" written before "New Hampshire," the poem as initially conceived was full of references to RF's other work as no poem in his oeuvre had been before.

      Incidentally, in the same discussion, RF taunted John Ciardi, the critic most responsible for popularizing the reading of "Stopping by Woods" as a death poem, with trying to explain how the poem, conceived when he "staggered outdoors" and saw the sunrise "and had a hallucination that is called 'Stopping by Woods on a Snowy Evening,'" came out of "New Hampshire."

213   *he admitted to veiling:* RF, conversation with Brower and students, March 25, 1958, recording.

214   *"pretend[ed] an inspiration":* RF to LU, Dec. 13, 1932, in *Letters,* 3:299.

214   *"Tradition and the Individual Talent": The Sacred Wood: Essays on Poetry and Criticism* (London: Methuen & Co., 1920), 42–53.

214   *"You're obliged to make your own quotable lines":* Cook, "Verbatim," July 2, 1949.

216   *calling himself a realist instead:* Cook, "Verbatim," July 2, 1949.

216   *"Nature is cruel":* From "In Harmony with Nature (to a Preacher)."

216   *another brief quotation from Arnold's poetry:* From "The Scholar Gipsy." In quoting Arnold, RF changed "takes" to "took."

218   *"Well, I must be getting on":* Cook, "Verbatim," June 2, 1958.

9. ASPENS IN RAIN

220   *On a sunny Sunday morning:* The trip is recounted by Romig in "Colorado Mornings."

220   *"Isnt it strange for me":* RF to LU, July 28, 1931, in *Letters,* 3:196–98.

221   *a rare lamentation:* EF to Edith Fobes, ca. Aug. 2, 1931, DCL 1178, box 12.

224   *neither total nor totally negative:* Poems mentioned, respectively: "Desert Places," "Spring Pools," "The Freedom of the Moon," "The Armful," "The Door in the Dark," "The Bear," "Atmosphere," in *CPPP,* 269, 224, 224, 245, 243, 247, 225.

227   *"I have always wanted to watch":* EF to Fobes, ca. May 5, 1931, DCL 1178, box 12.

228   *"goddam school boy":* RF to LF, July 18, 1950, VCL 6261, box 8.

228   *"painted Jezebel":* From a note excised from the proofs of *RFLU,* "After a Visit with [RF] at Ripton, [Sept. 20–21, 1960]," LOC MSS84950, box 10.

228   *"Please take the way with her":* RF to LF, Oct. 6, 1920, in *Letters,* 2:93.

229   *"the best poet in the family":* RF to Witter Bynner, April 5, 1926, in *Letters,* 2:519–20.

229 *"Marj has her ironies":* RF to Sidney Cox, Feb. 7, 1927, in *Letters,* 2:584.

229 *"the tendency to tuberculosis":* RF to Morris Tilley, Jan. 28, 1931, in *Letters,* 3:167.

230 *an unexpected guest:* Recounted by Romig in "Colorado Mornings."

230 *"the beautiful ideals":* Marjorie Frost to RF and EF, March 22, 1932, in *SL,* 382.

231 *"return to being 'Robert Frost's daughter'":* Marjorie Frost to Willard Fraser, ca. spring 1923, in McCarthy, *Afternoons in Montana,* 48.

231 *"like Aspen leaves in a gale":* Marjorie Frost to Helen Lawrie, July 11, 1933, DCL 886, box 1. Many details in this section are drawn from this collection.

231 *They were met by John and Margaret Bartlett:* Details and quotations in the remainder of the present section are drawn from Bartlett, Notes on conversations with RF, Aug. 8–9, 1934.

233 *a kind of toddler's game:* RF to LU, May 15, 1934, in *Letters,* 3:397–98.

233 *"kindness and friendship":* RF to Carol Frost, April 18, 1934, in *Letters,* 3:391–92.

234 *"pure and steadfast soul":* EF to LF, VCL 6261, box 8.

234 *"No death in war":* RF to LU, May 15, 1934, in *Letters,* 3:397–98.

234 *"her ruling passion must have been to be wise and good":* RF to LU, May 15, 1934.

234 *"Poor darling child!":* EF to Fobes, June 12, 1934, VCL 6261, box 8.

234 *"She wanted to live so badly":* EF to Fobes, July 15, 1934, VCL 6261, box 8.

235 *"of an almost straining loftiness":* RF to LU, May 15, 1934, in *Letters,* 3:397–98.

235 *"grim ironical and noble":* RF to LF, April 20, 1934, in *Letters,* 3:393.

235 *An early, untitled draft:* JL Series I.

235 *"Voice Ways":* CPPP, 274. In Aug. 1955, RF told Elizabeth Shepley Sergeant that the poem was "Between me and Marjorie. Sweet-cynical was Marjorie" (VCL 6538, box 18). Contextually, it seems likely that RF intended to use "Voice Ways" as the preface to the volume of Marjorie's poems eventually published in 1936, privately, as *Franconia.* RF mentions such a prefatory poem in his letter to LF of Oct. 8, 1935, but no draft of it, if ever sent, remains with the original of the letter (VCL 6261, box 8). Some have followed *Family Letters of Robert and Elinor Frost* in identifying the poem mentioned with "Voice Ways," and the identification is probably correct, although no poem of her father's would preface *Franconia* upon publication.

236 *"Let darkness keep her raven gloss":* Quoted in RF to Hervey Allen, April 12, 1938, in *SL,* 470.

236 *"They Were Welcome to Their Belief":* CPPP, 272.

236 *a bleak letter in June:* RF to Otto Manthey-Zorn, June 10, 1934, in *Letters,* 3:401–402.

238 *"Moon Compasses":* CPPP, 273. Ellipsis in original.

239 *"When I am sometimes unjustly praised":* Letters, 3:251–52.

239 *"Two Tramps in Mud Time":* CPPP, 251–52.

241 *the poem's main antecedent:* David Bromwich has also pointed out the deep influence on the poem of Wordsworth's "Resolution and Independence," whose leech-gatherer had also served as a model for Frost's "The Gum-Gatherer" in *Mountain Interval* (*A Choice of Inheritance: Self and Community from Edmund Burke to Robert Frost* [Cambridge: Harvard University Press, 1989], 218–31; *CPPP,* 134–35).

241 *"The Trial by Existence":* CPPP, 28–30.

10. THE WIND AND THE RAIN

244 *"We think they are lovely"*: EF to Romig, Feb. 16, 1936, VCL 10044-A, box 15.

245 *"spent an average of five hours a day"*: DeVoto to Kate Sterne, Jan. 29, 1936. Unless otherwise cited, letters from DeVoto to Sterne are quoted from *Selected Letters of Bernard DeVoto and Katharine Sterne*.

245 *"I am not an inordinately silent man"*: DeVoto to Sterne, Jan. 29, 1936.

246 *"the Amalgamated Adorers of Ezra Pound"*: DeVoto to Sterne, Jan. 29, 1936.

246 *"a really dreadful letter of abuse"*: RF to LU, May 8, 1936, in *Letters*, 3:649–51.

246–47 *debates between her and her husband*: Phyllis Gordon Frost to LT, March 23, 1967, VCL 10044-A, box 12.

247 *voting like her for the Republican Alf Landon*: RF to Bernard DeVoto, ca. Nov. 20, 1936, in *Letters*, 3:686–89.

247 *Jeannette and Bill Snow protested*: As recounted by Bill Snow in "Robert Frost I Knew."

247 *Frost's letter to Bill Snow*: RF to Snow, Jan. 2, 1938, printed in Snow, "Robert Frost I Knew."

247 *DeVoto's essay*: "The Critics and Robert Frost," *Saturday Review of Literature*, Jan. 1, 1938.

248 *"I said to Sidney Cox"*: RF to DeVoto, Dec. 29, 1937, in *SL*, 452–53.

248 *"She's a brave one"*: RF to LF, Sept. 30, 1937, in *Family Letters of Robert and Elinor Frost*, 188–89.

248 *"I have had almost too much"*: RF to LU, Oct. 4, 1937, in *RFLU*, 295–96.

249 *"You know how to read poetry"*: RF to Ted Davison, Oct. 3, 1937, DCL 1178, box 3.

249 *"I shall be taking her south"*: RF to Morrison, Oct. 2, 1937, DCL 1178, box 8.

249 *Frost responded by begging*: RF to Morrison, Feb. 12, 1938, DCL 1178, box 8.

249 *"You have no need of asking"*: Morrison to RF, Feb. 22, 1938, DCL 1178, box 8.

249 *shared with Kay after a visit*: Morrison to KM, July 21, 1936, Anne Morrison Smyth Papers.

250 *"I was the one I was bothered about"*: RF to Morrison, Feb. 27, 1938, DCL 1178, box 8.

250 *"A Prayer in Spring"*: CPPP, 21–22.

251 *He sent "Carpe Diem" to Untermeyer*: RF to LU, April 17, 1938, LOC MSS84950, box 3. The poem is slightly mistranscribed in *RFLU*, 307; "crushing" is crossed out and "crowding," not in RF's hand, is indicated as a replacement.

253 *"His face was drawn and pale"*: Notes by Katherine Canfield, Oct. 1977, ACL 00181, box 3.

254 *"Pretty nearly every one of my poems"*: RF to Alma and Roy Elliott, April 13, 1938, in *SL*, 471–72.

254 *Frost quoted two passages from Tennyson*: RF to Allen, April 12, 1938, in *SL*, 470.

254 *"I expect to have to go depths below depths"*: RF to DeVoto, April 12, 1938, in *SL*, 470–71.

255 *He thought he might move*: Newdick's notes on conversations with RF at Amherst, April 21–25, 1938, published as Item 21 in the appendixes to *Newdick's Season of Frost*.

255   *Otto drove Frost down to Derry:* Manthey-Zorn to KM, Dec. 26, 1962, DCL 1178, box 7.

255   *"I don't know myself yet":* RF to LU, May 16, 1938, LOC MSS84950, box 3.

255   *"I have nothing left":* RF to Newdick, July 20, 1938, VCL 6261, box 6.

256   *"So I told Kay":* RF to Morrison, July 29, 1938, DCL 1178, box 8.

256   *"a glorious subject for some sort of tragedy":* KM to Morrison, March 14, 1922, Smyth Papers. Various other biographical facts about KM and Ted Morrison are drawn from the collection as well.

256   *"I look up to you as a fixed star":* Morrison to KM, Oct. 18, 1927, Smyth Papers.

257   *He worried already:* Morrison to KM, Aug. 1927, Smyth Papers.

257   *two hours before Kay arrived:* KM to Morrison, May 23, 1935, Smyth Papers.

257   *his disdain for the trappings of "piosity":* Obituary for Robert Johnston, *Southern Churchman,* Sep. 14, 1935.

257   *"deep sensitivity for mankind":* Obituary for Robert Johnston, *The Churchman,* June 15, 1935.

257   *"I had the greatest enthusiasm":* Morrison to KM, May 23, 1935, Smyth Papers.

257   *"a poet—a poet of the love of God":* Alice Gregg to KM, May 27, 1935, Smyth Papers.

257   *to suspect Kay of an Oedipal attraction:* DeVoto to Sterne, Sept. 8, 1941. ("She has also found again the image of the Dean of Washington Cathedral who was too much her father.")

257   *"Loyal, tender, warm":* DeVoto to Sterne, April 25, 1938, *The Complete Letters of Bernard DeVoto and Katharine Sterne 1938,* University of Utah Press, Open Access.

258   *"Robert said, 'I hate those bastards!'":* DeVoto to Sterne, ca. Sept. 2, 1938.

258   *"that he went away as a woman":* Journal of Charles Foster, Aug. 29, 1938.

258   *"a veil between [himself]":* Journal of Charles Foster, Aug. 19, 1938.

259   *a "rebuke" from DeVoto:* DeVoto to Sterne, ca. Sept. 2, 1938.

259   *"I'm an old man":* Journal of Charles Foster, Aug. 28, 1938. Other details of the episode are drawn from the same entry in Foster's journal, which is factually consistent with DeVoto's more schematic (and dramatic) account in his letter to Sterne cited above. Foster's journal also recalls MacLeish in his lecture discussing *The Oxford Book of English Verse* with condescension, an affront to RF's taste that, though not expressly his object of grievance, could only have made matters worse.

259   *"You're a good poet":* LT, "Notes on Conversations," April 19, 1960, box 6.

260   *"but I don't think I will":* DeVoto to Sterne, Sept. 11, 1938.

260   *"These are terrible days":* DeVoto to Sterne, ca. Sept. 2, 1938.

260   *Writing to Kay from Concord Corner:* RF to KM, ca. Sept. 1, 1938, DCL 1211.

260   *like a drowning man:* Journal of Charles Foster, Aug. 19, 1938.

261   *"Tears in my heart":* RF to KM, ca. Sept. 1, 1938, DCL 1211.

261   *"I am where the wind":* RF to David McCord, Sept. 5, 1938, VCL 6538, box 2.

261   *another retracting it the next day:* RF to LF, Sept. 7, 1938, in *Family Letters of Robert and Elinor Frost,* 199. The retracted letter does not survive.

261   *a letter to Untermeyer in bafflement:* RF to LU, Sept. 6, 1938, in *RFLU,* 310–11.

262   *"The Wind and the Rain":* CPPP, 306–307.

264 *his old inspiration for "My Butterfly" and "Twilight":* In his letter to David McCord of Sept. 5, 1938, RF, "ruthlessly romantic . . . in mood," had discussed a number of Shelley's poems he was in the habit of rereading, including *Queen Mab* and *Epipsychidion* (VCL 6538, box 2). RF would go on to describe the end of "Ode to the West Wind," in a talk on April 13, 1939, as a false epiphany, an instance of "the rottenest Platonic thinking ever written," of which Shelley was guilty (VCL 10044-A, box 4).

267 *Great New England Hurricane:* In a coincidence whose symbolism would be too obvious for fiction, the storm blew the steeple off the Wesleyan University chapel in which an undergraduate LT was once enraptured by "The Freedom of the Moon."

I1. BLAKE'S PICTURE

268 *something like the same pen stroke:* RF to KM, Oct. 18, 1938, DCL 1211. The disavowal: RF to DeVoto, ca. Oct. 20, 1938, VCL 10044-A, box 3. "I object," RF would say in the spring, "to Platonic love, the having of one Iseult at home to bear your children and do the washing, and another 'perfect copy' or ideal in another man's bed" (from RF's talk to Norman Foerster's class, April 13, 1939, VCL 10044-A, box 4).

269 *"friendship and affection":* LU to RF, Nov. 30, 1938, VCL 10044-A, box 3.

269 *a kind of psychopathology:* LU to Merrill Moore, March 23, 1940, LOC MSS84950, box 3.

269 *"psychical adultery":* DeVoto to Sterne, Sept. 8, 1941.

270 *implausibly dated to his courtship:* The poem is manifestly written in RF's late, light style. DeVoto called it "one of the cryptic ones in the latter-day doggerel" and, in the same letter, recalled having seen the poem first in the fall of 1938, which is the earliest recollection of the poem by anyone other than RF (DeVoto to Sterne, Aug. 16, 1942). No manuscript of the poem exists from before Jan. 1942. LT reconciles the lateness of the style with a very early dating of the poem by citing testimony by RF that a version of the poem could have been published in *A Boy's Will* (*EY*, 512). Maybe so, but given RF's literary styles in the two decades preceding *A Boy's Will*, any earlier version that might have existed would have been a substantially different poem than the one that survives.

270 *"The Subverted Flower":* CPPP, 308–309.

270 *"The Inverted Flower":* MS in VCL 10044-B, box 1.

270 *"frigidity in women":* RF, interview by Richard Poirier, *Paris Review* (Summer–Fall 1960).

272 *"a literary life":* RF to LF, Sept. 26, 1917, in *Letters*, 1:573–74.

272 *"for this is all there is":* RF to LF, April 3, 1919, in *Letters*, 1:666–67.

272 *"Such grand writing":* VCL 6261, box 2.

272 *"ragged edge of the profession":* RF to LF, Feb. 1939, in *Family Letters of Robert and Elinor Frost*, 205–206.

272 *A representative letter:* LF to RF, ca. early 1935, DCL 1178, box 12.

273 *She planned to write his biography:* LF to RF, ca. May 1936: "The text-book idea sounds splendid. And of course I'll write a biography, as soon as this job is over. We'll plan it when I am in Amherst." DCL 1178, box 12.

273 *He told her in September:* RF to LF, Sept. 30, 1937, in *Family Letters of Robert and Elinor Frost*, 188–89.

273 *Elinor counted twenty-three cloudless days:* RF to Manthey-Zorn, March 1, 1938, ACL 00181, box 7.

273 *"You are late in overcoming":* RF to LF, Feb. 3, 1939, in *Family Letters of Robert and Elinor Frost*, 203–205.

273–74 *"a jester about sorrow":* RF to LF, March 1, 1939, in *Family Letters of Robert and Elinor Frost*, 209–11.

274 *exhausting and inexhaustible:* LF to KM, Jan. 19, 1940, DCL 1178, box 12.

274 *"With several things that need talking out":* LF to RF, March 2, 1939, DCL 1178, box 12.

275 *"Being out here with my faithful biographer":* RF to DeVoto, ca. Oct. 20, 1938, VCL 10044-A, box 3.

275 *"Over and over he told me":* Newdick to Cox, Nov. 1938, in *Newdick's Season of Frost*, 219–20.

275 *"Elinor's a fine mind":* Newdick's notes on conversations with RF from Oct. 1938, published as Item 30 in the appendixes to *Newdick's Season of Frost*.

276 *"She seems to have the same weakness":* RF to LU, Nov. 7, 1917, in *Letters*, 1:586–89.

276 *a letter to Frost after Elinor passed away:* Newdick to RF, March 27, 1938, in *Newdick's Season of Frost*, 170–71.

276 *the most important influence:* From a meditation Newdick was roused from sleep to write for himself, reprinted in *Newdick's Season of Frost*, 215–16.

276 *"I'll never forget my visit":* RF to Newdick, Dec. 2, 1938, VCL 6261, box 6.

276 *"a showdown" with Newdick:* Holmes to Newdick, March 12, 1939, in *Newdick's Season of Frost*, 230–31.

276 *He noticed a number of Frost's flaws:* Newdick prepared a list of "Points That Must Be Passed Over" in his writing on RF, including "Extreme sensitiveness to criticism," "Remembers old wrong," and "No ear for music, except that he likes ballads," *Newdick's Season of Frost*, 165.

277 *"My God, Sir":* James Fullington to RF, July 11, 1939, DCL 1178, box 8.

277 *her husband's last words:* Marie Newdick to RF, Dec. 18, 1953, DCL 1178, box 8: "Your biography will be written many times. I believe you would like to have available the results of the most meticulous as well as idolatrous research any scholar could make. As I told you, your name, not mine, were the last on my beloved husband's lips."

277 *"I was confronted with the paradox":* RF to LU, Oct. 12, 1939, LOC MSS84950, box 3.

278 *a scholar's poem:* William Meredith to LT, Aug. 23, 1970, VCL 10044-A, box 13. Meredith apparently misdates RF's comment to August 1940 rather than August

1939, when "The Schism," which Meredith refers to as from *The Atlantic* of "that summer," was published.

278 *One night:* Notecard on "To Earthward," VCL 10044-A, box 3.

278 *"a gorgeous crescendo of emotion":* LT to J. Donald Adams, Aug. 22, 1964, VCL 10044-A, box 5.

278 *"and went out of his head alone":* KM to LT, ca. early Jan. 1940, VCL 10044, box 4.

279 *"I hear you are resting":* LT to RF, Feb. 4, 1940, DCL 1178, box 11.

279 *"truly pitiable dependence":* LT to KM, ca. early March 1940 on internal evidence, VCL 10044, box 1. See chap. 1, sec. 6.

279 *her only surviving confession:* KM to LT, early March 1940, VCL 10044, box 4.

281 *"Your letter took a great weight":* LT to KM, March 13, 1940, VCL 10044, box 1.

282 *"Thank you for your letter":* KM to LT, March 15, 1940, VCL 10044, box 4.

282 *Larry felt moved:* LT to RF, Dec. 4, 1940, DCL 1178, box 11.

283 *an unusually clear point of inception:* LT, "Notes on Conversations," Feb. 19, 1963, box 6.

284 *Frost's letters to Carol:* See, for example, RF to Carol Frost, Sept. 9, 1933, in *Letters*, 3:346–47:

> I forgot to say that I wish I had in one holder the whole set of your poems to look over when inclined. Would it be too much trouble to make me a loose-leaf note book of them sometime this winter? The depth of feeling in them is what I keep thinking of. I've taken great satisfaction in your having found such an expression of your life. I hope as you go on with them, they'll help you have a good winter in the midst of your family.
>
> One thing I noticed in your hand written letter I never noticed before. You dont use a capital I in speaking of yourself. You write i which is awfully wrong. You begin a sentence with a small i too. You mustn't.

284 *"He had many fine qualities":* RF to Lillian LaBatt Frost, Oct. 1940, in *Family Letters of Robert and Elinor Frost*, 220–22.

284 *"He was splendid with animals":* RF to LU, Oct. 25, 1940, in *RFLU*, 322–24.

285 *a crescendo of moral disgust:* LT, "Notes on Conversations," July 28, 1941, box 5.

286 *"My, but there is the making of a fine novel":* LT, "Notes on Conversations," Aug. 27, 1941, box 5.

286 *"strained, empty, and forever changed":* DeVoto to Sterne, Sept. 8, 1941. Quotations in body text are drawn from this letter until otherwise cited.

287 *"some of the ugliest emotions":* DeVoto to Sterne, Aug. 16, 1942.

287 *the incident at Untermeyer's house:* LT, "Notes on Conversations," Dec. 27, 1941, box 5.

288 *his third or fourth:* Untermeyer had two non-consecutive marriages to his first wife, Jean Starr, RF's favorite. RF told her he wanted Louis to marry her at least every other time. LT, "Notes on Conversations," Aug. 22, 1946, box 5.

289 *"had been almost hysterical":* LT, "Notes on Conversations," Dec. 27, 1941.

289 *She did not want to get Frost in trouble:* Anne Morrison Smyth, interview by author, March 12, 2018.

289 A Masque of Reason: *CPPP*, 372–88.

289 *"Forty-third Chapter":* RF to Roy Elliott, Oct. 9, 1942, ACL 00181, box 6.

290 *"She's the kind of person":* Cook, "Verbatim," July 10, 1957.

291 *"Of course she is Thyatira":* LT, "Notes on Conversations," Aug. 28, 1957, box 5.

292 *his ambition for the work:* LT, "Notes on Conversations," Aug. 25, 1956, box 5.

292 *the singularly "great poem":* Cook, "Verbatim," July 28, 1955.

292 *integrate this scheme into biblical tradition:* In His opening argument in book 3 of *Paradise Lost*, God contends that the standards of justice apply to humanity because He created them free to choose in action and thought, in "will and reason (reason also is choice)." This is the premise that binds the treatment of justice in *Paradise Lost* with the drama of *Comus*. Its protagonist, the unnamed Lady, exemplifies virtue in her adherence to reason, resisting the eloquent temptations of the sorcerer Comus to drink of his potion and lose her awareness of herself in a numbing, sensuous indulgence. Comus is the devilish creature who comes upon the Lady in the dark Wood. His temptation of her mirrors Satan's temptation of Eve, whose capitulation in original sin is the reason for God's mercy first. The God of *Paradise Lost* urges the paramount importance of human responsibility for choices made despite the impossibility of choosing blamelessly on account of original sin. Reason, being choice, is hopelessly imperfect in our world. The Lady in *Comus* is a version of Eve who remains sinless because of the clarity of her reason. Had she taken the place of Eve in the book of Genesis, our reason could be untainted by sin and the standards of justice could apply untempered by mercy.

294 *mocks Milton's apologetics:* The joke is arch and often misunderstood. It is made by Satan, who, appearing near the end of *A Masque of Reason*, is permitted all of two lines in the play. His lines name the opening speech in book 3 of *Paradise Lost*, in which Milton worries that his blindness might preclude him from expressing God, then reflects that his condition, far from blinding him to the Light coextensive with God, leaves his vision unblemished by nature and receptive in its entirety to "thou celestial Light" shining inward, "that I may see and tell / Of things invisible to mortal sight." This looks like wishful thinking to Frost's Satan, whose lines in the masque are on the subject of the theological rationales humans offer for whatever befalls them, in response to Job's wife declaring, "Nothing has been brought out that for my part / I'm not prepared for or that Job himself / Won't find a formula for taking care of," to which Satan responds, "Like the one Milton found to fool himself / About his blindness." Satan's charge is an instance of the general thesis of RF's masque that, after Job, human reason lacks the capacity to comprehend the outcomes of justice. In the words of the God of the masque, "There's no connection man can reason out / Between his just deserts and what he gets." Directly following the speech in *Paradise Lost* at which Satan snubs his nose is God's disquisition on Reason and mercy that helped to inspire RF's second masque as well, *A Masque of Mercy*, which quotes lines about

mercy from that speech by Milton's God. For RF's fascination with the stretch of *Paradise Lost* including the opening parts of book 3, see note to *We are in something,* in chap. 6, sec.4.

12. ROBERT FROST AT MIDNIGHT

297 *five weeks of "Hell":* KM to LT, Oct. 16, 1945, VCL 10044, box 4.

297 *took an axe into his cabin:* LT, "Notes on Conversations," Aug. 21, 1946, box 5.

297 *"If Larry understands what has happened":* DeVoto to Sterne, June 19, 1942.

297 *what any gentleman would say:* LT, "Notes on Conversations," April 17, 1960, box 6.

298 *"bound together in the world's greatest love":* DeVoto to Sterne, April 20, 1943.

298 *"Her basic theory":* DeVoto to Sterne, June 6, 1943, *The Complete Letters of Bernard DeVoto and Katharine Sterne 1943,* University of Utah Press, Open Access.

298 *letters to the relevant parties:* KM to LT, May 26, 1943, VCL 10044, box 4; KM to Earle Bernheimer, May 26, 1943, DCL 1178, box 1.

298 *"Please see to it":* DeVoto to RF, June 7, 1943, in *SL,* 508–509.

298 *"injured and misunderstood":* RF to DeVoto, June 7, 1943, in *SL,* 509–10. Though *SL* asserts that "RF mailed a recopied version of [the letter]," no such version survives. Neither do references to it by DeVoto. Circumstantial evidence implies that RF never sent anything like the letter, which is conciliatory about DeVoto's accusation, given that RF was wondering how he could ever forgive DeVoto for the same charge as late as the summer of 1947. LT, "Notes on Conversations," Aug. 13, 1947, box 5.

298 *a rather self-flattering roman à clef: Mountain Time,* published in 1946 with a dedication to Ted Morrison. The part of the book drafted in 1938 and 1939 involved the psychology of Oedipal struggle between an older surgeon and his younger partner. The younger, Cy Kinsman, a displaced Utahan in New York, is as a surgeon intelligent, empirical, and scrupulous. The elder is, in contrast, a genius, albeit a genius entirely lacking in scruples. Kinsman is drawn toward a "showdown" with his superior partly out of a tension between the distinct intellectual values of someone who looked judiciously outward for evidence, rather like a writer of argumentative and historical prose, and an intuitive genius whose surgical performances are referred to as poetry. For an excellent discussion of the novel's role in DeVoto's working through his Oedipal conflict with RF, see Stegner, *Uneasy Chair,* 279–86.

After working through his relationship with RF in *Mountain Time,* DeVoto drafted a novel in which a woman's marriage, to a relatively undistinguished member of the faculty at Harvard, is psychologically disfigured by the more than secretarial duties she undertook for a famous older man after his wife's passing. The old eminence, publicly resplendent but privately desperate and volatile, will not be dissuaded from his deluded conviction in his secretary's love for him despite six years of her rebuffing his romantic advances. He compares her husband to a minor poet and insists they divorce. Her husband's friend, the novel's protagonist, accepts the secretary's denial of the rumors around Cambridge that there had been something physical between her and her boss, before wondering to himself, as DeVoto had for years, "But what dark bond held her to that foolish old man?" ("Assorted Canapes" MS, 329, Stanford Special Collections M0001, Box 89).

298 *a grand gesture of forgiveness:* LT chronicles the reconciliation in "Notes on Conversations," Aug. 13, 1947, box 5; Cook chronicles the rupture in "Verbatim," Sept. 17, 1947. DeVoto had made up with RF by putting his arm around him in front of the crowd gathered at the opening ceremony at the Bread Loaf Conference and saying, "Robert, I've been a damn fool and you've been a damn fool. Let's forget it and be friends." The rapprochement lasted until an episode at a cocktail party when DeVoto asked RF about the subject of his next masque and, finding insinuations in RF's answer of Nehemiah for reasons lost to history and perhaps owing to cocktails, took offense. They left the party "enemies," as Frost recounted shortly thereafter. (Nehemiah rebuilt the walls of Jerusalem in the eponymous book of the Old Testament.)

298 *the two were estranged once again:* Their relationship would resume its cordiality if not its intimacy. DeVoto gave two books of his to RF with warm inscriptions in the early 1950s, quoting RF's poetry loosely in each note. The two enjoyed a friendly visit in Ripton in June 1955, shortly before DeVoto's death. Cook, "Verbatim," June 24, 1955; DeVoto to William Sloane, July 5, 1955, Notecard in VCL 10044-A, Notecard box 6.

299 *a letter from Ripton:* RF to LU, Aug. 12, 1944, in *RFLU*, 335–40.

299 *insufficiently appreciated and understood:* "It gives [RF] great pleasure to have anyone like the Masque of Reason," KM wrote in a letter in Jan. 1960, indicating how seldom people had told him they did (KM to C. V. Huenemann, Jan. 18, 1960, DCL 1178, box 6). In a comment on a letter to RF by a serviceman in World War II who identified the "submission to unreason" in the masque with the soldier's need to take orders even from intellectual inferiors, Kay wrote, "It is strange that one of the few people to see this point should be this simple boy." Richard Brill to RF, May 15, 1945, DCL 1178, box 2.

299 *mistook the book for a critique:* See esp. LT, "Notes on Conversations," Sept. 13, 1953, box 5.

300 *the warning of a jealous Sidney Cox:* Cox to RF, March 31, 1947, in *RFSC*, 258–59.

300 *a phone call from Frost:* LT, "Notes on Conversations," April 11–13, 1947, box 5.

301 *The event precipitating Irma's collapse:* LT, "Notes on Conversations," Aug. 21, 1946, box 5.

301 *"The thing ought to be ended":* RF to John Cone, May 13, 1946, VCL 10044-A, box 4.

301 *whom he knew to have been adulterous:* RF to KM, April 29, 1948, DCL 1211.

301 *"extreme cruelty":* RF to John Cone, May 13, 1946.

301 *Frost suspected severe malnourishment:* RF to LF, July 18, 1950, VCL 6261, box 8.

301 *Moore had begun warning Frost:* LT to KM, Dec. 4, 1945, DCL 1178, box 11.

301 *"baffling":* RF to LF, April 3, 1945, VCL 6261, box 8.

301 *Moore strengthened his diagnosis:* LT to LU, Feb. 8, 1947, LOC MSS84950, box 3.

301 *"Any remark you could make":* KM to LT, ca. Jan. 1947, VCL 10044, box 4.

302 *she asked Moore for a pistol:* KM to LT, March 17, 1947, VCL 10044, box 4.

302 *"Merrill is for having Irma":* RF to LU, Jan. 1, 1947, in *RFLU,* 341–46.

302 *"we are specially anxious for":* RF to Bernheimer, Jan. 14, 1947, VCL 6261, box 5.

302 *"Now that Merrill Moore":* LT to LU, Feb. 8, 1947, LOC MSS84950, box 3.

303 *"This is a sorrowful business":* RF to Jackie Cone, July 17, 1947, VCL 10044-A, box 4.

303 *The situation came to crisis:* The days of crisis are recounted in entries from July 30 to Aug. 9 in LT, "Notes on Conversations," box 5, and entries of July 30, 1947, and Aug. 2, 1947, in Cook, "Verbatim."

303 *"Mishaps":* Lowell to J. F. Powers and Bucklin Moon, July 31, 1947, in *The Letters of Robert Lowell* (New York: Farrar, Straus and Giroux, 2005), 68.

304 *"a marvelous devil of a man":* Lowell to Gertrude Buckman, Aug. 16, 1947, in *Letters of Robert Lowell,* 68.

305 *Frost's stanzas included the following:* Chisholm Gentry, interview by author, Oct. 13, 2017. Gentry recalled the verse, not its performance on the occasion, which is inferred on the grounds that RF, never the most prolific, would have invented only so many alternate lines for the ballad and in his drunken glee gone through them all at least once.

306 *"Some people, Mr Frost said":* Sue Walcutt to LT, Jan. 12, 1948, VCL 10044-A, box 4.

306 *"the quince hedge":* Irma Frost to RF, ca. late March 1938, DCL 1178, box 12.

307 *"Directive":* CPPP, 341–42.

308 *"a momentary stay against confusion":* "The Figure a Poem Makes," in *CPPP,* 777.

308 *Lowell's sonnet "Robert Frost":* Robert Lowell, *Notebook 1967–68* (New York: Farrar, Straus and Giroux: 1969), 74. "Frost at Midnight" had served as a model for RF's early masterpiece "An Old Man's Winter Night," published first in *Mountain Interval. CPPP,* 105–106.

310 *"Come, come again":* Lowell to RF, May 21, 1949, DCL 1178, box 7. "MAY 21" written in Lowell's hand, year inferred from context.

310 *"I've seen my mother & father once":* Lowell to Allen Tate and Caroline Gordon, May 5, 1949, in *Letters of Robert Lowell,* 138–39.

311 A Masque of Mercy: CPPP, 389–417.

311 *the same passage on the primacy of mercy:* RF to Snow, Jan. 2, 1938, printed in Snow's "Robert Frost I Knew." See also note to *mocks Milton's apologetics,* in chap. 11, sec. 9.

312 *a sermon at his friend's synagogue:* Given at Rockdale Avenue Temple, Cincinnati, on Oct. 10, 1946, at the invitation of Rabbi Victor Reichert.

312 *one evening in December 1947:* Cook, "Verbatim," Dec. 13, 1947.

313 *Moore reassured Frost:* Moore to RF, Dec. 17, 1947, DCL 1178, box 8.

313 *"at once too insane":* RF to Margaret Bartlett, Dec. 26, 1947, VCL 6261, box 6.

313 *"The hardest thing for me":* RF to LF, July 18, 1950, VCL 6261, box 8.

313   *without understanding why she was there:* Irma Frost to Rastus Hewitt, Aug. 14, 1950, DCL 1178, box 12.

313   *She wanted to get out to a farm:* Irma Frost to Alma Elliott, April 20, 1951, DCL 1178, box 12.

313   *Larry returned to Ripton:* LT, "Notes on Conversations," June 22, 1948, box 5.

314   *what Frost had told Doc Cook:* Cook, "Verbatim," June 1, 1948.

13. THE BRINK OF MYSTERY

316   *"You probably felt as I did":* Alice Cox to RF, Dec. 16, 1956, DCL 1178, box 3.

317   *"Birches":* CPPP, 117–18.

317   *"One evening before my fire":* Cox, *Swinger of Birches*, 20–21.

320   *"stereoscopic":* From an interview of Cook by an anonymous "interlocutor" at the end of "Verbatim." The word is misspelled as "steroscopic" in the original.

321   *"New England Eclogues":* RF to Bartlett, ca. Aug. 1913, in which RF says of the manuscript that would become *North of Boston*, "I may decide to call it New England Eclogues" (*Letters*, 1:133–35). This was a variation on a suggestion by T. E. Hulme, who insisted that the book, which he greatly admired, be called "Yankee Eclogues": "I owe a little to T. E. Hulme. He wanted me to change the name of 'North of Boston' and call it 'Yankee Eclogues'—he was that much interested. But that would have been a mistake. That would be bad taste. But that was his way of looking at it: I was a Yankee, a Yankee Virgil or something—Theocritus." RF, ca. Oct. 1962, recording, LM0387, ACL 00181.

321   *not only by the pastoral* Eclogues: "One big metaphor with me," RF said in a talk in 1958, "is the eclogue. . . . Theocritus and Virgil have had a great influence on that. 'Birches' and the 'Mending Wall' are really eclogues." Talk at Johns Hopkins, Nov. 10, 1958, LM0032, ACL 00181.

321   *"Apples and pears rolled all around us":* From Idyll 7, trans. Anthony Verity.

322   *"the high-water mark of English Poesy":* Mark Pattison, *Milton* (New York: Harper & Brothers, 1880), 27. "In *Lycidas* (1637) we have reached the high-water mark of English poesy and of Milton's own production. A period of a century and a half was to elapse before poetry in England seemed, in Wordsworth's *Ode on Immortality* (1807), to be rising again towards the level of inspiration which it had once attained in *Lycidas*."

322   *Frost called it:* Cook, "Verbatim," July 17, 1950. RF also once used the phrase in a discussion of "Birches," saying, after reading the poem, "Now look . . . the wisdom there, see? I don't believe there's any wisdom that hasn't a brave touch of sadness to it. That is all our wisdom comes to. Something that approaches a jest about poetry. That is the height of poetry." From a talk given at Tufts on March 10, 1939, "Wisdom in Poetry," VCL 6261.

322   *on the summit of Mount Lafayette:* As relayed by Cox in "Walks and Talks with Robert Frost," 7. RF said something similar to Stewart Udall, whose notes have RF

climbing a mountain to *read* "Lycidas" alone (Bill Meredith to KM, Aug. 2, 1962, DCL 1178, box 7). Though other sources attest to RF's reciting large stretches of the poem from memory, one suspects he might have missed a line or two if he did indeed recite the height of poetry on a peak in Franconia.

322   *"Lycidas!"*: Cook, "Verbatim," June 1, 1949.

322   *"what you said to me about Lycidas"*: Cox to RF, Feb. 19, 1928, DCL 1178, box 3.

322   *his encounter with the poem*: Cook, "Verbatim," July 17, 1950.

326   *pagan image of harmonious existence*: "Birches" was not the first of RF's poems to draw on a poem of Milton's about the lost music of pagan poetry in days foregone. In RF's "Pan with Us," at first "Pan Desponds," from early in the Derry years (1902), Pan steps out of the woods by himself and casts aside his pipes in frustration, unable to play them in the new age of the world (*CPPP*, 32). In Milton's ode "On the Morning of Christ's Nativity," the music of Pan is also superseded by the dawn of a new epoch, in this case the entrance of Christ into human form, producing a music of the spheres far greater than the music ever made by Pan. The poems each picture Pan in his former glory—Milton's "the mighty Pan" sarcastically, RF's a "command[ing]" Pan sarcastically—each with Pan newly come to a pasture lawn used by shepherds, his music now with less power than a slight gust of air, a contrast drawn clearly by both Milton and RF. Pan appears in Milton's ode a stanza after Milton proclaims the sun himself ashamed at his newfound uselessness in light of the manifestation of this "greater Sun," more "Than his bright throne, or burning axletree could bear." RF's Pan lies down on "sun-burned earth."

"Pan with Us" stands toward "Birches" in the same general relation that Milton's ode stands to "Lycidas" (which RF also described as an ode). The former are poems of supersession of the pagan by the Christian, the latter poems of reclamation of a pagan form of transcendence within a broadly Christian cosmology. In a further demonstration that the recollected boy of "Birches" is a veiled figure for the pagan poet and his world-communing pipes, Pan occupies a markedly similar position in "Pan with Us" to that of the boy in "Birches," walking in and out of woods alone and looking for some way to "play." RF describes the boy in "Birches" as one "Whose only play was what he found himself," a discovery that turns out to answer a question posed at the end of "Pan with Us": "Play? Play?—What should he play?"

Pan had thrown away his pipes after realizing that they could do less than a small gust of air to sway even a little blue flower, let alone "the fruited bough of the juniper." The image of the tree branch laden with fruit points back to the fruit-laden branches of the harvest in the seventh Idyll of Theocritus, and those boughs dropping their bounty of apples and pears at the harvest-goers' feet point ahead to RF's companion poem for "Birches," a poem of bleary satiation after the former's longing expectancy: "After Apple-Picking." *CPPP*, 70–71.

"After Apple-Picking" is tied to "Birches" by a few parallels so obvious as to seem almost overstated. Its first two lines point to a long ladder still up in a tree, thus formerly climbed, its orientation described in the phrase of "Birches" and "Lycidas," "Toward heaven": "My long two-pointed ladder's sticking through a tree / Toward heaven still." Less obvious by a hair as parallels are the branches that "bend" in the breeze, the weariness from having had "too much" (though of gratification rather than responsibility), the graceful lowering of the fruit from the tree, avoiding a fall like the swinger.

If "Birches" offers largely sensory description with an intimation of spirit, "After Apple-Picking" offers a Judeo-Christian cosmology with nothing deeper than sensation. As such, the poem is a kind of reductio ad absurdum against the recourse only to material means for the fulfillment of spiritual longing. One can feel the sense of deflation this lack of spiritual imagination begets in the poem's last lines, in which the speaker insinuates an obvious concern with the fate of his soul in light of the apples that fell to the ground unsaved, "as of no worth." The poem gathers an array of spiritual questions, like many an ode, only to culminate in the fancy of a talking woodchuck—sensory description on the brink of mystery not elevated into a vision but deflated into a daydream.

327 *Following a passage in Schopenhauer:* Schopenhauer praises the myth of the transmigration of souls in sec. 63 of *The World as Will and Representation,* citing Plato, who discusses the subject in the Myth of Er at the end of *The Republic.* Though RF discussed the influences of Schopenhauer and Plato on his poem on several occasions, he did not mention Schopenhauer's treatment of transmigration itself despite its obvious influence on his poem. In Schopenhauer's discussion, the greatest reward for virtue in life is the soul's not having to reenter existence. In "The Trial by Existence," the soul's reward for its highest virtue, bravery, is the opportunity to reenter existence. The brave soul finds in the afterlife "that the utmost reward / Of daring should be still to dare"—that is, that the very opposite of Schopenhauer's idea is the truth.

David Bromwich has observed that "The Trial by Existence" owes a debt to "Palladium," a poem by Matthew Arnold. *A Choice of Inheritance,* 223–24. In "Palladium," the human condition is to depend on the great trials of our own souls obscured to us as if by their vast height. RF borrows this figure, substantially adapts it, and adds much to its tacit theology in "The Trial by Existence."

327 *"The Trial by Existence":* CPPP, 28–30.
328 *"The Constant Symbol":* CPPP, 786–91.
328 *"Spring Pools":* CPPP, 224.
328 *meet in excelsis:* For example, RF at New York University, March 23, 1956, recording, LM0013, ACL 00181.
328 *"play in excelsis":* RF at New York University, March 23, 1956, recording.
328 *"Play on the brink of mystery":* Cook, "Verbatim," July 3, 1957.

14. THE HEART OF ANY RELIGION

330 *the call from the hospital:* Many details in this and the following section are drawn from Anne Morrison Smyth, interviews by author, March 12, July 9, and Oct. 2, 2018.

333 *Her earliest sustained memory:* Jessamyn Smyth, interview by author, June 17, 2022.

333 *Once on a summer evening:* Chisholm Gentry, interview by author, Oct. 13, 2017.

334 *Anne was privy to whispers:* Anne Morrison Smyth, interview by author, Oct. 2, 2018.

334 *as he said himself:* DeVoto's crush is on display in his letter to Kate Sterne after his dinner with Kay and Ted following Elinor's memorial service (April 25, 1938). The ubiquity of such crushes in the past is mentioned in a letter of Sept. 8, 1941, in which, speaking of the writer Helen Everitt, DeVoto wrote, "It is clear that in the curiously interknit gangs I travel with Helen has succeeded to the place vacated by Kay Morrison, all us males are from twenty percent upwards in love with her."

DeVoto alleges more in a letter of July 5, 1955, to William Sloane. Contemplating the prospect of a return to Bread Loaf, DeVoto writes,

> There will be in fact all kinds of ghosts; among them a pretty and soft-spoken gal named Kay Morrison who had something other than venom in her heart and even looked kissable and, come to think of it, was. . . . Maybe the customers would like some of my reminiscences of a less tamed Bread Loaf and I am sure that the result would be informative to Ted. (Notecard in VCL 10044-A, Notecard box 6)

Posterity wishes that DeVoto had opted to clarify rather than insinuate for whom she was kissable, by whom she was kissed. Not by him, according to an entry in LT's "Notes on Conversations" about DeVoto's tendency to exaggerate intimacies:

> [RF] said Benny had always liked to think of himself as having a kind of harem, but that his harem-relationships was one of sisterly affection, along with the arms around his neck. Frost thought it innocent. (I did not tell him that Kay had described the innocence as impotence.) Then Kay had been included in this harem by Benny, very early. So when Frost had moved into the picture, with Kay, Benny had become jealous. He had accused Frost of breaking up—not Benny's harem but the Morrison marriage. (Aug. 28, 1957, box 5)

The description of "impotence," in context, clearly implies the frustration of the "crush" he had "always had" on Kay, revealed by her to Larry one week before

("Notes on Conversations," Aug. 21, 1957). RF's later biographer Jeffrey Meyers took "impotence" and "harem" literally and ascribed a sexual relationship to DeVoto and Kay on those grounds. Meyers, *Robert Frost*, 254.

335 *When Larry showed up in Ripton:* Many details in this section are drawn from LT, "Notes on Conversations," July–Aug. 1957, box 5. Misleadingly, Meyers in *Robert Frost*, 253–54 (and note 14 to the section) cites a pair of references in "Notes on Conversations" to the "Lady Chatterley's Lover" moniker as his evidence that KM was sleeping with Dragon, and as evidence that she was potentially sleeping with LT as well. Meyers neglects to mention that LT dismisses the allegations in the passages cited. In "Notes on Conversations," Aug. 12–19, 1961, LT describes driving up to Ripton as Stafford and KM were going off for "their weekly Sunday-afternoon-ride":

> I shouted, "Hi Kay, Hi Stafford." Stafford did not look back and did not answer. (He hates me, is jealous of me, and makes the tragedy comic by insisting that there is a love-affair between Kay and me. The townspeople gossip much, by the way, over those Sunday-afternoon-rides, and the more sophisticated summer-visitors refer to Stafford-the-man-Kay-hires as being "Lady Chatterley's Lover." I'm certain that they are wrong; but Betty Barker is certain that they are correct.)

LT gives the opinion of Barker, his sometime host in Ripton, as representative of the local gossip he gainsays. He was no more persuaded of KM's sexual entanglement with Dragon in the other entry Meyers cites, from July–Aug. 1957, in which LT describes Dragon's delusion as a consequence of KM's flirtation having been taken altogether too seriously:

> Kay was very friendly, and there was just so much to talk about; wouldn't I come down some time when we could talk, and when Stafford wasn't around because Stafford had insisted that when last I stayed there, the last night I was there, after the climb on Camel's Hump, Kay and I had slept together. (Relations with Stafford seem to have grown increasingly complicated for Kay, although she tries not to let Frost be aware of them. [Close parenthesis missing in original.] Kay's trouble in this regard is that she has always tried to butter up Stafford in ways which Stafford takes as "intimacies," and he has misinterpreted her butter-ups as justification for his subsequent jealousies. Nice variant on the D. H. Lawrence formula of relationships between the caretaker and the "lady."

Meyers lends a specious plausibility to the alleged affair by noting that "Stafford Dragon (the name itself was irresistible) was Frost's lively and handsome hired man"—for discussion of which rhetoric, see note on *he later reflected*, in chap. 14, sec. 5.

336 *"she must have had some kind of love for him"*: LT, "Notes on Conversations," Sept. 1, 1956, box 5.

337 *"with the intent to do honor"*: LT, "Notes on Conversations," Aug. 28, 1957, box 5.

337 *"Entree"*: DCL 1178, box 17.

338 *Peaks and troughs were both on display*: LT, "Notes on Conversations," Sept. 13, 1953, box 5.

339 *he later reflected*: LT's most extensive and revealing discussion of the conflict is in a note in "Notes on Conversations" from June 1962 though retrospectively dated "Summer 1949." Paramount is KM's fear about what LT has been told about her relationship with RF: "She hates me now, largely because she fears I know too much, and fears I don't accept her lies as truths." Secondary is his sense that his marriage made him less "charming" in her eyes: "So long as I was the carefree bachelor, with a bit of a record for being related to Don Juan and Lothario, Kay thought I was 'charming.' She said so to many of our mutual friends." LT notes KM's "dislike" of his wife and is unsure whether others in their circle were right to say it was "motivated in part by Kay's jealousy." Perhaps LT was too distracted by his own hatred of KM at the time of this entry to see that she was generally jealous of the emotional hold she had over the men in her life, to which LT's marriage was a threat, of which his wife was the very embodiment. With less of an emotional hold over him, KM was left with less power over what she feared he had heard from RF and come to believe in contrast to "her lies." LT, "Notes on Conversations," Summer 1949, box 5.

Tendentiously, Meyers quotes the entry above in his ascription of a prior sexual attachment to KM and LT (*Robert Frost*, 254–56). One would have to suppose LT was writing in code. Meyers makes his case for the relationship without citing any claims to that effect by parties involved or potentially witnessing, other than an allegation from Dragon that Meyers cites speciously, omitting to mention that LT recorded the accusation only to laugh at it (see note on *When Larry showed up in Ripton*, in chap. 14, sec. 4.). Neither does Meyers offer plausible or consistent ways to read between the lines of their writings, instead letting his audience read between the lines of a few suggestive details from their lives—LT's attractiveness, KM's "bitchiness" to LT and his wife, Janet (per the Summer 1949 entry quoted above), KM's visible surprise to learn the news of LT's engagement. Amid these details, Meyers asserts that the two were "lovers," as if that were the natural inference to draw given an attractive man and a woman who was mean to his wife ("I am sure that Janet was at fault," LT wrote in the same entry). The inference makes sense only with the tacit presumption that KM's every social impulse involving men was sexual and presumptively culminated in actual sex, as Meyers believed, on bad evidence, that it did with DeVoto and Dragon as well. That KM cared about social favor for reasons not entirely reducible to sexual interest, was socially ambitious for reasons unrelated to sex, was flirtatious for reasons of gratification and influence and mere intimacy, like anyone, seems not to have entered into the analysis.

For what it's worth, the story Meyers tells in which KM was shocked to learn about LT's engagement, as ostensibly recollected by Anne in an interview, was told by Anne, in an interview with the author, with Anne herself as the only one distressed to hear about the engagement, brought to tears because it meant she wasn't in fact going to grow up to marry LT as he had promised, giving her the pin off his naval uniform (Anne Morrison Smyth, interview by author, Oct. 2, 2018). In any case, Anne was seven, and one should hardly infer much about the existence of a clandestine affair on the strength of a momentary impression by a seven-year-old as recollected half a century later. (Meyers has her as eight at the time and dates the news to January 1945, but KM was told in late 1944, when Anne was seven, per LT to RF, Dec. 21, 1944, DCL 1178, box 11). The rupture of LT's faux engagement to Anne is marked by a letter of his to RF of Aug. 6, 1945, after his marriage, in which LT sends his best wishes to Anne "even if she has crossed me off her list" (DCL 1178, box 11).

339 *a startling proposal:* LT, "Notes on Conversations," July 19, 1954, box 5.

340 *"public humiliation":* LT, "Notes on Conversations," Oct. 7, 1965, box 6.

340 *"Now I've broken it down":* "The Enjoyment of Poetry," Jan. 9, 1955, recording, LM0112, ACL 00181.

341 *Frost had lately taken to blaming Larry:* LT, "Notes on Conversations," Aug. 3, 1959, box 6.

341 *"We have sized each other up":* RF to LT, July 11, 1959, DCL 1178, box 11. Of note, given tensions at the time, is that the letter was dictated to KM.

341 *Frost raised the problem:* LT, "Notes on Conversations," Aug. 4, 1959, box 6.

342 *"Knowledge of truth was impossible":* In context, RF (as paraphrased by LT) is referring not to truth categorically but to truths about "issues which could not be resolved." RF strikes a similar note in a notebook entry, ca. 1937, in which he writes "James common sense trial and error in the highest is most us," meaning that "in the highest" questions of the spirit he endorses William James's defense of willed belief in the absence of certainty, as argued in "The Will to Believe" (Notebook 29, ca. 1937–42, DCL 1178, box 16). RF's entry appears toward the end of a response to a novel by his old spiritual bête noire, George Santayana, *The Last Puritan* (1935), which prompted RF to turn the novel's titular phrase on its head, arguing that there will be Puritans as long as there are people unsparing in their commitment to truth:

> The last Puritan would be the final man to spare himself no disillusionment in his quest of the sense of truth. Perhaps that is like coldness on the nose a fish holds to the stream that is passing away. Everything aside in all directions. There is truth to feel somewhere. He will hug no delusion however comforting. There will be the harsh Protestant as long as their [sic] is the easy Catholic.

343 *a kind of singular extempore free verse:* Randall Jarrell, ca. Oct. 1962, recording, LM0225, ACL 00181.

344 *"town and gown audiences":* RF at New York University, March 23, 1956, recording.

344 *"Choose Something Like a Star":* CPPP, 365.

345 *"You don't know what I went through":* Talk by RF at the University of Miami, Coral Gables, Feb. 26, 1960, recording, LM0016, ACL 00181.

345 *"Forgive, O Lord":* CPPP, 440.

346 *On a given night:* May 19, 1960, to be precise. RF at Wesleyan University, recording, LM0014, ACL 00181.

346 *Having "got[ten] along so very well":* LT, "Notes on Conversations," postscript after March 28, 1961, box 6.

346 *"an accumulations [sic] of typically Frostian rages":* LT, "Notes on Conversations," Feb. 6, 1962, box 6.

346 *the two and a half weeks:* LT, "Notes on Conversations," Feb. 6–March 19, 1962, box 6.

347 *when the two saw each other:* LT, "Notes on Conversations," March 27, 1962, box 6.

347 *Kay, too, received a long round:* RF's eighty-eighth birthday, March 26, 1962, recording, LM0033, ACL 00181.

348 *Once was a tense day:* LT, "Notes on Conversations," Aug. 2, 1962, box 6.

348 *a consolatory letter:* RF to LT, Aug. 15, 1962, DCL 1178, box 11.

348 *when they saw each other at Trinity College:* LT, "Notes on Conversations," Dec. 3, 1962–Jan. 29, 1963, box 6.

348 *he had a friend in the crowd:* RF at Trinity College, Oct. 11, 1962, recording, LM0453, ACL 00181.

349 *"It was an impressive climax":* LT, "Notes on Conversations," ca. Jan. 30, 1963, box 6.

15. THE AGITATED HEART

350 *Bill Snow told the press:* "Tributes to Frost: Snow Praises Him as Great Poet and Friend," *Hartford Times,* Jan. 29, 1963.

350 *"unquestionably one of America's":* Syndicated in the *Hartford Times* as "Tributes to Frost: Untermeyer Calls Him One of 3 Top U.S. Poets," Jan. 29, 1963.

350 *"staunch support and care":* Bernie Mumford Jones to KM, Jan. 29, 1963, DCL 1178, box 6.

351 *"nobody seemed to go to pieces":* LT, "Notes on Conversations," early Feb. 1963, box 6.

351 *the "mythic image" of Frost:* LT, "Notes on Conversations," Feb. 11, 1963, box 6.

351 *unacknowledged edits of primary sources:* LT, "Notes on Conversations," July 15, 1964, box 6.

352 *the notes he left on the cutting-room floor:* LOC MSS84950, box 10.

352 *"You and I are not clever":* RF to LU, Nov. 11, 1915, in *Letters,* 1:385.

353 *"There's not much to add":* LU to LT, June 25, 1964, VCL 10044-A, box 16.

353 *loyal to him through it all:* Undated recording, ca. Oct. 1962, LM0451, ACL 00181.

353 *a visit of his to the farmhouse:* Cook, "Verbatim," Sept. 7, 1963.

354 *"Kay has always been willing to sacrifice":* LT, "Notes on Conversations," Aug. 30, 1963, box 6.

354 *"cover up the facts":* LT, "Notes on Conversations," Dec. 13, 1963, box 6.

354 *"One of my weaknesses":* LT, "Notes on Conversations," ca. July 1, 1964, box 6.

354 *the second dinner:* LT, "Notes on Conversations," Sept. 15, 1964, box 6.

355 *another bibulous dinner:* LT, "Notes on Conversations," June 29, 1964, box 6.

355 *a used "condrum":* LT, "Notes on Conversations," April 2, 1963, box 6.

355 *the question of the Gordons' credibility:* In the same visit, the Gordons repeated to LT a story they had heard from Lillian, who heard it from LF, who supposedly said that KM confessed to her the physicality of the relationship at Frost's funeral or in the hours afterward. One is asked to believe that KM revealed what she had scrupulously hidden for twenty-five years, at or shortly after a funeral at which she was conspicuously sad, to her lover's daughter whom she disliked. This bad piece of gossip reflects poorly on the Gordons' reliability as gossips.

355 *he had faked a raucous party:* LT, "Notes on Conversations," Jan. 10–12, 1947, box 5.

356 *"my love of . . . squandering fluid lust":* Undated prose fragment, DCL 1178, box 12. Handwriting and internal evidence date this fragment of a letter to the late 1940s or early 1950s, the period when RF had begun to talk and write about God as a "God of waste," as in the letter, which seems to have been written to KM.

356 *Larry picked up* Neurosis and Human Growth: LT, "Notes on Conversations," Oct. 7, 1965, box 6.

356 *a joke, which he would make:* For example, in an undated recording, ca. Oct. 1962, LM0250, ACL 00181.

357 *"orderly ways of dealing with dangerous conflicts":* EY, xxii.

358 *a more chaste encounter:* LY, 1–2.

358 *Frost's trip to the Great Dismal Swamp:* EY, 173–89. This tall tale from LT's first volume was, like the tall tale from the second, a story of a thematically significant journey. It was probably not a coincidence that the journeys embellished in volumes 1 and 2 were ones whose steps he had retraced in the years after RF's death. In LT's "Notes on Conversations," RF's retellings of the trip to the Dismal Swamp have the picaresque quality they have in his recounting elsewhere. No record exists of RF's telling LT the story with notes of terror, vindictiveness, or a death wish. As evidence for that sense of doom, LT cites a source, despite explaining its unreliability, purporting to quote RF having been menaced by the "Negro" walking behind him on the boardwalk (*EY,* 521). Perhaps LT had not seen a transcript of RF's recollection of the trip to a group of Southerners in March 1961: "Pretty soon, I was aware there was somebody walkin' behind me. . . . And all he was . . . was a pleasant Negro . . . with an axe on his shoulder. He'd been workin' somewhere" (Arthur Palmer Hudson to KM, April 4, 1961, DCL 1178, box 6). LT also claims that RF had never told him about the man despite this entry from LT's "Notes" in 1962: "A long talk . . . going over old ground. Nothing new. Big re-play of the trip through the Dismal Swamp 1894, and all about how the negro walked behind him in the moonlight carrying an axe on his shoulder and singing." LT, "Notes on Conversations," March 5, 1962, box 6.

359 *"been out of time":* RF to Susan Hayes Ward, Dec. 4, 1894, in *Letters,* 1:35.

359 *"I suppose it was all nothing":* RF to Jean Gould, Dec. 13, 1962, DCL 1178, box 5.

359 *The second tall tale:* YT, 507–10.

359 *learned only after Frost's death:* LT, "Notes on Conversations," Feb. 19, 1963, box 6. As his citation for the story, LT writes, "RF told LT, repeatedly, about this visit to the farm" (*YT,* 703). No records of such conversations exist in LT's vast archives. His story has RF telling his family that he has to go alone and mentions no one else with RF on what was ostensibly a solitary walk through his memories. LT suspected, as of Feb. 19, 1963, that Carol had driven him. Otto Manthey-Zorn, RF's old friend and colleague in Amherst, had actually driven him and walked the grounds with him. Manthey-Zorn to KM, Dec. 26, 1962, DCL 1178, box 7.

359 *"Robert Frost was so fascinated":* EY, xiii.

360 *"We all loved Larry":* Anne Morrison Smyth, interview by author, March 12, 2018.

360 *to be called "The Agitated Heart":* Morrison to LT, July 25, 1966, VCL 10044-A, box 14. Quotations of the essay herein are from the draft sent to LT, not the version published in *The Atlantic Monthly* (July 1967).

360 *"Revelation":* CPPP, 27–28.

361 *something closer to idolatry:* Ted, ever careful in public, made his criticism more forcefully in a letter responding to LT's urging that he be more direct and less suggestive in his essay on RF. "Salvation (for the reader or listener) consisted in total sympathy for Frost and his view of himself, and instant understanding of his mode of utterance. . . . And, damn it, the point does get us back to Concord, and to Perry's portrait of the Transcendental idea of friendship, based on communication (R.F. would say 'correspondence') that was so refined it practically destroyed itself and rendered its very purpose null and void" (Morrison to LT, July 25, 1966). Ted refers to *Consciousness in Concord* (1958), a hitherto unpublished journal of Thoreau's edited with acerbic commentary by Perry Miller, the preeminent intellectual historian of American Puritanism and its cultural heirs until his early death in the end of 1963, whereupon LT was offered his chair at Harvard. Miller had once inscribed his early masterpiece, *The New England Mind: The Seventeenth Century* (1939), "For Robert Frost / Who has said more in one page concerning the subject of this book than I have said in five hundred—this token of my deepest affection and profound esteem" (Robert Frost Library, NYU).

362 *"His life is a pursuit":* "Escapist—Never," in *CPPP,* 434.

362 *a tribute to Frost:* Recording in DCL 1178, box 39.

363 *used the same figure of a fixed star:* Morrison to KM, Oct. 18, 1927, Smyth Papers.

363 *"Larry, I hope you'll let me":* VCL 10044-A, box 10.

363 *"Othello-like":* Chalmers to LT, Sept. 17, 1964, VCL 10044-A, box 10.

364 *not only Lear and Job but Proteus:* Chalmers to LT, May 4, 1966, VCL 10044-A, box 10.

364 *"His endurance of the mystery":* Chalmers to LT, Sept. 17, 1964.

364 *"Your letter and its wonderful postscripts":* LT to Chalmers, Sept. 24, 1964, VCL 10044-A, box 10.

365   *an apparent digression:* Chalmers to LT, Dec. 30, 1968, VCL 10044-A, box 10.

365   *"You believe":* Chalmers to LT, ca. Dec. 25, 1968, on internal evidence, VCL 10044-A, box 10.

366   *So wrote the man:* Van Dore to LT, Nov. 16, 1966, VCL 10044-A, box 16.

367   *the interring article:* "Robert Frost," *New York Times Book Review,* August 9, 1970.

369   *"very intense and very loving":* Anne Morrison Smyth, interview by author, March 12, 2018.

369   *"the kind of lies":* LF to Francis Brown, Sept. 1, 1970, DCL 1178, box 12.

369   *Larry thought her letter was nonsense:* LT, "Notes on Conversations," Jan. 28, 1971, box 6.

370   *Kay imagined Larry's detractors:* KM to Edward Connery Lathem, May 8, 1971, DCL 965, box 23.

370   *Kay reported to Ed Lathem:* KM to Lathem, Aug. 18, 1969, DCL 965, box 23.

370   *"to offer a balanced portrait":* Typescript for lecture at Ripon College, Oct. 5, 1970, VCL, 10044-A, box 18.

370   *"a secret feeling of self-doubt":* LT to Mary Stegner, Feb. 11, 1971, VCL 10044-C/D.

370   *"too much of what must be said":* LT to Wallace Stegner, March 4, 1971, VCL 10044-C/D.

371   *"utterly overcome by the occasion":* Lathem to KM, June 15, 1973, DCL 965, box 23.

371   *"I've been as shattered":* KM to Lathem, June 16, 1973, DCL 965, box 23.

371   *"saved from death I suppose":* LT to I. L. Salomon, Feb. 28, 1972, VCL 10044-A, box 15.

371   *"May the Lord have mercy":* KM to Lathem, ca. early June 1972 on internal evidence, DCL 965, box 23. "As you must have heard from Jan, Larry has not yet been told."

371   *no particular interest in Frost:* Winnick, interview by author, Dec. 19, 2019.

371   *walked Roy privately through his approach:* LT dictating plans for *LY,* recordings, VCL 10044-A.

371   *"I am sure I'm going to suffer":* KM to Lathem, Oct. 1, 1973, DCL 965, box 23.

372   *her husband's rebuke:* Morrison to Winnick, Sept. 25, 1975, DCL 965, box 23.

373   *the review of* The Later Years*:* David Bromwich, "The Bleakest of Lords," *New York Times,* Jan. 16, 1977.

373   *the letter Kay wrote:* "Letters to the Editor: Robert Frost," March 6, 1977.

374   *"he laced his conversation":* Morrison, *Robert Frost,* 7.

374   *a whitewashing:* Audio recordings of LT, VCL 10044-A.

374   *"many threats to punish":* Morrison, *Robert Frost,* 5.

375   *"the reconsideration":* Morrison to Lathem, Oct. 27, 1984, DCL 965, box 23.

375   *Burnshaw cites a secondhand source:* The source is critic Denis Donoghue, who paraphrased LT to Burnshaw without purporting to quote him (*Robert Frost Himself,* 210). Donoghue's paraphrase might have meant something had he written it before the monster myth gained traction, but he wrote it in 1984, long after the myth had taken hold in the popular imagination. *Robert Frost Himself,* 319.

375   *Ted could not tell precisely:* Morrison to Lathem, Nov. 19, 1986, DCL 965, box 23.

16. MYRTLES AND ROSES

377 *the month Larry spent with Frost:* LT, "Notes on Conversations," May 19–June 22, 1957, box 5.

378 *"I suppose Larry is having to work":* RF to KM, May 23, 1957, DCL 1211.

378 *a letter to Frost days after their return:* LT to RF, June 25, 1957, DCL 1178, box 11.

379 *"I should like to have the name":* Letter to RF, Dec. 16, 1957, DCL 1178, box 8. The first name of the letter writer is largely illegible; the surname is O'Sullivan.

379 *The lines that came to him:* RF's conversation with Van Doren and Adams, ca. Oct. 1962, recording.

379 *"My very dear if mistaken love":* RF to KM, ca. late May 1957, DCL 1211.

379 *"I end as I began":* RF to KM, May 24, 1957, DCL 1211.

380 *"they've got one of his condrums":* Cook, "Verbatim," Aug. 25, 1949.

380 *Frost rejected Eliot's idea:* Cook, "Verbatim," Aug. 2, 1954.

380 *"scribes and Pharisees":* Cook, "Verbatim," Aug. 2, 1954.

380 *"I like to play at a level":* Sergeant, Notes on conversations with RF, 1956.

380 *he played euchre:* Quoted in *RFLU*, 321, and LU's *Bygones*, 46. LU describes the quotation in the former as spoken and in the latter as written.

380 *"You have been a great poet":* RF to Eliot, Sept. 2, 1957, in *SL*, 566–67.

380 *Eliot's climactic toast:* Audio recording, DCL 1178.

381 *Frost was fond of quoting:* For example, RF to Jessie Belle Rittenhouse, Aug. 16, 1919, in *Letters*, 1:704, and, more than forty years later, Cook, "Verbatim," July 27, 1960.

381 *Frost had at the same time been worried:* Sergeant, Notes on conversations with RF, Dec. 6, 1949.

382 *Frost's statement on behalf of Pound:* SL, 575–77. RF's appeal distinguished itself by its raised eyebrows at the relevant legal arguments in Pound's defense, even downplaying the relevance of "legal procedure" at all in the case. "I should think [a solution] would have to be reached more by magnanimity than by logic," wrote RF, "and it is chiefly on magnanimity I am counting." His litigation showed as shrewd a reserve as his verse, allowing the government to save face on matters of law while finding both virtue and prudence in taking up the call to demonstrate its greatness of soul.

382 *not wanting Pound to think:* Cook, "Verbatim," June 10, 1958.

382 *letter of gratitude:* Ezra Pound to RF, April 6, 1958, VCL 10044-A, box 5.

383 *"RF":* Pound to RF, June 19, 1958, VCL 10044-A, box 5.

383 *"Dear Mr. Frost":* JFK to RF, April 11, 1959, DCL 1178, box 6.

383 *"It's a Puritan named Kennedy":* "Robert Frost, on 85th Birthday, Romps Through Interview Here," *New York Times*, March 27, 1959.

384 *"There are plenty of good Puritans":* Notebook 29, ca. 1937–42, DCL 1178, box 16.

384 *Frost saw Puritanism:* RF, ca. Oct. 1962, recording, LM0227, ACL 00181.

384 *"reaches and makes the 'Divine'":* Bob Cotner to LT, May 16, 1971, VCL 10044-A, box 9.

384 *another session with reporters:* RF at Syracuse University, April 21, 1949, recording, LM0176, ACL 00181.

384   *Writing to Kay from Stanford:* RF to KM, Nov. 9, 1960, on internal evidence, DCL
      1211.
384   *Frost told Kennedy by telegram:* RF to JFK, Dec. 14, 1960, in *SL,* 586.
385   *"The Gift Outright":* CPPP, 316.
385   *Written in roughly 1935:* On a manuscript of the poem, RF wrote, "Written before
      1936." Crane, *Robert Frost,* 180.
387   *a necessary continuation:* Relatedly, Frost numbered Emancipation with the American
      Revolution as two of the three great political achievements of Puritanism in a
      talk in which he identified himself with "the Puritan party." (The third achieve-
      ment was the overthrow of Charles I.) RF's "Great Issues" lecture at Dartmouth,
      May 16, 1955, recording, DCL 12, box 10768.
388   *Frost's mood was dour:* LT, "Notes on Conversations," Jan. 19, 1961, box 6.
388   *"You cannot imagine how distinguished I feel":* Carter to RF, Jan. 24, 1961, DCL 1178,
      box 2.
389   *"A Monument to Afterthought Unveiled":* Lawrence High School *Bulletin,* June 1892.
389   *"Class Hymn":* Lawrence High School *Bulletin,* June 1892.
389   *"If Emerson had left us nothing else":* "On Emerson," in *CPPP,* 860–66.
389   *a pair of lines with which he thought:* RF's talk to American Academy of Arts and Sci-
      ences, Oct. 8, 1958, recording, LM0156, ACL 00181.
390   *he objected strongly:* Transcription of talk given at Exeter Academy, June 1, 1940,
      ACL 00181, box 2.
390   *brought an untold number of Americans:* See esp. Peter Wirzbicki, *Fighting for the Higher
      Law: Black and White Transcendentalists Against Slavery.*
390   *he tragically did much to bring about:* See esp. Nell Irvin Painter, *The History of White People.*
391   *an uncollected occasional poem:* Though RF tended to turn down requests to write verse
      for public occasions, he relented in 1920 for a pageant to be held the next year in
      Plymouth, Massachusetts, to mark the tercentenary of the landing at Plymouth
      Rock. His "Puritan Poem" as he called it, published as "The Return of the Pil-
      grims," bears a distinct, if subtle, resemblance to "Concord Hymn" (RF to Roy
      Elliott, *Letters,* 2:103; *The Pilgrim Spirit* [Boston: Marshal Jones Company, 1921],
      134–36). Emerson built his memorial to a spiritual calling of self-sacrifice for
      the sake of a free nation that the farmers in the colony of Massachusetts might
      themselves never know. RF built his monument to a hope of the Puritans that
      was their gift to future generations, something in their spirit that would bind the
      nation together no matter the racial backgrounds of its people.
         Yet RF was gravely disappointed by the poem, choosing never to republish it. He
      did, however, republish a lone stanza as a poem called "Immigrants" (*CPPP,* 240):

      No ship of all that under sail or steam
      Have gathered people to us more and more
      But Pilgrim-manned the *Mayflower* in a dream
      Has been her anxious convoy into shore.

Initially "races," not "people," were "gathered" (JL Series 3). The poem's single image is of a dream that both serves as inspiration and has its own reality, as if the spirit of the ship were truly present in immigrants' dreams. For this idea, RF drew on a hymn very different from Emerson's, an old devotional song by Thomas Campion called "O come quickly!" in *The Oxford Book of English Verse* (1900), in which the worshipper's spirit longs, more than any beaten vessel or weary pilgrim, for the Lord to take him in.

> Never weather-beaten sail more willing bent to shore,
> Never tirèd pilgrim's limbs affected slumber more,
> Than my wearied sprite now longs to fly out of my troubled breast:
> O come quickly, sweetest Lord, and take my soul to rest!

The Pilgrims, in RF's revision, are the ones called upon repeatedly to come, able to grant rest for the weary. They seem to stand for that in the spirit able to take anyone in—at least anyone who can "[hold] their meaning fast" and keep the "gift" the Pilgrims gave, as RF wrote in "The Return of the Pilgrims."

391 *"Kitty Hawk":* CPPP, 441–52.

391 *an integrationist in principle:* In the early summer of 1955, shortly after the Supreme Court ordered the desegregation of America's public schools in *Brown v. Board of Education*, RF chanced to talk over the ruling with Judge Learned Hand, a giant of liberal jurisprudence, who told RF that he had misgivings about what the court had just done. RF responded, "I haven't" (Cook, "Verbatim," July 28, 1955). RF shared the story with an audience at Bread Loaf that July, relaying Learned Hand's confession that his people had been anti-abolitionists, to which RF had responded, "My people were worse than that: they were Copperheads. They were wrong and your people were wrong." An anti-abolitionist, RF told his audience, was someone who couldn't stand the kind of "needling" that helped to bring about the Civil War and the ruling of the court, needling that was the product of a moral stubbornness he saw as part of the Puritan legacy like the impulse to travel south to spread education.

RF had undertaken such a trip in Jan. 1955, when, in a rare instance of his integrationism in practice, he gave a talk to the students of Morehouse and Spelman Colleges, arranged by Bill Snow in a year he spent there as visiting faculty. RF knew the risk he took with the segregationist white colleges in and near Atlanta, which stood to cancel his engagements on their campuses in light of his talk. He gave his talk anyway, for far less than his usual fee, to an integrated audience, leaving with the impression that the students with whom he talked into the small hours of the night had "show[n] themselves to be as keen as the students in white colleges." Snow to KM, winter 1955, DCL 1178, box 10.

RF's integrationism was likewise on display in his private support for Langston Hughes in 1950, when, in response to an editor at Holt unsure about publishing

Hughes in part on account of his attraction to communism, RF wrote, "I think he would be a credit to our list," calling Hughes "a negro I have thought pleasantly of as a first rate American," his racism nonetheless implicit in the premise that a "negro" being a first-rate American was worth remarking on at all (RF to Edward T. Rigg, July 25, 1950, DCL 1178, box 9). RF's pessimism about American race relations was evinced in 1959 when he declined to participate in a symposium on civil rights at the University of Minnesota.

His host would have been his former student Charles Foster. The year was 1959, and Foster had grown interested in the story of the abolitionist John Brown on the centenary of his raid on Harpers Ferry that was to have begun a revolt by American slaves. Foster had begun a book on John Brown, "the challenge" of which, he told RF, "is to see whether I can be bright enough to understand why good men like Thoreau, Emerson, [the minister Theodore] Parker, and T. W. Higginson supported and championed John Brown. I trace it all to your phrase for New England character: the residue of Cromwell and Milton" (Foster to RF, March 21, 1959, DCL 1178, box 4). For the centenary itself on Oct. 16, Foster proposed a panel on civil rights consisting of RF, William Faulkner, and Harry Truman, the former president mediating "the embodiment of New England and the embodiment of the south at a summit meeting." Foster was confident that Truman would say yes if RF would. He didn't even mind if RF didn't "like Brown any more than the general you are named for," hoping only that RF would speak on "what you think about the raid a century after and particularly what your wisdom tells you is the way through the present snarl concerning civil rights for the Negro." Other participants in the conference would include Martin Luther King Jr.

Thoreau and Emerson had called Brown a hero not for the practicality of his plan but for its complete disdain of practical considerations, Thoreau going so far as to write jeremiads against anyone so spiritually impoverished as not to recognize the nobility and heroism of Brown's giving himself entirely for a higher ideal. RF called it "an ugly form of idealism to dream of rousing the slaves against their masters," objecting to Brown on practical grounds (RF to Foster, June 18, 1959, DCL 1178, box 4). His skepticism about the possibilities for Brown's plot—shared at the time by others such as Frederick Douglass—was matched by a skepticism about the present hope for racial equality, whose prospects struck him as no better than those of Brown's raid: "The best we can say of our situation is that it insures [sic] us all of all the tragedy we need for the next thousand years." In his fatalism, in his prediction for the coming millennium, in his aesthetic reconciliation to the suffering of others, it was as if RF had become the minister in "The Black Cottage" whose moral vacuity he had exposed half a century earlier.

393   *a walk with friends in Ripton:* RF's conversation with Van Doren and Adams, ca. Oct. 1962, recording.

393 *Frost said it had begun:* Cook, "Verbatim," June 22, 1962.

394 *the beginnings of a poem about a king:* Notes by Anne Morrison Smyth, Jan. 21, 1963, VCL 10044-C/D.

394 *An agitation of another kind of love:* RF's conversation with Van Doren and Adams, ca. Oct. 1962, recording.

394 *Manichaean accounts of her childhood:* An almost unqualified joy in LF's recollection was "Our Family Christmas" (*Redbook*, Dec. 19, 1963). "I doubt whether any children, in any clime, in any Christian land, could have anticipated the joy of Christmas Eve and Christmas dawn (early dawn!) with any more excitement than the Frost children." Her beatific Christmas was tempered by a lone wistful memory: the one memory she had of her brother Elliott, who passed away in July 1900, before his fourth birthday. "He had been given a little metal train set that Christmas Day, and he was entertaining me with it, making me laugh, by running it rapidly up and down the floor below me as I sat on my mother's lap." Affecting as the memory was, it was a confabulation, to judge from her having been eight months old for the one Christmas she spent with Elliott. Perhaps her parents told her the story.

Earlier in 1963, she shared a memory with LT as demonic as her Christmas past was angelic. In another very early memory, included in volume I of the biography, her father got her out of bed, walked her down to the kitchen, and held up a revolver, asking her whom she wanted to live with, him or her mother, whereupon she burst into tears and her mother walked her back to her room (*EY*, 308–309). "I was stopped by a stiletto," Roberta Chalmers wrote LT, by "your taking what must have been an hallucination of Lesley's for gospel truths first as a maybe, maybe; then as a fact." "Children dream real—and Lesley's dreams, even when she was grown up and awake, were particularly vivid and her own. This incident is therefore not recordable as fact" (Chalmers to LT, Dec. 30, 1968, VCL 10044-A, box 10). Another skeptic of the story, on similar grounds, was LF's daughter Lesley Lee Francis (Parini, *Robert Frost*, 90).

395 *his short note to Hervey Allen:* RF to Allen, April 12, 1938, in *SL*, 470.

396 *the two cantos in the end of* In Memoriam: Cantos 122 and 123.

397 *"The new freedom is hard to report":* Notes by Anne Morrison Smyth, Jan. 27, 1963, VCL 10044-C/D.

398 *"I'm going to die tonight":* KM to Lathem, April 4, 1971, DCL 965, box 9.

398 *"great dream for all people":* Notes by Anne Morrison Smyth, Jan. 28, 1963, VCL 10044-C/D.

398 *"FINE. HOW'S IT GOING WITH HER?":* LT, "Notes on Conversations," Dec. 3, 1962–Jan. 29, 1963, box 6.

398 *"pleasure and comfort in having Anne":* Earle to KM, Jan. 30, 1963, DCL 1178, box 4.

398 *he and Kay liked to pretend:* Jessamyn Smyth, interview by author, June 17, 2022.

399 *At 4:00 a.m., Stafford called Doc Cook:* Cook, "Verbatim," Jan. 29, 1963.

Select Bibliography

I. WRITINGS BY ROBERT FROST

The Collected Prose of Robert Frost. Edited by Mark Richardson. Cambridge, Mass.: Harvard University Press, 2007.

Elected Friends: Robert Frost and Edward Thomas to One Another. Edited by Matthew Spencer. New York: Other Press, 2012.

Family Letters of Robert and Elinor Frost. Edited by Arnold Grade. Albany: State University of New York Press, 1972.

The Letters of Robert Frost. Vol. I, *1886–1920*. Edited by Donald Sheehy, Mark Richardson, and Robert Faggen. Cambridge, Mass.: Harvard University Press, 2014.

The Letters of Robert Frost. Vol. 2, *1920–1928*. Edited by Donald Sheehy et al. Cambridge, Mass.: Harvard University Press, 2016.

The Letters of Robert Frost. Vol. 3, *1929–1936*. Edited by Donald Sheehy et al. Cambridge, Mass.: Harvard University Press, 2021.

The Letters of Robert Frost to Louis Untermeyer. Edited by Louis Untermeyer. New York: Holt, Rinehart and Winston, 1963.

Robert Frost: Collected Poems, Prose, and Plays. Edited by Richard Poirier and Mark Richardson. New York: Library of America, 1995.

Robert Frost and Sidney Cox: Forty Years of Friendship. Edited by William Evans. Hanover, N.H.: University Press of New England, 1981.

Selected Letters of Robert Frost. Edited by Lawrance Thompson. New York: Holt, Rinehart and Winston, 1964.

II. ARCHIVES

Amherst College Archives and Special Collections, Amherst, Mass.

Bryn Mawr College Special Collections, Bryn Mawr, Pa.

Houghton Library, Harvard University, Cambridge, Mass.

Huntington Library, San Marino, Calif.

Jones Library Special Collections, Amherst, Mass.

Library of Congress Manuscript Division, Library of Congress, Washington, D.C.

Middlebury College Special Collections, Middlebury, Vt.

New York University Special Collections.

Plymouth State University Archives and Special Collections, Plymouth, N.H.

Princeton University Special Collections, Princeton, N.J.

Rauner Special Collections, Dartmouth College, Hanover, N.H.

Smyth, Anne Morrison. Papers. Private Collection, Belchertown, Mass.

University of Virginia Library Special Collections, Charlottesville.

III. BOSWELLIZING OF ROBERT FROST

Bartlett, John. Notes on conversations with Robert Frost. TS. VCL, Collection
    10044-A, box 19.

Cook, Reginald. "Verbatim." TS. MCL, Collection C-4, box 9.

Cox, Sidney. *Robert Frost: Original "Ordinary Man."* New York: Henry Holt, 1929.

————. *A Swinger of Birches: A Portrait of Robert Frost.* New York: New York University
    Press, 1957.

————. "Walks and Talks with Robert Frost." MS. DCL, Collection 392, box 5.

Foster, Charles. Journals of Charles Foster. Unpublished notes. VCL, Collection
    10044-A, box 3.

Hyde Cox, Edward. Notes on conversations with Robert Frost. Unpublished record-
    ing. DCL, Collection 1178, box 39.

Newdick, Robert. *Newdick's Season of Frost: An Interrupted Biography of Robert Frost.* Edited by
    William A. Sutton. Albany: State University of New York Press, 1976.

Pritchard, William H. *Frost: A Literary Life Reconsidered.* Amherst: University of Mas-
    sachusetts Press, 1993.

Romig, Edna Davis. "Colorado Mornings." MS. VCL, Collection 10044-A,
    box 15.

The Selected Letters of Bernard DeVoto and Katharine Sterne. Edited by Mark DeVoto. Salt Lake
    City: University of Utah Press, 2012.

Sergeant, Elizabeth Shepley. Notes on conversations with Robert Frost. TS. VCL,
    Collection 6538, box 19.

Thompson, Lawrance. "Notes on Conversations." Unpublished journals and type-
    script. VCL, Collection 10044, boxes 2, 5, 6.

N.B.: *Robert Frost: Life and Talks-Walking,* by Louis Mertins, though sometimes cited by
    scholars of Frost, is not included in the above as the author regards the source as
    unreliable.

IV. BIOGRAPHIES AND MEMOIRS

Francis, Lesley Lee. *The Frost Family's Adventure in Poetry: Sheer Morning Gladness at the Brim.*
    Columbia: University of Missouri Press, 1994.

————. *You Come Too: My Journey with Robert Frost.* Charlottesville: University of Virginia Press, 2015.

Frost, Lesley. *New Hampshire's Child: The Derry Journals of Lesley Frost.* Albany: State University of New York Press, 1969.

Hart, Henry. *The Life of Robert Frost: A Critical Biography.* Hoboken, N.J.: Wiley-Blackwell, 2017.

Meyers, Jeffrey. *Robert Frost: A Biography.* Boston: Houghton Mifflin, 1996.

Morrison, Kathleen. *Robert Frost: A Pictorial Chronicle.* New York: Holt, Rinehart and Winston, 1974.

Muir, Helen. *Frost in Florida: A Memoir.* Miami, Fla.: Valiant Press, 1995.

Munson, Gorham B. *Robert Frost: A Study in Sensibility and Good Sense.* New York: George H. Doran, 1927.

Parini, Jay. *Robert Frost: A Life.* New York: Henry Holt, 1999.

Reeve, F. D. *Robert Frost in Russia.* Boston: Little, Brown, 1964.

Sergeant, Elizabeth Shepley. *Robert Frost: The Trial by Existence.* New York: Holt, Rinehart and Winston, 1960.

Stegner, Wallace. *The Uneasy Chair: A Biography of Bernard DeVoto.* New York: Doubleday, 1974.

Thompson, Lawrance. *Robert Frost: The Early Years, 1874–1915.* New York: Holt, Rinehart and Winston, 1966.

————. *Robert Frost: The Years of Triumph, 1915–1938.* New York: Holt, Rinehart and Winston, 1970.

Thompson, Lawrance, and R. H. Winnick. *Robert Frost: The Later Years, 1938–1963.* New York: Holt, Rinehart and Winston, 1976.

Untermeyer, Louis. *Bygones: The Recollections of Louis Untermeyer.* New York: Harcourt, Brace and World, 1965.

————. *From Another World: The Autobiography of Louis Untermeyer.* New York: Harcourt, Brace, 1939.

Walsh, John Evangelist. *Into My Own: The English Years of Robert Frost.* New York: Grove Press, 1988.

V. CRITICISM AND SCHOLARSHIP

Anderson, Margaret Bartlett. *Robert Frost and John Bartlett: The Record of a Friendship.* New York: Holt, Rinehart and Winston, 1963.

Angyal, Andrew J. "Robert Frost's Poetry Before 1913: A Checklist." In *Proof 5: The Yearbook of American Bibliographical and Textual Studies.* Columbia, S.C.: J. Faust, 1977.

————. "Robert Frost's Poetry Written Before 1913: A Critical Edition." PhD diss., Duke University, 1976.

Atlas, Jay David. "Robert Frost: The Poetry, the Poet, the Philosopher of Language." MS. Draft of Sept. 2014.

Brodsky, Joseph, Seamus Heaney, and Derek Walcott. *Homage to Robert Frost.* New York: Farrar, Straus and Giroux, 1996.

Brower, Reuben. *The Poetry of Robert Frost: Constellations of Intention.* New York: Holt, Rinehart and Winston, 1965.

Burnshaw, Stanley. *Robert Frost Himself.* New York: George Braziller, 1986.

Buxton, Rachel. *Robert Frost and Northern Irish Poetry.* New York: Oxford University Press, 2004.

Cook, Reginald Lansing. *The Dimensions of Robert Frost.* New York: Rinehart, 1958.

Cramer, Jeffrey. *Robert Frost Among His Poems: A Literary Companion to the Poet's Own Biographical Contexts and Associations.* Jefferson, N.C.: McFarland, 1996.

Crane, Joan St. C., ed. *Robert Frost: A Descriptive Catalogue of Books and Manuscripts in the Clifton Waller Barrett Library, University of Virginia.* Charlottesville: University Press of Virginia, 1974.

Elder, John. *Reading the Mountains of Home.* Cambridge, Mass.: Harvard University Press, 1999.

Faggen, Robert. *Robert Frost and the Challenge of Darwin.* Ann Arbor: University of Michigan Press, 1997.

Jarrell, Randall. *No Other Book: Selected Essays.* Edited by Brad Leithauser. New York: Perennial, 2000.

———. *Poetry and the Age.* New York: Knopf, 1953.

Kearns, Katherine. *Robert Frost and a Poetics of Appetite.* Cambridge, U.K.: Cambridge University Press, 1994.

Kendall, Tim. *The Art of Robert Frost.* New Haven, Conn.: Yale University Press, 2012.

Kilcup, Karen. *Robert Frost and the Feminine Literary Tradition.* Ann Arbor: University of Michigan Press, 1998.

Logan, William. *Guilty Knowledge, Guilty Pleasure: The Dirty Art of Poetry.* New York: Columbia University Press, 2014.

McCarthy, Don. *Afternoons in Montana.* Aberdeen, S.D.: North Plains Press, 1971.

Muldoon, Paul. *The End of the Poem: Oxford Lectures.* New York: Farrar, Straus and Giroux, 2007.

O'Brien, Timothy. *Names, Proverbs, Riddles, and Material Text in Robert Frost.* New York: Palgrave Macmillan, 2010.

Orr, David. *The Road Not Taken: Finding America in the Poem Everyone Loves and Almost Everyone Gets Wrong.* New York: Penguin Press, 2015.

Oster, Judith. *Toward Robert Frost: The Reader and the Poet.* Athens: University of Georgia Press, 1994.

Poirier, Richard. *Poetry and Pragmatism.* Cambridge, Mass.: Harvard University Press, 1992.

———. *Robert Frost: The Work of Knowing.* New York: Oxford University Press, 1977.

Richardson, Mark. *The Ordeal of Robert Frost.* Urbana: University of Illinois Press, 1997.

———, ed. *Robert Frost in Context.* Cambridge, U.K.: Cambridge University Press, 2014.

Sanders, David. *A Divided Poet: Robert Frost, "North of Boston," and the Drama of Disappearance.* Rochester, N.Y.: Camden House, 2011.

Sheehy, Donald. "The Poet as Neurotic: The Official Biography of Robert Frost."
    American Literature 58, no. 3 (Oct. 1986).
————. "(Re)Figuring Love: Robert Frost in Crisis, 1938–1942." *New England Quarterly* 63, no. 2 (June 1990).
Thompson, Lawrance. *Fire and Ice: The Art and Thought of Robert Frost.* New York: Henry
    Holt, 1942.
Tuten, Nancy Lewis, and John Zubizarreta, eds. *The Robert Frost Encyclopedia.* Westport,
    Conn.: Greenwood Press, 2001.
Van Egmond, Peter, ed. *The Critical Reception of Robert Frost.* Boston: G. K. Hall, 1974.

Acknowledgments

My father gave me his copy of Frost's *Complete Poems* on my fifteenth birthday. If memory serves—and who knows—he first thought to read me "Into My Own" and then, seeing me take to it, declared the book mine, having gotten it for his own fifteenth birthday. I grabbed a Post-it note and copied out the inscription his father had written, struck by how much his graceless cursive matched my own.

They would not find me changed from him they knew— / Only more sure of all I thought was true. Nothing could have felt more reassuring as I sat at the end of childhood. Nothing could have felt more banal once I'd put childish ways behind me. So it was to my great surprise one afternoon in my mid-twenties, as I sat in my book-bestrewn cubicle in the offices of *The New Republic*, that I realized Frost had intended the banality in those lines as much as the reassurance; had intended the reassurance despite the banality; had done something so much richer and subtler than I had suspected or could explain. I had condescended to the simple-sounding poet, my taste and judgment formed on the giants of Modernism and their aesthetic descendants. Oh how little I knew.

I am grateful to the people who believed in this project in its earliest days. Ellen Umansky at the Poetry Foundation edited my first piece on Frost, warts and all. Leon Wieseltier, my boss at *The New Republic*, gave my second piece on Frost the kind of editorial treatment that is one of his great gifts to writers, a discerning encouragement that verges on inspiration for those of us otherwise alone with our strange and halfway articulated ideas. It was not the last time he'd inspire part of the book. Chris Benfey, Adam Kirsch, and Alec MacGillis all provided vital early encouragement and continued support. Frank Foer introduced me to my extraordinary agent, Melanie Jackson. Jonathan Galassi edited the book as only he could. Working with him on Frost has been one of the great things in my life.

Others provided editorial help in an unofficial capacity: Jon Baskin, Berit Erickson, Ben Greenberg, James and Marcy Plunkett, Fred Rossoff. Ben and Marcy (my mother) each read two drafts in their entirety and provided invaluable comments on both. Many others helped by talking through various aspects of the project over the years: Esther Breger, Heather Clark, Nate Cohn, Mark Hariz, Courtney Hutchison, Jessica Laser, Aidan Levy, David Plunkett, Leah Plunkett, Alice Robb, Oliver Sabot, Simon van Zuylen-Wood. Mari Erickson listened to more about Frost than anyone should ever have to. Other friends helped by talking through any number of things they surely didn't think had anything to do with Robert Frost: Levon Balayan, Zach Baron, Bob Beddor, Alexandra Blaney, Tim Brown, Nora Caplan-Bricker, Eric Chang, Aron Chilewich, Catherine Cypert, Leslie Cypert, Alex Efron, Dale Erickson, Debby Erickson, Seth Gannon, Chris Gomes, Merritt Graves, Jeff Guo, Sam Hamad, Carol Hamlin, Rick Hamlin, Will Hamlin, Sara Hoagland, Jake Izenberg, Puneet Jhaveri, Lech Kaiel, Kevin Kelley, Lauren Lederle, Nandi Levine, Zack Levine, Sean Levinger, Alana Lewis, Mike Lewis, Sam Lewis, Todd Logan, Marky Alexander Marcus, Maxim Massenkoff, Giorgio Mavroleon, Kaitlin Mondello, Melissa Munz, Eloise Ntekim, Marty Peretz, Ted Peters, Charles Petersen, Chanda Phelan, Michael Prude, Becky Randolph, Julia Sabot, Topher Sabot, Daniel Scinto III, Daniel Scinto IV, Francine Scinto, Steve Scinto, Thomas Scott-Railton, Jaden Slagle, Arvind Sohoni, Tom Stackpole, Andrew Sylvester, Ashley Toliver, Spencer Walsh, Diana Whitney. Daniel Scinto III, in particular, has taught me much more than he knows he knows about Frost. Jeff Weintraub has taught me and his other nephews much about what it means to understand traditions of ideas. Tim Duggan, Chad Harbach, Jed Perl, Deborah Rosenthal, Alex Star, Louisa Thomas, and Lindsay Whalen have all taught me more about publishing than they'd ever suspect. Caleb Crain put me on to the work of Melville scholars recovering erased marginalia, without which I could not have recovered Frost's dating of a number of his early poems.

While all things wrong with the book are, of course, my responsibility, many people contributed work in ways large and small. I am immensely grateful to Oona Holahan, Carrie Hsieh, Katie Liptak, and the whole team at Farrar, Straus and Giroux. Likewise the teams in special collections at the following libraries: Amherst College, Bryn Mawr, Dartmouth University, Harvard University, the Jones Library, the Library of Congress, Middlebury College, New York University, Princeton University, Stanford University, and the University of Virginia. I owe particular debts to Michael Kelly at Amherst, Morgan Swan at Dartmouth, Charlotte Priddle at NYU, Tim Noakes at Stanford, and everyone on the team at UVA who hosted me for all those happy weeks in their archives. Profound thanks as well to the many people who provided temporary research assistance, especially Laurainne Ojo-Ohikuare. The following institutions provided support for the book: the University of Virginia, which provided a Lillian Gary Taylor Visiting Fellowship; Eliot House, which provided a Writer's Residency; the Leon Levy Center for Biography at CUNY Graduate Center, at which I was a Biography Fellow; and the National Endowment for the Humanities, which awarded the book a Public Scholar grant. I remain grateful to Dana Hawkes, Clare Reihill, and Mary Rhinelander for the wonderful time at Eliot House. I never told them I was scared to be alone in that mansion at night. The Leon Levy Center has been an incredible source of ideas and professional friendships. Thank you to Kai Bird and Thad Ziolkowski for sustaining an institution like no other.

Frost understood better than any other poet in modernity the rich knowledge obtained through all varieties of practical work. I doubt I'd understand Frost as well if I hadn't always done such work along with research and writing. In addition to being grateful to all the great people at Lone Buffalo, I've learned an immense amount from many of them, especially K. C. Brown and Dave and Peggy Farrell. To Dave I owe an almost unspeakable amount. It is no exaggeration to say that without his help, his guidance, and his example I never could have written this book.

Mark Randolph bears an uncomfortable amount of responsibility for the book. Not only did he recommend me to the Farrells: he taught me to love poetry in tenth grade, which made my father think to read me a poem of Frost's when I turned fifteen. I will never stop being grateful to Mark and the other people who taught me how to think about poetry: Jay Atlas, Aaron Kunin, and Claudia Rankine. Though Jay taught philosophy, not literature, I learned more from him than from anyone else about ambiguity in language (as well as non-specificity, though I elide the distinction in writing for the general reader). And it was my bewilderingly good fortune to spend much of college reading poetry with Aaron and Claudia.

Billie Bozone and Jessamyn Smyth shared a simply extraordinary amount for the book, as did Anne Morrison Smyth before her passing. This book is dedicated in part to her memory, as it was written in memory of Alex and Dave.

To everyone I've forgotten to acknowledge, I quote the young Frost: "My thanks unlimited!"

Index

Dragon, Stafford, 333–35, 399, 452*n*,
    453*n*
"Dream, A" (Thomas), 177
dualism, 317

Earle, Laurel, 398
Ecclesiastes, 293
Eclogues (Virgil), 66, 321
Eden, 137, 184
editors, 207–208
"Education by Poetry" (Frost), 202–204
Edwards, Al, 340, 351
Eliot, T. S., 140, 162, 212, 214, 246,
    345; Frost and, 210–12, 249,
    379–81; "New Hampshire" and,
    216–17, 219; *The Sacred Wood*, 212,
    214; "Tradition and the Individual
    Talent," 214–15; *The Waste Land*,
    208–16
Elizabeth City, NC, 43
Elliott, Alma and Roy, 253, 398, 406*n*
Emerson, Ralph Waldo, 33, 63, 133,
    143, 145, 146, 242, 312, 314,
    391, 461*n*, 462*n*; "Circles,"
    148–49; "Concord Hymn," 389;
    "Concord Ode," 389–91; "Etienne
    de la Boéce," 147, 149–50, 152,
    156, 381, 428*n*; "Fate," 427*n*;
    as influence on Frost, 148–50;
    Parnassus, 135, 411*n*; "The Poet,"
    71–72; on Shakespeare, 70;
    "Uriel," 425*n*
emotions, 179, 264; thought and, 206
England: Frosts' life in, 130, 158–63,
    171–74, 176, 177, 187–88; Frost's
    trip to, 336, 337, 377–81
enthusiasm, 204
"Entree" (Frost), 337
Epipsychidion (Shelley), 33, 34, 42, 157, 206
Er, Myth of, 327, 450*n*
Erskine, John, 208

Essay on Man, An (Pope), 224
"Etienne de la Boéce" (Emerson), 147,
    149–50, 152, 156, 381, 428*n*
Euber farm, 339, 355
Europa, SS, 257
Eve, 137–39, 154, 192, 292, 424*n*, 444*n*
evil, 320
evolution, 203
existentialism, 332

Farjeon, Eleanor, 175
Farm-Poultry, The, 99
"Fate" (Emerson), 427*n*
Faulkner, William, 462*n*
Faxon, Henry, 279
"Figure a Poem Makes, The" (Frost), 52,
    435*n*
"Fire and Ice" (Frost), 425*n*
Fire and Ice (Thompson), 348
Fitzgerald, F. Scott, 210
Flint, F. S., 161, 164, 167
Florida, 244–45, 338, 346, 347, 393;
    Key West, 13–16, 22–23, 244,
    270, 279, 338, 365
"Flower-Gathering" (Frost), 47–52, 53,
    56, 64–65, 67–68, 74, 91, 94,
    250, 392, 411*n*, 426*n*
Fobes, Edith, 221, 223, 234
focus, 239–40
folk poetry, 163, 327
"For Annie" (Poe), 379, 393
"For Once, Then, Something" (Frost),
    139, 424*n*
Foster, Charles, 259, 462*n*
Francis, Dwight, 226
Franconia (Marjorie Frost), 244
Franconia, NH, 190, 198, 223, 260;
    Christmas tree woods in, 132,
    197; Frosts' farm in, 132–33,
    187–88
Franconia Range, 133

Permissions Acknowledgments